Reading Power

SIXTH EDITION

James I. Brown
University of Minnesota, Emeritus

Vivian Vick Fishco
President, Success Enterprise
Educational Consultant and Author

Houghton Mifflin Company
Boston *New York*

Editor in Chief: Patricia A. Coryell
Senior Sponsoring Editor: Mary Jo Southern
Associate Editor: Kellie Cardone
Editorial Associate: Danielle Richardson
Senior Project Editor: Tracy Patruno
Senior Manufacturing Coordinator: Jane Spelman
Marketing Manager: Annamarie Rice

Printed in the U.S.A.

Library of Congress Control Number: 2001131481

ISBN: 0-618-13901-X

123456789-CRS-05 04 03 02 01

As part of Houghton Mifflin's ongoing commitment to the environment, this text has been printed on recycled paper.

Contents

To the Student

This message from the authors can be as valuable to you as the Help Desk is in the computer lab. Don't skip over this resource! Read it before you begin your class.

SO-O-O-O, WHAT'S MOST WORTH KNOWING?

What's your top priority? Choose it carefully if you're going to use your time to best advantage. After all, you're in the middle of a knowledge explosion of unbelievable magnitude. Books, for example, pour from the world's presses at almost a thousand a day! Read only one today and you're already 999 books behind in your effort to keep informed. Now add newspapers, magazines—including almost 100,000 scientific journals—e-mails, and the flood of information from electronic databases. Overwhelming, isn't it? And it's *your* problem!

Well, what *is* most worth knowing? Knowing how to read! That was the answer back in the last century. Remember the three *R*s, with reading first? And that's still the answer today. A recent $14-million national survey revealed that roughly 80 million Americans over age 16—about half that category's total population—are, as far as most workplaces are concerned, basically unfit for employment. They can't really read—can't really access the information they need to do the job. So, what's most worth knowing? Knowing how to read!

MANAGING THE PRINT BLIZZARD

Makes sense, doesn't it? Keeping up is all-important, and being able to read quickly, efficiently, and critically is paramount these days. You must read *well* to accurately fill out forms in the doctor's office and at motor vehicle registration; to complete car and home loan applications; fill out scholarship applications; find your way through airports; learn about your credit card options; choose the best long-distance package; redeem frequent-flyer miles; compare the features of products; and learn about your rights and responsibilities in our society. At no other time in history has being an excellent reader been more important. How would you score yourself in handling the reading challenges of academic and non-academic life? If you need to improve, then *Reading Power* holds many tricks to make the job easier.

DID YOU KNOW?

Listening brings you information at about 100 words a minute, the average classroom lecture rate. But look at reading. The average reader gets information at about 250 words per minute, more than twice as fast as listening. That means you hear about 4,000 words in a forty-minute lecture but can read 10,000 words in that same time.

READING IS JUST THE BEGINNING

If reading comes first, what's next? To find out, put this page so close to your face that your nose actually touches it. Okay, it looks a little silly, but do it anyway. Now try to read it. Go ahead. Try it!

See? To read even one page, you need one more thing of key importance—perspective. You need to get back far enough to see the whole, not just a small fragment.

In a word, *perspective* is the key to this book, as it is to life. We have to see the present within the frame of both past and future. *Reading Power* allows you to explore what's serious and what's humorous, what's entertaining and what's useful, what's work and what's leisure. And since all work and no play means lack of perspective, the selections in this book touch not only on how to manage a rotten boss and how to write, listen, and talk to a difficult person, but also on vocational choices and how to maintain good health. In short, the thirty-six practice selections provide wide-ranging glimpses of life, from the practical to the exciting.

Furthermore, all the practice selections, those following the boldfaced Instructional Selections in the table of contents, fit into a broader perspective; they let you explore important reading rate and comprehension relationships. In short, they give you an ideal opportunity to apply newly learned reading skills to a variety of reading situations, including essential textbook reading.

GETTING THE MEANING

The very heart of reading—understanding—must also reflect desired perspective. It's not enough just to get the facts. You must see both the trees *and* the forest—the facts as well as the main ideas, the literal as well as the reflective. You'll find both in this book, laid out in gradual steps, bringing facts and meaning into balance. You must learn to crawl before you walk. In the same way, you must learn to get facts accurately before you can build complete comprehension. At the end of each selection, we have included ten comprehension check questions to measure your comprehension. The fourteen practice selections in Parts I, II, and III focus on getting the facts; the twenty-two practice selections in Parts IV and V focus on getting both facts and meaning.

THE POWER OF WORDS

An extensive vocabulary is an indispensable resource. Here, too, you need perspective. It's easy to focus on context and overlook word parts, or on the dictionary and overlook context. The exercises in this text focus on all three—context, word parts, and dictionary.

At times, context—even very limited context—practically defines a strange word for you; at other times it provides little or no help. In the Word Power Workout exercises in this book, the very brief contexts in Part A, "Leaning on Context," reflect the varying degrees of helpfulness and lay the groundwork for desired habits of attention to whatever clues are present. Add the heightened awareness of word parts, resulting from Part B, "Leaning on Parts," and you'll be even better prepared to unravel word meanings. Finally, in Part C, "Making the Words Yours," you'll find new sentence contexts, more conversational in nature, where you can fit the new words into place, making them indeed yours. This threefold attack on words ends, as it should, with application and use. As you know, best results come from doing—from actively using what you've learned.

OVER AND OVER AND OVER, AGAIN . . .

Finally, remember that reviewing plays an essential role in learning. To expedite that step, you'll find mini-reviews of all prefix, root, and suffix elements covered in Part B, plus an important mini-review of twenty other useful prefix shortcuts. You'll also find a description of the LDE formula—a formula that will let you deal with literally thousands of additional word parts. In addition, five vocabulary review quizzes have been added, structured to reinforce use of word parts in getting word meaning. Last, you'll find pronunciation aids, useful respellings to help you with words that might pose pronunciation problems.

So, as you work through this book, be assured you're using an approach that will bring a greatly improved vocabulary and the reading skill most worth having. In addition, you'll find increased awareness of how to fit what you read into better perspective. As a bonus, you're likely to become a better student and a more competent employee. It's a challenge worthy of your best efforts.

To the Instructor

Whether or not you have used *Reading Power* in previous editions, you will benefit from reading *To the Instructor,* as we have made many changes that reflect users' requests.

Goals

As with previous editions, our goals for writing this sixth edition of *Reading Power* are to

- stimulate heightened student interest in reading and vocabulary development.
- provide a practical classroom-tested program for achieving maximum reading proficiency and vocabulary growth.
- provide help in applying a wide range of specific reading and study techniques for better and more flexible management of textbook reading.
- fit reading into a broad framework, establishing it as an activity of prime importance both in and out of school, especially in the workplace.
- improve the reading skills needed to manage the information age explosion and the challenging world of work.

Teachers and students alike need a textbook that is both stimulating and practical. To provide that is our hope. This text has grown out of our firsthand teaching experiences with more than 15,000 reading students at universities and community colleges throughout the country. Add users of previous editions, and we would like to think *Reading Power* has helped hundreds of thousands of students deal more effectively with their reading problems.

Philosophy and Rationale

Reading Power is built on the premise that learners must have a clear understanding of their goals and a firm foundation on which to build new skills to become successful and efficient readers. Further, we believe that learning in context is lasting learning. The text is organized, then, so students move progressively from assessment in *The Check-up* through getting the facts in *The Start-up* to speeding up their reading in *The Speed-up* to the goal of the book—efficient comprehension and vocabulary skills—in *The Work-up.*

As in all subject areas, results in reading improvement tend to be unsatisfactory without high student interest. For that reason, we have continued to make interest a matter of prime concern. That means using an informal style in the instructional selections of *Reading Power* and drawing practice selections from bestsellers, popular magazines, textbooks, and works of high-profile authors. We have striven to include selections that will interest a diverse audience and provide opportunities to introduce your students to content that they might otherwise choose not to read.

Organization of the Text

This edition has retained eight practice selections that users agree are most effective and helpful and added twenty-eight entirely new ones, a sufficient number to permit choices in making assignments. We have maintained the same organizational format as before—a format well accepted by previous users. Each of the fifteen instructional articles, indicated in the table of contents by boldface type, is followed by two selections designed to provide immediate opportunities for applying the techniques covered. This application step, which builds successively upon previous skills presented, moves students quickly from theory into practice, accelerating growth.

The selections following each instructional article are ordered, insofar as possible, from easy to difficult, from shorter to longer. The average difficulty approximates the Standard English level on the Flesch Reading Ease scale. Exact Reading Ease figures are given for each of the selections on page 413 of the Appendix. The selections touch a wide variety of subjects: serious and humorous, personal and social concerns, technology, adventure, words, food, communicating, work, remembering, and personal narratives.

To meet teacher requests, we have added new features to this edition: ten new *Ultimate Review* selections and, for the first time, vocabulary pre- and post-tests, each designed to take a minimum of class time. The

50-item pre- and post-tests are structured to increase student awareness of the relationship between vocabulary and comprehension. For example, the two 25-item pre-tests contain one word from each of the first fifty selections, with the reminder that any word missed is a potential cause of misunderstanding content. Answers to these tests are not provided in the text, allowing teachers to use them as quick quizzes or progress reviews interspersed throughout instruction. For possible teacher use as class quizzes, the vocabulary post-test answers are not listed in the text but separately in the instructor's guide.

The text is divided into five carefully structured parts, each advancing the student step-by-step toward development of full reading potential.

Part I, *The Check-up,* introduced by the instructional article "Reading Power—Key to Personal Growth," focuses on diagnosis. The student makes informal explorations into the major factors of comprehension and rate. This part immediately involves students in self-exploration, generating increased interest and motivation. To supplement these informal explorations you need a standardized reading test such as the Nelson-Denny Reading Test for exact normative comparisons and a much more accurate evaluation of reading ability. The following two selections alert the student to the major problem to be faced as a reader, and tell exactly how to manage the problem of reading difficult material—useful advice for helping students handle the reading responsibilities of school and work.

The next check-up is on vocabulary, introduced by the selection "How Should You Build Up Your Vocabulary?" The following two selections continue the focus on vocabulary—the first on a more detailed look at word parts, an amazing shortcut to vocabulary development, and the second on a brief look at how words reveal feelings as well as express ideas.

The vocabulary approach incorporates significant research done by Holmes and Singer, who attempted to discover exactly what factors led to comprehension. They learned that the single most important first-order factor contributing to comprehension was *vocabulary in context.* It contributed 39 percent, considerably more than even *intelligence,* which contributed only 27 percent. Developing skill in dealing with context aids comprehension more than any other first-order factor. Second- and third-order factors provide additional evidence of the importance of vocabulary: V*ocabulary in isolation* contributes 47 percent, *prefixes* 11 percent, and *suffixes* 10 percent. In short, to improve comprehension, improve vocabulary.

The vocabulary exercises in this text strongly reflect the Holmes-Singer findings. Students are led gradually from *vocabulary in isolation* with no context to *vocabulary in minimal context,* and finally to *vocabulary in full context* as found in the selection being read.

Before reading a selection, students work through the exercise "Leaning on Context," built around ten potentially troublesome words drawn from the selection—words with minimal context. Such exercises uncover words that pose difficulties, which students are encouraged to resolve at that time by further study. To reinforce word mastery, they do yet another exercise over those same words: "Making the Words Yours." That exercise provides ten informal, more complete contexts, requiring students to choose the appropriate word from those being studied—a valuable double check to solidify their effective use of those words. This minimizes any potential word blocks to understanding before the actual reading of the selection.

In addition to those two exercises, a third, "Leaning on Parts," focuses on the important prefix, root, and suffix elements found in more than 14,000 words of desk-dictionary size, an invaluable shortcut.

Part II, *The Start-up,* launched by "How Do You Best Get the Facts?" leads the student along the reading for facts road, laying a solid foundation for the subsequent move into in-depth comprehension. If readers have trouble getting the facts, they inevitably have trouble drawing accurate conclusions or making accurate evaluations. All judgments based on faulty or incomplete grasp of details will lack accuracy.

Part III, *The Speed-up,* appeals strongly to students, who usually face major problems in finding time to cover all the required reading in college. The selections in this part concentrate on helping them manage their study time better through use of such techniques as surveying, skimming, and scanning, and by learning how to increase reading speed without sacrificing comprehension—invaluable aids to academic success.

Therefore, the readings through Part III concentrate on establishing a solid foundation of factual accuracy before moving on to the in-depth comprehension.

Part IV, *The Work-up,* makes the all-important transition from factual to in-depth comprehension. "Reading for Meaning" starts the process. That and all the remaining selections—twenty-one in all—have comprehension tests balancing factual with inferential, judgmental, and critical questions. Concentrated attention is given to reading words, paragraphs, and entire selections more effectively, an ordering to encourage metacognitive skills development. Techniques for getting better grades and developing special interests in varied academic areas conclude this part.

Finally, Part V, *The Round-up,* provides the opportunity to pull together all the newly developed reading and vocabulary suggestions—the separate strands of content—for final application and reinforcement in one of the most troublesome areas for college students, textbooks. Of the nine selections in this part, eight come directly from college textbooks—samples of the reading students must do effectively to succeed in school. These selections are also appropriate for students to practice SSQ, a study technique introduced on page 294 of this text.

Using This Text as a Customized Teaching Tool

The sixth edition of *Reading Power* follows the format and philosophy of previous editions. To allow for differences in instructors' teaching methods, we have developed the text so selections are complementary but not necessarily interdependent. While the book is organized according to proven pedagogical sequence—assessment, explanation of concepts/skills, application of knowledge, skills practice, and evaluation—the book is laid out so that you can use selections in any order that fits your teaching style and the needs of your students. Feel free to bundle instructional passages, applications, reading selections, and assessment pieces in any order that works for you. To ensure the greatest flexibility, we have included more selections than you are likely to use in a sixteen-week semester, which will allow you to omit some pieces if they do not appeal to the interests of your students.

Textbook Selections

PURPOSE FOR THE TEXT EXCERPTS

The textbook excerpts in Part V are included at the suggestion of users of previous editions of *Reading Power.* Presenting these passages gives you an opportunity to dispel many myths about the task of reading textbooks. Some students think that a text is difficult because it is long. Others think that a text is easy if it has many pictures, graphs, and charts. Still others think that they can comprehend the text without mastering the discipline's unique vocabulary. We have written an introductory note to students on pages 345–346 explaining the value of reading textbooks efficiently. Ensure that students read this blurb before tackling the selections that follow.

As in the previous edition, we have included passages from eight college textbooks, and here, too, we have kept interest uppermost, selecting passages of particular appeal. While a single college reading assignment averages 2,500–5,000 words, we have held the text excerpts in this edition to 920–1,650 words, typifying the structure, layout, vocabulary, and syntax of college texts.

Some selections will appeal to all readers, and other excerpts will either be quite difficult or of less interest. For instance, selection 46, "Short Stories," is an overview of a topic that many students find difficult to understand. It is by no means an in-depth treatment and should not replace class discussions of literary elements; to save you the time-consuming task of locating material to illustrate a point, we have included the original in-text examples. However, to reinforce these ideas, you may wish to provide your students examples of literary elements from writings that may be more familiar to them than the ones embedded in the excerpt. You may also choose to use selection 9, "The Three Who Found Death" (though our primary purpose for including this selection in *The Check-up* is to emphasize the importance of recognizing factual information) along with selections 35 and 36 to give students an additional opportunity to apply their knowledge of literary elements.

Likewise, selection 49, "Matter and Energy", is an excerpt from a science text dealing with another less-than-popular topic that most students must study. You may choose to enliven this assignment by asking a science instructor to team teach this class with you, or introduce the topic with a **short** and **interesting** video on the subject. Helping students approach an assignment that they are less than enthusiastic about with tolerance and curiosity fosters an attitude toward learning that will pay off for years to come.

TEXTBOOK VOCABULARY

Since texts are usually written with a degree of formality and pomposity, the text excerpts present you with the opportunity to discuss the different levels of language usage and focus on academic prose versus informal, peer language. This discussion will help students succeed with *The Work-up* and all textbook readings once they understand the role vocabulary plays in readers' understanding of academic subject matter. Before assigning the first selection in *The Work-up*, you may want to take an excerpt from one of the texts used in an introductory course at your institution and illustrate how the author has chosen precise language to express her or his ideas. Also point out that all fields have a unique vocabulary, and learning that vocabulary is critical to learning the discipline. For example, demonstrate how crucial specific words such as *byte, cursor, memory, hard drive,* and *mouse* are to the field of computer science. If the author of the text has provided embedded assistance with the passage's key vocabulary, point out those aids and encourage students to use them.

HELPING STUDENTS DEVELOP INTEREST *BEFORE* THEY TACKLE AN ASSIGNMENT

As every teacher knows, strong student interest promotes academic success and commitment to learning. So when you ask students to read a text excerpt in which they have little interest, they often choose not to read it or complain bitterly while doing the task. When this happens, we suggest that you whet their appetites by giving them interesting bits of information about the subject, suggest that they go on the Internet to seek general information before doing the assignment, teach them study strategies appropriate for the text, or require them to ask a couple of specific questions of at least one authority on the subject before the next class. For instance, if your students complain that they are not interested in the topic of selection 47, "Bureaucratic 'Pathologies,'" do SQ3R on the piece *with* them. Once students are involved with the topic, assign the selection for study.

SHOULD YOU TIME TEXT EXCERPTS?

Maybe you should, and maybe you shouldn't. We have included the word count for each text selection in case you or the students want to assess the rate at which they read complex and challenging content. You might want to time students on the first text selection, provide them strategies for making the task easier and more efficient over the next six, then time the last selection to determine if rate has improved. However, students should understand that texts must be *studied* not just read for effective comprehension and recall. To emphasize this point, you might consider assigning *Ultimate Review* selection 8, "Developing a Study Plan," when students begin working with text selections.

The Ultimate Review

This section of the text has become one of its most popular features. The selections are short, helpful, and appealing to adult readers. You may choose to use them intermittently throughout the semester, a few at the end of each text division, as a finale of reading comprehension exercises, or as students choose them to satisfy a specified number of additional readings.

Regardless of the way you use the *Ultimate Review*, students will benefit from seeing how effectively they are able to apply the skills presented in *Reading Power*.

Internet Activities

Because so much of the reading and research people do today is onscreen, we decided to provide students an opportunity to hone their skills while using this medium. The brief overview of key vocabulary and search engines will help novices launch their first Internet searches with confidence. The six assignments, arranged from easiest to most challenging, provide students ample opportunities to apply the skills presented in the *Ultimate Review*, selection 20, page 531.

The Appendix

The appendix, in addition to the Difficulty Rating Index, contains progress record charts to help students visualize improvement and a conversion table for changing reading time to word-per-minute rate. The Answer Key contains answers for all the exercises, except the Vocabulary post-tests and the *Ultimate Review*, and comprehension tests to provide immediate feedback.

In short, this book is an eminently practical text, emphasizing both reading and study procedures. Flexibility is a central concept, with specialized techniques, different kinds of comprehension questions, and a wide variety of short, highly interesting articles and stories contributing to that objective. The book *leads* the student in a step-by-step progression toward achieving his or her full potential as a reader.

Instructor's Resource Manual

Available with this edition is an Instructor's Resource Manual, which offers suggestions for using the text, vocabulary quizzes, master words activities and tests, and reading and writing discussion questions for each text selection.

Acknowledgments

We wish to thank the following individuals who reviewed the manuscript and made helpful suggestions for improving the text: Terrence Foley, Henry Ford Community College; Lois Hassan, Henry Ford Community College; Damaris Matthews, Crafton Hills College; Constantinos E. Scaros, Interboro Institute. We especially want to thank Ruth Brown for her perceptive insights on the teaching of reading—insights from her training and experience as a certified tutor and teacher of reading that continue to be strongly reflected in this edition of the text.

J. I. B
Prescott, Arizona

V. V. F.
Prescott, Arizona

PART I

The Check-up

CHECK-UP ON YOU THE READER

As you start your reading improvement program, ask yourself three all-important questions; (1) How fast do I read? (2) How much do I comprehend? (3) How much word power do I now have?

Those are the big three questions. Once you know the answers, you can see more clearly the best route to follow for maximum reading improvement. Obviously, you won't know when you've doubled your reading rate unless you know what your present rate is. And you can't know when you've improved comprehension or word power unless you also know what those levels are now. These next few pages will begin to give you some answers.

Begin by checking your current reading rate and comprehension. Of course, such a check-up is complicated by the fact that you're at least three readers rolled into one. And all three need to be carefully checked.

First, there's you the normal reader. Suppose you're at home and see an interesting magazine article. You read it normally, not thinking about reading rate or comprehension. In that normal situation, how fast do you read and how much do you comprehend? That's the first reader you must get acquainted with—you the relaxed, unpressured, normal reader. What's true in that situation?

Next, check up on yourself as a speed reader. It's the same you, but different. What happens when you read as fast as you possibly can? That's something you need to know. What is your absolute top rate and how much comprehension do you get? Sometimes you haven't time to read normally. You have to turn on top speed. So—check up on yourself as a speed reader. How fast can you read and how much comprehension do you get in that situation?

Finally, there's still another reader to be checked—you the serious reader. As a student or career reader, comprehension is all-important. And you want to get top comprehension in one careful reading. In that situation, what happens to speed? And do you get the desired comprehension? Remember—only one reading for best possible comprehension.

Individual differences abound. You may read fast and comprehend little or much. You'll find out which only by checking up on yourself. In general, speed suggests carelessness. In reading, however, often the faster you read, *within limits,* the better your comprehension. But those limits vary widely with individuals and you'll have to discover what those limits are for you.

To understand why this is so, compare reading with driving. Driving along a country road at 20 mph invites relaxation and wandering attention. But swing onto a freeway and zoom up to 75 mph and you're forced to give driving your full, concentrated attention. In the same way, slow reading can invite wandering attention and loss of comprehension. Within limits, faster reading usually means improved comprehension.

In the three readings that follow, take a threefold look at yourself: (1) as a normal reader, (2) as a speed reader, and (3) as a reader for comprehension. You'll then see yourself as a complete reader, discovering strong and weak points so that your efforts to improve will be focused to best advantage for making progress.

Now do your first reading—"Reading Power—Key to Personal Growth." Read it only once, normally. Don't try for speed or comprehension. See what happens when you just relax and read normally. Use a stop watch or clock with a sweep second hand to get an accurate time for your reading. When you reach the end of the selection, check the minutes and seconds to see how long it took you. Then take the following ten-item comprehension test without looking back at the selection. This gives you a comprehension score. Finally, when you finish that test, turn to the conversion table on page 421 and convert your reading time into words per minute (wpm)—your reading rate score.

Continue on with the next two selections, doing each exactly as directed to get a threefold picture of you the reader. These scores will mark your present performance levels—your beginning point for progress in all three reading situations.

1

Reading Power—Key to Personal Growth

BEGIN TIMING

Power! Could you get through a single normal day without using some? Take electrical power. Without it, your TV and radio would be soundless. And you might as well not own an electric refrigerator, toaster, mixer, or stove, not to mention a telephone or doorbell. And that dependable car of yours, minus a storage battery, is dead—utterly and completely. We're indeed heavily dependent on power, whether it be electric, gasoline, water, or nuclear.

Most people, however, overlook the most important power of all: reading power. Through reading we get knowledge; and according to Bacon, "Knowledge itself *is* power." Voltaire agreed. He said, "Books rule the world." Engineers, for example, must rely on knowledge to plan, build, and maintain all varieties of power systems.

But here's the important question. What can reading power do for you personally, now and for the rest of your life?

Reading Power = Learning Power

First, reading power generates learning power. As Carlyle said: "All that mankind has done, thought, gained or been: it is lying as in magic preservation in the pages of books." Reading provides the key.

Reading will help you know yourself better. You'll know your potential better—your strengths and weaknesses, including those in the area of reading. A recent comprehensive survey of 418 institutions of higher education was most revealing. From 64 to 95 percent of the students had trouble with their reading. That means that when you take steps to improve your reading, you soon gain a distinct advantage over those who don't.

Reading will also help you know others better. Back in 1926, Tunney challenged Dempsey, world heavyweight boxing champion, to a match. Tunney, an avid reader, read everything he could about his formidable opponent. He discovered that Dempsey's fists were once clocked at 135 miles an hour. To minimize Dempsey's hammerlike blows, Tunney practiced running backward. Soon he ran as lightly and surely backward as forward. And it paid off. Tunney won. He became the new world champion. Knowing others helps you win friends and influence people as well as win championships—extremely valuable knowledge.

Finally, reading helps you understand past, present, and future more clearly. "Cultures which see no further than themselves bear the seeds of their own destruction." Similarly, individuals who see no further than themselves bear the seeds of their own difficulties. The past provides perspective for both present and future. "Future shock" is not nearly so traumatic or unsettling.

In those three areas—knowing self, others, and the broad sweep of time—reading power brings you added learning power. You can understand and cope more effectively with the sum total of life.

Reading Power = Earning Power

Your reading power activates a second power of crucial importance: your earning power. The move from learning power to earning power is easy to understand. An individual with know-how is obviously worth more than one without know-how. Suppose you have car trouble. You'll certainly want a technician who has read the various detailed instructional manuals. He should be able to solve your car problems quickly and efficiently.

Reading power helps in two ways. It helps you get a better job. And it helps you succeed better on the job.

William Anderson, Navy submarine officer, was called in for an interview with Hyman Rickover, Admiral of the Navy, about a special hush-hush assignment. During the interview, Rickover said, "Anderson, name the books and their authors that you have read in the last two years."

Anderson was struck completely dumb by this unexpected question. He couldn't remember a single title. Finally he stammered out the name of one book that came to mind, but he couldn't remember the author. Rickover frowned, then said with finality, "Good-bye."

When Anderson got home, he told his wife about the interview. He added, "I don't know what job he had in mind, but I do know I will never get it."

Later, he wandered into his library. He then began jotting down titles of the books he remembered reading. Just so Rickover wouldn't think him too easygoing and not sufficiently concerned with personal growth through reading, Anderson mailed him the list of twenty-four books.

Apparently Rickover had all but rejected him. But when he received his reading list, Rickover "changed his mind," Anderson says. So, Anderson got the position—commander of the world's first nuclear-powered submarine.

Reading contributes equally well to improved on-the-job performance. You'll find pertinent manuals, texts, and articles to help with any job. Technical information pours out at a rate of 60 million pages a year. Obviously, it takes a good reader to keep abreast of developments and make him- or herself genuinely indispensable.

Reading Power = Yearning Power

Getting or keeping a job may not be as important as making your own job. That takes some not-so-impossible dreaming—some yearning, so to speak. That's still another benefit from reading. Reading serves well as a catalyst for creativity.

Reading can actually make you a billionaire. You'll see how. Just read on. You'll discover exactly where to find millions in gold and silver that you have a legal right to. The figures are from Rachel Carson's book *The Sea Around Us.* In every cubic mile of sea water you'll find about $93,000,000 in gold and $8,500,000 in silver. There it waits. Of course, you'll have to do some more reading to develop sufficient know-how to get it. But you can be certain that one of these days, some purposeful reader will work out the necessary details. He or she will make a fortune. It's like buried treasure. It's waiting for the right person to move from yearning to earning.

In short, don't overlook the role reading power can play in your life from now on. In school, use it to achieve heightened scholastic success. Afterward, use it to bring on-the-job success.

In fact, probably everything you do can be done somewhat better by some appropriate reading. So, make reading power your key to learning, earning, and yearning power. Make it your key to personal growth and achievement.

Length: 1000 words.
Reading Time: __________
See Conversion Table, p. 421.
Enter WPM Rate on p. 416.

1 Reading Power—Key to Personal Growth

COMPREHENSION CHECK

1. What kind of power is *not* specifically mentioned? (a) earning power (b) atomic power (c) electrical power (d) nuclear power — 1. ____

2. Specific mention is made of whom? (a) Hitler (b) Bacon (c) Churchill (d) Shakespeare — 2. ____

3. The survey mentioned is of (a) junior colleges. (b) private colleges. (c) secondary schools. (d) institutions of higher learning. — 3. ____

4. What did Tunney practice? (a) running backward (b) ducking (c) side-stepping (d) making lightning jabs — 4. ____

5. Dempsey's fists were clocked at (a) 60 mph. (b) 85 mph. (c) 100 mph. (d) 135 mph. — 5. ____

6. "Cultures which see no further than themselves bear the seeds of their own . . ." what? (a) death (b) dominance (c) destruction (d) stability — 6. ____

7. Rickover is spoken of as (a) a Navy Captain. (b) Admiral of the Navy. (c) Secretary of War. (d) a General. — 7. ____

8. Anderson (a) was demoted. (b) got a tentative appointment only. (c) did not get the job. (d) got the job. — 8. ____

9. Technical information pours out at a rate of how many million pages a year? (a) 20 (b) 40 (c) 60 (d) 80 — 9. ____

10. A single cubic mile of sea water contains about how much money in gold? (a) $120,000,000 (b) $93,000,000 (c) $28,000,000 (d) $8,500,000 — 10. ____

Check your answers with the Key on p. 451. Give yourself 10 points for each one right and enter your comprehension score on p. 414.

Comprehension Score: ________

Read this selection at your top reading speed, checking both rate and comprehension as with the earlier selection. No rereading. Just one reading at top speed.

2

Surviving the Information Avalanche

JAMES I. BROWN

How fortunate you are to be living in the information age. Right? Better think again. This information age has spawned a veritable avalanche of print that threatens to bury us all alive. Unless? Yes, read on for possible help.

BEGIN TIMING

Our overwhelming flood of words is both wonderful and impossible. So wonderful to have this unbelievable wealth of knowledge! So impossible to deal with it! Actually, it's a two-fold problem—print-on-paper, print-on-screen.

Print-on-paper has been growing ever since Solomon's day. You remember what he said, "Of making many books there is no end." He couldn't begin to know that the Library of Congress now reports over 300,000 different titles a year. You'd have to read more than a book a minute to keep up with that avalanche of print. And that's only books. What about magazines, newspapers, brochures, and letters? One expert, talking about technical information, said it was coming out at a rate of 60 million pages a year. Reading eight hours a day, he added, it would take you until 3363 to finish one year's outpouring.

Add to that the relatively new print-on-screen avalanche. Surf the World Wide Web. What information is out there in cyberspace? Suppose you want to know about "senior citizen health." You go to the search engine Excite. You type in that subject. The screen tells you there are exactly 2,808,486 finds! And that's only one subject. What a challenge screen reading is. How wonderful! How impossible!

Obviously, time is of the essence. A 48-hour day would help. But time, that most precious commodity, comes only in 24-hour segments—no more, no less. What's the solution? *Making time.* That's quite different from adding to time, an impossibility. As little as fifteen to thirty minutes a day can do the trick. That thin sliver of time can make you well over twenty-one additional hours a week.

Here's how it works. Suppose you now read at 250 words per minute (wpm). And suppose you read three hours a day on average—on paper or on screen. By doubling your reading rate, you have, in a sense, made yourself twenty-one extra hours a week. You can now do forty-two hours of reading in twenty-one hours' time. In a year that means you've made yourself 1,092 hours. And don't think you have to stop with doubling your rate. Many readers triple or quadruple their rate; that means 2,184 or 3,276 extra hours a year.

But, improving your reading speed should, in fact, serve three functions, not one. It should act as time-stretcher or hour-maker, problem-solver, and experience-extender. Carlyle catches that broad perspective so well. Remember? He wrote, "All that mankind has done, thought, gained, or been; it is lying as in magic preservation in the pages of books."

Let's be specific. Exactly how can you increase your reading rate? By taking off the brakes! You wouldn't think of driving your car with both hand and foot brake on. Yet, as a reader, you probably have several brakes on. Let's check the three most common.

Regressing

The first brake is regressing. That's looking back every now and then at something already read. It's like stepping backward every few yards as you walk—hardly the way you move ahead in a hurry. Why do readers regress? It may be pure habit. After all, when we started reading we looked back all the time. It may just be lack of confidence or mind wandering. It may be a vocabulary deficiency or an actual missing of a word or phrase. See what it does to—it does to a complex sentence—complex sentence like this, which seems even more tangled—more tangled than usual as the—the eyes frequently—eyes frequently regress—regress. Obviously, this all-too-common habit plays havoc with reading speed, comprehension, and efficiency.

Eye movement photographs of some 12,000 readers show that college students regress on the average of fifteen times in reading only 100 words. To be sure, they performed better than the average ninth grader, who regressed twenty times. In short, regressions probably consume one-sixth or more of your precious reading time. That makes them a major retarding factor. Release this brake; enjoy an immediate spurt in reading speed. Class results show that an awareness of this problem, which you now have, plus application of the suggestions to follow, should bring an 80 percent decrease in regressions.

Vocalizing

A second common brake is vocalizing—pronouncing the words to yourself as you read. As beginning readers we were probably taught to pronounce words, syllables, and even letters. No wonder traces of this habit persist, interfering later on with general reading efficiency. To see for yourself how vocalizing slows reading speed, read these words slowly, pronouncing aloud as you read, sounding the syl - la - bles and even l - e - t - t - e - r -s.

At the lip level, vocalizing pulls reading down to the speed of speech, probably well below 175 wpm. To diagnose, put a finger over your lips as you read silently. Do you feel any movement? To rid yourself of the habit, keep a memory-jogging finger on your lips as you read.

Vocalizing at the voice-box level is far more common and much less obvious. If your top reading rate was close to 275 wpm, you have reason to suspect that kind of vocalizing. Check further by placing your thumb and forefinger lightly on each side of your voice box. If, as you read silently, you feel faint movements, you know your problem, an important step toward its solution.

Word-for-Word Reading

The third major brake is word-for-word reading. To move 200 books, you certainly wouldn't take 200 trips, one book a trip. Ten trips, twenty books a trip would be more likely. As a reader, keep that same principle in mind.

Eye movement photographs show that in reading, the eyes move jerkily along a line of print, making a series of short stops to permit reading a portion of print. Research indicates that even college students without special training are word-by-word readers, taking in only 1.1 words per fixation or look. Obviously one way to double or triple your rate is by learning to take in two or three words at a glance instead of the usual one.

There they are—the three major causes of reading inefficiency, the three brakes that hold your reading to a snail's pace. Release them and enjoy immediate returns. Fortunately, one single key principle, properly applied, will do the job.

The Solution

Every successful reading improvement course relies heavily on this key principle—faster-than-comfortable reading. This principle automatically reduces regressions. You're pushing ahead too fast to look back. Furthermore, you have less time to vocalize; that bad habit begins to disappear. Finally, the added speed actually forces you to deal with word groups, not single words.

Put this principle to immediate use. Practice faster-than-comfortable speeds with the selections in this book. Don't worry too much at first about comprehension. That will come later as you gain added experience and skill at the faster speeds. Keep an accurate record of your rate with each selection in the back of the book. Make yourself hundreds of additional hours. The need is imperative.

One word sums up our times better than any other. The word *change!* But hasn't change always been present? True. But never at such breakneck speed. Today it's more than change. It's unprecedented change, revealed largely through the information avalanche. At such a time, reading gives you the best tool possible for keeping up in a world continually being remade.

Length: 1210 words.
Reading Time: ________
See Conversion Table, p. 421.
Enter WPM Rate on p. 416.

2 Surviving the Information Avalanche

COMPREHENSION CHECK

1. The article mentions (a) Moses. (b) Solomon. (c) Samson. (d) Shakespeare. 1. ____

2. What search engine was mentioned? (a) Yahoo! (b) Expedia (c) Pico Search (d) Excite 2. ____

3. Doubling your reading rate makes you how many extra hours a week? (a) 12 (b) 14 (c) 21 (d) 42 3. ____

4. Improving your reading speed serves how many functions? (a) only one (b) two (c) three (d) four 4. ____

5. How many different brakes were discussed? (a) 2 (b) 3 (c) 4 (d) 5 5. ____

6. In reading 100 words, college students regressed an average of how many times? (a) 15 (b) 18 (c) 20 (d) 23 6. ____

7. College students were called (a) omnivorous readers. (b) careful readers. (c) word-by-word readers. (d) fast readers. 7. ____

8. Vocalizing at the voice-box level is suspected if your top reading rate is close to what speed? (a) 240 wpm (b) 260 wpm (c) 275 wpm (d) 295 wpm 8. ____

9. A comparison was made between reading and (a) driving. (b) skimming. (c) moving books. (d) thinking. 9. ____

10. What one word was said to sum up our times best? (a) speed (b) computer (c) change (d) frustration 10. ____

Check your answers with the Key on p. 451. Give yourself 10 points for each one right and enter your comprehension score on p. 414.

Comprehension Score: ________

Read this selection once only for the best possible comprehension. Check both rate and comprehension as with the earlier two selections. Remember! Once only for maximum comprehension.

3

How to Read a Difficult Book

MORTIMER J. ADLER

Adler has been a prime mover of a new way to become educated—an education no one gets in an educational institution today. His concern is not with credits, degrees, and diplomas; it's with reading the finest written creations of the human mind—fifty-seven volumes in all—the Great Books. Now you know why he's helping us read difficult books.

BEGIN TIMING

The most important rule about reading is one I have told my great books seminars again and again: In reading a difficult book for the first time, read the book through without stopping. Pay attention to what you can understand, and don't be stopped by what you can't immediately grasp. Keep on this way. Read the book through undeterred by the paragraphs, footnotes, arguments, and references that escape you. If you stop at any of these stumbling blocks, if you let yourself get stalled, you are lost. In most cases you won't be able to puzzle the thing out by sticking to it. You have a much better chance of understanding it on a second reading, but that requires you to read the book *through* for the first time.

This is the most practical method I know to break the crust of a book, to get the feel and general sense of it, and to come to terms with its structure as quickly and as easily as possible. The longer you delay in getting some sense of the over-all plan of a book, the longer you are in understanding it. You simply must have some grasp of the whole before you can see the parts in their true perspective—or often in any perspective at all.

Shakespeare was spoiled for generations of high school students who were forced to go through *Julius Caesar, Hamlet,* or *Macbeth* scene by scene, to look up all the words that were new to them, and to study all the scholarly footnotes. As a result, they never actually read the play. Instead, they were dragged through it, bit by bit, over a period of many weeks. By the time they got to the end of the play, they had surely forgotten the beginning. They should have been encouraged to read the play in one sitting. Only then would they have understood enough of it to make it possible for them to understand more.

What you understand by reading a book through to the end—even if it is only 50 percent or less—will help you later in making the additional effort to go back to places you passed by on your first reading. Actually you will be proceeding like any traveler in unknown parts. Having been over the terrain once, you will be able to explore it again from vantage points you could not have known about before. You will be less likely to mistake the side roads for the main highway. You won't be deceived by the shadows at high noon, because you will remember how they looked at sunset. And the mental map you have fashioned will show better how the valleys and mountains are all part of one landscape.

There is nothing magical about a first quick reading. It cannot work wonders and should certainly never be thought of as a substitute for the careful reading that a good book deserves. But a first quick reading makes the careful study much easier.

This practice helps you to keep alert in going at a book. How many times have you daydreamed your way through pages and pages only to wake up with no idea of the ground you have been over? That can't help happening if you let yourself drift passively through a book. No one ever understands much that way. You must have a way of getting a general thread to hold onto.

A good reader is active in his efforts to understand. Any book is a problem, a puzzle. The reader's attitude is that of a detective looking for clues to its basic ideas and alert for anything that will make them clearer. The rule about a first quick reading helps to sustain this attitude. If you follow it, you will be surprised how much time you will save, how much more you will grasp, and how much easier it will be.

Length: 650 words.
Reading Time: ________
See Conversion Table, p. 421.
Enter WPM Rate on p. 416.

3 How to Read a Difficult Book

COMPREHENSION CHECK

1. Adler mentions his (a) honor students. (b) college teaching. (c) graduate students. (d) seminars. 1. ____

2. Specific reference is made to (a) italics. (b) footnotes. (c) central idea. (d) subheadings. 2. ____

3. You're specifically told to get a sense of the (a) over-all plan. (b) main idea. (c) outline. (d) author's purpose. 3. ____

4. Adler refers to (a) *Merchant of Venice.* (b) *King Lear.* (c) *Julius Caesar.* (d) *Romeo and Juliet.* 4. ____

5. For high school students reading Shakespeare bit by bit, Shakespeare was (a) ruined. (b) spoiled. (c) mismanaged. (d) harmed. 5. ____

6. You are told to read a book through even if you understand (a) only 50 percent or less. (b) only 20 percent. (c) only 10 percent. (d) almost nothing. 6. ____

7. You are specifically told that a first quick reading was (a) magical. (b) not magical. (c) optional. (d) wonder-working. 7. ____

8. Specific mention is made of (a) side roads. (b) trails. (c) freeways. (d) gravel roads. 8. ____

9. Adler writes about holding on to what? (a) an idea (b) a general thread (c) a ruling purpose (d) an outline 9. ____

10. Adler specifically likens reading a book to a (a) paradox. (b) mystery. (c) puzzle. (d) riddle. 10. ____

Check your answers with the Key on p. 451. Give yourself 10 points for each one right and enter your comprehension score on p. 414.

Comprehension Score: ________

Interpreting Your Reading Check-up

Now take your three sets of scores—your three-fold diagnosis of you the reader—and enter them in the appropriate blanks that follow. Then look at the descriptive labels below to get help in evaluating your three performances. Finally, check on your flexibility as directed. The descriptive labels are based on normative data from reading classes at the University of Minnesota, classes with a mixture of freshman through senior students. Such comparisons may not be as appropriate for you as others might be, but you can still use them as rough estimates to help you evaluate your reading performance.

You can see immediately how you are coping with the information avalanche. In addition, you'll know whether your three performances tend to be somewhat on a par or whether one is much better than another. For example, some readers may find that they are "average" when reading normally but only "fair" at top speed.

The last check—the check of flexibility—should provide additional useful insights. If you had a one-speed car that would only run at 40 mph, you would be a most dissatisfied owner. If you find you are almost a one-speed reader, as some people are, you'll want to know so you can start building added reading flexibility. Some things deserve fast reading, some slow. You want to manage both well.

1. My normal reading rate was ______.

175 wpm or less	Very poor
175–210 wpm	Poor
210–240 wpm	Fair
240–275 wpm	Average
275–320 wpm	Very good
320–400 wpm	Excellent
400 wpm or more	Outstanding

2. My top reading rate was ______.

230 wpm or less	Very poor
230–300 wpm	Poor
300–330 wpm	Fair
330–390 wpm	Average
390–420 wpm	Very good
420–500 wpm	Excellent
500 wpm or more	Outstanding

3. My comprehension reading rate was ______.

125 wpm or less	Very poor
125–160 wpm	Poor
160–180 wpm	Fair
180–210 wpm	Average
210–245 wpm	Very good
245–280 wpm	Excellent
280 wpm or more	Outstanding

4. Check of reading flexibility
   Fastest reading rate: ______
   Slowest reading rate: ______
   Subtract to get the difference: ______

50 wpm or less	Very poor
50–100 wpm	Poor
100–125 wpm	Fair
125–150 wpm	Average
150–200 wpm	Very good
200–300 wpm	Excellent
300 wpm or more	Outstanding

This extended check on yourself as a reader is so important that you will be repeating the same process after the next three readings to provide even more substantial insights to build on as you progress through this text.

Use these scores to set up a target for yourself. Take aim at either rate or comprehension and at normal speed, top speed, or comprehension reading. The lower your score in any area, the more room you have for improvement. A sharp, clear focus on what most needs your attention should do much to speed your progress.

Furthermore, no matter how good you are in any area, you always have room for improvement. A comprehension score of 70 is good but a move up to 80 or 90 is much better. A reading rate of 250 wpm is good, but increasing your rate to 500 wpm is much to be desired.

Remember, the better you read, the better you feel about yourself. Traces of uncertainty or inferiority tend to disappear, to be replaced by feelings of self-confidence and assurance. To be sure, it takes effort. But a blood, sweat, and tears approach soon brings improved skill, success—and smiles. It does pay off.

Beginning with the next selection, you should follow this step-by-step procedure:

1. **Word Power Workout.** Always complete this three-part exercise *before* reading the selection that follows. This helps you resolve major word problems before doing the reading, equivalent to stretching before running. Actually, there are two kinds of words—those you know and those you don't. These exercises are designed to move as many words as possible from the don't-know to the do-know category. And, remember, words are like muscles—use them or lose them. So even if a word is one you already know, use it again, don't lose it.
2. **Selection.** Read the selection, always timing yourself to get an accurate measure of reading rate.
3. **Comprehension Check.** Complete the ten-item test after doing the reading. Don't look back at the selection for help. The comprehension score should measure what you got in one reading. Use the Answer Key on pages 451–452 to get your comprehension score.
4. **Conversion Table.** To convert reading time to wpm rate, use the Conversion Tables on pages 421–436.
5. **Progress Record Chart.** To see graphically what progress you're making, enter both rate and comprehension scores for every reading on the Progress Record Charts on pages 414–419.

CHECK-UP ON YOU THE WORD-USER

Words are at the very heart of you the communicator, whether you read, write, speak, or listen. That means you need to take a careful look at your present vocabulary level. Some years ago the *New York Times* carried an editorial titled "Vocabulary and Marks," which began by asking if there was any magic formula for getting high marks in college. It went on to say that a research study showed that freshmen who worked on vocabulary got better marks in all their sophomore courses than did their fellow classmates. Conversely, those who did not work on vocabulary averaged 7.5 places nearer the bottom of their class their sophomore year. Looks like a new word a day keeps the low grades away. And that's exactly why this book is designed as it is—to give your vocabulary and your reading maximum improvement.

Those results suggested the need to check further. We took several sections of the University of Minnesota Efficient Reading class for which we had standardized Nelson-Denny reading test scores at the beginning and end of the course. That meant we knew exactly how much progress each student had made. On the last day of class students were asked how frequently they had used a dictionary during the quarter. Those who said they used the dictionary once a week or less averaged 11 percentile points improvement. But those who said they used a dictionary once a day or more averaged 26 percentile points improvement—45 percent more than those consulting the dictionary less frequently. Make the dictionary your best friend, academically speaking. Keep it handy. Use it often. Obviously it pays off!

Now it's time to find out how much word power you have. The following two tests measure what might be called a basic knowledge of words. You have nothing to help you arrive at meaning but the word itself. Take the tests without help from your dictionary. See how many you know right now without further study.

VOCABULARY PRE-TEST A

This twenty-five item test is made up of one word from each of the first twenty-five selections in this text. Each item you miss means a possible misreading or misunderstanding of a part of that selection. Your score will let you know how much attention you should give to developing more word power. Enter the letter of the correct answer in the space at the right.

1. potential — (a) convenient (b) fragrant (c) possible (d) tempting (e) helpful — 1. _____

2. essence — (a) combination (b) major part (c) odor (d) elimination (e) feeling — 2. _____

3. stalled — (a) lingered (b) stained (c) shoved (d) stopped (e) cleared — 3. _____

4. predilection — (a) prediction (b) session (c) preference (d) election (e) section — 4. _____

5. maxim — (a) size (b) increase (c) meaning (d) saying (e) measure — 5. _____

6. competent — (a) complex (b) adequate (c) painful (d) patient (e) adaptable — 6. _____

7. abysmally — (a) safely (b) extremely (c) modestly (d) absently (e) rudely — 7. _____

8. sham — (a) disgrace (b) fraud (c) amazement (d) hatred (e) change — 8. _____

9. dirk — (a) ornament (b) pin (c) dagger (d) label (e) dent — 9. _____

10. relented — (a) respected (b) delayed (c) combined (d) gave in (e) saved — 10. _____

11. attain — (a) stretch (b) attempt (c) achieve (d) supply (e) travel — 11. _____

12. conned — (a) crossed (b) attempted (c) quieted (d) tricked (e) settled — 12. _____

13. veritable — (a) changeable (b) actual (c) substantial (d) imaginary (e) shaky — 13. _____

14. unalterable (a) unchangeable (b) unimaginable (c) unlikely (d) unfinished (e) unhealthy 14. ____

15. vulnerable (a) vague (b) helpless (c) crude (d) grasping (e) voluntary 15. ____

16. repertoire (a) show (b) sound (c) range of skills (d) retreat (e) pattern 16. ____

17. platitudes (a) level stretches (b) bridges (c) plates (d) proverbs (e) commonplaces 17. ____

18. berated (a) judged (b) returned (c) asked (d) separated (e) scolded 18. ____

19. feasible (a) flexible (b) factual (c) workable (d) reasonable (e) answerable 19. ____

20. malevolent (a) antagonistic (b) crazy (c) ignorant (d) careless (e) relevant 20. ____

21. equanimity (a) sadness (b) strangeness (c) calmness (d) wisdom (e) care 21. ____

22. ambiguity (a) energy (b) hugeness (c) admiration (d) artistry (e) uncertainty 22. ____

23. ovation (a) overture (b) greeting (c) welcome (d) burst of applause (e) small opening 23. ____

24. verge (a) trial (b) sense (c) vagueness (d) brink (e) hope 24. ____

25. havoc (a) war (b) horror (c) shelter (d) hatred (e) confusion 25. ____

4 points for each correct answer.
See Key on p. 440.
Vocabulary Pre-Test A Test Score: ________

VOCABULARY PRE-TEST B

For this test, one word has been selected from each of the last twenty-five selections in this text. Again, any item missed means a potential misreading or misunderstanding of a portion of the selection containing that word.

26. repress	(a) redo (b) suppress (c) hold up (d) save (e) approve	26. ____
27. contiguity	(a) result (b) complaint (c) conduct (d) nearness (e) strength	27. ____
28. abound	(a) are plentiful (b) attack (c) enter (d) help (e) remain	28. ____
29. culled	(a)created (b) crossed (c) selected (d) sampled (e) calmed	29. ____
30. epiphany	(a) preclude (b) harmony (c) flash of insight (d) concert (e) cloud burst	30. ____
31. facilitate	(a) fasten (b) hold up (c) release (d) continue (e) assist	31. ____
32. pang	(a) spot (b) beginning (c) bruise (d) look (e) twinge	32. ____
33. quizzical	(a) questioning (b) quaint (c) uncertain (d) hopeful (e) far	33. ____
34. arduous	(a) eager (b) difficult (c) direct (d) original (e) ancient	34. ____
35. pariah	(a) outcast (b) priest (c) partner (d) player (e) deserter	35. ____
36. agile	(a) aged (b) tall (c) supple (d) grand (e) tender	36. ____
37. culmination	(a) end (b) beginning (c) summation (d) outline (e) highest	37. ____
38. ironic	(a) metallic (b) awkward (c) sad (d) intense (e) contradictory	38. ____
39. imperative	(a) impudent (b) suggestive (c) unexpected (d) compelling (e) imaginative	39. ____

40. outstanding (a) upright (b) stable (c) sharp (d) remarkable (e) proud 40. ____

41. norm (a) standard (b) sum (c) nostril (d) feeling (e) note 41. ____

42. emulate (a) face (b) copy (c) enter (d) sign (e) fasten 42. ____

43. archaic (a) accidental (b) crooked (c) poisonous (d) crippled (e) ancient 43. ____

44. vanguard (a) rear (b) barrier (c) forefront (d) brace (e) vehicle 44. ____

45. exemplify (a) extract (b) empty (c) illustrate (d) complicate (e) earn 45. ____

46. cumbersome (a) combined (b) bent around (c) casual (d) complicated (e) separated 46. ____

47. dour (a) dark (b) blind (c) severe (d) ancient (e) small 47. ____

48. amorphous (a) amorous (b) sleepy (c) lively (d) solid (e) shapeless 48. ____

49. paramount (a) primary (b) fixed (c) active (d) artistic (e) ageless 49. ____

50. philanthropic (a) benevolent (b) hearty (c) thoughtful (d) lovely (e) rich 50. ____

4 points for each correct answer.

See Key on p. 440.

Vocabulary Pre-Test B Test Score: ________

Word Power Beginnings

Now for your first step toward greater word power! It's the first of forty-seven such word power workouts, each with an in-depth coverage of ten of the most difficult words from the selection that follows. Complete all forty-seven; make your vocabulary 470 words richer.

At first in every exercise you'll meet each word in the briefest of contexts exactly as found in the selection to be read. Sometimes that context supplies no more than an indication of part of speech. You match words and definitions with context help. Next you make the words yours by turning to the longer sentence-length contexts, approximating the English you yourself might use. Fit each word into its appropriate sentence. Then repeat the sentence a time or so to make it seem natural. These steps sharpen your awareness of meaning and provide useful reinforcement before you meet the word for the third time as you read it in its full, complete context.

To make a word yours, use it three times. Once isn't enough. That's only a good beginning. Twice and it's almost within your grasp. It's the third time that does the trick, that makes it rememberable. That's the rationale behind these exercises.

To be sure, you already know some of those 470 words. Even so, the exercises will bring such words closer to the tip of your tongue or pen for easier use. That's called *fluency*—a very important facet of word power. After all, you don't want to waste time groping for words. You want them ready for immediate use.

You'll also find exercises to sharpen your ability to deal with word parts—all-important prefix, root, and suffix elements. They provide shortcuts to the meanings of over 14,000 words of desk dictionary size or an estimated 100,000 words in the big unabridged volume.

In short, when you finish this book, your vocabulary should be well over ***14,470*** words stronger. That includes new words, new meanings for old words, old words raised to a more fluent level, plus some dramatically useful shortcuts to word meanings. That all adds up to increased confidence and satisfaction with your improved ability to communicate—in reading, writing, speaking, and listening.

So, do each exercise carefully, checking your answers with the Key. Clear up any word difficulties before reading on. If needed, get additional help from your dictionary. Always enter your score for each part on the Progress Record Charts, pages 414–415.

NAME ______________________ CLASS ____________________ DATE _____________

4 How Should You Build Up Your Vocabulary?

WORD POWER WORKOUT

A. LEANING ON CONTEXT

In each of the blanks provided, place the letter that precedes the best definition of the underlined word in context to the left.

Words in Context

1. _____ <u>consolidated</u> his findings
2. _____ research <u>corroborates</u> that fact
3. _____ <u>discrimination</u> contributes more to speed of reading
4. _____ strange words <u>hinder</u> comprehension
5. _____ <u>hybrid</u> corn combines the best qualities
6. _____ to <u>expedite</u> your use of word parts
7. _____ a <u>tentative</u> definition
8. _____ a <u>predilection</u> for reading
9. _____ dynamic <u>interplay</u> of approaches
10. _____ vocabulary in <u>context</u>

Definitions

a. confirms; makes certain
b. hasten; speed up
c. preference
d. noting of differences
e. prevent
f. interaction
g. surrounding words, phrases, and sentences
h. mixed origin
i. combined
j. temporary

Check your answers with the Key on p. 442 before going on. Give yourself 10 points for each one right and enter your score on the chart under A on p. 420. Review any that you have missed.

A Score: ________

Pronunciation aids: **1. kuhn-SOL-uh-dayt'd** **2. kuh-ROB-uh-rayts** **6. EK-spuh-dyts** **8. pred-uh-LEK-shun**

B. LEANING ON PARTS

See how prefix meaning relates to word meaning by supplying the missing word or word part in each of the following sentences.

1. To heat "before" is to pre________.
2. To make ready "beforehand" is to pre________.
3. In our government, the one before all others is called pre________.
4. The pre________ *pre-* is a shortcut to the meanings of over 4000 words in the big unabridged dictionary.
5. To precede means to go ________ someone else.

C. MAKING THE WORDS YOURS

In each blank below, enter the most appropriate word from the ten words in context in the first exercise, substituting it for the word(s) in parentheses. Use these words: *consolidated, context, corroborated, discrimination, expedite, hybrid, bindered, interplay, predilection, tentative.*

1. In order to make a profit, the two companies were (combined) ____________.
2. Most (mixed origin) ____________ flowers are larger.
3. He tried to (hasten) ____________ his trial.
4. Her dishonesty (prevented) ____________ her from receiving a promotion.
5. The lie detector (confirmed) ____________ his guilt.
6. The group had a strong (preference) ____________ for rock music.
7. The high team morale was due to the (interaction) ____________ of many factors.
8. She made (temporary) ____________ arrangements for her transportation.
9. The (noting of differences) ____________ among synonyms can sometimes be troublesome.
10. A good reader uses (the surrounding words, phrases, and sentences) ____________ to help understand an unknown word.

Check your answers with the Key on p. 443.

B Score: ________

C Score: ________

Enter your scores on p. 420.

Again, with this selection check your normal reading rate and comprehension. Read it once only. Don't try to read faster or slower or to comprehend more or less than you would normally in relaxed fashion at home. See how you perform normally.

4

How Should You Build Up Your Vocabulary?

BEGIN TIMING

Exactly what do you do during a normal day? How do you spend your time? Paul T. Rankin very much wanted an answer to that question. To get it, he asked sixty-eight individuals to keep an accurate, detailed record of what they did every minute of their waking hours. When he consolidated his findings, he discovered that the average individual spent 70 percent of his or her waking time doing *one* thing only—*communicating.* That meant either reading, writing, speaking, or listening.

Put that evidence alongside of the research findings uncovered by the Human Engineering Laboratories. In exploring aptitudes and careers involving, among other things, data from 30,000 vocabulary tests given yearly, they discovered that big incomes and big vocabularies go together. Vocabulary, more than any other factor yet known, predicts financial success.

And it all fits. Each word you add to your vocabulary makes you a better reader, writer, speaker, and listener. Furthermore, linguistic scientists are quick to point out that we actually think with words. If that is so, new words make us better thinkers as well as communicators. No wonder more words are likely to mean more money. What better reason for beginning right now to extend your vocabulary?

Take reading. What exactly do you read? Common sense says you read words. Research corroborates that fact. "Vocabulary in context" contributes 39 percent to comprehension. That's more than any other factor isolated and studied—even more than intelligence. And "word discrimination" contributes more to speed of reading than any other factor—28 percent. In short, your efforts to improve vocabulary will pay off in both comprehension and speed.

Suppose, as you're reading along, you lumtebs across a strange word. Did you find yourself stopping for a closer look at *lumtebs?* Pardon the spelling slip. That's actually the word *stumble.* The letters just got mixed around. Obviously you now know that strange words do slow you down—or even stop you completely. Furthermore, strange words hinder comprehension. Which is easier to understand, "Eschew garrulity" or "Avoid talking too much"?

What you need is a vital, dynamic approach to vocabulary building. Hybrid corn combines the best qualities of several varieties to ensure maximum productivity. A hybrid approach to vocabulary should, in the same way, ensure maximum results. That's why you should use the CPD Formula.

Through Context

When students in a college class were asked what should be done when they came across an unknown word in their reading, 84 percent said, "Look it up in the dictionary." If you do, however, you short-circuit the very mental processes needed to make your efforts most productive.

But there's another reason. Suppose someone asks you what the word *fast* means. You answer, "speedy or swift." But does it mean that in such contexts as "*fast* color," "*fast* woman," or "*fast* friend"? And if a horse is fast, is it securely tied or galloping at top speed? It could be either. It all depends. On the dictionary? No, on context, on how the word is actually used. After all, there are over twenty different meanings for *fast* in the dictionary. But the dictionary doesn't tell you which meaning is intended. That's why it makes such good sense to begin with context.

Through Word Parts

Now for the next step. Often unfamiliar words contain one or more parts, which, if recognized, provide definite help with meaning. Suppose you read that someone "had a predilection for reading mysteries." The context certainly isn't too helpful. But do you see a prefix, suffix, or root that you know? Well, there's the familiar prefix *pre-*, meaning "before." Look back at the context and try inserting "before." Reading mysteries apparently comes "before" other kinds of reading. Yes, a pre-dilection—or *pre*ference—is something put "before" something else.

Or take the word *monolithic.* Try to isolate the parts. There's the prefix *mono-,* meaning "one," and the root *lith,* meaning "stone." Finally, there's the suffix *-ic,* meaning "consisting of." Those three parts add up to this definition: "consisting of one stone."

To expedite your use of word parts, you will be introduced to the fourteen most important words in the English language. The prefix and root elements in those few words are found in over 14,000 words of desk dictionary size. With those amazingly useful shortcuts, you can build vocabulary, not at a snail's pace, one word at a time, but in giant strides, up to a thousand words at a time.

Your second step, then, is to look for familiar word parts. If they do not give you exact meanings, they should at least bring you much closer.

Through the Dictionary

Now you can see why you should consult the dictionary last, not first. You've looked carefully at context. You've looked for familiar word parts. Now you play Sherlock Holmes—an exciting role. You hypothesize. In light of context or context and word parts, you try to solve a mystery. What exactly does that strange word mean? Only after you go through the mental gymnastics to come up with a tentative definition should you open the dictionary to see if you're right.

After all, those first two steps or approaches spark a stronger than usual interest in that dictionary definition. You're now personally involved. Did you figure out the word meaning? Your heightened interest will lead to better memory of both word and meaning. It also encourages your development of the habits needed to accelerate your progress. And when you see in black and white the definition you had expected, what a feeling of accomplishment is yours. In that way, the CPD Formula provides the exact dynamic interplay of approaches for maximum effectiveness.

Well, there it is, your new formula: Context, Parts, Dictionary. Use it! The exercises that follow will give you specific, step-by-step help in sharpening your awareness of contextual clues, learning the most useful word parts, and using the dictionary with increased accuracy and ease. The results will be like money in the bank.

Length: 1000 words.
Reading Time: __________
See Conversion Table, p. 421.
Enter WPM Rate on p. 416.

4 How Should You Build Up Your Vocabulary?

COMPREHENSION CHECK

1. What percent of the average person's waking time is spent in communication? (a) 30 percent (b) 45 percent (c) 60 percent (d) 70 percent — 1. ____

2. Specific reference is made to the (a) Scientific Energy Corporation. (b) Municipal Research Division. (c) Human Engineering Laboratories. (d) Human Resources Center. — 2. ____

3. With respect to comprehension, *vocabulary in context* contributes (a) less than intelligence. (b) the same as intelligence. (c) more than intelligence. (d) an unspecified amount. — 3. ____

4. "Eschew garrulity" means (a) stop shouting. (b) speak louder. (c) look up words. (d) avoid talking too much. — 4. ____

5. One of the words mentioned is said to have over how many different meanings? (a) 10 (b) 15 (c) 20 (d) 25 — 5. ____

6. As a shortcut to vocabulary, you will be introduced to how many important words? (a) 14 (b) 22 (c) 35 (d) 50 — 6. ____

7. To suggest the importance of context, which word is discussed? (a) fast (b) slow (c) sharp (d) trip — 7. ____

8. In the CPD Formula, the *C* stands for (a) confirm. (b) correct. (c) classification. (d) context. — 8. ____

9. Who is mentioned by name? (a) Einstein (b) Tom Sawyer (c) Johnny Cash (d) Sherlock Homes — 9. ____

10. When you meet a strange word, you are told to consult your dictionary (a) first. (b) last. (c) as a second step. (d) at no set time. — 10. ____

Check your answers with the Key on p. 451. Give yourself 10 points for each one right and enter your comprehension score on p. 414.

Comprehension Score: ________

MAKING THE APPLICATION

Now that you know how important context is in determining word meaning, why not check to see how well you use contextual clues? That's a skill well worth developing to the fullest. The exercises in this text should help you develop real skill in defining words through use of contextual clues.

To check, we'll use a two-step procedure. First you'll take a vocabulary test—ten items without any context to help. Then you'll take the same test but this time you'll have the help of sentence contexts. Research has shown that Vocabulary in Context, contributing 39 percent to comprehension, was actually more important than Intelligence, which contributed only 27 percent. Context then deserves *major* attention.

Put your answers for the first time through the test in column A. These are difficult words—words that you'd need contextual help in getting meaning. You may not answer a single one right the first time through. Answer all ten items. Then continue as directed.

CONTEXT VOCABULARY TEST

		A	B
1. Refectory means (a) kitchen. (b) mirror. (c) dining room. (d) pantry. (e) living room.	1.	____	____
2. Preferment means (a) burial. (b) precision. (c) health. (d) choice. (e) advancement.	2.	____	____
3. Camaille means (a) mob. (b) dog hospital. (c) hell. (d) campus. (e) students.	3.	____	____
4. Glabrous means (a) large. (b) bald. (c) round. (d) sharp. (e) glamorous.	4.	____	____
5. Capriole means (a) whim. (b) leap. (c) capture. (d) trot. (e) buck.	5.	____	____
6. Halcyon means (a) sunny. (b) memorable. (c) bright. (d) tranquil. (e) warm.	6.	____	____
7. Mephitic means (a) intoxicating. (b) soothing. (c) harmful. (d) methodical. (e) mystical.	7.	____	____
8. Epergne means (a) centerpiece. (b) entry. (c) sword. (d) classical poem. (e) salad.	8.	____	____
9. Abecedarian means (a) expert. (b) grammarian. (c) stranger. (d) beginner. (e) teacher.	9.	____	____

10. Mawkish means (a) modest. (b) sickening. (c) awkward. (d) colorful. (e) humorous. 10. ____ ____

Now for the second step. Here are sentence contexts for each of the preceding words. Study each, then go back to the test and enter the answer that seems to fit the context best in column B. Don't change any answers in column A. Sometimes, of course, you may have the same answer in both columns.

1. Sometimes the helper worked inside, sweeping crumbs off the refectory floor from around the tables.
2. If you want preferment, work so hard you'll stand out above all others.
3. The unruly, shouting camaille burst into the palace, smashing down the doors.
4. That night as he walked down the street, his glabrous head reflected the street lights.
5. The spectators marveled as the horse executed a perfectly timed capriole.
6. They thought of their restful days in the mountains as halcyon days indeed.
7. A stupefying mephitic gas came pouring out of the overhead vent into the crowded room, with devastating consequences.
8. As they entered the dining room, they noticed a beautiful epergne in the middle of the table.
9. Well, remember you've had years of skiing experience; I'm just an abecedarian.
10. That movie was so mawkish, we left in the middle—we just couldn't take it any longer.

Now you should have two sets of answers. Score each set separately, counting 10 points for each correct answer. If you made a perfect use of context, you should score 100 in column B. The difference between scores indicates how well you now use contextual clues and sharpens your awareness of context importance. Key is on page 440.

MASTER-WORD VOCABULARY TEST

To prepare you for the next selection and for a new way to get word meaning, take this difficult test. Put your answers in column A. Get an answer down for each word, even if it's a guess.

			A	B
1. effete	(a) athletic (b) difficult (c) shut in (d) worn out (e) wealthy	1.	____	____
2. elide	(a) omit (b) slide (c) glisten (d) enter (e) soften	2.	____	____
3. expunge	(a) dive in (b) soak (c) erase (d) swim (e) fold	3.	____	____
4. ebullition	(a) blackness (b) boiling out (c) seeping in (d) repair (e) entry	4.	____	____
5. exostosis	(a) outgrowth (b) leg bone (c) paralysis (d) bruise (e) insertion	5.	____	____

Try five more items, even more difficult for they are French words, not English.

6. éditeur	(a) reporter (b) collector (c) publisher (d) official (e) athlete	6.	____	____
7. évincer	(a) eject (b) enter (c) establish (d) serve (e) save	7.	____	____
8. ébaucher	(a) brace (b) bend (c) arise (d) damage (e) outline	8.	____	____
9. écarte	(a) lonely (b) earnest (c) careful (d) clear (e) full	9.	____	____
10. éclater	(a) applaud (b) delay (c) turn in (d) comfort (e) burst out	10.	____	____

You'd be lucky to know even one of those words. Yet if you had a certain technique for dealing with strange, even foreign, words, you could have made a good score. By chance, as you took that test, did you think of the common prefix *ex-*, meaning "out"? Most test takers wouldn't, yet each of those ten words contains a form of that prefix.

Now go back and retake that test, putting your answers this time in column B. See how much better you score when you reply on the prefix knowledge that *ex-* means "out." When you finish, check both sets of answers with the Key on page 441. You will have discovered for yourself just how helpful prefix knowledge can be in dealing with words. You'll get more complete details in the next selection, "The Master-Word Approach to Vocabulary."

NAME ______________________ CLASS ____________________ DATE ______________

5 The Master-Word Approach to Vocabulary

WORD POWER WORKOUT

A. LEANING ON CONTEXT

In each of the blanks provided, place the letter that precedes the best definition of the underlined word in context to the left.

Words in Context

1. _____ furnished <u>invaluable</u> background
2. _____ giving you a <u>technique</u>
3. _____ the big <u>unabridged</u>
4. _____ *Precept* <u>literally</u> means
5. _____ a <u>maxim</u> or rule
6. _____ as changeable as a <u>chameleon</u>
7. _____ of a <u>variant</u> form
8. _____ the strange word <u>explication</u>
9. _____ <u>intricacies</u> of our language
10. _____ and leads <u>eventually</u> to

Definitions

a. different

b. finally

c. priceless

d. explaining

e. method

f. complications

g. lizard

h. not shortened

i. actually

j. saying

Check your answers with the Key on p. 442 before going on. Give yourself 10 points for each one right and enter your score on the chart under A on p. 420. Review any that you have missed.

A Score: ________

Pronunciation aids: **6. Kuh-MEEL-yen**

9. IN-tri-kuh-sees

B. LEANING ON PARTS

Try to supply the missing word or word part in each of the following sentences. Notice also how prefix meaning relates to word meaning.

1. If you move away from town, you leave or de____________.
2. To climb down a mountain is to de____________.
3. To put money down on a purchase is to make a de____________.
4. To be down in spirits is to be de____________.
5. If you decline an invitation, you turn it ____________.

C. MAKING THE WORDS YOURS

In each blank below, enter the most appropriate word from the ten words in context in the first exercise, substituting it for the word(s) in parentheses. Use these words: *chameleon, eventually, explication, intricacies, invaluable, literally, maxim, technique, unabridged, variant.*

1. The (complications) ____________ of the present tax code are obvious.
2. Don't worry! I'll (finally) ____________ get my term paper written.
3. To perform any task well, you should know the most helpful (method) ____________ to use.
4. At the zoo we were amazed to watch the (lizard) ____________ change color.
5. The British (different) ____________ spelling of *center* is *centre.*
6. The speaker's (explaining) ____________ of how the new law affected both rich and poor was clearly done.
7. The thief managed to get away with one of the museum's most (priceless) ____________ paintings.
8. I think my friend's (saying) ____________ is this: "What you don't know, can't hurt you."
9. That word isn't in my desk dictionary so I guess I'll have to consult the (not shortened) ____________ one.
10. When I said he'd spilled the beans, I meant figuratively, not (actually) ____________.

Check your answers with the Key on p. 443.

B Score: ________

C Score: ________

Enter your scores on p. 420.

For this selection, once again check your performance when you read as fast as you possibly can. Knowing yourself well as a reader is so important that you should double-check results in this reading situation.

5

The Master-Word Approach to Vocabulary

JAMES I. BROWN

You probably know what a master key is. With one of those a custodian doesn't have to carry around a hundred keys for a hundred offices—just one master key. Master-words work the same way. Each one unlocks not one but hundreds of word meanings. Read on to see how to put them to work.

BEGIN TIMING

You have two ways to build a vocabulary. The slow way—one word at a time! Or, the master-word way—over a thousand at a time! Start work on the second method right away.

How do you do it? On page 43 you'll find a list of fourteen words—the most important in the English language to speed you along a superhighway toward vocabulary and success. They're keys to the meanings of well over 14,000 words of desk dictionary size, or an estimated 100,000 from the big unabridged volume. They also furnish invaluable background for further word study, giving you a technique—a master key—with endless possibilities.

You see, most of our English words aren't English at all, but borrowings from other languages. Furthermore, 80 percent of those borrowed words come from Latin and Greek sources, making up about 60 percent of our English language. That means those elements most frequently borrowed make amazingly useful shortcuts for vocabulary growth. These master-words, by actual count, contain prefix and root elements found in over 14,000 English words of desk dictionary size.

To see for yourself just how useful a single prefix can be, look at the first word on the list of fourteen—*precept.* That's a shortcut to how many English words? When you finish reading this selection, turn to your desk dictionary and check. You'll find about nine pages of *pre-* words. Then check the big unabridged volume. One such dictionary contains over 17 pages of *pre-* words, including a listing at the bottom of over 2,400 words—over 4,000 in all. Those words aren't defined, just listed. They don't need defining. If you know that *pre-* means "before," you can comprehend all of them, from *preabsorb* to *prewrap.* That single prefix is your shortcut to understanding thousands of English words. And you haven't added the words from the root shortcut, *capere.*

How exactly do you put these master-words to work? How can you best convert them into keys to the meanings of thousands of English words?

First, look up each of the fourteen words in your dictionary. One a week would be ideal. Note both prefix and root meanings. For example, look up *precept.* You'll find it comes from Latin *prae* or *pre,* meaning "before," plus the Latin root *capere,* meaning "to take." *Precept* literally means "to take before." By definition a precept is "a maxim or rule meant to govern conduct." "Be industrious" is such a precept. Then look for the idea of "before." Obviously you have to *have* a precept "before" you can start applying it.

Next, zero in on each part. For example, take *pre-*. You'll find four different meanings—before in time, before in place, before in rank, and preliminary to or in preparation for something. Now you know the various ways of thinking about *pre-*. Next, take a closer look at the Latin root *capere.* Unfortunately, you can't look up Latin words in your English dictionary. You have to think of some other prefixes to use in place of *pre-*. Go back to your fourteen words. Try the next prefix, *de-*. Make *decept.* When you look for that word, you don't find it—but you see *deception.* And you're told to look at *deceive.* Both words are from *capere.* When you deceive someone, you take "away" some of the needed facts and deceive. That's deception, since *de-* means "down or away."

When you look up a prefix, you'll find some as changeable as chameleons. *Pre-* has only two forms—*pre-* and *prae-*. But look up *ob-*. Then look up *offer.* The prefix *ob-* actually becomes *of-* in *offer* because *offer* is so much easier to say. The dictionary makes such changes clear. The same with the word *cooperation,* "to operate or work together." But isn't the prefix *com-,* not just *co-?* And doesn't *com-* mean "together"? Yes, but *comoperation* is more awkward to say. This prepares you for the changes that come when *com-* is added to *-stant, -relation, -laboration,* and *-cil* to make *constant, correlation, collaboration,* and *council.* Use pronunciation as a help. And check your dictionary to keep you accurate.

There's your background for recognizing similar chameleon-like changes of *in-, ad-, ex-,* and others. When you look up the prefix, the dictionary will always spell out those changes.

Gradually you'll also begin to notice root variations, as with *deceive* and *deception.* Try to use some intelligent guessing. Take the root *plicare,* meaning "to fold," as in *complicated.* Think of other prefixes to add. There's *application, implication,* and *duplication.* Let *duplication* suggest *duplex* as well as *perplex* and *complex. Complex* may open the way to *comply,* which may in turn suggest *apply, imply, supply, pliant, deploy,* and *employ.* Each discovery you make of a variant form adds that much to your background and understanding of the large family of words for which that root is key. Your dictionary will always keep your guesses in line with facts. And you'll find the idea of folding always present. If something is *implied,* it's folded into what's said. If it's *pliant,* it's folded.

So much for method. First look up each word. Next look more closely at each word part—both prefix and root. Now, just how useful is your newly acquired knowledge of prefixes and roots?

Suppose you see the strange word *explication.* You know *ex-* means "out" and *plicare* means "to fold." To fold out or unfold! You read the sentence, "His explication was confused and hard to follow." Lean on the prefix and root—"fold out." His attempt to "fold out" something was hard to follow. You hardly need the dictionary definition "to make clear, to explain fully." Yes, knowing only one part of a word is sometimes enough. When you read of a person's predilection for novels, you need only the *pre-* to know that he put novels "before" other kinds of books—a preference for them. Take another example. Is a precocious child one who develops before or after normal children? Again the prefix lets you know.

The master-word approach also makes spelling easier. Suppose you continually misspell *prescription* with a *per—perscription.* Use prefix meaning to help. Prescriptions are written out "before" you can fill them, hence *prescription.* You'll also know how to spell such demons as *misspell* or *misstep,* for you'll know they are combinations of *mis-* plus *spell* and *mis-* plus *step.* You'll not write *mispell* or *mistep.* And what about someone who migrates into this country? Is she an immigrant or an emigrant? Since she's coming *into* the country, she's an inmigrant, or, by assimilation, an immigrant. Assimilation is a technical term, describing how the first letter of the root changes the last letter of the prefix. The *m* in *migrant* changes, or assimilates, the *n* in *in* to *m.*

In this way you begin to understand the intricacies of our language. At first you may have trouble spotting the root *facere* in *benefactor.* But soon you'll be a regular Sherlock Holmes, able to ferret out that root in such varied disguises as *artifice, affair, feature, affection, facsimile, counterfeit, fashion,* and *facilitate.* And you'll soon have no trouble finding *ex-* in *effect* or *dis-* in *differ,* more examples of assimilation at work.

Best of all, your master-word technique will help with countless other classical elements. Yours is the magic touchstone—curiosity about derivations—which brings life to all words and leads eventually to an awareness of words reached by a very few.

Length: 1230 words.
Reading Time: __________
See Conversion Table p. 421.
Enter WPM Rate on p. 416.

5 The Master-Word Approach to Vocabulary

COMPREHENSION CHECK

1. How many master-words are there? (a) ten (b) twelve (c) fourteen (d) sixteen — 1. ____

2. Master-words are keys to an estimated how many words of unabridged dictionary size? (a) 20,000 (b) 40,000 (c) 70,000 (d) 100,000 — 2. ____

3. In the English language, words derived from Latin and Greek make up what percent? (a) 20% (b) 40% (c) 60% (d) 80% — 3. ____

4. The Latin root *capere* means (a) to take. (b) to find. (c) to work. (d) to send. — 4. ____

5. How many different forms does the prefix *pre-* have? (a) only one (b) two (c) three (d) four — 5. ____

6. You were told to put what prefix in place of *pre-* in *precept* to get help with *capere?* (a) *sub-* (b) *re-* (c) *de-* (d) *com-* — 6. ____

7. The prefix *com-* means (a) together. (b) inside. (c) outside. (d) close. — 7. ____

8. The Latin verb *plicare* means to (a) push. (b) pull. (c) fold. (d) care. — 8. ____

9. Which of the following words was *not* discussed? (a) predilection (b) explication (c) cooperation (d) prevarication — 9. ____

10. Assimilation involves what letter of a root? (a) the last (b) the first (c) the second (d) the middle — 10. ____

Check your answers with the Key on p. 451. Give yourself 10 points for each one right and enter your comprehension score on p. 416.

Comprehension Score: ________

MAKING THE APPLICATION

YOUR MASTER WORDS

Well, here they are, the fourteen words you've been reading about—the most important words in the English language to speed your vocabulary growth. They provide a vocabulary superhighway to *over* 14,000 words of desk dictionary size and an estimated 100,000 *plus* words from the big unabridged volume.

Words	Prefix	Common Meaning	Root	Common Meaning
precept	pre-	(before)	capere	(take, seize)
detain	de-	(away, down)	tenere	(hold, have)
intermittent	inter-	(between)	mittere	(send)
offer	ob-	(against)	ferre	(bear, carry)
insist	in-	(into)	stare	(stand)
monograph	mono-	(one)	graphein	(write)
epilogue	epi-	(upon)	legein	(say, study of)
aspect	ad-	(to, toward)	specere	(see)
uncomplicated	un-	(not)	plicare	(fold)
	com-	(together)		
nonextended	non-	(not)	tendere	(stretch)
	ex-	(out of)		
reproduction	re-	(back, again)	ducere	(lead)
	pro-	(forward)		
indisposed	in-	(not)	ponere	(put, place)
	dis-	(apart from)		
oversufficient	over-	(above)	facere	(make, do)
	sub-	(under)		
mistranscribe	mis-	(wrong)	scribere	(write)
	trans-	(across, beyond)		

To further your advantage of these amazing shortcuts to meaning, you'll find forty-seven special exercises cover the twenty prefixes and fourteen roots in those master words. Those special Word Power exercises are introduced with selection 4 and labeled Part B: Leaning on Parts. They will speed your awareness of these word parts and hasten their vocabulary-building usefulness.

In addition, take advantage of the following four steps to supplement the Part B exercises. You may find it desirable to take one word a week, concentrating that long on one single word. Write the word on a 3 × 5 card and, during each day, try using words with the prefix or root you're studying. Then follow these important steps.

1. *Look up the master word in your dictionary.* Especially notice the derivational material. Look for the relationship between the literal meaning of prefix and root and the definitions given for the word. The parts don't always add up to the exact meaning, but there's usually a close relationship, an ideal memory aid.
2. *Look up each prefix.* Note the meanings given and the various spellings so that you will spot them more quickly.
3. *List five words containing the prefix or prefixes being studied.* Check your list with the dictionary to avoid mistakes. And don't overlook the less common forms in the dictionary entry.
4. *List five words containing the root being studied.* Again, check your list with the dictionary to ensure accuracy. For example, take *reproduction.* The root is *ducere,* meaning "to lead." It may be easy to think of *produce, reduce,* or *induce. Induce* may lead you to another form—*induct* or *abduct. Conduct* may lead you to *conduit.* And you may stumble on *duke* and *duchess,* still other forms of *ducere.* After all, a duke is a leader. Remember Mussolini, Il Duce?

To expedite still further your mastery of these elements, you'll find helpful Mini-Reviews and a special LDE Formula later in this text.

NAME ____________ CLASS ____________ DATE ____________

6 Words That Laugh and Cry

WORD POWER WORKOUT

A. LEANING ON CONTEXT

In each of the blanks provided, place the letter that precedes the best definition of the underlined word in context to the left.

Words in Context	Definitions
1. _____ capacity of written words	a. put
2. _____ are mere symbols	b. adequate
3. _____ symbols with no more feeling	c. ability
4. _____ he might affect	d. portion
5. _____ possess remarkable facility	e. only
6. _____ commit to paper	f. skill
7. _____ copy goes to the printer	g. influence
8. _____ exhibition of weakness	h. representations
9. _____ parcel of written language	i. manuscript
10. _____ any competent poet	j. display

Check your answers with the Key on p. 442 before going on. Give yourself 10 points for each one right and enter your score on the chart under A on p. 420. Review any that you have missed.

A Score: ________

B. LEANING ON PARTS

Fill in the missing word or word part in each of the following blanks. Notice also how knowing the meaning of *inter-* helps with word meanings.

1. The highway going between states is known as the inter____________.
2. The period between acts of a play is called the inter____________.
3. If you mediate a problem, you become an inter____________or.
4. To break into someone's discussion or talk is to inter____________ it.
5. An international agreement is an agreement ____________ nations.

C. MAKING THE WORDS YOURS

In each blank below, enter the most appropriate word from the ten words in context in the first exercise, substituting it for the word(s) in parentheses. Use these words: *affect, capacity, commit, competent, copy, exhibition, facility, mere, parcel, symbols.*

1. My test scores were (only) ____________ fractions of a point from getting an A.
2. The words I speak are but (representations) ____________ of my true feelings about this matter.
3. Will the arthritis (influence) ____________ his ability to play on the football team?
4. Some students do not yet have the (ability) ____________ to deal with computer programming.
5. I marveled at her (skill) ____________ in using the Italian language.
6. Now (put) ____________ yourself to running for class president.
7. Do you think that a freshman is (adequate) ____________ to be captain of our basketball team?
8. Finally I have the (manuscript) ____________ ready for the editor of the school paper.
9. I was sorry to see his (display) ____________ of anger when his idea was rejected by the rest of the committee.
10. My dad just bought a (portion) ____________ of land on which to build a new house.

Check your answers with the Key on p. 442.

B Score:________

C Score:________

Enter your scores on p. 420.

For this selection, repeat your check of reading for comprehension. Read the selection once only for the best possible comprehension, checking both rate and comprehension.

6

Words That Laugh and Cry

CHARLES A. DANA

***Words laugh and cry. They can also smile and snarl. If you see a thin woman who attracts you, you'll probably call her* slender. *If she doesn't attract you, you'll probably call her* skinny. *Yet both words mean the same thing—thin. Yes, you can call her a* vision*—or call her a* sight.**

BEGIN TIMING

Did it ever strike you that there was anything queer about the capacity of written words to absorb and convey feelings? Taken separately they are mere symbols with no more feeling to them than so many bricks, but string them along in a row under certain mysterious conditions and you find yourself laughing or crying as your eye runs over them. That words should convey mere ideas is not so remarkable. "The boy is fat," "the cat has nine tails," are statements that seem obvious enough within the power of written language. But it is different with feelings. They are no more visible in the symbols that hold them than electricity is visible on the wire; and yet there they are, always ready to respond when the right test is applied by the right person. That spoken words, charged with human tones and lighted by human eyes, should carry feelings, is not so astonishing. The magnetic sympathy of the orator one understands; he might affect his audience, possibly, if he spoke in a language they did not know. But written words: How can they do it? Suppose, for example, that you possess remarkable facility in grouping language, and that you have strong feelings upon some subject, which finally you determine to commit to paper. Your pen runs along, the words present themselves, or are dragged out, and fall into their places. You are a good deal moved; here you chuckle to yourself, and half a dozen lines farther down a lump comes into your throat, and perhaps you have to wipe your eyes. You finish, and the copy goes to the printer. When it gets into print the reader sees it. His eye runs along the lines and down the page until it comes to the place where you chuckled as you wrote; then he smiles, and six lines below he has to swallow several times and snuffle and wink to restrain an exhibition of weakness. And then someone else comes along who has no feelings, and swaps the words about a little, and twists the sentences; and behold the spell is gone, and you have left a parcel of written language duly charged with facts, but without a single feeling.

No one can juggle with words with any degree of success without getting a vast respect for their independent ability. They will catch the best idea a man ever had as it flashes through his brain, and hold on to it, to surprise him with it long after, and make him wonder that he was ever man enough to have such an idea. And often they will catch an idea on its way from the brain to the pen point, turn, twist, and improve on it as the eye winks, and in an instant there they are, strung hand in hand across the page, and grinning back at the writer: "This is our idea, old man; not yours!"

As for poetry, every word that expects to earn its salt in poetry should have a head and a pair of legs of its own, to go and find its place, carrying another word, if necessary, on its back. The most that should be expected of any competent poet in regular practice is to serve a general summons and notice of action on the language. If the words won't do the rest for him, it indicates that he is out of sympathy with his tools.

But you don't find feelings in written words unless there were feelings in the man who used them. With all their apparent independence they seem to be little vessels that hold in some puzzling fashion exactly what is put into them. You can put tears into them, as though they were so many little buckets; and you can hang smiles along them, like Monday's clothes on the line, or you can starch them with facts and stand them up like a picket fence; but you won't get the tears out unless you first put them in. Art won't put them there. It is like the faculty of getting the quality of interest into pictures. If the quality exists in the artist's mind, he is likely to find means to get it into his pictures, but if it isn't in the man no technical skill will supply it. So, if the feelings are in the writer and he knows his business, they will get into the words; but they must be in him first. It isn't the way the words are strung together that makes Lincoln's Gettysburg speech immortal, but the feelings that were in the man. but how do such little, plain words manage to keep their grip on such feelings? That is the miracle.

Length: 800 words.
Reading Time: ________
See Conversion Table, p. 421.
Enter WPM Rate on p. 416.

6 Words That Laugh and Cry

COMPREHENSION CHECK

1. Words, taken separately, are likened to (a) building blocks. (b) bricks. (c) windows. (d) arrows. 1. ____

2. The author uses what sentence as an example? "The boy is (a) large." (b) fat." (c) heavy." (d) big." 2. ____

3. The author says feelings are invisible like (a) temperature. (b) air. (c) electricity. (d) humidity. 3. ____

4. The author refers to (a) an orator. (b) a politician. (c) an actress. (d) a preacher. 4. ____

5. The author compares (a) the pen and the sword. (b) the thinker and the dreamer. (c) newsmen and newsmakers. (d) spoken and written words. 5. ____

6. As you write, you were said to (a) laugh out loud. (b) frown. (c) look sad. (d) chuckle to yourself. 6. ____

7. Words were sometimes said to say, "This is our (a) idea." (b) belief." (c) thought." (d) intention." 7. ____

8. Mention was made of (a) novels. (b) biographies. (c) poetry. (d) history. 8. ____

9. Words were said to have (a) glamour. (b) independent ability. (c) egotism. (d) picturesque origins. 9. ____

10. Mention was made of (a) Washington. (b) Lincoln. (c) Roosevelt. (d) Jefferson. 10. ____

Check your answers with the Key on p. 451. Give yourself 10 points for each one right and enter your comprehension score on p. 414.

Comprehension Score: ________

Interpreting Your Second Reading Check-up

As with selections 1, 2, and 3, enter your scores for the second set of selections as you did with the first set. Use the chart below. Then fill in the numbers from both charts on page 51. Compare the two sets of figures to make sure there is a definite pattern of performance that will serve to guide your efforts most effectively as you work to improve.

In comparing the two sets of scores, you should see evidence already of some improvement—a foreshadowing of what you can expect as you continue work with this text. And you should now know definitely where to put major emphasis to get maximum results.

1. My normal reading rate was ______.

175 wpm or less	Very poor
175–210 wpm	Poor
210–240 wpm	Fair
240–275 wpm	Average
275–320 wpm	Very good
320–400 wpm	Excellent
400 wpm or more	Outstanding

2. My top reading rate was______.

230 wpm or less	Very poor
230–300 wpm	Poor
300–330 wpm	Fair
330–390 wpm	Average
390–420 wpm	Very good
420–500 wpm	Excellent
500 wpm or more	Outstanding

3. My comprehension reading rate was ______.

125 wpm or less	Very poor
125–160 wpm	Poor
160–180 wpm	Fair
180–210 wpm	Average
210–245 wpm	Very good
245–280 wpm	Excellent
280 wpm or more	Outstanding

4. Check of reading flexibility
   Fastest reading rate: ______
   Slowest reading rate: ______
   Subtract to get the difference: ______

50 wpm or less	Very poor
50–100 wpm	Poor
100–125 wpm	Fair
125–150 wpm	Average
150–200 wpm	Very good
200–300 wpm	Excellent
300 wpm or more	Outstanding

Now it's time to take a look at your check-up results in order to discover strengths and weaknesses and know how to make the best possible progress in both reading and comprehension.

First, let's look at you as a reader. Enter your scores below:

	Rate	Comp.		Rate	Comp.
Normal (Sel. #1)	______	______	Normal (Sel. #4)	______	______
For speed (Sel. #2)	______	______	For speed (Sel. #5)	______	______
For comp. (Sel. #3)	______	______	For comp. (Sel. #6)	______	______

My normal reading rate was ______. (Add selection 1 and selection 4 figures.)

Based on data from reading classes at the University of Minnesota, here's how to interpret your normal reading rate scores:

175 wpm or less	Very poor
175–210 wpm	Poor
210–240 wpm	Fair
240–275 wpm	Average
275–320 wpm	Very good
320–400 wpm	Excellent
400 wpm or more	Outstanding

My top reading rate was ______. (Add selection 2 and selection 5 figures.)

Here's how to interpret your top reading rate:

230 wpm or less	Very poor
230–300 wpm	Poor
300–330 wpm	Fair
330–390 wpm	Average
390–420 wpm	Very good
420–500 wpm	Excellent
500 wpm or more	Outstanding

My comprehension reading rate was ______. (Add selection 3 and selection 6 figures.)

Here's how to interpret your reading for comprehension score:

125 wpm or less	Very poor
125–160 wpm	Poor
160–180 wpm	Fair
180–210 wpm	Average
210–245 wpm	Very good
245–280 wpm	Excellent
280 wpm or more	Outstanding

Look at your results in still another way, this time to check your reading flexibility in terms of rate.

First three checks:

Fastest reading rate ______

Slowest reading rate ______

Subtract to get difference ______

Next three checks:

Fastest reading rate ______

Slowest reading rate ______

Subtract to get difference ______

Check your rating below.

50 wpm or less	Very poor
50–100 wpm	Poor
100–125 wpm	Fair
125–150 wpm	Average
150–200 wpm	Very good
200–300 wpm	Excellent
300 wpm or more	Outstanding

Unfortunately, we can't do with comprehension what we can with reading rate. Comprehension is affected by difficulty level, subject matter, and type of material far more than is reading rate. But you will want to start noticing habitual differences in comprehending exposition, narration, persuasion, and literary works.

PART II

The Start-up

NAME ____________ CLASS ____________ DATE ____________

7 How Do You Best Get the Facts?

WORD POWER WORKOUT

A. LEANING ON CONTEXT

In each of the blanks provided, place the letter that precedes the best definition of the underlined word in context to the left.

Words in Context	Definitions
1. _____ dominates his every move	a. false, untrue
2. _____ sensory experience	b. receptive
3. _____ comprehension was abysmally poor.	c. extremely, immeasurably
4. _____ fallacious notion	d. chief
5. _____ blurred . . . details	e. vocabulary, terms
6. _____ he knows . . . the terminology	f. connected
7. _____ prime purpose	g. rules
8. _____ closely related	h. suitable
9. _____ appropriate reading rate	i. the greatest possible
10. _____ brings maximum comprehension	j. hazy, unclear

Check your answers with the Key on p. 442 before going on. Give yourself 10 points for each one right and enter your score on the chart under A on p. 420. Review any that you have missed.

A Score: ________

Pronunciation aids: **2. SEN-so-ree**

3. uh-BIZ-muh-lee

4. fuh-LAY-shus

B. LEANING ON PARTS

The prefix *ob-* (also spelled *oc-, of-, op-,* or *o-*) means "against" or "to." Supply the missing word or word part in each of the following blanks.

1. If you're against some plan, you ob__________ to it.
2. A barrier that stands against your progress is an ob__________.
3. If you're against a candidate, you can always voice your ob__________.
4. Don't let the darkness ob__________ your vision of the road.
5. To obfuscate someone is to work __________ his or her understanding.

C. MAKING THE WORDS YOURS

In each blank below, enter the most appropriate word from the ten words in context in the first exercise, substituting it for the word(s) in parentheses. Use these words: *abysmally, appropriate, blurred, dominates, fallacious, maximum, prime, related, sensory, terminology.*

1. One student constantly (rules) __________ the discussion.
2. The weather was (extremely) __________ poor during the whole vacation.
3. The class read at its (greatest possible) __________ speed.
4. Better make yourself the (chief) __________ candidate for the job.
5. You'd better test your eye (receptive) __________ levels before starting flying lessons.
6. The lack of description in the article left many (hazy) __________ ideas.
7. Those (false) __________ statements caused tension in the group.
8. My reading rate was (suitable) __________ for my grade level.
9. How closely (connected) __________ are those two family members?
10. My friend knows the (vocabulary) __________ of football.

Check your answers with the Key on p. 442.

B Score: ________

C Score: ________

Enter your scores on p. 420.

7

How Do You Best Get the Facts?

BEGIN TIMING

How do you get factual information? Well, one thing is certain. You're not born with it. You have to acquire it. John Locke explained the process in this way. Our mind is at birth like a blank sheet of paper. Gradually, everything we see, feel, taste, hear, and smell—our total sensory experience—writes on that blank sheet. That's what gives us mind and memory. That's how Locke focuses attention on the countless bits of reality called facts. In reading, how do we get them?

The Role of Factual Information

As a first step, look closely at the role of facts. They form the base or foundation half of comprehension. They're the raw material or ingredients, such as are used in making an angel food cake. If a single ingredient is missing, the end results may be disastrous. Similarly, in reading, missing a fact may make quite a difference.

Facts *are* important. But isn't what they add up to even more important? See the problem? Which is more important, the ingredients or the cake? How do you add 3 and another number if you don't know the other number? As a reader, how do you evaluate the facts if you don't get all of them? Apparently the place to start is with the facts.

Setting the Purpose

Next, establish purpose. A good hunter, for example, doesn't rush into the woods and start shooting blindly in all directions, hoping somehow to hit something. No! If the hunter is hunting deer, that purpose dominates every move. So it is with reading. Don't just open a book and begin. Without a crystal-clear purpose, your comprehension will inevitably suffer.

Let's restate in terms of purpose what was said about facts. One purpose is to get the facts, accurately and completely. That's perhaps the prime purpose in school as well as in much of life. The second purpose, very closely related, is to get an understanding of those facts—a move into depth. Sherlock Holmes was a genius at both noting details and adding them together into a case-solving hypothesis.

Exactly how does purpose affect end results? To see, try reading the following short passage. Your purpose? To find out exactly how many men stepped out of the elevator at the top floor. Read with that purpose uppermost.

Here's the passage: Six men and three women got into the waiting elevator at the bottom floor. At the next stop, four more men entered and two women got out. At the next stop, five men got out and three men entered. At the next stop, two men got out and three entered. At the top floor everyone got out.

1. How many men got out? 2. Now, without rereading, do you know exactly how many women got out? 3. And do you know how many stops the elevator made?

This should let you see for yourself the importance of setting purpose. It pays! You can also see that too specific a purpose may actually keep you from getting some facts. A more general purpose such as "get *all* the facts" should make it easier to answer *all* three questions. Always set purpose!

Setting Your Reading Rate

As a third step, set an appropriate reading rate.

With many things, the faster you do them, the worse the results. If a typist hurries too much, for example, accuracy suffers. From this, you might assume that the way to get all the facts is to read very slowly. Let's examine that idea.

In one of my classes, one student after two weeks showed almost no progress. His starting speed was 170 words per minute (wpm). His in-class reading had never gone beyond the 190 wpm mark. Furthermore, his comprehension was abysmally poor. Before class one day, I suggested that he step up his speed by 50 to 100 wpm. He looked at me sadly and shook his head. "I only get 30 to 40 percent comprehension when I read slowly. I wouldn't get anything if I went any faster." See? There's that fallacious notion, the slower the better.

"With reading," I said, "it's a bit different. Within limits, the faster you read, the better you comprehend. Try it." He did. He read the next article at 260 wpm—for him a breakneck speed. To his surprise and pleasure, his comprehension soared to an all-time high of 70.

Compare rapid reading with rapid driving and you'll understand why. When driving along a country lane at 20 miles an hour, you literally invite your attention to wander. Now step up briefly to 60 miles an hour on a freeway. See how that speed forces concentration on the road.

So it is with reading. The slower you read, the more you encourage your mind to wander. *Within limits,* faster reading forces improved concentration.

What are those limits? For most students, increasing speed from 50 to 175 wpm above their normal rate still means improved comprehension. Of course, you'll have to discover your own limits. When you have, you'll know exactly what rate brings maximum comprehension.

Building Improved Background

As a final step, plan mini-reading programs to improve weak background areas. For example, take an avid baseball fan. With her background, reading a news account of a game seems almost effortless. She knows the players by name, the teams, the leagues, the terminology. As she reads, the details form a sharp, clear picture.

By contrast, take someone who has never seen a game. He doesn't know what RBI or AB stand for. He doesn't know what players are on each team or what city to connect with, say, the White Sox. In short, when he reads the same account, he gets a fuzzy, out-of-focus picture. Why? He lacks background.

Well, there you are. To sharpen your ability to get the facts, just apply these suggestions. Set your purpose. Use an appropriate reading rate. Build improved backgrounds. Soon, with practice, blurred or missed details will begin to come through, sharp and clear.

Length: 1000 words.
Reading Time: __________
See Conversion Table, p. 421.
Enter WPM Rate on p. 416.

7 How Do You Best Get the Facts?

▶ COMPREHENSION CHECK

1. Mention is made of (a) Walter Logan. (b) John Locke. (c) Thomas Hobbes. (d) Voltaire. 1. ____

2. Reference is made to what kind of cake? (a) fruit cake (b) sponge cake (c) angel food cake (d) devil's food cake 2. ____

3. For one illustration, mention is made of a (a) hunter. (b) fisher. (c) scuba diver. (d) pianist. 3. ____

4. One purpose is to get the facts, the other is to (a) recall them. (b) understand them. (c) relate them. (d) combine them. 4. ____

5. One illustration is of (a) a bus. (b) an elevator. (c) a train. (d) an airplane. 5. ____

6. You are told always to (a) set purpose. (b) check carefully. (c) reread. (d) avoid distractions. 6. ____

7. The starting rate for the slow reader mentioned is (a) 100 wpm. (b) 140 wpm. (c) 170 wpm. (d) 190 wpm. 7. ____

8. That slow reader's comprehension is (a) poor. (b) average. (c) good. (d) not discussed or mentioned. 8. ____

9. Reading is compared to (a) eating. (b) speaking. (c) walking. (d) driving. 9. ____

10. In one illustration, reference is made to (a) football. (b) hockey. (c) baseball. (d) tennis. 10. ____

Check your answers with the Key on p. 451. Give yourself 10 points for each one right and enter your comprehension score on p. 414.

Comprehension Score: ________

MAKING THE APPLICATION

By this time you have probably taken comprehension tests over seven different selections, with a total of 70 questions. Why not see what kinds of facts come through well and what kinds you tend to miss? Some people can remember telephone numbers with almost no effort. Others have to rely on a directory or list of numbers frequently called.

Suppose we set up some categories to let you see if there is a definite pattern in your answers.

1. *Names of people* (such as John Locke, Abraham Lincoln, Francis Bacon, etc.)

   Number of errors:_____
2. *Names of places* (such as Brazil, Ohio, etc.)

   Number of errors:_____
3. *Statements* (such as "our mind is like a blank sheet of paper")

   Number of errors:_____
4. *Figures* (such as one student's starting figure for reading—170 wpm)

   Number of errors:_____
5. *Details* (such as dates, colors, abbreviations, addresses, phone numbers, etc.)

   Number of errors:_____
6. *Organizational facts* (such as number of points, main divisions, or subdivisions)

   Number of errors:_____

Go back over the preceding seven comprehension tests to find two questions under each of the six categories indicated. Then tally the number of errors you have made in each category. As one expert said, a problem well-identified is a problem half-solved. If you know from this survey that you tend not to notice organizational facts, you will obviously be more aware of them in the readings that follow, and be more likely to improve in comprehending them.

Before reading selections 8 and 9, set your purpose mentally, as clearly as possible. Take advantage of the survey you just made. In case you tended not to note organizational facts, set that as a special purpose before beginning to read. Note particularly anything that suggests major divisions or subdivisions. Or, if you tend to miss figures, see if you can set your purpose to get more of them with accuracy.

To help you develop an improved subject matter grounding for comprehending what you read, complete the following exercise:

1. List your most difficult subject:_______________
2. Check the library to find three easy, popular books in that subject matter area. You can usually tell from the title whether it is a textbook or a popular book. For example, the title *Our Friend the Atom,* by Heinz Haber, lets you know that this is probably a popular, easily read book on atomic physics. List three books by title that should provide better background, yet be relatively easy readings in your difficult subject matter area. Your instructor may have a suggestion here.

   ____

   ____

   ____

3. List three specific moves you can now make to improve your background further for this difficult subject.

   ____

   ____

   ____

   ____

NAME ____________ CLASS ____________ DATE ____________

8 Short Words Are Words of Might

WORD POWER WORKOUT

A. LEANING ON CONTEXT

In each of the blanks provided, place the letter that precedes the best definition of the underlined word in context to the left.

Words in Context	Definitions
1. _____ hold more <u>sham</u>	a. unusual happening
2. _____ and give <u>zest</u>	b. attention to; notice
3. _____ with <u>naught</u> but	c. fraud; pretense
4. _____ an odd <u>freak</u>	d. pert, saucy girl
5. _____ by our <u>sires</u>	e. relish; keen enjoyment
6. _____ we <u>wail</u>	f. cover with gold; beautify
7. _____ you are a <u>minx</u>	g. lament; mourn
8. _____ is <u>bound</u> to be made	h. nothing
9. _____ <u>gild</u> dirt	i. male ancestors
10. _____ not much <u>heed</u>	j. sure

Check your answers with the Key on p. 442 before going on. Give yourself 10 points for each one right and enter your score on the chart under A on p. 420. Review any that you have missed.

A Score: ________

Pronunciation aids: **3. naut**
7. mingks

B. LEANING ON PARTS

Supply the missing word or word part in the following sentences. Note also how the meaning of *in-* (also spelled *il-, ir-,* or *im-*) relates to word meanings.

1. One who is not dependent is in__________.
2. One who is not capable of doing something is in__________.
3. A situation that is not formal is in__________.
4. If you do not like the direct route, try the in__________.
5. Someone who is insufferable is __________ sufferable.

C. MAKING THE WORD YOURS

In each blank below, enter the most appropriate word from the ten words in context in the first exercise, substituting it for the word(s) in parentheses. Use these words: *bound, freak, gild, heed, minx, naught, sham, sires, wail, zest.*

1. Did you (pay attention to, notice) __________ that advice?
2. Don't mix with that crowd; it's full of (fraud, pretense) __________ and ignorance.
3. You're (sure) __________ to see someone you know at the party.
4. The change of traffic regulations brought (nothing) __________ but grief to the drivers.
5. Let us pay tribute to our (male ancestors) __________, who brought law and order to the West.
6. (Relish, keen enjoyment) __________ for reading marks those who find greatest satisfaction in living.
7. You should have heard the child (lament, mourn) __________ when her toy got broken.
8. You (cover with gold, beautify) __________ the wreath after you've formed it.
9. Nothing quiet and demure about her—she's a veritable (pert, saucy girl)__________.
10. That (unusual happening) __________ meeting with an old high school friend will never be forgotten.

Check your answers with the Key on p. 444.

B Score: ________

C Score: ________

Enter your scores on p. 420.

8

Short Words Are Words of Might

LOUISE ANDREWS KENT

How should you say it? "Eschew polysyllabic verbal symbols" or "Avoid big words"? Kent advocates short words. And she proves her point amazingly well, as you'll soon see, by using* only *words of one syllable, a tremendous strain on anyone's vocabulary. She always manages to make her short word the right word. And that's the important thing. Be sure you always use the right words, whether short or long, to express your ideas accurately. Above all, when you write, don't avoid short words of might.

BEGIN TIMING

This is a plea for the use of short words in our talk and in what we write. Through the lack of them our speech is apt to grow stale and weak and, it may be, hold more sham than true thought. For long words at times tend to hide or blur what one says.

What I mean is this: If we use long words too much we are apt to talk in ruts and use the same old, worn ways of speech. This tends to make what we say dull, with no force nor sting. But if we use short words we have to say real things, things we know; and say them in a fresh way. We find it hard to hint or dodge or hide or half say things.

For short words are bold. They say just what they mean. They do not leave you in doubt. They are clear and sharp, like signs cut in a rock.

And so, if you would learn to use words with force and skill it is well first to use short words as much as you can. It will make your speech crisp and give zest and tang to what you say or write.

To prove that this is true, let us see what can be done here and now with short words. If I tell what I have to say in this plain way—that is, with naught but short words—you may think of it as but an odd freak of mine. But I hope it is more than a mere stunt. I shall try to show that one can say much that is true and live and with good strong meat of thought in it, in a way that does not come from books; that does not, as the phrase goes, "smell of the lamp."

Of course I need not be quite so strict and hold to a hard and fast rule. Some long words might be used and I could, I think, still prove my point. But I have thought that one might learn more and feel more sure that I am right from a talk which shows by its own form just what I would teach. And to do that I have made that form just as pure as it can be.

Well then, first, let us see just what place short words have in our tongue.

Short words must have been our first words when the world was young. The minds of men were raw, like that of a child. Their needs were few and so their thoughts were crude. Life for a man was in the main but a hunt for food, a fight with foes, a quest for a mate and a search for a place to rest safe from the storm and wild beasts. And for his mate there was thought but of their brat, the fire pot on the fire, the skins with which to make clothes.

Their first words were, no doubt, mere grunts or growls, barks, whines, squeals like those of the beasts. These rough, strange sounds were made to show how they felt. They meant joy or pain or doubt or rage, or fear—things like that. But these sounds came, in time, to grow more and more plain as real words. They were short words, strong and clear. And these first short words, used by our sires, way, way back in the dark of time, still have strength and truth. They are bred in our flesh and bone. We may well call such words the life blood of our speech.

And so when we feel, we still use short words. If we know joy we say, "I love you more than all the world! Kiss me!" In our pride we cry, "I have got it! I have won!" With glee we shout, "Good for you! That is right!" And if we fear we use short words. We yell, "The house is on fire! Come quick!" We moan in our woe, "Oh, why have you done this!" or weep, "She is gone. She has left me!" We wail, "I am sick. I feel bad." All fierce moods, too, use short words. We snarl, "I hate you! You are a minx." We growl, "I will kill you!"

Most words we call bad are short words, too. A curse or an oath is bound to be made of short words. That is why such terms as damn and hell and worse words that stink of filth seem full of force to one who has the mind of a child—or a beast.

And words which to most seem still more vile, coarse sex words, they are short, as well. They must needs be since they tell of the stark, raw facts and acts of life. But at least they are not pale and weak. They do not slide off the truth. Nor do they gild dirt or mask low thoughts by sly tricks of speech as do some long words. What they mean they say right out and you know where you are with them.

Short words, you see, come from down deep in us—from our hearts or guts, not from the brain. For they deal for the most part with things that move and sway us, that make us act. And so they are said with not much heed of their use. We think out loud, that is all; and the words come to our lips as do smiles or scowls. At times we do not quite know how we use them—just as we do not know, much of the time, that we breathe; just as we walk, too, at times, with no care for our steps. That, I think, is why short words tend to make our thoughts more live and true. . . .

Long words have their use, of course. If you can say just what you mean in short words, those are the best words to use. But there are things that can not be said in short words. Then it is well to use the long words, of course; but strive to use just as few as you can. Do not use a long or strange word when a short well-known word will do just as well. That is if the main end you wish is to be clear.

Length: 1080 words.
Reading Time: __________
See Conversion Table, p. 421.
Enter WPM Rate on p. 416.

8 Short Words Are Words of Might

COMPREHENSION CHECK

1. The author expresses concern (a) only about writing. (b) only about talking. (c) about neither one specifically. (d) about both writing and talking specifically. 1. ____

2. If we use long words we are apt to (a) get into ruts. (b) repeat. (c) digress. (d) develop bad habits. 2. ____

3. Short words are likened to (a) diamonds. (b) the rays of the sun. (c) signs cut in a rock. (d) arrows straight to the mark. 3. ____

4. The author refers to her essay specifically as a (a) challenge. (b) trial. (c) stunt. (d) demonstration. 4. ____

5. Kent specifically mentions (a) hunting bears. (b) ice fishing. (c) skins to make clothes. (d) caves for shelter. 5. ____

6. She refers to early words as (a) songs from the heart. (b) food and drink. (c) blind stabs. (d) life blood. 6. ____

7. The author discusses (a) songs. (b) oaths. (c) fads. (d) plays. 7. ____

8. She specifically mentions (a) safe words. (b) sane words. (c) soul words. (d) sex words. 8. ____

9. She says short words come from our (a) actions. (b) past. (c) brain. (d) heart. 9. ____

10. She ends by saying that short words are best for (a) interest. (b) simplicity. (c) directness. (d) clarity. 10. ____

Check your answers with the Key on p. 451. Give yourself 10 points for each one right and enter your comprehension score on p. 414.

Comprehension Score: ________

NAME ______________ CLASS ______________ DATE ______________

9 The Three Who Found Death

WORD POWER WORKOUT

A. LEANING ON CONTEXT

In each of the blanks provided, place the letter that precedes the best definition of the underlined word in context to the left.

Words in Context	Definitions
1. ____ range of brawls	a. request
2. ____ heard a knell	b. dagger
3. ____ a great score	c. number
4. ____ all stark mad	d. fights
5. ____ "Churl," said one	e. bottle-shaped containers
6. ____ grant me this boon	f. death bell
7. ____ one of the knaves	g. treasure
8. ____ by the hoard	h. rogues
9. ____ with your dirk	i. completely
10. ____ flasks of wine	j. peasant

Check your answers with the Key on p. 442 before going on. Give yourself 10 points for each one right and enter your score on the chart under A on p. 420. Review any that you have missed.

A Score: ________

Pronunciation aids: 2. nell

B. LEANING ON PARTS

The prefix *mono-* means "one" or "alone." Supply the appropriate word or word part in each of the following sentences.

1. An airplane with only one wing is called a mono__________.
2. A word of only one syllable is a mono__________.
3. If some company has exclusive control, it has a mono__________.
4. Doing one and the same thing day after day soon becomes mono__________.
5. A monochrome is a painting or drawing done in __________ color.

C. MAKING THE WORDS YOURS

In each blank below, enter the most appropriate word from the ten words in context in the first exercise, substituting it for the word(s) in parentheses. Use these words: *boon, brawls, churl, dirk, flasks, board, knaves, knell, score, stark.*

1. The word (peasant) __________ is certainly not as commonly used now as it was years ago.
2. The (rogues) __________ lay in ambush to rob those returning from an evening meeting.
3. Avoid that disreputable tavern with its nightly (fights)__________.
4. The museum contained some beautifully decorated (bottle-shaped containers) __________ of Greek origin.
5. The sound of the (death bell) __________ scared me.
6. Why not ask the king to grant you safe conduct as a special (request) __________?
7. A (number) __________ of years passed before they met again.
8. A long-handled (dagger) __________ was the only weapon available for the mission.
9. One disaster after another finally drove the leader (completely) __________ mad.
10. The (treasure) __________ stolen from the palace was soon well hidden in a remote mountain cave.

Check your answers with the Key on p. 444.

B Score: ________

C Score: ________

Enter your scores on p. 420.

9

The Three Who Found Death

GEOFFREY CHAUCER

Try reading the oldest story in English that you've probably ever read—or ever will read. Over 600 years old! Of course, Chaucer's English isn't ours. Here's an excerpt from his Canterbury Tales:

> ***Whan that Aprill with his shoures soote***
> ***The droghte of March hath perced to the roote.***

Obviously Chaucer had a spelling problem! So, we're retelling his story in a more modern way. See how you like it.

BEGIN TIMING

In the dim past, near the North Sea, a group of young men took a hand in a whole range of brawls and fool's tricks. They drank. They fought. They bet on the dice. Night and day this was their sport. They ate and drank far more than they should. They drank toasts to the Foul Fiend from Hell. The oaths they swore were great and foul—vile things to hear.

The three worst were now in a bar at the inn—drunk, their mugs half full in front of them. Then they heard a knell—men on their way to take a corpse to the grave. One of the drunks called to a lad who was near.

"Go and ask," said he, "what corpse is that they bear? And bring us word."

"Sir," said the boy, "I need not ask. I heard who it was. He was an old friend of yours. As he sat here on this bench last night—drunk—he was killed. There came a thief called Death, who kills in these parts. Death struck him to the heart, then went his way. He said not a word. He has slain all who stand in his way. Sir, when you come to meet him, I think it best you should watch out for this black foe. Be on guard. So my folks taught me."

"By St. John," said the man whose inn this was, "the child speaks truth. For this year, in a large town a mile hence, Death came and killed a great score. I think he must be near. It were a wise man to be on guard to keep from ill."

Then with a vile oath did one rogue say, "Is there such risk to cross his path? I vow to hunt him in all parts—all streets in each town." He turned to his two friends. "Hear me. Let us all three join hands to seek out this fiend Death and slay him!"

And so, all stark mad and drunk, they swore on oath, then left and went to the town of which the man at the inn had told them.

They had gone but half a mile when they met a poor old man. He was meek but spoke to them. "Churl," said one of the three, "what do you do here at your old age? Why don't you die?"

The old man spoke, his eyes on the face of the one who had asked. "I cannot find a man who will change his youth for my great age. So I must bear my age as long as it is the will of God I should do so. Death will not take my life. And I walk on earth like a sad wretch. On the ground, which is like the door to the one who gave me birth, I knock with my staff. I say to her, 'Please let me in! See how thin and weak I am. When shall I have rest? I would that I could go to my grave down by you and lie in peace.'

"Yet she will not grant me this boon. Pale and sad is my face. But, sirs, it is not right for you to do wrong to an old man who has not said or done you ill. Harm not this old man. You would not like to be harmed in your old age. So, God be with you. Now I must go on my way."

"Nay, nay, old churl," said one of the knaves. "By St. John we do not part so fast. You spoke just now of that fiend Death that goes here and there and kills all our friends. By my truth, tell us where he is. Do you wish him to kill us? Are you his spy?"

"Sirs," said he, "if it be your wish to find Death, turn up yon path that winds back and forth. On my faith, I left him in that grove by a tree, and there he will be for some time. I know he will not hide from you in spite of all your bold talk. Do you see that oak? There you will meet with him. And God keep you," said the old man.

The three rogues ran up the path till they came to the tree. There they found a large heap of fine gold coins. They sought no more for Death, so glad they were at the sight of those bright gold coins. Down they sat by the hoard.

One of the three said that as they had found gold, they should now live in mirth and fun for the rest of their lives. "But," said he, "if we take all this gold home now, we shall run the risk that men will think us thieves—and we may be hanged. We had best take the gold home at night so as not to be seen. In the meantime, let us draw lots to see who shall go to the next town to buy bread and wine. The other two will stay and guard the gold."

So, they drew lots. The lot fell to the young one. As soon as he was out of sight on his way to town, one said, "You know that we three have long been sworn friends. Now if you will hear me, I will show you how all this gold for us three, shall be for just us two."

"How can that be? Our sworn friend trusts us and knows where the coins are."

"Here is what we will do. Two are more strong than one. When he comes back and sits down, you must push him as if in play and try to get him down. I will watch my chance while you seem to play, and stab him in the ribs. See that you do the same with your dirk. Then, my dear friend, all this gold will be for just us two and we may do with it what we please." In that way did the rogues plan to kill their young friend.

As the young one went on to town, he thought of all that gold. "O, Lord," he said. "If I could but have all that gold as my own, not a man on earth would be as glad as I."

Then did the great foe of man—the Foul Fiend—put it in his head to buy a strong drug to kill his two friends. He found a drug, one drop of which would strike a man dead.

He then bought three flasks of wine. He put the drug in two of them, then put wine in all three. When he came back to his mates, he thought to kill them and take all the gold home as his own that night.

What need I to go on with my tale? As the two did plan, they killed him. Then they sat down to feast. When they were done they would dig a hole and put the dead one out of sight. But, by chance, they got one of the flasks with the drug to drink.

What pain they had as they died. And so the lives of all these rogues did end. They did in truth find Death.

Length: 1220 words.
Reading Time: __________
See Conversion Table, p. 421.
Enter WPM Rate on p. 416.

9 The Three Who Found Death

COMPREHENSION CHECK

1. This story occurred near which Sea? (a) Irish (b) Celtic (c) Baltic (d) North — 1. ____

2. When the three heard a knell, they (a) sent a lad to find out who had died. (b) went out to sea. (c) asked the innkeeper. (d) heard someone say the name. — 2. ____

3. The dead man was a (a) visitor. (b) stranger. (c) friend. (d) townsman. — 3. ____

4. Speaking of Death, the innkeeper tells them (a) not to worry. (b) to be on guard. (c) that Death comes nightly. (d) that Death always wears black. — 4. ____

5. The three ask the old man they meet (a) where he's going. (b) where he's been. (c) where he lives. (d) why he doesn't die. — 5. ____

6. The old man's mother (a) died ten years ago. (b) lives in another village. (c) is dead. (d) lives with her son. — 6. ____

7. The old man told them that Death is by what kind of tree? (a) beech (b) oak (c) maple (d) fir — 7. ____

8. They don't take the gold home immediately for fear that people would (a) rob them. (b) gossip about them. (c) think them thieves. (d) arrest them. — 8. ____

9. Which one left for food? (a) the youngest (b) the oldest (c) the smallest (d) the fattest — 9. ____

10. The poison was said to have brought (a) sudden death. (b) a lingering death. (c) an easy death. (d) a painful death. — 10. ____

Check your answers with the Key on p. 451. Give yourself 10 points for each one right and enter your comprehension score on p. 414.

Comprehension Score: ____________

PART III

The Speed-up

NAME ____________ CLASS ____________ DATE ____________

10 How Can You Speed Up Your Reading?

WORD POWER WORKOUT

A. LEANING ON CONTEXT

In each of the blanks provided, place the letter that precedes the best definition of the underlined word in context to the left.

Words in Context	**Definitions**
1. ____ student <u>plodded</u> along	a. gave in, yielded
2. ____ comprehension suffers <u>temporarily</u>	b. moved slowly
3. ____ <u>reinforce</u> your bad habits	c. strengthen
4. ____ your latest <u>entry</u>	d. recording
5. ____ single <u>key</u> principle	e. beginning
6. ____ I finally <u>relented</u>	f. basic
7. ____ <u>sliver</u> of time	g. small splinter
8. ____ strange <u>phenomenon</u>	h. reduce
9. ____ <u>minimize</u> those brakes	i. fact, happening
10. ____ your <u>initial</u> rate	j. for a time

Check your answers with the Key on p. 442 before going on. Give yourself 10 points for each one right and enter your score on the chart under A on p. 420. Review any that you have missed.

A Score: ________

Pronunciation aids: **3. ree-in-FORS**

8. fuh-NOM-uh-nun

B. LEANING ON PARTS

The Greek prefix *epi-* means "upon." Supply the appropriate word or word part in each of the following sentences.

1. A commemorative inscription upon a tomb is an epi____________.
2. The outer layer of your skin is called the epi____________.
3. A nervous disorder characterized by convulsions is called epi____________.
4. A rapidly spreading disease is often spoken of as an epi____________.
5. The epilogue contained comments ____________ the meaning of the play.

C. MAKING THE WORDS YOURS

In each blank below, enter the most appropriate word from the ten words in context in the first exercise, substituting it for the word(s) in parentheses. Use these words: *entry, initial, key, minimize, phenomenon, plodded, reinforces, relented, sliver, temporarily.*

1. To lose weight, (reduce) ____________ the amount of food you eat.
2. He (moved slowly) ____________ through the material.
3. Reading for facts instead of ideas (strengthens) ____________ poor reading habits.
4. A (small splinter) ____________ of wood caught under my fingernail.
5. The store was (for a time) ____________ out of meat.
6. After thinking things over, the father (gave in) ____________.
7. Being attacked by a giant bird was an unbelievable (happening) ____________.
8. A (basic) ____________ element in successful reading is concentration.
9. On what line do I make the (recording) ____________ of the new balance?
10. The speaker's (beginning) ____________ remarks caught everyone's attention.

Check your answers with the Key on p. 444.

B Score: ________

C Score: ________

Enter your scores on p. 420.

10

How Can You Speed Up Your Reading?

BEGIN TIMING

At this point you should be progressing nicely. You've checked reading strengths and weaknesses. You've started to build vocabulary and improve factual comprehension. It's time now to speed up your reading.

How do you do that? By taking off the brakes! Remember the three brakes: *regressing,* or looking back as you read, *vocalizing,* or pronouncing words to yourself, and *word-for-word* reading instead of phrase reading.

To be sure, you've read all that before. But this approach is so important it deserves repeating—but with a new twist, as you'll soon see. So read on.

Faster-Than-Comfortable Reading

How can you eliminate or minimize those brakes that hold your reading to a snail's pace? Fortunately, one single key principle, properly applied, will do the job. Try faster-than-comfortable reading.

Faster-than-comfortable reading reduces regressions. You just don't have time to look back. Furthermore, you have less time to vocalize, so that bad habit begins to disappear. Finally, that extra speed forces you into dealing with word groups, not single words.

Put a faster-than-comfortable reading plan into effect immediately. Set aside fifteen minutes a day for practice. To be sure, you've practiced reading for years, but probably never the uncomfortable variety. That means you've probably done little more than reinforce your bad habits. You can practice twenty years at 200 wpm and *never* develop skill at double that rate. Push uncomfortable speeds with the selections in this book, as well as with other easy reading. Keep a careful record of changes in rate. If those practice sessions don't tire you, you know you're not pushing hard enough to get maximum results.

Whenever you first push into faster speeds, you will probably feel you are not actually reading. Remember, you need new experience to make those faster speeds comfortable. And don't worry if comprehension suffers temporarily. It will improve as soon as you gain sufficient additional experience.

Pacing

At some point in your development, you're going to find yourself just unable to read any faster. Continual checks of your Progress Record Charts in the back of this book will help you know when that point is reached. The minute your latest entry is less than 20 wpm faster than the preceding one, you know you need added impetus. That's true especially if you find yourself saying, "I just can't push myself any faster!"

That's when you need the special technique of pacing. Almost without exception, there are hidden potentials in all of us that become available only under crisis or unusual pressure. Pacing provides the key for unlocking such resources. For that reason it is the oldest, most widely used, yet newest approach for speeding your reading.

Why is pacing so common? The answer is simple. It works. This was brought dramatically home to me in one of my adult efficient reading classes at the university. At our first session, one student plodded along at 80 wpm while the rest of the class patiently waited for him to finish.

After class, I told him he'd better cancel. In desperation, he said, "I need this more than anyone." I had to agree, but added that it seemed hardly fair to make all the others wait for him to finish. He begged to stay, saying, "All right. Don't wait for me. Let me get what I can." I finally relented.

As the course progressed, I noted an amazing change. While the class moved up nicely from 254 to 481 wpm, the plodder had shot up from 80 to 460 wpm! "What are you doing?" I asked him. He explained. He told me he had wired his electric clock to the radio. Every time the sweep second hand passed 12, the radio came on briefly to let him know a minute had passed.

Every night, without fail, for only fifteen minutes, he used that device to pace himself in the *Reader's Digest,* which contains about 500 words per full page. At first he tried to read half a column in a minute—125 words. When he could manage that, he tried a full column, then a full page. The results were spectacular.

Why not enjoy similar results yourself? Use a fifteen-minute sliver of time. Have someone pace you by saying "next" every minute. Pace at speeds at least 75 wpm faster than your last entry on the Progress Record Chart. In this way you will gradually build the ability to read quite effectively at the faster speeds.

Add pacing to faster-than-comfortable reading. It's like firing what might be called a second-stage rocket to blast you into speedier orbit.

Swing Two Bats

As a booster rocket, tap an important psychological principle. If you've never once driven at 100 mph, imagine how that would feel. As you accelerate beyond your usual 65 mph, can't you feel the tension build, your grip on the steering wheel tighten? One slip would be fatal. After a time, when you dropped back to your usual 65 mph, you would notice a strange phenomenon. That 65 mph speed would seem much slower—almost like a leisurely 50 mph. In essence, that's the same psychological principle a baseball player uses when he swings two bats before dropping one and stepping up to the plate. The one remaining bat seems much lighter and easier to swing.

Capitalize on this to develop increased reading speed. When you're reading normally at 250 wpm, practice at 350 to make yourself more comfortable at 300 wpm. Your top reading speed will always be uncomfortable. That's why you should practice at even faster speeds. Suppose you double your initial rate, moving from 250 to 500 wpm. Be sure to make yourself comfortable at 500 wpm by practicing some at a 600 to 700 figure. This ensures maximum progress.

Judging from class results here at Minnesota, when you finish this program you should read at least twice as fast, with the same or better comprehension. Of our students, about 72 percent double their rate, 20 percent triple it, and 8 percent quadruple it.

Length: 1000 words.
Reading Time: __________
See Conversion Table, p. 421.
Enter WPM Rate on p. 416.

10 How Can You Speed Up Your Reading?

COMPREHENSION CHECK

1. To speed your reading you are told to (a) set a new purpose. (b) think speed. (c) take off the brakes. (d) analyze yourself. 1. ____

2. One slowing-down factor mentioned is (a) fatigue. (b) drowsiness. (c) lack of concentration. (d) regressing. 2. ____

3. Another factor mentioned is (a) vocalizing. (b) background deficiency. (c) eyestrain. (d) inattention. 3. ____

4. You are told to keep a careful record of (a) material read. (b) changes in rate. (c) time spent in reading. (d) special reading difficulties. 4. ____

5. You are cautioned not to (a) lose any comprehension. (b) read too fast. (c) worry over temporary loss of comprehension. (d) read too long at any one time. 5. ____

6. Pacing is commonly used because (a) it works. (b) it is simple. (c) it is convenient. (d) it requires minimal equipment. 6. ____

7. A normal full page of the *Reader's Digest* contains about how many words? (a) 200 (b) 300 (c) 400 (d) 500 7. ____

8. Pacing is likened to (a) a super-charged engine. (b) a second-stage rocket. (c) a second-wind effort. (d) high gear on a car. 8. ____

9. You are asked to imagine yourself (a) driving at 100 mph. (b) piloting a jet plane. (c) speeding down a mountainside on skis. (d) steering a toboggan. 9. ____

10. You are told that your top speed would (a) eventually become comfortable. (b) be impossible to sustain. (c) always be uncomfortable. (d) have to be practiced frequently. 10. ____

Check your answers with the Key on p. 451. Give yourself 10 points for each one right and enter your comprehension score on p. 414.

Comprehension Score: ________

MAKING THE APPLICATION

Pacing suggestions: To estimate the number of words per page, take any book or magazine that you plan to use for pacing. Turn to a full page and count up to 100 words. A word is any letter or combination of letters that stands alone, *I* and *a* as well as longer ones. Count the number of lines in that 100-word sample and use that figure to estimate the number of words on a full page. A magazine the size of the *Reader's Digest,* for example, has about 500 words per full page, which gives you an idea of what to expect with other page sizes.

To pace, first select an easy, popular book that you want to read. Pace for about ten minutes a session a day. You can enlist the help of a roommate or friend—someone who will say "begin reading" and say "next" at the end of every minute for ten minutes. You, the reader, try to cover each page so that at the word "next" you are just reading the last words. If you are a bit slow, skip to the next page and read faster, gradually adjusting rate to the pacing figure settled on. For your first pacing, if you read at about 250 wpm, try a 500-wpm rate. This would mean reading ten 500-word pages in ten minutes or twelve-and-a-half 400-word pages.

Pacing can also be done with your textbooks. Here your first move is to read the text for exactly one minute to see what your usual wpm rate is for that text. Suppose you find it to be 125 wpm. You then pace yourself through an assignment at about 250 wpm. Determine the number of words per page as discussed and figure the number of pages you must read in ten minutes to read at 250 wpm. Divide that number by ten to know where you should be at the command of "next."

Even if you don't have a friend or roommate to help, you can still pace yourself. Place a marker at the point of the book where you should be in exactly ten minutes. See if you can make it. If not, go slightly faster for the next ten minutes.

Pacing both with easy reading as well as with more difficult reading will encourage you to develop real flexibility of rate, a flexibility that can be readily modified by purpose to your advantage. The added concentration that comes from pacing should let you handle faster speeds with real effectiveness.

A pacing record similar to the one that follows should point up progress. Under the heading *Subjective Feeling,* enter a descriptive word or phrase to indicate your feeling—such as *impossibly fast, frustrating, manageable,* or *understandable.* It is most satisfying to see a given speed become *manageable,* when at first it was quite *frustrating.*

Title of book used for pacing: ______________________

	Minutes of Pacing	Pacing Rate	Subjective Feeling
Week 1	________	________	________
Week 1	________	________	________
Week 1	________	________	________
Week 2	________	________	________
Week 2	________	________	________
Week 2	________	________	________
Week 3	________	________	________
Week 3	________	________	________
Week 3	________	________	________

NAME ______________ CLASS ______________ DATE ______________

11 The All-Important Question

WORD POWER WORKOUT

A. LEANING ON CONTEXT

In each of the blanks provided, place the letter that precedes the best definition of the underlined word in context to the left.

Words in Context

1. ____ this most crucial
2. ____ you can attain
3. ____ almost any goal
4. ____ you may prefer
5. ____ why I'm convinced
6. ____ babble meaninglessly
7. ____ only utter gibberish
8. ____ sponsoring a wordless TV program
9. ____ acronym for Compact Disk
10. ____ fasten around your loin

Definitions

a. choose
b. of supreme importance
c. underwriting
d. achieve
e. intention
f. persuaded
g. talk incoherently
h. speak
i. lower part of back
j. word formed by first letters of other words

Check your answers with the Key on p. 442 before going on. Give yourself 10 points for each one right and enter your score on the chart under A on p. 420. Review any that you have missed.

A Score: ________

Pronunciation aids: 9. AK-rah-nim

B. LEANING ON PARTS

The prefix *ad-* (also spelled *ac-, af-, ag-, al-, an-, ap-, ar-, as-, at-,* or *a-*) means "to" or "toward." Supply the proper word or word parts in the following.

1. When one surface sticks to another, it ad__________ to it.
2. This ticket will ad__________ you to the next performance.
3. Two buildings next to each other can be said to be ad__________ent.
4. The army ad__________ very slowly toward enemy positions.
5. An adjunct is an unessential thing added __________ something else.

C. MAKING THE WORDS YOURS

In each blank below, enter the most appropriate word from the ten words in context in the first exercise, substituting it for the word(s) in parentheses. Use these words: *acronym, attain, babble, convinced, crucial, goal, loin, prefer, sponsoring, utter.*

1. I (persuaded) __________ them to take a different route going home.
2. He was injured in the (lower part of the back) __________.
3. Do you know the words that form the (word formed by first letters of other words) __________ for radar?
4. The more you (talk incoherently) __________, the less attention you get.
5. They tried (underwriting) __________ a campaign to clean up the environment.
6. Never try to (achieve) __________ a lasting record in an endurance run.
7. Don't (speak) __________ a single word about this accident to anyone.
8. It's (of supreme importance) __________ that you get a good mark on your final exam.
9. Do you (choose) __________ your pie with or without ice cream?
10. My (intention) __________ is to be captain of the football team next year.

Check your answers with the Key on p. 444.

B Score: ________

C Score: ________

Enter your scores on p. 420.

11

The All-Important Question

JAMES I. BROWN

Someone once said, "Every time you learn all the answers, they change all the questions." Well, here's the most important question of all. It certainly deserves an all-important answer. And no questioning of the question!

BEGIN TIMING

If you knew the answer to one question, you could have almost anything you want—friends, success, health, happiness, power, recognition, you name it. Just one question rightly raised and answered would do it. What's this most crucial of all questions? Well, read on.

WHAT KNOWLEDGE IS MOST WORTH HAVING?

Answer that question right and you can attain almost any goal you desire. Now I'm not talking about the million and one things you already know, or the billions upon billions of things in the world that you could learn. I'm talking *only* about those bits of knowledge most *worth your* knowing—nothing more, nothing less. What's your answer to that all-important question?

I'll give you mine. WORDS! To me, words make up that knowledge most worth having.

Perhaps you don't agree. You may prefer another answer. But at least let me explain why I'm convinced that's the right answer. And let me overdramatize a bit. Suppose with the snap of a finger we could eliminate all words—every single one, written or spoken, from the face of the earth. Snap—just like that.

What would happen? Well, I could no longer write these words to you as I'm now doing. And you couldn't read these or any other words from paper or your computer screen. Why? Because now there aren't any words. Even if I were to meet you I could only babble meaninglessly—only utter gibberish, if that.

Look around. Do you see a TV set anywhere? Get rid of words and you get rid of TV. What company would waste money sponsoring a wordless TV program? You need words to indicate a sponsor or, even more important, to attract and sell a customer.

And what about computers? Without words, what use are they? The information superhighway demands words, otherwise it's closed permanently. No more Web surfing. No more e-mail. No more Internet.

Computers, however, deserve a closer look. For example, the American Airlines reservation system uses a computer to store some 4.4 trillion bytes. That's the equivalent of 4 million million characters on a computer hard disk. Put those words into regular book form and you'd have a book of more than 2 million pages. See what you'd lose when you eliminate words? You lose computers. They're now worthless. And your CD-ROM, acronym for Compact Disk–Read Only Memory, that also becomes worthless.

Let's look further. Without words, no telephone, no fax. Talk about change! Also, no words, no radio. Advertisers couldn't advertise. You need words to sell. And now there aren't any. That brings us to business. There, too, no words, no business. Business depends on words—ads, letters, phone calls, sales representatives.

No words, no government. Prime Minister Benjamin Disraeli once said, "It is with words that we govern." *Fortune* magazine reminds us that our government presently collects about 3 billion bits of information a year. Collecting, reviewing, and storing those words costs about $500 per person yearly. Get rid of words and you get rid of government.

No words, and no books, magazines, or newspapers. They're gone. You realize, of course, that you've just wiped out our whole educational system—students, teachers, and administrators. Without words education becomes an impossibility.

You go ahead. Add to my list. No more pleasant conversations! No laws to obey—or disobey! No way to know what's going on in other parts of the world! That all depends on words.

What's left? Well, grab a cloth to fasten around your loin and head for the nearest cave. We've just turned the clock back to prehistoric times. You can see it clearly now—no words, no civilization.

Now you know why I say that knowledge of words is indeed that knowledge most worth having.

Length: 620 words.
Reading Time: __________
See Conversion Table p. 421.
Enter WPM Rate on p. 416.

11 The All-Important Question

COMPREHENSION CHECK

1. Answering the question right was said to let you attain what specific goal? (a) money (b) position (c) freedom (d) success — 1. ____

2. Specific mention was made of the (a) million and one things you know. (b) CD-ROM to be consulted. (c) countless experiences you've had. (d) encyclopedia you should consult. — 2. ____

3. The selection speaks specifically of (a) imagining. (b) pretending. (c) overdramatizing. (d) overstating. — 3. ____

4. The selection refers to (a) mumbling nonsense. (b) babbling meaninglessly. (c) whistling. (d) saying nothing. — 4. ____

5. Mention is made of (a) Northwest Airlines. (b) Delta Airlines. (c) American Airlines. (d) America West Airlines. — 5. ____

6. How many trillion bytes were stored? (a) 5.5 (b) 4.4 (c) 3.3 (d) 2.2 — 6. ____

7. The *M* in ROM stands for (a) measure. (b) memory. (c) meaning. (d) microprocessing. — 7. ____

8. Mention was made of (a) the information superhighway. (b) the World Wide Web. (c) WordPerfect. (d) Windows 98. — 8. ____

9. Who was quoted? (a) Winston Churchill (b) Margaret Thatcher (c) Benjamin Disraeli (d) Queen Victoria — 9. ____

10. Mention was made of a (a) bow and arrow. (b) spear. (c) loin cloth. (d) club. — 10. ____

Check your answers with the Key on p. 451. Give yourself 10 points for each one right and enter your comprehension score on p. 414.

Comprehension Score: ________

NAME ________________ CLASS ________________ DATE ____________

12 Words Can Be Slippery

WORD POWER WORKOUT

A. LEANING ON CONTEXT

In each of the blanks provided, place the letter that precedes the best definition of the underlined word in context to the left.

Words in Context	**Definitions**
1. ____ can be a plea	a. water-soaked
2. ____ term of endearment	b. roll about
3. ____ marital relations	c. entreaty
4. ____ on the tinker's trail	d. arranged
5. ____ We wallow	e. scheming
6. ____ crammed the general air	f. affection
7. ____ conned by the anti-logic	g. traveling repairman's
8. ____ connivance of the wool-pullers	h. matrimonial
9. ____ the sodden plasticity	i. stuffed
10. ____ We have negotiated it	j. trickery

Check your answers with the Key on p. 442 before going on. Give yourself 10 points for each one right and enter your score on the chart under A on p. 420. Review any that you have missed.

A Score: ________

Pronunciation aids: **3. MAR-ih-tl**
8. kuh-NI-vens

B. LEANING ON PARTS

Well over a thousand words contain the prefix *un-,* meaning "not." Supply the missing word or word part in each of the following blanks.

1. If a story or article is not usual, call it un__________.
2. If you are not certain about something, you are un__________.
3. If your actions are not wise, they can be called un__________.
4. If I am not worthy of praise, I am un__________.
5. If you are unconscious, that means you are __________ conscious.

C. MAKING THE WORDS YOURS

In each blank below, enter the most appropriate word from the ten words in context in the first exercise, substituting it for the word(s) in parentheses. Use these words: *conned, connivance, crammed, endearment, marital, nego-tiated, plea, sodden, tinker's, wallow.*

1. I like to watch the pigs (roll about) __________ in the mud.
2. The salesman's (trickery) __________ led him to invest in a worth-less gold mine.
3. That boy's mischievous behavior seemed (an entreaty) a __________ for attention.
4. She used (scheming) __________ to get the committee to make a yes vote.
5. The owners (arranged) __________ a good price for their big ranch.
6. You'd better use some words of (affection) __________ if you want action.
7. They (stuffed) __________ all their camping gear into their car.
8. Hope you don't have any (matrimonial) __________ difficulties.
9. That sudden deluge made his clothes (water-soaked) __________.
10. Why not look in the (traveling repairman's) __________ truck to see what's there.

Check your answers with the Key on p. 444.

B Score: __________

C Score: __________

Enter your scores on p. 420.

12

Words Can Be Slippery

FRANK G. JENNINGS

Words! Not only slippery but highly revealing! Say a dozen words and you've said much more than you thought. Those few words whisper volumes about your age, your background, your education—who you are, where you've been, and how you look on life.

BEGIN TIMING

There is no one sovereign way of getting information. Pictures are good. So are smells, yells and bellyaches. But information is the raw material of communication. Information isn't even that unless it is used or a use is contemplated for it. Communication is a social act. It is always concerned with other people. It can be done with a grunt, a bump or a glance. It can be rich with "meanings" or with feeling or with a mixture of both. The *what* of things can be reduced to the simple symbols of mathematics but the *why* and its *worth* needs the poets' magic and the shared remembrance of dreams and hopes. The crudest television commercial pays homage to this when the dancing bottles or marching cigarettes picket the screen with little signs, pleading for closer attention.

Words are slippery things. They won't stay put. They pick up meanings and colors not "intended" for them. They suffer or profit by the company they keep. In the mouth of one man the word "love" can be a plea. Other lips can make it a curse. Its meaning can be reduced to the equivalent of "like" or expanded to mean "worship." The word *red* may mean truth, beauty or falsehood. *Liberty* can become a dirty name; *chain* a term of endearment.

What happens to words can and does happen to any symbol. A flag, a statue or a city can "stand for" opposite things for different peoples. But we trust the words we share with others until we or they are misunderstood and even then we distrust them more than their words. We often have a very firm belief that the words that we use are the same as and as real as the things they stand for or the acts they represent. Languages are filled with reverent remarks like "I give you my word!" The tyranny of the two-letter word *is* forces us to act, sometimes as if the word we use for a thing is as real as the thing in itself. This causes us to misjudge the nature of the actual world. It worries us and even makes us sick. Some people in this world, not of course as civilized as we are, even think that it is dangerous to let anyone know their real names for fear that the name-knower would have power over them. But let any man call another a fool or a liar or question the social regularity of his parents' marital relations and he will act as violently as any other primitive.

We are a nation of loudmouths. We got that way on the tinker's trail and at the boasting parties around frontier campfires. We have more tall tales in our folklore than you can find in all of Europe. But our tallest tales have become merely conservative estimates of our actual performances. Pecos Bill rode a tornado. His great-grandchild rides a Thunderjet at ten times the speed. Paul Bunyan's Blue Ox would be worn out by a medium sized bulldozer and Johnny Inkslinger couldn't even feed the cards to an obsolete IBM bookkeeping machine.

We wallow in this flood of words, but it's of our own making. We've painted the clouds with ads for soap, curtained the countryside with billboards for baby foods, and crammed the general air with electronic declarations about the benefits of laxatives and deodorants. But the anxiety we should suffer in the face of this flood is only apparent in the warnings of the permanently disenchanted.

Of course it is true that the shell game is played on us every day in the year by peddlers, purveyors and produces of everything that we need and use and a lot that we don't need, never wanted but cannot do without.

It is certainly true that our intelligences, however great or meager, are insulted and conned by the anti-logic of the huckster but it is about time that someone blew the whistle on the anxious applicants for our intellectual guardianship. This is not to say that there should be no concern about the connivance of the wool-pullers and pharmaceutical wolf-criers but, rather, than those individuals with off-center sensitivity over the sodden plasticity of the masses ought to learn to read their dials and counters with more accuracy and objectivity. The mass mind is a myth.

The mass media for communication, and we have invented and perfected all of them here, are effective upon the masses only so far as distribution of "information" is concerned. The only apparent mass movement that television has so far been able to effect is the concerted and collective use of plumbing during the commercials. Mass action can still only be effected where there are masses. The motion picture could do this, but we lack the indecency of Hitler's Leni Reifensthal; besides, our whole population is never anxious about the same thing at the same time. We rarely suffer more than a few mob scenes during any year, and these are engineered by methods that were invented by the old Greeks and still require a man with leather lungs and a ruptured psyche.

No, we live splendidly and dangerously in this word ocean of ours. Its currents are strong. Its shoals are treacherous but it is not the whole of our environment. We inhale and exhale words for our social living, but we do this for purposes, to make or change things or keep them as they are. To do this we must take thought and to think we must be able to hold ideas still long enough to compare them. To make comparisons we must be able to choose and choice requires that we have preferences. None of these acts are possible if we cannot manage and master the words that we use. The mastery that we have gained is the measure of the cultural distance we have traveled from the cave. It is a long long way. We have negotiated it through our ability to make, read and act upon signs. Early man was a good sailor on the sea of life. We are navigators.

Length: 990 words.
Reading Time: __________
See Conversion Table, p. 421.
Enter WPM Rate on p. 416.

12 Words Can Be Slippery

▶ COMPREHENSION CHECK

1. What way of getting information is *not* mentioned? (a) listening (b) pictures (c) yells (d) smells — 1. ____

2. Communication is said to be what kind of act? (a) meaningful (b) necessary (c) social (d) frequent — 2. ____

3. What specific word is discussed? (a) book (b) justice (c) red (d) hate — 3. ____

4. What important two-letter word is mentioned? (a) is (b) it (c) in (d) be — 4. ____

5. Boasting parties were (a) community potlucks. (b) cocktail parties. (c) neighborhood picnics. (d) around frontier campfires. — 5. ____

6. The article specifically mentions (a) laxatives. (b) soaps. (c) shampoos. (d) computers. — 6. ____

7. The writer says that by hucksters our intelligence is (a) ignored. (b) shamed. (c) insulted. (d) ridiculed. — 7. ____

8. The mass mind is called (a) bitter truth. (b) mistake. (c) figment of the imagination. (d) myth. — 8. ____

9. Specific mention was made of (a) Hitler. (b) Mussolini. (c) Roosevelt. (d) Eisenhower. — 9. ____

10. We are called (a) navigators. (b) sailors. (c) prospectors. (d) pilgrims. — 10. ____

Check your answers with the Key on p. 451. Give yourself 10 points for each one right and enter your comprehension score on p. 414.

Comprehension Score: ________

YOUR LDE FORMULA

Can you get meanings for strange words or word parts without your dictionary? Certainly! It's just a matter of harnessing brain power to word power and applying the LDE Formula. Here's how it works.

Take the strange Latin word *omnis,* which gives us the prefix *omni-*. What does it mean? You don't know? You've never taken Latin? When dealing with words, never say, "I don't know." That shuts the door to important vocabulary growth. You probably do know, but just don't know that you do. Think again. What's an omnidirectional radio receiver? One that receives sound waves from all directions, you say. Now if you know that, you really know what *omni-* means. It means "all."

That kind of reasoning lies behind the LDE Formula. Your first step when meeting a strange prefix, root, or suffix is to LIST several words containing that element. With *omni-,* let's say you listed *omnidirectional* and *omnipotent.* Maybe that's all you thought of. Or perhaps you also listed *omnipresent* and *omniscient.* You don't necessarily need that many. Some times one word is enough, although usually the more the better. That's step one of the formula: LIST.

The second step? DEFINE each word you listed. Let's say you define *omnidirectional* as "in all directions," *omnipotent* as "all-powerful," *omnipresent* as "always present," and *omniscient* as "all-knowing." That's step two: DEFINE.

The third and last step is to EXTRACT the common denominator or meaning. What do the *omni-* words have in common? The meaning "all"! The formula made you aware of that meaning. From now on when you see a word beginning with *omni-,* look for that meaning. An omnivorous reader has to be a reader of "all" kinds of things.

That's how the three-step LDE Formula works. It's not only three-step, it's also three-way—to be used with all three kinds of word parts: prefixes, roots, and suffixes. Furthermore, if one word part can be a shortcut to the meanings of over a thousand words, this formula deserves the label *super-shortcut,* for it works with all elements. You'll be more than pleased with the way it speeds your vocabulary growth, not one word at a time but up to a thousand.

That doesn't mean you'll always arrive at the right meaning, but you should always be closer. Even if the formula works only 70 percent of the time, that gives you a 70 percent advantage over those who don't apply it—an advantage well worth having.

(To develop added skill with the formula, do the exercise on page 156.)

NAME ______________ CLASS ______________ DATE ______________

13 Speeding by Surveying

WORD POWER WORKOUT

A. LEANING ON CONTEXT

In each of the blanks provided, place the letter that precedes the best definition of the underlined word in context to the left.

Words in Context	**Definitions**
1. ____ we <u>obviously</u> demand choices	a. succeeding
2. ____ a <u>veritable</u> avalanche of print	b. brief
3. ____ a neat manageable <u>capsule</u>	c. clearly
4. ____ <u>compressed</u> the essentials of chapters	d. small case
5. ____ amazingly <u>concise</u> indication	e. condensed, brought together
6. ____ This chapter <u>zeros in</u>	f. focuses
7. ____ <u>apportion</u> to each article	g. to the point
8. ____ <u>subsequent</u> reading rate	h. distribute, allot
9. ____ seems more <u>pertinent</u>	i. actual
10. ____ book <u>jacket</u>	j. cover

Check your answers with the Key on p. 442 before going on. Give yourself 10 points for each one right and enter your score on the chart under A on p. 420. Review any that you have missed.

A Score: ________

Pronunciation aids: **2. VAIR-uh-tuh-bul** **5. kun-SYS** **3. CAP-sul** **9. PUR-ten-ent**

B. LEANING ON PARTS

The prefix *com-* (also spelled *col-, cor-, con-,* or *co-*) means "together" or "with." Supply the missing word or word part in each of the following blanks.

1. Pressing leaves together makes a more com__________pile.
2. A person traveling with you is called a traveling com__________.
3. To com__________two things more easily, put them side by side.
4. Salt, composed as it is of two elements, is a chemical com__________.
5. A compromise is sometimes necessary to bring two sides __________.

C. MAKING THE WORDS YOURS

In each blank below, enter the most appropriate word from the ten words in context in the first exercise, substituting it for the word(s) in parentheses. Use these words: *apportion, capsule, compressed, concise, jacket, obviously, pertinent, subsequent, veritable, zeros in.*

1. His father tried to (distribute, allot) __________ the money equally.
2. Watch the hunter as he (focuses) __________ on the moving deer.
3. A description of the novel was written on the book (cover) __________.
4. The (brief) __________ summary made the chapter clear.
5. The speaker (condensed) __________ the speech in order to save time.
6. Doing these exercises will help you with the (succeeding) __________ readings.
7. It is (clearly) __________ time to make some changes.
8. That (actual) __________ wall of water demolished the houses.
9. Six vitamins and four minerals are packed inside this one (small case) __________.
10. I had to collect some (to the point) __________ facts for my term paper.

Check your answers with the Key on p. 445.

B Score: ________

C Score: ________

Enter your scores on p. 420.

13

Speeding by Surveying

BEGIN TIMING

Rapid reading is good, but not good enough. Of necessity, you should also know and use three superspeeds—*surveying, skimming,* and *scanning.* This chapter zeros in on the first of the three—surveying. Let's see exactly what it is, how it works, and when to use it.

To put surveying into better perspective, ask yourself a question. Who would buy a car—even a racy sports model—if it ran at only one speed? No one! In traveling we obviously demand choices, such as going by jet, by car, by bicycle, or on foot. Each choice has its own speed range, its own advantages and disadvantages, and serves quite different needs.

What about reading speeds? Here a variety of speeds is even more important. You face a veritable avalanche of print. Without a fantastically wide range of speeds, you'll soon feel buried alive. That's why you need superspeeds.

What Is Surveying?

Surveying is a specialized technique for getting a mountaintop view of an article, chapter, or entire book. With it, you catch a broad, overall picture of basic essentials. You speed through material anywhere from ten to over fifty times faster than with ordinary reading. That means you can survey up to fifty articles, chapters, or books in the time it usually takes to read just one. Obviously, a most useful technique!

How Does It Work?

Written communication has, fortunately, certain characteristics that make surveying possible. Usually, for example, the title of an article provides an amazingly concise indication of article content. The first paragraph normally adds substance, suggesting more exactly what is to follow.

From that point on, major divisions are often marked with headings. Other especially important points are apt to appear in italics, graphs, or tables. Finally, more often than not, the last paragraph will summarize or suggest key implications or applications.

Now translate those characteristics into action. You'll soon see exactly how to survey. *Read the title, the first paragraph, all headings, italicized words, graphs, and tables, and the last paragraph.* Simple? Yes. And you'll usually end up with the best possible overview with a minimal investment of time.

Stop right here. Survey this entire article before reading on. To guide you, the key words are all underlined. Just read all underlined words, starting with the title. Then come back to this spot and continue with your timing of this chapter.

Now you can see for yourself. You do have the essentials. A survey functions much as an abstract. It compresses the essentials of a full-length chapter into a neat, manageable capsule.

With certain modifications, you can also survey an entire book. To do this, read the title and table of contents. If there is a book jacket, read the material on the front, back, and inside flaps. This provides a broad overview of the entire book. Then go ahead to survey each chapter individually, as described earlier. Read the chapter title, first paragraph, headings, italicized words, graphs, tables, and last paragraph. That's how it works.

Surveying as a Reading Expeditor

One important use for surveying is to facilitate your reading. Think back to what happened when you surveyed this chapter. You caught the essentials and the writer's plan.

In planning a car trip, you normally get out maps to see exactly what route to travel. Reading an article without an overview is much like traveling a strange highway. You don't know what towns or cities to expect or what intersections or junctions to note. Surveying serves as a road map. Obviously, when you know the road even slightly, you travel it more confidently and easily. So it is with reading. When you know in general where the writer is going, you can follow more easily.

In short, surveying should actually increase your subsequent reading speed. After all, you're traveling a more familiar road. It should also improve comprehension. You have the advantage of double coverage of key parts. Use surveying, then, as a prereading step, to gain added speed and comprehension.

Surveying as a Decision Expeditor

Still another use for surveying focuses on an age-old problem. Sir Francis Bacon put it this way. "Some books are to be tasted, others to be swallowed, and some few to be chewed and digested." Unfortunately, Bacon left the heart of the problem untouched. How do you decide which books belong where? Well, who knows your own personal background, interests, problems, and specific needs best? You yourself, of course. Yet, how can you tell, before you read a book, exactly what attention it deserves?

Surveying is your answer. A quick survey provides an ideal basis for deciding intelligently whether to taste, swallow, or chew and digest.

Actually, you have four possibilities—to skip, skim, read, or study. Suppose your initial survey reveals no information of interest. Well, you've already given it all the attention it deserves. Put it aside. Remember—that decision was not made blindly. You know what's there.

If the material seems more pertinent, put it into the next category. Skim it. Skimming takes much less time than reading yet brings more information than surveying. The third choice is to read it. Do this with material deserving even more attention. Finally, it may be so important as to deserve careful study. Many make the mistake of trying to read almost everything—an impossible task. Only after reading an entire book do they realize it was a waste of time.

To remember these choices, put them into a formula—the <u>*SD4 Formula.*</u> You <u>*Survey*</u> in order to <u>*Decide*</u> which of <u>*4*</u> things to do—<u>*skip, skim, read,*</u> or <u>*study*</u>.

To summarize, surveying lets you apportion to each article or book precisely the time it deserves—no more, no less. Furthermore, that decision is solidly based on evidence gained in a minimum of your precious time.

<u>Here's your first superspeed. Let it help you read more rapidly, comprehend better, and decide more intelligently what attention you should give to all the reading material around you. Put it to immediate use</u>.

Length: 1000 words.
Reading Time: __________
See Conversion Table, p. 421.
Enter WPM Rate on p. 416.

13 Speeding by Surveying

▶ COMPREHENSION CHECK

1. Surveying is said to be about how many times faster than ordinary reading? (a) 5 to 8 times (b) 20 to 30 times (c) 10 to 50 times (d) not specifically mentioned — 1. ____

2. Mention is made of a (a) 10-speed bicycle. (b) racing car. (c) turtle. (d) one-speed car. — 2. ____

3. To survey, you read (a) every other paragraph. (b) the first paragraph. (c) no paragraph completely. (d) all paragraphs in part. — 3. ____

4. Specific reference is made to (a) italicized words. (b) headings. (c) graphs and tables. (d) all of the preceding. — 4. ____

5. You are told how to survey a (a) letter. (b) book. (c) report. (d) summary. — 5. ____

6. Reference is made to (a) road maps. (b) patterns. (c) recipes. (d) guidelines. — 6. ____

7. Specific reference is made to (a) William Shakespeare. (b) Francis Bacon. (c) Alexander Pope. (d) the Bible. — 7. ____

8. After the quick survey, how many choices are mentioned? (a) one (b) two (c) three (d) four — 8. ____

9. What does the *D* in SD4 stand for? (a) determine (b) demand (c) decide (d) describe — 9. ____

10. What is the first choice mentioned? (a) study (b) select (c) skip (d) save — 10. ____

Check your answers with the Key on p. 451. Give yourself 10 points for each one right and enter your comprehension score on p. 414.

Comprehension Score: ________

MAKING THE APPLICATION

You know in theory, now, exactly how to survey an article. But that is only a beginning. How do you move effectively from theory to practice? How do you make yourself a superb surveyor? Try these three steps.

One: Using a colored felt-tip pen, turn back to the selection you just read, "Speeding by Surveying." Highlight in color all the underlined words. This provides a much clearer visualization of what is read in a survey, thus reinforcing the pattern to be used.

Two: Now turn immediately to a chapter in a textbook or to an explanatory article. Again, using your colored felt-tip pen, highlight the portions to be read in surveying the material.

Three: This last step is the pay-off and is of most importance, deserving special attention and thought. How well can you read between the paragraphs and headings? How accurately can you arrive at conclusions about the unread portions? Here's where practice and experience will pay off to best advantage.

You will find it helpful to use a heading like this to provide the proper mental set: *Assumptions about the content of the unread portions.* Under that general heading, list from four to six assumptions based on your survey.

Repeat these steps often enough to become a genuinely skilled surveyor. You will soon see that this view down the road ahead makes any subsequent reading that much easier. Use surveying frequently.

A. VOCABULARY REVIEW QUIZ

This quiz contains ten words drawn from the preceding Word Power Workouts, but with other possible meanings of the word. The focus is on words with important prefixes so as to reinforce your awareness of prefixes as aids to word meaning.

1. consolidates (a) soothes (b) remains (c) joins (d) strengthens (e) injures
Consolidates contains the prefix ______, meaning ______. 1. ____

2. explication (a) making clear (b) planning (c) practicing (d) helping (e) repairing
Explication contains the prefix ______, meaning ______. 2. ____

3. commit (a) memorize (b) order (c) judge (d) give up (e) bind
Commit contains the prefix ______, meaning ______. 3. ____

4. related (a) worked (b) connected (c) granted (d) worked hard (e) read
Related contains the prefix ______, meaning ______. 4. ____

5. reinforces (a) attacks (b) takes in (c) imagines (d) strengthens (e) contains
Reinforces contains the prefix ______, meaning ______. 5. ____

6. attain (a) suggest (b) remind (c) advise (d) satisfy (e) reach
Attain contains the prefix ______, meaning ______. 6. ____

7. connivance (a) underhandedness (b) theorizing (c) advancing (d) criticizing (e) agility
Connivance contains the prefix ______, meaning ______. 7. ____

8. apportion (a) detain (b) collect (c) distribute (d) admire (e) prepare
Apportion contains the prefix ______, meaning ______. 8. ____

9. compressed — (a) sent down (b) shortened (c) led (d) favored (e) examined — 9. ____
Compressed contains the prefix ______, meaning _____.

10. prefer — (a) like better (b) investigate (c) feel pain (d) involve (e) search around — 10. ____
Prefer contains the prefix ______, meaning _____.

10 points for each correct answer.
See Key on p. 441.
Vocabulary Review Score: ________

NAME ____________ CLASS ____________ DATE ____________

14 The First Rule of Conversation

WORD POWER WORKOUT

A. LEANING ON CONTEXT

In each of the blanks provided, place the letter that precedes the best definition of the underlined word in context to the left.

Words in Context	Definitions
1. _____ able to respond	a. complaints
2. _____ less frivolous questions	b. additions
3. _____ logical extensions	c. speaker
4. _____ first and foremost	d. achievements
5. _____ his wife's permission	e. unmindful
6. _____ Republican spokesman	f. consent
7. _____ unalterable opposition	g. unchangeable
8. _____ Regardless of your views	h. chief
9. _____ his pet peeves	i. superficial
10. _____ and their accomplishments	j. answer

Check your answers with the Key on p. 442 before going on. Give yourself 10 points for each one right and enter your score on the chart under A on p. 420. Review any that you have missed.

A Score: ________

Pronunciation aids: 2. FRIV-uh-lus

B. LEANING ON PARTS

The prefix *non-* means "not," as in *nonexistent.* Fill in the blanks in the following sentences with the appropriate word or word part.

1. Things that are not essential to life can be called non__________.
2. A person not conforming to accepted behavior is a non__________.
3. Books are often classified in two ways, as fiction or non__________.
4. If something is unbelievably foolish, call it utter non__________.
5. A nonresident is, of course, __________ a resident.

C. MAKING THE WORDS YOURS

In each blank below, enter the most appropriate word from the ten words in context in the first exercise, substituting it for the word(s) in parentheses. Use these words: *accomplishments, extensions, foremost, frivolous, peeve, permission, regardless, respond, spokesman, unalterable.*

1. She is the (chief) __________ suspect in this murder trial.
2. Who is the (speaker) __________ for the teacher's union?
3. How are you going to (answer) __________ to the candidates's false statement?
4. Winning an Olympic gold medal in swimming was one of his (achievements) __________.
5. You shouldn't waste your time with such (superficial) __________ details.
6. My special (complaint) __________ is having someone blow smoke in my face.
7. Her (additions) __________ to these plans need reworking.
8. His opposition to adding a sales tax is (unchangeable) __________.
9. (Unmindful) __________ of her father's wishes, she continued to date Bill.
10. Do you have official (consent) __________ to serve another term?

Check your answers with the Key on p. 445.

B Score: __________

C Score: __________

Enter your scores on p. 420.

14

The First Rule of Conversation

LARRY KING

Who wouldn't like to know how to talk to anyone, anytime, anywhere? Who wouldn't like to know the secrets of good communication? And, for that matter, who can give such advice better than Larry King. After all, he makes his living by conversing—by interviewing.

BEGIN TIMING

My first rule of conversation is this: I never learn a thing while I'm talking. I realize every morning that nothing *I* say today will teach me anything, so if I'm going to learn a lot today, I'll have to do it by listening.

As obvious as this sounds, you run across proof every day that people simply do not listen. Tell your family or friends your plane will arrive at eight and before the conversation ends they'll ask, "What time did you say your plane is coming in?" And try to estimate the number of times you have heard someone say, "I forgot what you told me."

If you don't listen any better than that to someone, you cannot expect them to listen any better to you. I try to remember the signs you see at railroad crossings in small towns and rural areas: "Stop—Look—Listen." Show the people you talk to that you're interested in what they're saying. They will show you the same.

To be a good talker, you must be a good listener. This is more than just a matter of showing an interest in your conversation partner. Careful listening makes you better able to respond—to be a good talker when it's your turn. Good follow-up questions are the mark of a good conversationalist.

When I watch Barbara Walters's interviews I'm often disappointed, because I think she asks too many "so what" questions, like "If you could come back, what would you like to be?" In my opinion Barbara would be much better if she asked less frivolous questions and better follow-ups, logical extensions of the answer to her previous question. That comes from listening.

I was pleased by something Ted Koppel said to *Time* magazine a few years ago. "Larry listens to his guests," he said. "He pays attention to what they say. Too few interviewers do that." Even though I'm known as a "talking head," I think my success comes first and foremost from listening.

When I interview guests on the air, I make notes ahead of time about the kinds of questions I will ask them. But often I'll hear something in one of their responses that leads me into an unexpected question—and a surprising answer.

Example: When Vice President Dan Quayle was my guest during the 1992 presidential campaign, we talked about the laws governing abortion. He said it made no sense at all for his daughter's school to require his or his wife's permission for their daughter to miss a day of school, but not to get an abortion. As soon as he said that, I was curious about Quayle's personal angle on this political topic. So I asked what his attitude would be if his daughter said she was going to have an abortion. He said he would support her in whatever decision she made.

Quayle's reply made news. Abortion was a white-hot issue in that campaign, and here was President Bush's very conservative running mate, the national Republican spokesman for his conservative wing's unalterable opposition to abortion, suddenly saying he would support his daughter if she decided to have one.

Regardless of your views on that issue, the point here is that I got the response from Quayle because I wasn't just going through a list of questions. I was listening to what he was saying. That was what led me to the newsworthy answer.

The same thing happened when Ross Perot came on my show on February 20, 1992, and denied several times that he was interested in running for president. I kept hearing that his denials were less than complete, and when I put the question differently near the end of the show—bang! Perot said he'd run if his supporters succeeded in registering him on the ballot in all fifty states.

All of that happened not because of what I said, but because of what I *heard.* I was listening.

The late Jim Bishop, the popular writer, columnist, and author, was another New Yorker who spent a lot of time in Miami when I was there. He told me once that one of his pet peeves was people who ask you how you are but then don't listen to your answer. One man in particular was a repeat offender on this subject, so Jim decided to test just how poor a listener this fellow was.

The man called Jim one morning and began the conversation the way he always did: "Jim, how are ya?"

Jim says, "I have lung cancer."

"Wonderful. Say, Jim. . ."

Bishop had proved his point.

Dale Carnegie put it effectively in his book *How to Win Friends and Influence People,* which has now sold fifteen million copies: "To be interesting, be interested."

He added, "Ask questions that other persons will enjoy answering. Encourage them to talk about themselves and their accomplishments. Remember that the people you are talking to are a hundred times more interested in themselves and their wants and problems than they are in you and your problems. A person's toothache means more to that person than a famine in China which kills a million people. A boil on one's neck interests one more than forty earthquakes in Africa. Think of that the next time you start a conversation."

Length: 880 words.
Reading Time: __________
See Conversion Table, p. 421.
Enter WPM Rate on p. 416.

14 The First Rule of Conversation

COMPREHENSION CHECK

1. King writes that "while I'm talking, I never (a) learn a thing." (b) worry." (c) wonder what to say." (d) look at my notes." 1. ____

2. What time is the plane said to arrive? (a) seven (b) eight (c) nine (d) ten 2. ____

3. King mentions (a) *Time.* (b) *Newsweek.* (c) *The New Yorker.* (d) *Life.* 3. ____

4. King is known as a (a) talking head. (b) talking genius. (c) star talker. (d) master talker. 4. ____

5. What presidential campaign year is mentioned? (a) 1984 (b) 1988 (c) 1992 (d) 1996 5. ____

6. Abortion is specifically called a (a) white-hot issue. (b) news-maker issue. (c) hush-hush issue. (d) conservative issue. 6. ____

7. Who is *not* mentioned? (a) Ross Perot (b) Ronald Reagan (c) Dan Quayle (d) Ted Koppel 7. ____

8. Jim bishop was a (a) Minnesotan. (b) Floridian. (c) New Yorker. (d) Californian. 8. ____

9. To test a poor listener, Bishop says on the phone that he had (a) skin cancer. (b) prostate cancer. (c) lung cancer. (d) diabetes. 9. ____

10. Dale Carnegie said that to be interesting, you had to (a) listen. (b) ask about problems. (c) read widely. (d) be interested. 10. ____

Check your answers with the Key on p. 451. Give yourself 10 points for each one right and enter your comprehension score on p. 414.

Comprehension Score: ________

SHORTCUTS TO WORD MEANINGS

Vocabulary, like Rome, isn't built in a day. If you lived to the ripe old age of 80 and learned one new word every single day of your life, you would have a vocabulary of only 29,200 words—less than 14 percent of the 400,000 words found in our largest dictionary. That's why you need a shortcut, a way of learning words not one at a time but hundreds at a time. Prefix, root, and suffix elements—the building blocks for the bulk of our English vocabulary—provide just that.

Suppose someone speaks of a "precocious youngster." You can look *precocious* up in the dictionary and learn its meaning. Or, better yet, you can put a shortcut to work. Look up *precocious* but notice that *pre-* means "before." In that way, you'll learn not only the meaning of *precocious* but also the meanings of hundreds of other words with that prefix.

For example, you'll know that a reader with a PREdilection for mysteries prefers mysteries "before" other kinds of books. You'll know that someone with rare PREscience knows things "before" they happen (has foresight, as we'd say). One unabridged dictionary lists 2,791 words with the prefix *pre-*, in addition to defining 13 pages of other *pre-* words. *Pre-* is your amazing shortcut to all such words. While it may not always bring you the exact dictionary definition, it will bring you closer to meaning—a big advantage.

Take the prefix *com-* (also spelled *col-*, *cor-*, *con-*, or *co-*) meaning "together." That knowledge provides you with a shortcut to almost two thousand words of desk dictionary size. For example, when you COMpose a theme, you put your ideas "together," so says the prefix. If things are CONcatenated, you know from the prefix they're "together," or, as the dictionary says, "linked or joined together." If two things are CONcomitant, they happen "together."

So, beginning now, whenever you look up a word, notice any prefix, root, or suffix meanings. Turn each element into a useful shortcut for defining hundreds of related words besides the one you looked up. Start by memorizing the all-important elements in this text (see page 43). Begin using them immediately in dealing with unfamiliar words.

NAME ______________ CLASS ______________ DATE ______________

15 How to REALLY Talk to Another Person

WORD POWER WORKOUT

A. LEANING ON CONTEXT

In each of the blanks provided, place the letter that precedes the best definition of the underlined word in context to the left.

Words in Context	Definitions
1. ____ The <u>resultant</u> damage	a. summarized
2. ____ Bill, <u>arrogantly</u> insists	b. misleading
3. ____ argument is <u>valid</u>	c. clear up
4. ____ <u>recapped</u> each position	d. following
5. ____ met with <u>indifference</u>	e. coolness
6. ____ You feel <u>vulnerable</u>	f. conceitedly
7. ____ the other person <u>initiates</u>	g. results
8. ____ appearances are <u>deceptive</u>	h. sound
9. ____ very serious <u>repercussions</u>	i. begins
10. ____ to <u>clarify</u> matters	j. helpless

Check your answers with the Key on p. 442 before going on. Give yourself 10 points for each one right and enter your score on the chart under A on p. 420. Review any that you have missed.

A Score: ________

Pronunciation aids: **1. re-ZUL-tent**
6. VUL-ner-uh-bul
9. re-pur-KUSH-uns

B. LEANING ON PARTS

The prefix *ex-* (also spelled *ec-, ef-, es-,* or *e-*) means "out" or "out of." Supply the missing word or word part in each of the following blanks.

1. When you breathe out, do you inhale or ex___________?
2. The way out of the building is marked with an ex___________ sign.
3. If you're completely worn out after work, you're ex___________.
4. The dynamite caused a tremendous ex___________.
5. If you exclude them from the meeting, you keep them___________.

C. MAKING THE WORDS YOURS

In each blank below, enter the most appropriate word from the ten words in context in the first exercise, substituting it for the word(s) in parentheses. Use these words: *arrogantly, clarify, deceptive, indifference, initiates, recapped, repercussions, resultant, valid, vulnerable.*

1. It's hard to believe the (coolness) ___________ she showed at the tragedy.
2. He looked like an athlete, but I soon saw appearances were (misleading) ___________.
3. It took years to assess the (following) ___________ effects of the new law.
4. Being late with the payment had unexpected (results) ___________.
5. Do you have a (sound) ___________ reason for suspecting treachery?
6. They (conceitedly) ___________ tried to force their way into the meeting.
7. You need to (clear up) ___________ your reasons for going south for vacation.
8. He (begins) ___________ action to bring the matter to court.
9. Most older people feel quite (helpless) ___________ when dealing with scam artists.
10. I think the teacher (summarized) ___________ the various reports quite well.

Check your answers with the Key on p. 445.

B Score: ________

C Score: ________

Enter your scores on p. 420.

15

How to REALLY Talk to Another Person

MALCOLM BOYD

Someone once said, "There are very few people who don't become more interesting when they stop talking." Is that, in essence, what the author of the following selection is saying? At any rate, we should know how to **really** ***talk to people. And that's what you'll soon find out.***

BEGIN TIMING

One of my favorite news clippings of all time was written early in the century and concerns the first two automobiles ever to have appeared on the streets of a major American city. Its opening sentence went something like this:

"The only two automobiles in town collided today at the intersection of State and Main."

But we don't need to be in cars to collide. People bump into one another all the time—in their families, their jobs, their social relationships and in the public arena. Somehow, we get our signals crossed because we just don't communicate clearly. This article will offer seven basic rules to help keep you collision-free when exchanging ideas.

Communication failures are stumbling blocks to good living. We hear examples of them every day: "I didn't mean to say that." "She misunderstood me." "He lied."

The resultant damage to human feelings, to business, to property and finances—even to international relations—is inestimable. We can avoid all this only by communicating clearly, honestly and effectively.

Strangely enough, I have found that the secret of being heard—of how to really talk to another person—is, for the most part simply to *listen.*

Listening to others is a sure way to get yourself heard—and it can capture more attention than a string of crackling firecrackers. Picture a roomful of people all shouting their message. Finally, a gavel pounds, order is restored. One by one, each shouter is given a chance to speak. The first, Bill, arrogantly insists that only his argument is valid. He bars any compromise. Eileen, a speaker with an opposing point of view, watches sullenly as Bill holds forth. Gene, waiting for his turn to grab the spotlight, rehearses what he will say. Among them, *nobody is listening!* You can bet that, even as each takes a turn at the microphone, he or she will not be heard by the others. You'd have an even surer bet that, if John Doe got up and recapped each position given and then addressed them, the shouters *would* listen to John Doe. Why? Because John would have practiced one of the prime rules of communication.

One of the first lessons taught most schoolchildren is, "Stop, look and listen before you cross the street." That way, they're told, they'll avoid accidents. If, before we talk, we learn to stop, look (at how people talk, both with their faces and bodies) and listen (to the sounds of people's voices as well as their words), we'll probably avoid collisions in communications.

Sometimes we hear more with our eyes than with our ears and hear more from tones than from words. That's why it is important to follow this rule:

1. **Listen with an inner ear—to hear what actually is meant, rather than what is said with words.** War, peace, love, hate—at crucial times, everything may hang on this ability. Of course, people should say what they mean, but sometimes they just can't. Only by listening carefully and deeply to others—and observing their actions, as well as their words—can we truly communicate.
2. **Listen to the concerns of others. Don't concentrate solely on your own ideas.** You already *know* what *you* think. Find out what others think and address *their* ideas. You might learn something, and others, seeing that you take them seriously, may be moved to take you seriously in return. Nothing is more deadly than I-I/me-me. Make it *we* and *us.* You'll get a bigger audience than a skywriter does—and people may even be willing to help you cross your *T*s in the process.
3. **It is important to know when *just* to listen.** Sometimes, a barrier suddenly falls between two people with a very close relationship. When it happens to you, try not to panic. No matter how close two people may be with one another, there are times when one person withdraws. This may occur for any reason—from midlife crisis to job anxiety to personal pain to a deep sense of loss. Usually it has nothing to do with *you,* specifically. Yet it affects you acutely.

   Suddenly, words fail. Coldness replaces warmth. Silences seem threatening: You wonder: "Is this the end? Can I possibly save this situation?" Familiar ways of bonding are met with indifference. Your signaled need for closeness meets with rejection. You feel vulnerable, and the sense of alienation grows.

   If ever there was a time to listen, this is it. Be patient and supportive. Be quiet and wait. Be ready to respond to communications the other person initiates. Sometimes, by simply listening, you say more about how you feel than any words could say. The other person will hear you and be grateful.

Try always to listen with a clear head and an open mind, which leads to the next rule:

4. **Assume nothing.** Too often we assume something is one thing and later find that it is something else entirely.

We all have found that appearances are deceptive. We assume: *This* person couldn't possibly cheat. (But he does!) *That* relationship is more solid than the Rock of Gibraltar. (But it isn't.) Pat, the well-groomed, smiling man, obviously is bright, and Mike, the thrown-together one, is a dolt. (The reverse is true.)

Making assumptions in human relations—and letting them affect our point of view, untested—can be fatal. Did you ever have a feeling that someone was out to "get" you? It's too easy to persuade ourselves that someone is telling a lie, gossiping maliciously, being unfaithful or trying to get our job. However, if we act on an assumption as though it were fact and make a false judgment, not only might we end up with egg on our faces, but we also could create very real losses for ourselves.

Misreading signs of human behavior can have very serious repercussions. I learned long ago that a seemingly unfriendly attitude might indicate nothing more than that someone is suffering—from a toothache or a troubled life at home. Look for the real (not the assumed) person behind the stranger you meet. It's important to remember always that we're communicating with another distinctively individual human being who lives and breathes and feels the need to like and be liked.

An elderly woman, blind and nearly deaf, lived in a retirement home I visited. She scared me by acting scared when I drew near. But, one day, I greeted her gently.

"Who are you?" she whispered.

"I've come to visit you," I said.

"Oh, how nice," she responded.

I described her dress, so she too could "see" its hues of bright turquoise, burnt orange and gold. Her face lit up.

"People do need each other," she said. "Together, we're not so lonely."

We've explored listening as a surefire way to be heard. Now let's address *how to talk to another person.* And the cardinal rule here is this:

5. **Say what you mean.** It never ceases to amaze me that some people offhandedly tell such outright lies as: "I like it." "Your job is safe." "I'll be back in five minutes." They say things they don't mean. Result: hurt, confusion, resentment. Once we stop telling the truth about small things, it's just a small step to spinning a veritable spiderweb of

falsehoods. Then, finding we're caught in that web, we start to tell bigger lies. Saying what we mean keeps confusion to a minimum.

At a recent meeting, a dozen professional men and women gathered to draft a statement about long-range plans. It became painfully clear that the discussion was getting nowhere, growing ever more abstract and unrealistic. Finally, I asked: "Why don't we say what we mean?" A silence fell. Then someone laughed sheepishly and said, "But that's so hard to do."

6. **Before speaking, always ask yourself: What is the message that's needed?** It wouldn't be quite so hard to communicate clearly if we first answered these questions: What do those I'm talking to need to know? What is the best way for me to say it and to get straight to the point? How do I get them to listen?

   The rules for talking and listening are very similar. The key to the deepest secret of communication lies in *truly understanding what must be communicated.* If, for example, you are trying to *give* information to others, you must first find out what they need to know. If you are trying to *get* information, ask clearly for what you need to know. If, after listening carefully, you don't get what you need—or you don't understand what you get—say so and ask questions to clarify matters. Too often, we short-circuit our messages by telling people what we think they ought to know, rather than finding out what it is they need to know.

7. **Remember that communication is in the present.** "I should've said" just doesn't cut it. This moment—now—might change your life forever. Be open to communicating with that person who comes your way today. Don't miss your chance!

Length: 1510 words.
Reading Time: __________
See Conversion Table, p. 421.
Enter WPM Rate on p. 416.

15 How to REALLY Talk to Another Person

COMPREHENSION CHECK

1. Where did the two-car collision occur? (a) New York (b) Chicago (c) Detroit (d) unnamed city — 1. ____

2. You are asked to picture what? (a) a roomful of shouting people (b) two angry people (c) a noisy schoolroom (d) a noisy town meeting — 2. ____

3. You are specifically told to listen with your (a) subconscious. (b) mind. (c) inner ear. (d) eyes. — 3. ____

4. Sometimes what specifically comes between two people? (a) a barrier (b) a barricade (c) a fence (d) a wall — 4. ____

5. Mention is made of the (a) Rock of Ages. (b) Rock of Gibraltar. (c) Berlin Wall. (d) Washington Monument. — 5. ____

6. One episode is about (a) a school teacher. (b) an elderly woman. (c) a receptionist. (d) a barber. — 6. ____

7. What quotation is used? (a) I agree. (b) Don't worry. (c) Your job is safe. (d) You'll get a raise. — 7. ____

8. The professional group was trying to draft (a) company policy. (b) next year's budget. (c) community action. (d) a long-range plan. — 8. ____

9. Communication is specifically said to be in the (a) here and now. (b) present. (c) eyes of the beholder. (d) desired result. — 9. ____

10. How many rules were given? (a) five (b) six (c) seven (d) eight — 10. ____

Check your answers with the Key on p. 451. Give yourself 10 points for each one right and enter your comprehension score on p. 414.

Comprehension Score: ________

NAME ______________________ CLASS ______________________ DATE ______________

16 Speeding by Skimming

WORD POWER WORKOUT

A. LEANING ON CONTEXT

In each of the blanks provided, place the letter that precedes the best definition of the underlined word in context to the left.

Words in Context

1. ____ to your <u>repertoire</u>
2. ____ <u>reiterates</u> the topic idea
3. ____ skip completely <u>intervening</u> paragraphs
4. ____ effectively <u>counteract</u> an hour of slow reading
5. ____ improve learning <u>productivity</u>
6. ____ develop such <u>exceptional</u> skill
7. ____ <u>cultivate</u> different skimming patterns
8. ____ <u>snatch</u> the key words
9. ____ <u>superficial</u> careless reading
10. ____ give this pattern top <u>priority</u>

Definitions

a. take
b. range of skills
c. preference
d. surface, limited
e. repeats
f. offset, change
g. abundant or favorable production
h. coming between
i. outstanding, excellent
j. form, refine

Check your answers with the Key on p. 442 before going on. Give yourself 10 points for each one right and enter your score on the chart under A on p. 420. Review any that you have missed.

A Score: ________

Pronunciation aids: **1. REP-ur-twahr** **2. ree-IT-uh-rayts** **3. in-tur-VEEN-ing** **9. soo-pur-FISH-ul** **10. pry-OR-uh-tee**

B. LEANING ON PARTS

The prefix *re-*, found in over 1,000 words, means "back" or "again." Supply the missing word or word part in each of the following blanks.

1. To turn back and read an article again is to re____________ it.
2. If you appear again, you can be said to re____________.
3. To go back home is to re____________ home.
4. To repair something is to put it ____________ into good condition.
5. To rewrite a report is to write it ____________.

C. MAKING THE WORDS YOURS

In each blank below, enter the most appropriate word from the ten words in context in the first exercise, substituting it for the word(s) in parentheses. Use these words: *counteract, cultivated, exceptional, intervening, priority, productivity, reiterate, repertoire, snatched, superficial.*

1. In a year of wide reading he (formed) ____________ many new interests.
2. Her top (preference) ____________ was college.
3. Both classical and rock music were within his (range of skills) ____________.
4. Often a boxer's desire to win will (offset) ____________ physical disadvantages.
5. The paragraphs (coming between) ____________ need not be read.
6. A (limited) ____________ knowledge could be dangerous.
7. High-grade seed and fertile land are important factors for (favorable production) ____________.
8. (Repeat) ____________ your point if you want people to remember it.
9. The third baseman (took) ____________ the ball from the ground and threw it home.
10. She was termed an (excellent) ____________ student.

Check your answers with the Key on p. 445.

B Score: ________

C Score: ________

Enter your scores on p. 420.

16

Speeding by Skimming

BEGIN TIMING

It's time now to add a second superspeed to your repertoire. *Skimming.* This technique speeds you through print at three to five times your usual reading speed. The secret? Paragraph structure.

A paragraph is a paragraph because it explains or develops *one* single idea. When you're served a big, juicy T-bone steak, you normally concentrate on the meat—not the bone, fat, or gristle. Similarly, skimming concentrates your attention on the meat of the paragraph—the important part, the essentials.

How Do You Skim?

Let's see how skimming works. Try it on the next paragraph. Instead of reading it as usual, word by word, read *only* the underlined parts. Skip the other two-thirds.

<u>How exactly do you get paragraph meaning without reading the paragraph?</u> You use <u>skimming</u>. Fortunately, 55 to 85 percent of the paragraphs you read are <u>expository</u>. They explain. Most textbooks are, of course, expository in nature. They explain such things as a theory, process, procedure, technique, development, or situation. From 60 to 90 percent of <u>such paragraphs</u> have the <u>topic sentence first</u>. The <u>next</u> most <u>likely spot</u> is the <u>last sentence</u>. And if the last sentence is not the topic sentence, more often than not it summarizes or reiterates the topic idea. <u>In between</u> the first and last sentences you'll normally find <u>key words</u> or phrases that expand, clarify, or further support the main idea. <u>Capitalize on these common paragraph characteristics and get the heart of the paragraph without reading it word by word</u>.

That's how you skim a single, fairly long paragraph. You read the first and last sentences and snatch the key words in between. Done properly, skimming is a far cry from superficial, careless reading. It is a careful reading of selected parts. Based on characteristics common to written communication, it helps you zero in on essentials.

But what about skimming an entire article or chapter? To do that, just add paragraph skimming to the survey technique that you already know. You remember how. You read the title, first paragraph, subheadings, tables, graphs, italicized words, and the last paragraph. You skip completely all the intervening paragraphs.

To skim an *entire article,* you don't skip a single paragraph. That's the difference. You skim all paragraphs except the first and last, which you read.

Two Skimming Patterns

Actually, you should cultivate two somewhat different skimming patterns to match the two common styles of writing—formal and informal.

The formal style, typical of most textbooks, is characterized by such things as long paragraphs, involved sentences, and few personal pronouns. The specially marked paragraph above, containing over 130 words, is closer to the formal style in length. With such paragraphs, read both first and last sentences, plus key words. You're still reading less than a third of the paragraph.

For more informal writing, such as in this text, with its shorter paragraphs, read only the first sentence and, possibly, key words. Even for the longer paragraphs, you may want to give this pattern top priority. It will usually give you the essentials. Furthermore, it is an easier and faster pattern to apply.

Skimming—Your Reading Substitute

Take this situation. You've surveyed an article. You feel it doesn't merit reading but seems too important to discard. That's when you need skimming. That kind of in-between coverage serves ideally as a reading substitute.

Remember also that skimming skills vary widely. You may develop such exceptional skill in skimming that you can actually skim an article at 2,000 wpm and get more out of it than an average or poor reader, plodding along at 200 wpm. So, in deciding when to skim and when to read, keep your own level of skill development in mind.

Skimming—Your Reading Speed Generator

Here you are—working to improve reading ability. Perhaps you practice rapid reading thirty minutes every day, conscientiously. But you may also be reading other things more slowly for two hours daily. You're practicing slow reading more than rapid reading. Progress is bound to suffer. How can this be avoided?

If you want to teeter-totter with a thirty-pound youngster, yet you weigh four times more, what do you do? That's easy. You sit closer to the fulcrum, where you can both balance perfectly. Similarly, why not use skimming to balance the slowing pull of normal reading. Ten minutes of skimming should effectively counteract an hour of slower reading.

Let's look at one specific way to ensure frequent use of skimming. Suppose you're going to read an important 4,000-word article. Reading it at 200 wpm will take exactly twenty minutes. Here's how to introduce skimming without taking any additional time. Skim the article first at 1,000 wpm, a four-minute task. Then read the article once at 250 wpm, a sixteen-minute task. Four plus sixteen equals twenty minutes.

That skim-read combination takes no more time than one slightly slower reading. But it has two advantages. First, comprehension should be better; second, reading rate should be improved.

Skimming—Your Review Aid

Make skimming serve still a third function. When you open a psych text and spot the Ebbinghaus curve of forgetting, you're bound to feel discouraged. His research indicates that thirty minutes after you've barely learned something, you will have forgotten half of it. In eight hours, two-thirds will be gone.

Take a typical situation—a test over three chapters of chemistry. Last night you studied them and felt rather well prepared. But here it is, fourteen hours later. When you start the test you soon realize how much you have forgotten.

This suggests another important use of skimming. In a free hour just before the test, skim all three chapters. You haven't time to read them, but you have plenty of time to skim them. Now as you take the test, you should notice greatly improved sureness and confidence—and improved grades.

So, begin now. Develop added skimming skill. Be sure to make skimming a daily activity. Use it (1) to reduce your reading load, (2) to generate added speed, and (3) to improve learning productivity.

Length: 1000 words.
Reading Time: __________
See Conversion Table, p. 421.
Enter WPM Rate on p. 416.

16 Speeding by Skimming

COMPREHENSION CHECK

1. The secret of skimming lies in (a) paragraph structure. (b) sentence structure. (c) outlining. (d) word usage. 1. ____

2. Skimming lets you cover print how many times faster than usual? (a) two to three (b) three to five (c) four to eight (d) not specifically mentioned 2. ____

3. The most common paragraphs you read are (a) expository. (b) narrative. (c) persuasive. (d) descriptive. 3. ____

4. In skimming, what part of a paragraph do you read? (a) no sentence in entirety (b) both first and last sentences (c) first sentence only (d) last sentence only 4. ____

5. To skim an article, you (a) skip every other paragraph. (b) skim every paragraph. (c) skim all but the first and last paragraphs. (d) skip all but the first and last paragraphs. 5. ____

6. Skimming is spoken of as a reading (a) refresher. (b) stimulus. (c) supplement. (d) substitute. 6. ____

7. One illustration involves a (a) pair of scales. (b) teeter-totter. (c) balloon. (d) fishing line. 7. ____

8. In reading an important 4,000-word article, it is suggested that you (a) read it once at 200 wpm. (b) read it once at 250 wpm. (c) skim it first, then read it. (d) read it first, then skim it. 8. ____

9. The part about forgetting indicates that we forget how much in the first thirty minutes after learning something? (a) 15 percent (b) 30 percent (c) 42 percent (d) half 9. ____

10. Specific mention is made of (a) improving grades. (b) taking tests. (c) taking chemistry. (d) all the preceding. 10. ____

Check your answers with the Key on p. 451. Give yourself 10 points for each one right and enter your comprehension score on p. 414.

Comprehension Score: ________

MAKING THE APPLICATION

This is the time to compare surveying, skimming, and reading to sharpen your awareness of the role each technique should play. To do so, take a selection you have not yet read, one further on in this text—selection 29, "How to Work for a Rotten Boss." We'll now guide you through a surveying, then a skimming, of that selection. At that point you're to take the ten-item comprehension test to see exactly what surveying and skimming contribute to comprehension. Don't check your answers until you have read the selection and taken the test a second time, seeing how comprehension is affected. Here is what you get from a survey.

SURVEYING

Title How to Work for a Rotten Boss

First paragraph Want to send silent party guests rushing into riproaring conversation? Well, toss out the topic of rotten bosses, sit back and watch the sparks fly.

Headings and italics

The Bulldog

The Overbearing Blowhard

The Heel-Grinder

Never forget—he or she is your boss.

Management will judge you by how well you get along with your boss.

Don't try to change the boss.

Stand your ground.

Don't argue, but do disagree.

The Ogre

The Fire Eater

The Super-Delegator

The Staller

The Perfectionist

Last paragraph To cope, learn to follow and to lead; let your relationship work for you.

What kind of overview do you have? What would you infer is said between the first and last paragraphs, based on the sketchy information you have? That is the mental process you go through to make surveying the effective aid it should be.

SKIMMING

Now see what you get from skimming the same selection. Use the pattern most useful with informal writing, reading only the first sentence of each paragraph.

Title	How to Work for a Rotten Boss
First paragraph	(Reread the first paragraph as printed under the *Surveying* heading, then read the following first sentences.)
First sentence of all following paragraphs up to the last paragraph	Do you have an impossible boss?
	If you have a boss who's sending you up in smoke every day, you're probably not smiling often or sleeping much.
	There really are such "killer" bosses—too many of them, of both sexes.
	In the '80s, at the Center for Creative Leadership in Greensboro, N.C., the behavioral researchers Michael Lombardo, Morgan McCall, Jr., and Ann Morrison listened to executives' stories about their bosses.
	A good way to start is to learn about the demands your boss has to meet:
	Above all, learn your boss' schedule and rhythms:
	Some bosses are more difficult than others.
	The Bulldog He not only takes responsibility, he sinks his teeth into it.
	The Overbearing Blowhard This boss is on a constant ego trip.
	The Heel-Grinder This one likes to bully and humiliate.
	The successful executives and near-perfect bosses interviewed by Lombardo, McCall, and Morrison said that coping with bad bosses had helped them form their own best-management approaches.

Those are hard lessons to master while trying to survive and get ahead, yet most of the successful executives interviewed had managed it.

Before you quit or your rotten boss retires, here are tips from Lombardo, McCall, and Morrison to help you cope:

Never forget—he or she is your boss.

Management will judge you by how well you get along with your boss.

Don't try to change the boss.

The boss may be 100 percent to blame for the conditions under which you struggle.

Rotten bosses come in an infinite number of varieties—most of them known to Robert Bramson, a management consultant in Oakland, Calif., and an author.

Bramson adds that the bullying boss learns better behavior once it's clear that you respect him or her as the boss and that *you* have self-respect too.

Stand your ground.

Don't argue, but do disagree.

"Attack" type bosses include:

The Ogre This boss likes to yell and appear powerful.

The Fire Eater This boss seems emotionally uneven—prone to mood swings that may begin with grumblings and end with eruptions.

Then there are those bosses who just "aren't there" for you.

The Super-Delegator This type seems to give you lots of responsibility, but, even when pressed, he or she won't say what's expected of you.

The Staller This one is so afraid of stress—anybody's—that he or she puts off telling others anything they might find stressful.

Last but not least are the types of bosses who hold the reins too tightly.

The Perfectionist This boss *must* be flawless and sees mistakes everywhere.

Last paragraph (Now reread the last paragraph as printed under the *Surveying* heading.)

Now turn to page 233 and take the usual ten-item comprehension test. Do not check your answers, however. You just want to see exactly how much you get out of surveying and skimming an article. When you have finished the test, then turn to page 229 and read the selection as usual, timing yourself and taking the same test over again. This will let you compare the comprehension you've been getting from one reading with that from surveying, skimming, and reading. Also notice your wpm rate for the reading. Most students find that they tend to read material faster after skimming it than when just reading it. In short, the time you invest in skimming may be repaid wholly or in part by the faster reading you do after skimming.

NAME ______________ CLASS ______________ DATE ______________

17 Two Ways of Looking at Life

WORD POWER WORKOUT

A. LEANING ON CONTEXT

In each of the blanks provided, place the letter that precedes the best definition of the underlined word in context to the left.

Words in Context

1. ____ The startle reflex
2. ____ ruminating about the baby's hearing
3. ____ soundless isolation
4. ____ jail, divorce, dismissal
5. ____ long bouts of listlessness
6. ____ temporary and surmountable
7. ____ After a reversal
8. ____ unfazed by defeat
9. ____ debilitating tendencies
10. ____ mouthing platitudes

Definitions

a. layoff
b. realizable
c. automatic response
d. not disturbed
e. brooding
f. change of fortune
g. commonplaces
h. weakening
i. solitude
j. spells

Check your answers with the Key on p. 442 before going on. Give yourself 10 points for each one right and enter your score on the chart under A on p. 420. Review any that you have missed.

A Score: ________

Pronunciation aids: 2. ROO-muh-nay-ting

B. LEANING ON PARTS

The prefix *pro-* means "forward," as in *proceed.* Supply the missing word or word part in each of the following blanks.

1. For the parade, the marching band led the pro____________.
2. To show this film, you'll need a movie pro____________.
3. With proper diet and care you can pro____________ your life.
4. Motorboats are usually driven through the water by a pro____________.
5. If *regress* means to go back, *progress* should mean go ____________.

C. MAKING THE WORDS YOURS

In each blank below, enter the most appropriate word from the ten words in context in the first exercise, substituting it for the word(s) in parentheses. Use these words: *bouts, debilitating, dismissal, isolation, platitudes, reflex, reversal, ruminating, surmountable, unfazed.*

1. While camping I suffered (spells) ____________ of hunger.
2. I was late to work three mornings in a row and got my (layoff) ____________.
3. The doctor checked my (automatic response) ____________ by tapping my knees.
4. The speaker couldn't think of how to answer the question well and resorted to (commonplaces) ____________.
5. Despite the seriousness of the accident, the driver was (not disturbed) ____________.
6. That serious problem caused me to do much (brooding) ____________.
7. That newly formed company started well but soon ran into a bad (change of fortune) ____________.
8. The pneumonia caused the patient to fall into a (weakening) ____________ condition.
9. The problem is difficult, but I think it's (realizable) ____________.
10. The splinter group faced (solitude) ____________ because of their radical ideas.

Check your answers with the Key on p. 445.

B Score: ________

C Score: ________

Enter your scores on p. 420.

17

Two Ways of Looking at Life

MARTIN E. P. SELIGMAN

How do you look at life? Is it as an optimist or a pessimist? Think about some of your friends. Can you classify them into those two groups? Here's your chance to focus on a family representing both ways. It will help you decide where you belong.

BEGIN TIMING

The father is looking down into the crib at his sleeping newborn daughter, just home from the hospital. His heart is overflowing with awe and gratitude for the beauty of her, the perfection.

The baby opens her eyes and stares straight up.

The father calls her name, expecting that she will turn her head and look at him. Her eyes don't move.

He picks up a furry little toy attached to the rail of the bassinet and shakes it, ringing the bell it contains. The baby's eyes don't move.

His heart has begun to beat rapidly. He finds his wife in their bedroom and tells her what just happened. "She doesn't seem to respond to noise at all," he says. "It's as if she can't hear."

"I'm sure she's all right," the wife says, pulling her dressing gown around her. Together they go into the nursery.

She calls the baby's name, jingles the bell, claps her hands. Then she picks up the baby, who immediately perks up, wiggling and cooing.

"My God," the father says. "She's deaf."

"No she's not," the mother says, "I mean, it's too soon to say a thing like that. Look, she's brand-new. Her eyes don't even focus yet."

"But there wasn't the slightest movement, even when you clapped as hard as you could."

The mother takes a book from the shelf. "Let's read what's in the baby book," she says. She looks up "hearing" and reads out loud: "'Don't be alarmed if your newborn fails to startle at loud noises or fails to orient toward sound. The startle reflex and attention to sound often take some time to develop. Your pediatrician can test your child's hearing neurologically.'"

"There," the mother says. "Doesn't that make you feel better?"

"Not much," the father says. "It doesn't even mention the other possibility, that the baby is deaf. And all I know is that my baby doesn't hear a thing. I've got the worst feeling about this. Maybe it's because my grandfather was deaf. If that beautiful baby is deaf and it's my fault, I'll never forgive myself."

"Hey, wait a minute," says the wife. "You're going off the deep end. We'll call the pediatrician first thing Monday. In the meantime, cheer up. Here, hold the baby while I fix her blanket. It's all pulled out."

The father takes the baby but gives her back to his wife as soon as he can. All weekend he finds himself unable to open his briefcase and prepare for next week's work. He follows his wife around the house, ruminating about the baby's hearing and about the way deafness would ruin her life. He imagines only the worst: no hearing, no development of language, his beautiful child cut off from the social world, locked in soundless isolation. By Sunday night he has sunk into despair.

The mother leaves a message with the pediatrician's answering service asking for an early appointment Monday. She spends the weekend doing her exercises, reading, and trying to calm her husband.

The pediatrician's tests are reassuring, but the father's spirits remain low. Not until a week later, when the baby shows her first startle, to the backfire of a passing truck, does he begin to recover and enjoy his new daughter again.

This father and mother have two different ways of looking at the world. Whenever something bad happens to him—a tax audit, a marital squabble, even a frown from his employer—he imagines the worst: bankruptcy and jail, divorce, dismissal. He is prone to depression; he has long bouts of listlessness; his health suffers. She, on the other hand, sees bad events in their least threatening light. To her, they are temporary and surmountable, challenges to be overcome. After a reversal, she comes back quickly, soon regaining her energy. Her health is excellent.

The optimists and the pessimists: I have been studying them for the past twenty-five years. The defining characteristic of pessimists is that they tend to believe bad events will last a long time, will undermine everything they do, and are their own fault. The optimists, who are confronted with the same hard knocks of this world, think about misfortune in the opposite way. They tend to believe defeat is just a temporary setback, that its causes are confined to this one case. The optimists believe defeat is not their fault: Circumstances, bad luck, or other people brought it about. Such people are unfazed by defeat. Confronted by a bad situation, they perceive it as a challenge and try harder.

These two habits of thinking about causes have consequences. Literally hundreds of studies show that pessimists give up more easily and get depressed more often. These experiments also show that optimists do much better in school and college, at work and on the playing field. They regularly exceed the predictions of aptitude tests. When optimists run for office, they are more apt to be elected than pessimists are. Their health is unusually good. They age well, much freer than most of us from the usual physical ills of middle age. Evidence suggests they may even live longer.

I have seen that, in tests of hundreds of thousands of people, a surprisingly large number will be found to be deep-dyed pessimists and another large portion will have serious, debilitating tendencies toward pessimism. I have learned that it is not always easy to know if you are a pessimist, and that far more people than realize it are living in this shadow. Tests reveal traces of pessimism in the speech of people who would never think of themselves as pessimists; they also show that these traces are sensed by others, who react negatively to the speakers.

A pessimistic attitude may seem so deeply rooted as to be permanent. I have found, however, that pessimism is escapable. Pessimists can in fact learn to be optimists, and not through mindless devices like whistling a happy tune or mouthing platitudes ("Every day, in every way, I'm getting better and better"), but by learning a new set of cognitive skills. Far from being the creations of boosters or of the popular media, these skills were discovered in the laboratories and clinics of leading psychologists and psychiatrists and then rigorously validated. . . .

Twenty-five years of study has convinced me that if we *habitually* believe, as does the pessimist, that misfortune is our fault, is enduring, and will undermine everything we do, more of it will befall us than if we believe otherwise. I am also convinced that if we are in the grip of this view, we will get depressed easily, we will accomplish less than our potential, and we will even get physically sick more often. Pessimistic prophecies are self-fulfilling.

Length: 1120 words.
Reading Time: __________
See Conversion Table, p. 421.
Enter WPM Rate on p. 416.

17 Two Ways of Looking at Life

COMPREHENSION CHECK

1. Specific reference is made to a (a) diaper. (b) doll. (c) teddy bear. (d) crib. 1. ____

2. The mother initially consults a (a) friend. (b) neurologist. (c) pediatrician. (d) baby book. 2. ____

3. The father mentions his own (a) grandfather. (b) uncle. (c) brother. (d) father. 3. ____

4. What does the mother *not* do during the weekend? (a) her exercises (b) entertain guests (c) read (d) calm her husband 4. ____

5. The father is said to (a) plan action. (b) imagine the worse. (c) check with a doctor. (d) develop a headache. 5. ____

6. How many years has the author studied this subject? (a) ten (b) fifteen (c) twenty-five (d) thirty 6. ____

7. Optimists are specifically said to blame defeat on (a) fate. (b) chance. (c) circumstances. (d) themselves. 7. ____

8. What specific kind of pessimists are mentioned? (a) deep-dyed (b) chronic (c) absolute (d) dyed-in-the-wool 8. ____

9. To become an optimist the author advocates (a) taking a course. (b) getting some special tapes. (c) learning new cognitive skills. (d) using hypnotism. 9. ____

10. The author says that if we believe as a pessimist, we believe that misfortune is (a) unavoidable. (b) widespread. (c) common. (d) our fault. 10. ____

Check your answers with the Key on p. 451. Give yourself 10 points for each one right and enter your comprehension score on p. 414.

Comprehension Score: ________

NAME ____________ CLASS ____________ DATE ____________

18 Two Words to Avoid, Two to Remember

▶ WORD POWER WORKOUT

A. LEANING ON CONTEXT

In each of the blanks provided, place the letter that precedes the best definition of the underlined word in context to the left.

Words in Context	**Definitions**
1. _____ flash of <u>insight</u>	a. undestroyable
2. _____ of several <u>miscalculations</u>	b. distinct
3. _____ an <u>eminent</u> psychiatrist	c. scolded
4. _____ as <u>indestructible</u> as ever	d. awareness
5. _____ at his <u>perceptiveness</u>	e. prominent
6. _____ he <u>berated</u> himself	f. ability to know
7. _____ a <u>perverse</u> streak	g. wrong impressions
8. _____ shook my head <u>ruefully</u>	h. get back
9. _____ <u>audible</u> click	i. sorrowfully
10. _____ to <u>retrieve</u> anything	j. contrary

Check your answers with the Key on p. 442 before going on. Give yourself 10 points for each one right and enter your score on the chart under A on p. 420. Review any that you have missed.

A Score: ________

B. LEANING ON PARTS

The prefix *in-* (also spelled *il-*, *ir-*, or *im-*) means "in" or "into." Supply the missing word or word part in each of the following blanks.

1. Don't stay outside in the cold; come in__________ by the fire.
2. Have you tried to in__________ the key in the lock the other way?
3. For the best possible return, you must in__________ your money well.
4. Does this typed list in__________ the names of all members?
5. To indoctrinate is to instruct __________ some theory or belief.

C. MAKING THE WORDS YOURS

In each blank below, enter the most appropriate word from the ten words in context in the first exercise, substituting it for the word(s) in parentheses. Use these words: *audible, berated, eminent, indestructible, insight, miscalculations, perceptiveness, perverse, retrieve, ruefully.*

1. Her (ability to know) __________ put her at the top of her class.
2. With everything going wrong, I developed a (contrary) __________ tendency to do nothing.
3. The leader brought considerable (awareness) __________ to bear on the complex problem.
4. He explained (sorrowfully) __________ that his house was still flooded.
5. The (prominent) __________ chemist was awarded special honors at the convocation.
6. I used my fishing pole to (get back) __________ my hat, which was floating in the lake.
7. When their mother (scolded) __________ them, they started to cry.
8. This new plastic is practically (undestroyable) __________.
9. His (wrong impressions) __________ led him to miss his scheduled flight.
10. The strange sound outside was (distinct) __________ to everyone inside.

Check your answers with the Key on p. 445.

B Score: ________

C Score: ________

Enter your scores on p. 420.

18

Two Words to Avoid, Two to Remember

ARTHUR GORDON

Most people sometime in their lives feel the need to change themselves—for the better, of course. And here's an author who knows just how to do it. He needs only four words—two to avoid and two to remember. If you think you'll ever need a change, read on to learn his secret.

BEGIN TIMING

Nothing in life is more exciting and rewarding than the sudden flash of insight that leaves you a changed person—not only changed, but changed for the better. Such moments are rare, certainly, but they come to all of us. Sometimes from a book, a sermon, a line of poetry. Sometimes from a friend. . . .

That wintry afternoon in Manhattan, waiting in the little French restaurant, I was feeling frustrated and depressed. Because of several miscalculations on my part, a project of considerable importance in my life had fallen through. Even the prospect of seeing a dear friend (the Old Man, as I privately and affectionately thought of him) failed to cheer me as it usually did. I sat there frowning at the checkered tablecloth, chewing the bitter cud of hindsight.

He came across the street, finally, muffled in his ancient overcoat, shapeless felt hat pulled down over his bald head, looking more like an energetic gnome than an eminent psychiatrist. His offices were nearby; I knew he had just left his last patient of the day. He was close to 80, but he still carried a full case load, still acted as director of a large foundation, still loved to escape to the golf course whenever he could.

By the time he came over and sat beside me, the waiter had brought his invariable bottle of ale. I had not seen him for several months, but he seemed as indestructible as ever. "Well, young man," he said without preliminary, "what's troubling you?"

I had long since ceased to be surprised at his perceptiveness. So I proceeded to tell him, at some length, just what was bothering me. With a kind of melancholy pride, I tried to be very honest. I blamed no one else for my disappointment, only myself. I analyzed the whole thing, all the bad judgments, the false moves. I went on for perhaps 15 minutes, while the Old Man sipped his ale in silence.

When I finished, he put down his glass. "Come on," he said. "Let's go back to my office."

"Your office? Did you forget something?"

"No," he said mildly. "I want your reaction to something. That's all."

A chill rain was beginning to fall outside, but his office was warm and comfortable and familiar: booklined walls, long leather couch, signed photograph of Sigmund Freud, tape recorder by the window. His secretary had gone home. We were alone.

The Old Man took a tape from a flat cardboard box and fitted it onto the machine. "On this tape," he said, "are three short recordings made by three persons who came to me for help. They are not identified, of course. I want you to listen to the recordings and see if you can pick out the two-word phrase that is the common denominator in all three cases." He smiled. "Don't look so puzzled. I have my reasons."

What the owners of the voices on the tape had in common, it seemed to me, was unhappiness. The man who spoke first evidently had suffered some kind of business loss or failure; he berated himself for not having worked harder, for not having looked ahead. The woman who spoke next had never married because of a sense of obligation to her widowed mother; she recalled bitterly all the marital chances she had let go by. The third voice belonged to a mother whose teen-age son was in trouble with the police; she blamed herself endlessly.

The Old Man switched off the machine and leaned back in his chair. "Six times in those recordings a phrase is used that's full of subtle poison. Did you spot it? No? Well, perhaps that's because you used it three times yourself down in the restaurant a little while ago." He picked up the box that had held the tape and tossed it over to me. "There they are, right on the label. The two saddest words in any language."

I looked down. Printed neatly in red ink were the words: *If only.*

"You'd be amazed," said the Old Man, "if you knew how many thousands of times I've sat in this chair and listened to woeful sentences beginning with those two words. 'If only,' they say to me, 'I had done it differently—or not done it at all. If only I hadn't lost my temper, said that cruel thing, made that dishonest move, told that foolish lie. If only I had been wiser, or more unselfish, or more self-controlled.' They go on and on until I stop them. Sometimes I make them listen to the recordings you just heard. 'If only,' I say to them, 'you'd stop saying *if only,* we might begin to get somewhere!'"

The Old Man stretched out his legs. "The trouble with 'if only,'" he said, "is that it doesn't change anything. It keeps the person facing the wrong way—backward instead of forward. It wastes time. In the end, if you let it become a habit, it can become a real roadblock, an excuse for not trying anymore.

"Now take your own case: your plans didn't work out. Why? Because you made certain mistakes. Well, that's all right: everyone makes mistakes. Mistakes are what we learn from. But when you were telling me about them, lamenting this, regretting that, you weren't really learning from them."

"How do you know?" I said, a bit defensively.

"Because," said the Old Man, "you never got out of the past tense. Not once did you mention the future. And in a way—be honest, now!—you were enjoying it. There's a perverse streak in all of us that makes us like to hash over old mistakes. After all, when you relate the story of some disaster or disappointment that has happened to you, you're still the chief character, still in the center of the stage."

I shook my head ruefully. "Well, what's the remedy?"

"Shift the focus," said the Old Man promptly. "Change the key words and substitute a phrase that supplies lift instead of creating drag."

"Do you have such a phrase to recommend?"

"Certainly. Strike out the words 'if only'; substitute the phrase 'next time.'"

"Next time?"

"That's right. I've seen it work minor miracles right here in this room. As long as a patient keeps saying 'if only' to me, he's in trouble. But when he looks me in the eye and says 'next time,' I know he's on his way to overcoming his problem. It means he has decided to apply the lessons he has learned from his experience, however grim or painful it may have been. It means he's going to push aside the roadblock of regret, move forward, take action, resume living. Try it yourself. You'll see."

My old friend stopped speaking. Outside, I could hear the rain whispering against the windowpane. I tried sliding one phrase out of my mind and replacing it with the other. It was fanciful, of course, but I could hear the new words lock into place with an audible click.

"One last thing," the Old Man said. "Apply this little trick to things that can still be remedied." From the bookcase behind him he pulled out something that looked like a diary. "Here's a journal kept a generation ago by a woman who was a schoolteacher in my hometown. Her husband was a kind of amiable ne'er-do-well, charming but totally inadequate as a provider. This woman had to raise the children, pay the bills, keep the family together. Her diary is full of angry references to Jonathan's weaknesses, Jonathan's shortcomings, Jonathan's inadequacies.

"Then Jonathan died, and all the entries ceased except for one—years later. Here it is: 'Today I was made superintendent of schools, and I suppose I should be very proud. But if I knew that Jonathan was out there somewhere beyond the stars, and if I knew how to manage it, I would go to him tonight.'"

The Old Man closed the book gently. "You see? What she's saying is 'if only'; if only I had accepted him, faults and all; if only I had loved him while I could." He put the book back on the shelf. "That's when those sad words are the saddest of all: when it's too late to retrieve anything."

He stood up a bit stiffly. "Well, class dismissed. It has been good to see you, young man. Always is. Now, if you will help me find a taxi, I probably should be getting on home."

We came out of the building into the rainy night. I spotted a cruising cab and ran toward it, but another pedestrian was quicker.

"My, my," said the Old Man slyly. "If only we had come down ten seconds sooner, we'd have caught that cab, wouldn't we?"

I laughed and picked up the cue. "Next time I'll run faster."

"That's it," cried the Old Man, pulling his absurd hat down around his ears. "That's it exactly!"

Another taxi slowed. I opened the door for him. He smiled and waved as it moved away. I never saw him again. A month later, he died of a sudden heart attack, in full stride, so to speak.

More than a year has passed since that rainy afternoon in Manhattan. But to this day, whenever I find myself thinking "if only," I change it to "next time." Then I wait for that almost-perceptible mental click. And when I hear it, I think of the Old Man.

A small fragment of immortality, to be sure. But it's the kind he would have wanted.

Length: 1600 words.
Reading Time: ________
See Conversion Table, p. 421.
Enter WPM Rate on p. 416.

18 Two Words to Avoid, Two to Remember

COMPREHENSION TEST

1. The story starts in (a) Boston. (b) Manhattan. (c) the Bronx. (d) Chicago. 1. ____

2. The Old Man was a (a) psychiatrist. (b) consultant. (c) psychologist. (d) philosopher. 2. ____

3. The Old Man was close to (a) 60. (b) 70. (c) 80. (d) 90. 3. ____

4. One tape was of a mother who had a son with (a) marriage problems. (b) police problems. (c) business problems. (d) school problems. 4. ____

5. "If only" is called (a) killer words. (b) stumbling blocks. (c) toxic thinking. (d) subtle poison. 5. ____

6. "If only" is specifically said to keep one (a) off balance. (b) facing the wrong way. (c) unhappy. (d) disillusioned. 6. ____

7. The phrase "next time" is said to supply (a) lift. (b) hope. (c) help. (d) movement. 7. ____

8. From his bookcase the Old Man pulled out a (a) letter. (b) textbook. (c) pamphlet. (d) journal. 8. ____

9. The night was (a) foggy. (b) rainy. (c) windy. (d) snowy. 9. ____

10. The Old Man left in (a) a bus. (b) a streetcar. (c) a taxi. (d) his car. 10. ____

Check your answers with the Key on p. 451. Give yourself 10 points for each one right and enter your comprehension score on p. 414.

Comprehension Score: ________

NAME ____________ CLASS ____________ DATE ____________

19 Speeding by Scanning

WORD POWER WORKOUT

A. LEANING ON CONTEXT

In each of the blanks provided, place the letter that precedes the best definition of the underlined word in context to the left.

Words in Context	Definitions
1. _____ the proverbial needle-in-a-haystack	a. adequate
2. _____ an accelerator surpasses that	b. desirable
3. _____ goals are feasible	c. not understood
4. _____ jog your memory	d. many-sided
5. _____ a versatile reader	e. typical
6. _____ uncover relevant information	f. exceeds
7. _____ most enviable position	g. refresh
8. _____ develop sufficient scanning skill	h. pertinent
9. _____ such elusive things	i. workable
10. _____ mass of undigested material	j. evasive

Check your answers with the Key on p. 442 before going on. Give yourself 10 points for each one right and enter your score on the chart under A on p. 420. Review any that you have missed.

A Score: ________

Pronunciation aids: **1. pruh-VUR-bee-ul** **3. FEE-zuh-bul** **5. VUR-suh-tul** **6. REL-uh-vunt** **7. EN-vee-uh-bul** **9. ih-LOO-siv**

B. LEANING ON PARTS

The prefix *dis-* (also spelled *dif-*, or *di-*) means "apart" or "away." Supply the needed word or word part in each of the following blanks.

1. If the two sides are far away from agreement, they dis____________.
2. If you send a message away, you can be said to dis____________ it.
3. To scatter or drive away a crowd is to dis____________ it.
4. The students were dis____________ early from school.
5. If attention is distracted, it's drawn ____________ in another direction.

C. MAKING THE WORDS YOURS

In each blank below, enter the most appropriate word from the ten words in context in the first exercise, substituting it for the word(s) in parentheses. Use these words: *elusive, enviable, feasible, jog, proverbial, relevant, sufficient, surpasses, undigested, versatile.*

1. Try a mnemonic device to (refresh) ____________ your memory.
2. My ability as a skier (exceeds) ____________ that of my brother.
3. Their answers were (evasive) ____________.
4. I make a quite (adequate) ____________ salary.
5. A doctor has a very (desirable) ____________ position.
6. A (workable) ____________ plan is needed for success.
7. A novel that is (not understood) ____________ may be criticized by the reader.
8. The one who hid his money under the bed was a (typical) ____________ miser.
9. A (many-sided) ____________ athlete will be successful.
10. Are these statistics (pertinent) ____________ to your question?

Check your answers with the Key on p. 446.

B Score: ________

C Score: ________

Enter your scores on p. 420.

19

Speeding by Scanning

BEGIN TIMING

Now for the third and last superspeed technique. It's called *scanning*. To function effectively, a mechanic needs many tools. So does a reader. The different techniques are the tools. After all, you don't tighten bolts with a file or loosen screws with a wrench. And you don't *read* an entire article just for *one single fact*.

What Is Scanning?

Scanning is the special technique you use to find one specific bit of information within a relatively large body of printed matter. It's the proverbial needle-in-a-haystack situation. Of all the superspeeds, this is the highest gear of all.

Notice how it fits into place with the other techniques. The survey is like a quick, high-altitude glimpse of a large city from a plane. Skimming is a lower-altitude view, with more details observable. And scanning is a supersonic zooming in for a close glance at only one specific house.

Your Scanning Speed Potential

How fast should you scan? To answer that question, let's look at students in efficient reading classes at the University of Minnesota. Without special training, classes will, on the average, scan initially at about 1,800 wpm. Of course, they vary. Since 1972 class averages have ranged from 1,569 to 2,924 wpm. Accuracy has hovered around 75 percent, with a range from 65 to 89.

Later in the quarter, we spend an entire class period in practice. Students try one scanning problem after another, with instructional tips in between to hasten progress. That single practice session is sufficient to push scanning speeds from 1,800 wpm to 15,000 wpm. Some students even reach speeds of 24,000 wpm with 100 percent accuracy.

At the end of the quarter we asked this question: "What do you feel is your probable upper-rate limit for scanning, if you were to develop your full potential?" The answer was 18,959. Individual figures ranged from 1,700 to 75,000 wpm. These figures suggest three things: (1) how quickly scanning speeds can be improved, (2) how much individuals differ, and (3) what goals are feasible.

How Do You Scan?

You have certainly noticed how, in looking over a new telephone directory, your own name tends to jump out at you. It's almost like magic. This psychological fact suggests the first of four tips for ensuring accuracy in scanning.

1. *Visualize the thing to be spotted.* If you are scanning for the date 1970, for example, visualize exactly how those four numbers will look in print. That clear mental picture will make the date stand out, just like your own name.
2. *Use all available clues.* If, for example, you are scanning for a proper name, use the inevitable capital letter as an aid. With other problems, use quotation marks, hyphens, or italics. And for more complex scanning, resort to computerlike search techniques. Think of possible synonyms or key words that will lead you to the desired information.
3. *Use paragraph topical clues.* To locate average rainfall figures, find the paragraph dealing with weather.
4. *Use systematic scanning patterns.* To scan material printed in columns, as newspapers and some magazines, run your eyes rapidly down the middle of each column, using a slight zigzag motion. For solid pages of print, use a wider side-to-side movement.

Judging from class results, you should scan at about ten times your present rate. To develop that facility, however, you must practice. It's not automatic. One or two scanning problems every day will do wonders. Let it grow naturally out of your usual reading. Whenever you finish reading something, ask yourself a question. Was there mention of a name, date, formula, or statement that you're not sure about? A quick scan will bring that bit of information into sharp focus. Even more important, that daily scanning will gradually make you enviably proficient.

Functions of Scanning

Generally speaking, scanning serves two functions. It uncovers relevant information. It also accelerates your reading speed and flexibility.

Since scanning is the fastest coverage of all, its role as an accelerator surpasses that of skimming. In breezing through an article at 18,000 wpm, you are definitely breaking out of the usual reading straitjacket. You'll find it much easier to slip from reading into skimming and into scanning, as purpose dictates. And that's one true mark of a versatile reader.

Common Situations

Actually, two fairly common situations demand scanning. They're alike—yet different. In one situation you deal with the *known,* in the other with the *unknown.*

One has already been mentioned. Remember? That's where you're after such elusive things as a date, formula, name, statement, or list. For example, you *know* that this chapter contains four scanning tips. But do you remember *exactly* what they are? If not, scan to jog your memory. In situations of this kind, scanning serves an important review function.

In the other situation, you're looking for something—but a yet unknown something. Here, you won't *know* exactly until you find it. The dilemma faced by a sales manager for a large firm is typical. Every month, salesmen would mail in lengthy reports, piling up over two feet high on his desk. Ninety-nine percent of that information was purely routine. But every month somewhere in that mass of undigested material there would be three or four bits of important information. Read them? Impossible! But he could and did develop sufficient scanning skill to get what he wanted. Similarly, in school use scanning to get you through a mountain of material to uncover details for a term paper or speech.

There it is. Your third superspeed. Most readers never take time to become skilled in a variety of different techniques. With practice, you can soon develop outstanding ability to apply the right technique at the right time. If the situation demands reading, you read. If it demands scanning, you use your highly developed scanning skills to bring success with a minimum of time and effort. That puts you into a most enviable position. Make the most of it!

Length: 1000 words.
Reading Time: ___________
See Conversion Table, p. 421.
Enter WPM Rate on p. 416.

19 Speeding by Scanning

COMPREHENSION CHECK

1. Reading techniques are likened to (a) tools. (b) medicines. (c) foods. (d) exercises. 1. ____

2. Which is like a quick, high-altitude glimpse of a city from a plane? (a) reading (b) scanning (c) skimming (d) surveying 2. ____

3. One in-class practice session is enough to push scanning speeds up to about what figure? (a) 2,800 wpm (b) 5,000 wpm (c) 9,000 wpm (d) 15,000 wpm 3. ____

4. Mention is made of looking into (a) an encyclopedia. (b) a dictionary. (c) a telephone directory. (d) an index. 4. ____

5. You are told to (a) squint your eyes. (b) hold material at a distance. (c) visualize appearance. (d) blink often. 5. ____

6. You are told to use what as clues? (a) quotation marks (b) hyphens (c) italics (d) all of the preceding 6. ____

7. In scanning, you are directed to (a) come straight down the middle of the page. (b) run the eyes along each line. (c) use systematic patterns. (d) use no set eye pattern. 7. ____

8. Scanning is said to serve how many functions? (a) one (b) two (c) three (d) four 8. ____

9. One illustration involves (a) an accountant. (b) a sales manager. (c) a personnel director. (d) a vice-president. 9. ____

10. You are told to scan to get material for a (a) speech. (b) lab report. (c) take-home final. (d) book review. 10. ____

Check your answers with the Key on p. 451. Give yourself 10 points for each one right and enter your comprehension score on p. 414.

Comprehension Score: ________

MAKING THE APPLICATION

You should discover your present scanning speed, now that you have completed the instructional selection on scanning. For this, you will probably need help from your teacher or friend. A stopwatch is almost a necessity.

Here are two problems, either of which will serve to check both scanning speed and accuracy. Both require you to scan the 1,000-word selection 19, "Speeding by Scanning."

Problem 1: In this entire selection how many dates are given—year dates, that is, such as 1972 or 1888? Visualize your problem, then at a given signal, scan the article for the answer. Divide 1,000 (the number of words) by your scanning time in seconds; multiply the resulting figure by 60 to get a wpm scanning figure.

Problem 2: How many times in this entire selection is there a specific reference to *superspeed* or *superspeeds?* Count them as you scan. Again, wait for the given signal. Keep track of the time and figure your scanning rate.

To develop more accuracy or added speed, try one or both of the following problems based on selection 1, "Reading Power—Key to Personal Growth," 1,000 words in length.

Problem 1: How many times in that selection is the proper name *Anderson* repeated? Divide 1,000 by your scanning time; multiply the result by 60 to get your scanning rate. Check accuracy.

Problem 2: How many times in that selection is the word *And* repeated, with the *A* capitalized? Follow the same procedure.

As soon as possible, start using this technique as a review device in your regular textbook reading to spot names, dates, formulas, or other facts that you want to fix in your mind after finishing the assignment. Soon you will find this an indispensable review tool.

APPLYING THE LDE FORMULA

Work through this exercise so you can use the LDE Formula (page 97) to better advantage.

What does the prefix *syn-* mean? First, list some *syn* words. Suppose you list *synchronize, synonym,* and *synthesize.* Now define each. To synchronize two watches is to bring them together in time. Synonyms are words that belong together in meaning. And to synthesize is to bring separate parts together into a whole. Finally, extract the common meaning. You see that *syn-* probably means "together."

Now try the formula with another prefix: *hyper-*. What does it mean? Again, make a list—perhaps *hyperactive, hypertension,* and *hypersensitive.* Define each. *Hyperactive* means "more active than normal." *Hypertension* means "abnormally high tension"; and *hypersensitive,* "excessively sensitive." Extract the common meaning and you have "more" or "above normal" as meanings of *hyper-*.

Now try the formula with some roots. What does *gress* (from Latin *gradi*) mean? First, make a list. Since you may not think of any words beginning with *gress,* try adding some prefixes. Let's say you list *progress, regress,* and *digress.* If you progress, you "move forward." If you regress, you "move back"; and if you digress, you "move away" from the subject or point you're making. Extract the common denominator and you get "move" as the meaning of *gress.* Actually *gress* means "step," but if you got "move" or "go," that's close enough.

Try another: the Latin root *tractus.* What does it mean? Take off the ending to get closer to the English form, in this case *tract.* Suppose you list *tractor, attract,* and *contract.* Define them, filling in the blanks below.

1. A tractor is a vehicle for ____________ loads.
2. To attract is to ____________ attention to.
3. A contract is an agreement ____________ up between two or more parties.

The Latin word *tractus* apparently means "to draw."

Finally, try the formula on a suffix. What does *-ic* mean? Let's say you list *metallic* and *angelic.* You define them: *metallic* is "like metal" and *angelic* is "like an angel." Extracting the common meaning *-ic* apparently means "like."

Never say that you don't know what any and all such elements mean. Just put the LDE Formula to work and discover the meanings.

NAME ____________ CLASS ____________ DATE ____________

20 Watching a Veterinarian at Work

WORD POWER WORKOUT

A. LEANING ON CONTEXT

In each of the blanks provided, place the letter that precedes the best definition of the underlined word in context to the left.

Words in Context	**Definitions**
1. _____ cantankerous Aberdonian	a. elaborate, magnificent
2. _____ he niggled constantly	b. place of punishment
3. _____ a long recital	c. bad-tempered
4. _____ predatory colleagues	d. worked fussily
5. _____ a malevolent glance	e. humble request
6. _____ a most imposing creation	f. twists
7. _____ pretty well immobilized	g. detailed account
8. _____ an attitude of supplication	h. antagonistic
9. _____ a few contortions	i. pinned down
10. _____ a new purgatory	j. advantage-taking

Check your answers with the Key on p. 442 before going on. Give yourself 10 points for each one right and enter your score on the chart under A on p. 420. Review any that you have missed.

A Score: ________

Pronunciation aids: **1. kan-TANG-ker-US** **4. PRED-uh-tor-ee** **5. muh-LEV-uh-lent** **8. sup-li-KA-shun** **9. kon-TOR-shun** **10. PUR-ga-tor-ee**

B. LEANING ON PARTS

The useful and easily identified prefix *over-* means "above." Supply the needed word or word part in each of the following sentences.

1. To price a thing above its proper retail value is to over__________ it.
2. If someone is far above normal weight, the person is over__________.
3. A coat worn above other clothes is called an over__________.
4. If a river rises above its banks, it over__________.
5. When you drive under an overpass, the overpass is __________ you.

C. MAKING THE WORDS YOURS

In each blank below, enter the most appropriate word from the ten words in context in the first exercise, substituting it for the word(s) in parentheses. Use these words: *cantankerous, contortions, immobilized, imposing, malevolent, niggled, predatory, purgatory, recital, supplication.*

1. Our friendly director has now turned (ill-tempered) __________.
2. The initiation put the new members into a veritable (place of punishment) __________.
3. The bad auto accident kept the driver almost completely (pinned down) __________.
4. Unfortunately, the new foreman constantly (worked fussily) __________ when working with the men.
5. My friend was in (twists) __________ because of his intense musculature pain.
6. Always watch out for (advantage-taking) __________ money leaders.
7. The worker came before the board in (humble request) __________ for another chance.
8. The major appeared in (elaborate, magnificent) __________ full dress uniform.
9. Give us a (detailed account) __________ of the accident.
10. When I disagreed with him publicly, he gave me a(n) (antagonistic) __________ look.

Check your answers with the Key on p. 446.

B Score: ________

C Score: ________

Enter your scores on p. 420.

20

Watching a Veterinarian at Work

JAMES HERRIOT

What's probably the most important choice you'll make in life? Your career choice or choices! What you're going to do in life! Knowing what that involves is crucial. Firsthand observation is best but not easy to come by. One book may be the equivalent of years of observation, as this sample episode suggests.

BEGIN TIMING

As I came into the operating room I saw that Siegfried had a patient on the table. He was thoughtfully stroking the head of an elderly and rather woebegone border terrier.

"James," he said, "I want you to take this little dog through to Grier."

"Grier?"

"Vet at Brawton. He was treating the case before the owner moved into our district. I've seen it a couple of times—stones in the bladder. It needs an immediate operation and I think I'd better let Grier do it. He's a touchy devil and I don't want to stand on his toes."

"Oh, I think I've heard of him," I said.

"Probably you have. A cantankerous Aberdonian. Since he practices in a fashionable town he gets quite a few students and he gives them hell. That sort of thing gets around." He lifted the terrier from the table and handed him to me. "The sooner you get through there the better. You can see the op and bring the dog back here afterwards. But watch yourself—don't rub Grier the wrong way or he'll take it out of you somehow."

At my first sight of Angus Grier I thought immediately of whisky. He was about fifty and something had to be responsible for the fleshy, mottled cheeks, the swimmy eyes and the pattern of purple veins which chased each other over his prominent nose. He wore a permanently insulted expression.

He didn't waste any charm on me; a nod and a grunt and he grabbed the dog from my arms. Then he stabbed a finger at a slight, fairish youth in a white coat. "That's Clinton—final-year student. Do ye no' think there's some pansy-lookin' buggers coming in to this profession?"

During the operation he niggled constantly at the young man and, in an attempt to create a diversion, I asked when he was going back to college.

"Beginning of next week," he replied.

"Aye, but he's awa hame tomorrow," Grier rasped. "Wasting his time when he could be gettin' good experience here."

The student blushed. "Well, I've been seeing practice for over a month and I felt I ought to spend a couple of days with my mother before the term starts."

"Oh, I ken, I ken. You're all the same—canna stay away from the titty."

The operation was uneventful and as Grier inserted the last stitch he looked up at me. "You'll no' want to take the dog back till he's out of the anaesthetic. I've got a case to visit—you can come with me to pass the time."

We didn't have what you could call a conversation in the car. It was a monologue; a long recital of wrongs suffered at the hands of wicked clients and predatory colleagues. The story I liked best was about a retired admiral who had asked Grier to examine his horse for soundness. Grier said the animal had a bad heart and was not fit to ride, whereupon the admiral flew into a fury and got another vet to examine the horse. The second vet said there was nothing the matter with the heart and passed the animal sound.

The admiral wrote Grier a letter and told him what he thought of him in fairly ripe quarter-deck language. Having got this out of his system he felt refreshed and went out for a ride during which, in the middle of a full gallop, the horse fell down dead and rolled on the admiral who sustained a compound fracture of the leg and a crushed pelvis.

"Man," said Grier with deep sincerity, "man, I was awfu' glad."

We drew up in a particularly dirty farmyard and Grier turned to me. "I've got a cow tae cleanse here."

"Right," I said, "fine." I settled down in my seat and took out my pipe. Grier paused, half way out of the car. "Are you no' coming to give me a hand?"

I couldn't understand him. "Cleansing" of cows is simply the removal of retained afterbirth and is a one-man job.

"Well, there isn't much I can do, is there?" I said. "And my Wellingtons and coat are back in my car. I didn't realize it was a farm visit—I'd probably get messed up for nothing.

I knew immediately that I'd said the wrong thing. The toadskin jowls flushed darker and he gave me a malevolent glance before turning away; but half way across the yard he stopped and stood for a few moments in thought before coming back to the car. "I've just remembered. I've got something here you can put on. You might as well come in with me—you'll be able to pass me a pessary when I want one."

It sounded nutty to me, but I got out of the car and went round to the back. Grier was fishing out a large wooden box from his car.

"Here, ye can put this on. It's a calving outfit I got a bit ago. I haven't used it much because I found it a mite heavy, but it'll keep ye grand and clean."

I looked in the box and saw a suit of thick, black, shining rubber. I lifted out the jacket; it bristled with zip fasteners and press studs and felt as heavy as lead. The trousers were even more weighty, with many clips and fasteners. The whole thing was a most imposing creation, obviously designed by somebody who had never seen a cow calved and having the disadvantage that anybody wearing it would be pretty well immobilized.

I studied Grier's face for a moment but the watery eyes told me nothing. I began to take off my jacket—it was crazy but I didn't want to offend the man.

And, in truth, Grier seemed anxious to get me into the suit because he was holding it up in a helpful manner. It was a two-man operation. First the gleaming trousers were pulled on and zipped up fore and aft, then it was the turn of the jacket, a wonderful piece of work, fitting tightly round the waist and possessing short sleeves about six inches long with powerful elastic gripping my biceps.

Before I could get it on I had to roll my shirt sleeves to the shoulder, then Grier, heaving and straining, worked me into it. I could hear the zips squeaking into place, the final one being at the back of my neck to close a high, stiff collar which held my head in an attitude of supplication, my chin pointing at the sky.

Grier's heart really seemed to be in his work and, for the final touch, he produced a black rubber skull cap. I shrank away from the thing and began to mouth such objections as the collar would allow, but Grier insisted. "Stand still a wee minute longer. We might as well do the job right."

When he had finished he stood back admiringly. I must have been a grotesque sight, sheathed from head to foot in gleaming black, my arms, bare to the shoulders, sticking out almost at right angles. Grier appeared well satisfied. "Well, come on, it's time we got on wi' the job." He turned and hurried towards the byre; I plodded ponderously after him like an automaton.

Our arrival in the byre caused a sensation. There were present the farmer, two cowmen and a little girl. The men's cheerful greeting froze on their lips as the menacing figure paced slowly, deliberately in. The little girl burst into tears and ran outside.

"Cleansing" is a dirty, smelly job for the operator and a bore for the onlooker who may have to stand around for twenty minutes without being able to see anything. But this was one time the spectators were not bored. Grier was working away inside the cow and mumbling about the weather, but the men weren't listening; they never took their eyes away from me as

I stood rigid, like a suit of armor against the wall. They studied each part of the outfit in turn, wonderingly. I knew what they were thinking. Just what was going to happen when this formidable unknown finally went into action? Anybody dressed like that must have some tremendous task ahead of him.

The intense pressure of the collar against my larynx kept me entirely out of any conversation and this must have added to my air of mystery. I began to sweat inside the suit.

The little girl had plucked up courage and brought her brothers and sisters to look at me. I could see the row of little heads peeping round the door and, screwing my head round painfully, I tried to give them a reassuring smile; but the heads disappeared and I heard their feet clattering across the yard.

I couldn't say how long I stood there, but Grier at last finished his job and called out, "All right, I'm ready for you now." The atmosphere became suddenly electric. The men straightened up and stared at me with slightly open mouths. This was the moment they had been waiting for.

I pushed myself away from the wall and did a right turn with some difficulty before heading for the tin of pessaries. It was only a few yards away but it seemed a long way as I approached it like a robot, head in the air, arms extended stiffly on either side. When I arrived at the tin I met a fresh difficulty; I could not bend. After a few contortions I got my hand into the tin, then had to take the paper off the pessary with one hand; a new purgatory. The men watched in fascinated silence.

Having removed the paper, I did a careful about turn and paced back along the byre with measured tread. When I came level with the cow I extended my arm stiffly to Grier who took the pessary and inserted it in the uterus.

I then took up my old position against the wall while my colleague cleaned himself down. I glanced down my nose at the men; their expressions had changed to open disbelief. Surely the mystery man's assignment was tougher than that—he couldn't be wearing that outfit just to hand over a pessary. But when Grier started the complicated business of snapping open the studs and sliding the zips they realized the show was over; and fast on the feeling of letdown came amusement.

As I tried to rub some life back into my swollen arms which had been strangulated by the elastic sleeves, I was surrounded by grinning faces. They could hardly wait, I imagined, to get round to the local that night to tell the tale. Pulling together the shreds of my dignity, I put on my jacket and got into the car. Grier stayed to say a few words to the men, but he wasn't holding their attention; it was all on me, huddling in the seat. They couldn't believe I was true.

Back at the surgery the border terrier was coming out of the anaesthetic. He raised his head and tried bravely to wag his tail when he saw me. I wrapped him in a blanket, gathered him up and was preparing to leave when I saw Grier through the partly open door of a small store room. He had the wooden box on a table and he was lifting out the rubber suit, but there was something peculiar about the way he was doing it; the man seemed to be afflicted by a kind of rigor—his body shook and jerked, the mottled face was strangely contorted and a half stifled wailing issued from his lips.

I stared in amazement. I would have said it was impossible, yet it was happening right in front of me. There was not a shadow of a doubt about it—Angus Grier was laughing.

Length: 1990 words.
Reading Time: __________
See Conversion Table, p. 421.
Enter WPM Rate on p. 416.

20 Watching a Veterinarian at Work

COMPREHENSION CHECK

1. Grier practiced in a (a) fashionable town. (b) nearby city. (c) village. (d) small town. 1. ____
2. Grier was about how old? (a) 45 (b) 50 (c) 55 (d) 60 2. ____
3. Grier's student helper was named (a) Wilson. (b) Clinton. (c) Clarke. (d) Williams. 3. ____
4. Grier diagnosed the admiral's horse as having (a) a bad heart. (b) a bad liver. (c) heaves. (d) lung disease. 4. ____
5. Herriot excused himself from helping because (a) he would get messed up. (b) it was a one-man job. (c) he didn't know the farmers. (d) he was tired. 5. ____
6. The sleeves in the rubber suit were how long? (a) 4 inches (b) 5 inches (c) 6 inches (d) 7 inches 6. ____
7. When Herriot appeared in his rubber suit, the little girl (a) grabbed her father's hand. (b) laughed. (c) backed away. (d) burst out crying. 7. ____
8. The pessaries were in a (a) sealed packet. (b) box. (c) tin. (d) plastic container. 8. ____
9. As Grier was leaving, the farmers (a) looked on in amazement. (b) grinned. (c) looked at one another laughing. (d) shook James's hand. 9. ____
10. When the border terrier saw Herriot, it (a) whined. (b) barked softly. (c) tried to wag its tail. (d) licked his hand. 10. ____

Check your answers with the Key on p. 451. Give yourself 10 points for each one right and enter your comprehension score on p. 414.

Comprehension Score: ________

NAME ____________ CLASS ____________ DATE ____________

21 Watching a Surgeon at Work

WORD POWER WORKOUT

A. LEANING ON CONTEXT

In each of the blanks provided, place the letter that precedes the best definition of the underlined word in context to the left.

Words in Context	Definitions
1. _____ <u>classical</u> signs	a. characteristic
2. _____ to establish <u>eligibility</u>	b. reluctant
3. _____ disturb his <u>equanimity</u>	c. turned upside down
4. _____ handed me the <u>scalpel</u>	d. infinitely small
5. _____ make the <u>incision</u>	e. suitability
6. _____ not to be <u>hesitant</u>	f. small knife
7. _____ <u>reverted</u> to my earlier tack	g. calmness
8. _____ usual <u>infinitesimal</u> attack	h. cut
9. _____ an <u>abnormal</u> position	i. returned
10. _____ stump is <u>inverted</u>	j. unusual

Check your answers with the Key on p. 442 before going on. Give yourself 10 points for each one right and enter your score on the chart under A on p. 420. Review any that you have missed.

A Score: ________

Pronunciation aids: **2. EL-uh-ja-bil-uh-tee**
3. e-kwa-NIM-uh-tee
8. in-fin-i-TES-uh-mal

B. LEANING ON PARTS

The prefix *sub-* (also spelled *suc-, suf-, sum-, sup-, sur-,* or *sus-*) means "under." Supply the missing word or word part in each of the following blanks.

1. The basement under the main basement is the sub__________.
2. Any school under the required scholastic standards is sub__________.
3. Traveling under the speed of sound? Not supersonic but sub__________!
4. A secondary or explanatory book title is called a sub__________.
5. To subjugate a country is to bring it __________ control or subdue it.

C. MAKING THE WORDS YOURS

In each blank below, enter the most appropriate word from the ten words in context in the first exercise, substituting it for the word(s) in parentheses. Use these words: *abnormal, classical, eligibility, equanimity, hesitant, incision, infinitesimal, inverted, reverted, scalpel.*

1. The surgeon had trouble making the (cut) __________ because of the thick fat layer.
2. The (infinitely small) __________ change in the adjustment caused a disaster.
3. The police soon noticed (characteristic) __________ signs of drug abuse.
4. Unfortunately, the container holding the acid was (turned upside down) __________, letting some acid escape.
5. Some people never let anything ruffle their (calmness) __________.
6. (Suitability) __________ jeopardized his place on the football team.
7. The warmth of that day in the dead of winter was (unusual) __________.
8. The patient (returned) __________ to his old drinking habits as soon as he left the hospital.
9. The surgeon used a (small knife) __________ to make the incision.
10. The guide was (reluctant) __________ to take us along the trail at the edge of the cliff.

Check your answers with the Key on p. 446.

B Score: ________

C Score: ________

Enter your scores on p. 420.

21

Watching a Surgeon at Work

WILLIAM A. NOLEN

So you might choose to be a surgeon? To help make that career choice, why not watch an operation? That's difficult to arrange and even if you managed, you'd probably not know what was going on? Let reading come to your rescue. Here you'll know exactly what's going on as a surgeon performs his first appendectomy.

BEGIN TIMING

The patient, or better, victim, of my first major surgical venture was a man I'll call Mr. Polansky. He was fat, he weighed one hundred and ninety pounds and was five feet eight inches tall. He spoke only broken English. He had had a sore abdomen with all the classical signs and symptoms of appendicitis for twenty-four hours before he came to Bellevue.

After two months of my internship, though I had yet to do anything that could be decently called an "operation," I had had what I thought was a fair amount of operating time. I'd watched the assistant residents work, I'd tied knots, cut sutures and even, in order to remove a skin lesion, made an occasional incision. Frankly, I didn't think that surgery was going to be too damn difficult. I figured I was ready, and I was chomping at the bit to go, so when Mr. Polansky arrived I greeted him like a long-lost friend. He was overwhelmed at the interest I showed in his case. He probably couldn't understand why any doctor should be so fascinated by a case of appendicitis: wasn't it a common disease? It was just as well that he didn't realize my interest in him was so personal. He might have been frightened, and with good reason.

At any rate, I set some sort of record in preparing Mr. Polansky for surgery. He had arrived on the ward at four o'clock. By six I had examined him, checked his blood and urine, taken his chest x-ray and had him ready for the operating room.

George Walters, the senior resident on call that night, was to "assist" me during the operation. George was older than the rest of us. I was twenty-five at this time and he was thirty-two. He had taken his surgical training in Europe and was spending one year as a senior resident in an American hospital to establish eligibility for the American College of

Surgeons. He had had more experience than the other residents and it took a lot to disturb his equanimity in the operating room. As it turned out, this made him the ideal assistant for me.

It was ten o'clock when we wheeled Mr. Polansky to the operating room. At Bellevue, at night, only two operating rooms were kept open—there were six or more going all day—so we had to wait our turn. In the time I had to myself before the operation I had reread the section on appendectomy in the *Atlas of Operative Technique* in our surgical library, and had spent half an hour tying knots on the bedpost in my room. I was, I felt, "ready."

I delivered Mr. Polansky to the operating room and started an intravenous going in his arm. Then I left him to the care of the anesthetist. I had ordered a sedative prior to surgery, so Mr. Polansky was drowsy. The anesthetist, after checking his chart, soon had him sleeping.

Once he was asleep I scrubbed the enormous expanse of Mr. Polansky's abdomen for ten minutes. Then, while George placed the sterile drapes, I scrubbed my own hands for another five, mentally reviewing each step of the operation as I did so. Donning gown and gloves I took my place on the right side of the operating-room table. The nurse handed me the scalpel. I was ready to begin.

Suddenly my entire attitude changed. A split second earlier I had been supremely confident; now, with the knife finally in my hand, I stared down at Mr. Polansky's abdomen and for the life of me could not decide where to make the incision. The "landmarks" had disappeared. There was too much belly.

George waited a few seconds, then looked up at me and said, "Go ahead."

"What?" I asked.

"Make the incision," said George.

"Where?" I asked.

"Where?"

"Yes," I answered, "where?"

"Why, here, of course," said George and drew an imaginary line on the abdomen with his fingers.

I took the scalpel and followed where he had directed. I barely scratched Mr. Polansky.

"Press a little harder," George directed. I did. The blade went through the skin to a depth of perhaps one sixteenth of an inch.

"Deeper," said George.

There are five layers of tissue in the abdominal wall: skin, fat, fascia (a tough membranous tissue), muscle and peritoneum (the smooth, glistening, transparent inner lining of the abdomen). I cut down into the fat. Another sixteenth of an inch.

"Bill," said George, looking up at me, "this patient is big. There's at least three inches of fat to get through before we even reach the fascia. At the rate you're going, we won't be into the abdomen for another four hours. For God's sake, will you cut?"

I made up my mind not to be hesitant. I pressed down hard on the knife, and suddenly we were not only through the fat but through the fascia as well.

"Not that hard," George shouted, grabbing my right wrist with his left hand while with his other hand he plunged a gauze pack into the wound to stop the bleeding. "Start clamping," he told me.

The nurse handed us hemostats and we applied them to the numerous vessels I had so hastily opened. "All right," George said, "start tying."

I took the ligature material from the nurse and began to tie off the vessels. Or rather, I tried to tie off the vessels, because suddenly my knot-tying proficiency had melted away. The casual dexterity I had displayed on the bedpost a short hour ago was nowhere in evidence. My fingers, greasy with fat, simply would not perform. My ties slipped off the vessels, the sutures snapped in my fingers, at one point I even managed to tie the end of my rubber glove into the wound. It was, to put it bluntly, a performance in fumbling that would have made Robert Benchley blush.

Here I must give my first paean of praise to George. His patience during the entire performance was nothing short of miraculous. The temptation to pick up the catgut and do the tying himself must have been strong. He could have tied off all the vessels in two minutes. It took me twenty.

Finally we were ready to proceed. "Now," George directed, "split the muscle. But gently, please."

I reverted to my earlier tack. Fiber by fiber I spread the muscle which was the last layer but one that kept us from the inside of the abdomen. Each time I separated the fibers and withdrew my clamp, the fibers rolled together again. After five minutes I was no nearer the appendix than I had been at the start.

George could stand it no longer. But he was apparently afraid to suggest I take a more aggressive approach, fearing I would stick the clamp into, or possibly through, the entire abdomen. Instead he suggested that he help me by spreading the muscle in one direction while I spread it in the other. I made my usual infinitesimal attack on the muscle. In one fell swoop George spread the rest.

"Very well done," he complimented me. "Now let's get in."

We each took a clamp and picked up the tissue-paper-thin peritoneum. After two or three hesitant attacks with the scalpel I finally opened it. We were in the abdomen.

"Now," said George, "put your fingers in, feel the cecum [the portion of the bowel to which the appendix is attached] and bring it into the wound."

I stuck my right hand into the abdomen. I felt around—but what was I feeling? I had no idea.

It had always looked so simple when the senior resident did it. Open the abdomen, reach inside, pull up the appendix. Nothing to it. But apparently there was.

Everything felt the same to me. The small intestine, the large intestine, the cecum—how did one tell them apart without seeing them? I grabbed something and pulled it into the wound. Small intestine. No good. Put it back. I grabbed again. This time it was the sigmoid colon. Put it back. On my third try I had the small intestine again.

"The appendix must be in an abnormal position," I said to George. "I can't seem to find it."

"Mind if I try?" he asked.

"Not at all," I answered. "I wish you would."

Two of his fingers disappeared into the wound. Five seconds later they emerged, cecum between them, with the appendix flopping from it.

"Stuck down a little," he said kindly. "That's probably why you didn't feel it. It's a hot one," he added. "Let's get at it."

The nurse handed me the hemostats, and one by one I applied them to the mesentery of the appendix—the veil of tissue in which the blood vessels run. With George holding the veil between his fingers I had no trouble; I took the ligatures and tied the vessels without a single error. My confidence was coming back.

"Now," George directed, "put in your purse string." (The cecum is a portion of the bowel which has the shape of half a hemisphere. The appendix projects from its surface like a finger. In an appendectomy the routine procedure is to tie the appendix at its base and cut it off a little beyond the tie. Then the remaining stump is inverted into the cecum and kept there by tying the purse-string stitch. This was the stitch I was now going to sew.)

It went horribly. The wall of the cecum is not very thick—perhaps one eighth of an inch. The suture must be placed deeply enough in the wall so that it won't cut through when tied, but not so deep as to pass all the way through the wall. My sutures were alternately too superficial or too deep, but eventually I got the job done.

"All right," said George, "let's get the appendix out of here. Tie off the base."

I did.

"Now cut off the appendix."

At least in this, the definitive act of the operation, I would be decisive. I took the knife and with one quick slash cut through the appendix—too close to the ligature.

"Oh oh, watch it," said George. "That tie is going to slip."

It did. The appendiceal stump lay there, open. I felt faint.

"Don't panic," said George. "We've still got the purse string. I'll push the stump in—you pull up the stitch and tie. That will take care of it."

I picked up the two ends of the suture and put in the first stitch. George shoved the open stump into the cecum. It disappeared as I snugged my tie. Beautiful.

"Two more knots," said George. "Just to be safe."

I tied the first knot and breathed a sigh of relief. The appendiceal stump remained out of sight. On the third knot—for the sake of security—I pulled a little tighter. The stitch broke; the open stump popped up; the cecum disappeared into the abdomen. I broke out in a cold sweat and my knees started to crumble.

Even George momentarily lost his composure. "For Christ's sake, Bill," he said, grasping desperately for the bowel, "what did you have to do that for?" The low point of the operation had been reached.

By the time we had retrieved the cecum, Mr. Polansky's peritoneal cavity had been contaminated. My self-confidence was shattered. And still George let me continue. True, he all but held my hand as we retied and resutured, but the instruments were in my hand.

The closure was anticlimactic. Once I had the peritoneum sutured, things went reasonably smoothly. Two hours after we began, the operation was over. "Nice job," George said, doing his best to sound sincere.

"Thanks," I answered, lamely.

The scrub nurse laughed.

Mr. Polansky recovered, I am happy to report, though not without a long and complicated convalescence. His bowel refused to function normally for two weeks and he became enormously distended. He was referred to at our nightly conferences as "Dr. Nolen's pregnant man." Each time the reference was made, it elicited a shudder from me.

During his convalescence I spent every spare moment I could at Mr. Polansky's bedside. My feelings of guilt and responsibility were overwhelming. If he had died I think I would have given up surgery for good.

Length: 2060 words.
Reading Time: ________
See Conversion Table, p. 421.
Enter WPM Rate on p. 416.

21 Watching a Surgeon at Work

COMPREHENSION CHECK

1. Mr. Polansky weighed how many pounds? (a) 180 (b) 190 (c) 200 (d) 210 — 1. ____

2. How old was Nolen? (a) 25 (b) 32 (c) 36 (d) 39 — 2. ____

3. Before the operation Nolen spent time (a) checking another patient. (b) tying knots. (c) talking with George about procedure. (d) assuring Polansky. — 3. ____

4. Prior to surgery Nolen (a) called the family. (b) helped the nurse prepare. (c) ordered a sedative. (d) checked blood pressure. — 4. ____

5. Nolen then looked for (a) the swelling. (b) the landmarks. (c) the monitor connection. (d) some sterile gauze. — 5. ____

6. Mention was made of (a) Bob Hope. (b) Robert Benchley. (c) Frank Sinatra. (d) Laurel and Hardy. — 6. ____

7. George helped Nolen (a) spread the muscles. (b) tie blood vessels. (c) get the right clamps. (d) staunch the blood. — 7. ____

8. How many attempts did Nolen make to find the appendix? (a) one (b) two (c) three (d) four — 8. ____

9. What happened with the knots? (a) they slipped (b) one was pulled too tight (c) they were tied too loosely (d) a suture broke — 9. ____

10. What did George say at the end? (a) better luck next time (b) fine (c) great (d) nice job — 10. ____

Check your answers with the Key on p. 452. Give yourself 10 points for each one right and enter your comprehension score on p. 414.

Comprehension Score: ________

PART IV

The Work-up

NAME ______________ CLASS ______________ DATE ______________

22 Reading for Meaning

WORD POWER WORKOUT

A. LEANING ON CONTEXT

In each of the blanks provided, place the letter that precedes the best definition of the underlined word in context to the left.

Words in Context	Definitions
1. ____ fascinating new <u>in-depth</u> side	a. elusive, difficult to detect
2. ____ in the <u>margins</u>	b. overly proud
3. ____ sensitive to context and <u>ambiguity</u>	c. stress
4. ____ to <u>insinuation</u> and implication	d. charge
5. ____ same words could be an <u>accusation</u>	e. edges
6. ____ special <u>emphasis</u> on meaning	f. thorough
7. ____ a <u>mature</u> reader	g. sly hint
8. ____ usually they're more <u>subtle</u>	h. uncertainty
9. ____ men are always <u>conceited</u>	i. fully developed
10. ____ a <u>variety of</u> meanings	j. number of different

Check your answers with the Key on p. 442 before going on. Give yourself 10 points for each one right and enter your score on the chart under A on p. 420. Review any that you have missed.

A Score: ________

Pronunciation aids: **3. am-buh-GYOO-uh-tee**
4. in-SIN-yoo-ay-shun
8. SUT- l

B. LEANING ON PARTS

The prefix *mis-* means "wrong" or "wrongly." Supply the missing word or word part in each of the following sentences.

1. Wrong behavior is, of course, mis__________.
2. To lead you in the wrong direction is to mis__________ you.
3. They laughed when they heard you mis__________ the speaker's name.
4. To deal cards improperly is to mis__________ them.
5. An act of misfeasance is an act of __________doing.

C. MAKING THE WORDS YOURS

In each blank below, enter the most appropriate word from the ten words in context in the first exercise, substituting it for the word(s) in parentheses. Use these words: *accusation, ambiguity, conceited, emphasis, in-depth, insinuations, margins, mature, subtle, variety.*

1. When I next saw her, there was a very (elusive) __________ difference in her attitude.
2. A star athlete may be (overly proud) __________.
3. The (stress) __________ was placed on reading comprehension.
4. (Uncertainty) __________ in writing can cause the reader to lose interest.
5. An authority should have (a thorough) __________ knowledge of his subject.
6. Certain (sly hints) __________ led me to think he was guilty.
7. There are a (number) __________ of ways to stay physically fit.
8. The (charge) __________ was unfounded.
9. Leave more space in the (edges) __________.
10. (Fully developed) __________ judgment is not found in children.

Check your answers with the Key on p. 446.

B Score: ________

C Score: ________

Enter your scores on p. 420.

22

Reading for Meaning

BEGIN TIMING

Comprehension, when you think of it, has a top side and an under side, just as an ocean. The view from above, sun sparkling on the waves, is totally different from the view from below, with schools of fish darting about the weeds and rocks. Yet, it's the same ocean. So it is with comprehension.

Reading for details or facts focuses on the top side of comprehension—what's on the surface. That's already been discussed. *Reading for meaning* opens up a fascinating new in-depth side of comprehension. Here you plunge into a whole world of previously hidden or partially hidden meaning.

The Detail-Meaning Relationship

One side is not enough. You need both. After all, you build meaning by fitting details together. At this point, reading and thinking become inseparable. Adler, in his book *How to Read a Book,* writes that complete comprehension is always present in one situation. When people "are in love and are reading a love letter, they read for all they are worth . . . they read between the lines and in the margins; they read the whole in terms of the parts, and each part in terms of the whole; they grow sensitive to context and ambiguity, to insinuation and implication. . . . Then, if never before or after, they read." Neither side of comprehension is neglected.

Let's examine more closely the detail-meaning relationship. Two are speaking. One says, "It's ten o'clock." What does he mean? Well, that's easy, you say. He means it's ten o'clock. It's just a pure statement of fact—a detail.

Let's dive in for a below-surface look at some possibilities. You know exactly what he *said.* But what did he *mean?*

Well, he could mean, "Let's go for our usual ten o'clock coffee break." To be sure, that's not what he said; it's what he meant, though. His friend understood perfectly and replied, "Right! Let's go. What are we waiting for?"

Again, those same words could be an accusation. He might mean, "You said you'd be here at nine. You're a whole hour late!" Or he might be expressing surprise. "How come you're so early? You weren't supposed to arrive until ten-thirty." Again, he might mean, "Your watch is slow." Obviously, what's *said* and what's *meant* can be quite different. Beneath the world of surface detail, you can glimpse a truly fascinating new world opening up.

Getting Main Ideas

In the world of meaning, what's most important? It's getting the main or central idea of a book, chapter, paragraph, or example. Some readers can't see the forest for the trees. They get all the details accurately, but don't see how they add up. When they hear a story, they're likely to miss the point. Yes, getting the main idea deserves top priority.

How do you manage that? Just ask the right question. Ask yourself "What's the point?" That question will start you along the road to the answer. For example, think back to the bit about "It's ten o'clock." Now raise the question. What's the point of that discussion? A variety of different meanings were advanced. But they all pointed up the need to consider both sides of comprehension—detail *and* underlying meaning, with special emphasis on meaning.

Drawing Inferences

Such words as *infer* and *imply* suggest still other areas in the world of meaning. To infer means to reason something out from given evidence. If someone *says* he's pleased, you *know* it. If he smiles, you have to *infer* it. That's the difference.

Try your hand at inferring with this story. A foreman hustled over to the construction site. "How long have you been working here?" he asked one man. The worker replied, "Ever since you arrived."

What inferential leap can you make? Well, you could infer that the worker was both lazy and stupid. True, he didn't actually say so. You'd have to infer it. An inference is that kind of thing—a leap from the known into the unknown.

Reaching Conclusions

As a mature reader, you'll also want to become proficient in building a chain of reasoning, the last step of which brings you to a logical finish—a conclusion. Someone yawns, his head nods, and his eyes close. Conclusion? He's sleepy.

Take another illustration. A Texan built three swimming pools in his spacious back yard. One he filled with warm water, another with cool. The third was empty. When asked about that, he explained. "The empty one is for two of my friends who can't swim." Conclusion? The Texan was *more* than rich. He was "filthy rich."

Here, as with the main idea, just ask the right question: What conclusion can I make? With that question in mind, read on. She: "Handsome men are always conceited." He: "Not always. I'm not." What's your conclusion about him? And why?

Determining Importance

Can you think of still another important area of meaning? Well, a really good reader should certainly know what points are most or least important.

How can you tell? Fortunately, writers rely heavily on three devices. First, they come right out and tell you what's most or least important. Usually, however, they're more subtle. You're likely to remember best the first or last point in a series. Writers know that and tend to put their most important points in those positions. Again, if you talk more about one thing than another, you suggest which you consider most important. Again, writers do the same. Lean on those three clues: (1) statement, (2) position, and (3) amount. They really help.

Fortunately, you've already taken the two best steps to improve reading for meaning. You know some specifics. You know what questions to raise. After all, a problem well identified is a problem half solved. You're aware of getting the main ideas, drawing inferences, reaching conclusions, and evaluating importance. Other areas, such as making generalities, classifying, or determining purpose, will gradually be included. It all adds up to more enjoyment with that fascinating in-depth side of comprehension.

Length: 1000 words.
Reading Time: __________
See Conversion Table, p. 421.
Enter WPM Rate on p. 416.

22 Reading for Meaning

COMPREHENSION CHECK

GETTING THE FACTS

1. Comprehension is likened to (a) a coin. (b) an ocean. (c) a sheet of paper. (d) a face. 1. ____

2. What specific time is mentioned? (a) 8 o'clock (b) 9 o'clock (c) 10 o'clock (d) 11 o'clock 2. ____

3. Details are likened to (a) the forest. (b) raindrops. (c) the trees. (d) particles of sand. 3. ____

4. A leap from the known into the unknown is (a) an inference. (b) a suggestion. (c) a guess. (d) a hope. 4. ____

5. Writers tend to put important points (a) first. (b) last. (c) first or last. (d) in the middle. 5. ____

GETTING THE MEANING

6. This selection is mainly about (a) determining what things are important. (b) understanding what complete comprehension means. (c) making the detail-meaning relationship clear. (d) getting the main idea. 6. ____

7. The quoted bit about reading a love letter is to show (a) the importance of getting the essentials. (b) the importance of noting word meanings. (c) how inferences are made. (d) when complete comprehension occurs. 7. ____

8. The discussion of "it's . . . o'clock" is intended to point up the (a) confusion of communication. (b) difficulty of getting meaning. (c) two aspects of comprehension. (d) importance of getting what's said. 8. ____

9. Apparently the most important thing is to (a) read between the lines. (b) draw proper inferences. (c) draw logical conclusions. (d) get the main idea. 9. ____

10. Regarding facts and meaning, what is more important? (a) getting details. (b) getting meaning. (c) Both. (d) Both are equally important. 10. ____

Check your answers with the Key on p. 452. Give yourself 10 points for each one right and enter your comprehension score on p. 414.

Comprehension Score: ________

MAKING THE APPLICATION

At this point in your development of reading skills, notice what changes, if any, occur in your comprehension scores. Up to this time all ten questions have covered how well you were getting the facts. From now on, five of the ten questions will check your ability to get meaning, for most readers a much more difficult task.

This presents such an important change in your reading development that you should look closely and carefully at what is happening in the first selections with this new and different emphasis. Use the following chart for entering the results of selections 22 through 31. Total your findings to see exactly how well you are managing both kinds of questions.

Selection	22	23	24	25	26	27	28	29	30	31	Total errors
Number of errors in items 1 through 5											=
Number of errors in items 6 through 10											=

In these same ten readings, how many times did you miss test item 6, always a main idea item? _______

What conclusions can you draw about your present reading habits?

Think over the various kinds of questions that require more than just noting facts. Here are some *general* questions to consider. Space is left under each for you to move into a *specific* example relating to a specific reading. The general questions should apply to all selections, either in entirety or in part.

1. What's the main idea? (Specific example: How would you phrase the main idea for selection 11, "The All-Important Question.")

____

____

2. What specific evidence would you mention to justify your statement of the main idea in selection 11?

____

____

3. What inference can you draw?

____

____

4. What bias did you note?

____

____

5. What purpose does the author have?

____

____

6. What generalization can you make?

____

____

7. What plan of organization do you see?

____

____

8. What words mark structural elements?

____

____

9. What are facts and what are opinions?

____

____

10. Is there a cause-effect relationship apparent?

____

____

NAME ________________ CLASS ________________ DATE ____________

23 The Juggler

WORD POWER WORKOUT

A. LEANING ON CONTEXT

In each of the blanks provided, place the letter that precedes the best definition of the underlined word in context to the left.

Words in Context	Definitions
1. _____ asked for refuge	a. burst of applause
2. _____ a tear of compassion	b. took in
3. _____ in his generosity	c. significant
4. _____ wear his jester outfit	d. shelter
5. _____ began his routine	e. expressive
6. _____ gave him a standing ovation	f. regular procedure
7. _____ do an encore	g. willingness to give
8. _____ meaningful moment of silence	h. professional fool
9. _____ eloquent instructive silence	i. favor, pity
10. _____ we absorbed the power	j. repeat performance

Check your answers with the Key on p. 442 before going on. Give yourself 10 points for each one right and enter your score on the chart under A on p. 420. Review any that you have missed.

A Score: ________

Pronunciation aids: **1. REF-yooj** **6. oh-VAY-shun** **7. AHN-kor** **9. EL-uh-kwent**

B. LEANING ON PARTS

The prefix *trans-* means "across" or "beyond." Supply the needed word or word part in each of the following sentences to see that prefix at work.

1. They went across the Atlantic in a trans__________ liner.
2. This ticket allows you to trans__________ across to another bus.
3. If you lose too much blood, you'll need a blood trans__________.
4. If you can't read French, find someone to trans__________ this letter.
5. If it transcends expectations, it goes __________ what you expected.

C. MAKING THE WORDS YOURS

In each blank below, enter the most appropriate word from the ten words in context in the first exercise, substituting it for the word(s) in parentheses. Use these words: *absorbed, compassion, eloquent, encore, generosity, jester, meaningful, ovation, refuge, routine.*

1. The court (professional fool) __________ entertained people royally.
2. The guest artist's last number received such applause that she returned for an (a repeat performance) __________.
3. One delegate's report went to the very heart of the matter—a particularly (significant) __________ contribution.
4. One speaker demonstrated an unusually (expressive) __________ manner of delivery.
5. When the downpour commenced we took (shelter) __________ under a conveniently close awning.
6. The student (took in) __________ the lecture information well.
7. (Willingness to give) __________ seemed a common trait in that close-knit community.
8. To renew your driver's license just follow the (regular procedure) __________ you've followed before.
9. After the superbly sung solo, the guest artist received an outstanding (burst of applause) __________.
10. The whole country showed special (pity, favor) __________ for the suffering victims of the flood.

Check your answers with the Key on p. 446.

B Score: ________

C Score: ________

Enter your scores on p. 420.

23

The Juggler

ROBERT FULGHUM

Can you always tell what's real and what's imagined? How much communicating is done with words, and how much without? Quintilian said, "It is feeling and force of imagination that make us eloquent." Conrad agrees, calling imagination "the supreme master of art as of life." With imagination that important, how can you put it to work for yourself? Let the juggler show you how.

BEGIN TIMING

My friend Willy reminds me of a juggler who came to our church one Christmas Eve for the midnight service. I wanted to read an old story from long ago about a wandering juggler who happened into a monastery in deep winter and asked for refuge. You may know this story. If memory serves me well, I think it's a French tale called "Our Lady's Juggler."

The story says that the monks were busy making gifts to lay before the high altar of the monastery chapel in honor of the Virgin Mary. Because if she was pleased, her statue would shed a tear of compassion for humanity. But when the gifts were presented at the Feast of the Nativity, the statue did not respond. In the middle of the night, the juggler, who thought he had no gift to give, went in alone and juggled before the statue—and juggled to the very limit of his capacity. To make a long story short, the statue of the Virgin Mary shed a tear—and the baby Jesus in her arms smiled—because the juggler had given everything he had, holding back nothing in his generosity. So goes the story.

To bring the story to life, I wanted to have a real juggler perform for the congregation first, and then I'd tell the story and turn it into my Christmas sermon. A little show-business pizzazz for the midnight service.

When time for the service came, the juggler had not arrived. Not until the middle of the second carol did I see him working his way up the crowded side aisle. But no costume. I had specifically asked him to wear his jester outfit. And no juggling equipment, either. What a disappointment. So much for magic at midnight.

While the congregation headed into the last verse of "O Little Town of Bethlehem," the juggler and I held a whispered conference. His car had been stolen, with all his possessions and equipment. But not to worry. A friend had brought him and would take him home afterward. In the meantime, he had an idea. All I had to do was tell the fairy story, and he, the juggler, would take it from there.

No time to argue. The carol was done, and the service had to go on. I assumed that when it came time for his performance, the juggler would explain his circumstances and use some things he had found in the church kitchen for a short act. Reasonable enough. However, Christmas Eve is not a time for reasonableness. I ought to know that by now.

So I read the story.

And the juggler stepped into the light from out of the congregation. Slim young man, the wiry, athletic kind. Black tennis shoes, jeans, green turtleneck shirt. Solemn expression and freckles on his face in place of the expected makeup. Longish brown hair. Nothing special to look at. And no tools of his trade.

He smiled. And began his routine. In fact, he went through his entire routine just as if he had brought balls and clubs and knives and scarves with him. We had all seen enough juggling to know what was going on. And in each part of the routine, he went one step further than he had ever juggled and we had ever seen. Seven balls is supposed to be the limit for the very best professional juggler. Our guy did eight, and we knew it when he did it and applauded the moment of triumph. On through twelve silk scarves in the air at once and seven knives, and we even knew when he set his torches on fire and got eight torches in the air all at once and caught them without burning himself. We laughed and shouted encouragement and applauded this remarkable performance. We couldn't see it, but we believed it. We gave him a standing ovation. On Christmas Eve in church—a standing ovation. He held up his hand for silence, and the congregation sat down. The juggler wasn't through. He was going to do an encore.

He started juggling things we couldn't quite recognize. What's this? Chickens? Birds? Some kind of tree. Rings. One off of each finger. Five? Five gold rings. Got it! "The Twelve Days of Christmas." He was going to juggle one of everything in the Twelve Days. The partridge, the pear tree, and all the rest. Impossible. But he was doing it. A swan. A goose and an egg. I was thinking, he will never get the maid and the cow off the ground, but with a great heaving effort, he did it. After that, the leaping lady and the dancing lord and the drum and drummer were a piece of cake. Every gift was in the air—way, way up in the air, because this was a lot of stuff. And as each piece came around, we knew what it was and shouted out its name as he caught it and threw it back into the air again. Fantastic! Nobody had ever done this before. The juggler was laughing. The congregation cheered like a crowd at a championship game when a last-minute score won it for the home team. The juggler suddenly clapped his hands loudly and stood still. One finger in front of his lips called for silence. And silence came.

We stood looking at him and he at us in the most powerful and meaningful moment of quiet I've witnessed at Christmas Eve. The sermon was supposed to follow the juggler. And it did. But it was not I who spoke. We were all addressed by a sermon of eloquent instructive silence. The silence in which we absorbed the power of the vision we had of the impossible event we had wished into being. The silence in which we thought about our capacity to realize things we can sometimes only imagine. Some of the most wonderful things have to be believed to be seen. Like flying reindeer and angels. Like peace on earth, goodwill, hope, and joy. Real because they can be imagined into being. Christmas is not a date on a calendar but a state of mind.

Someone—I don't know who—began to sing "Silent Night." As was our tradition, people on the first row lit their small candles from the big candle on the altar, and then passed the flame on to the candles of those in rows behind them. The church filled with light. And we filed out of the church singing into the night and went home, taking our light with us.

Length: 1100 words.
Reading Time: __________
See Conversion Table, p. 421.
Enter WPM Rate on p. 416.

23 The Juggler

COMPREHENSION CHECK

GETTING THE FACTS

1. In origin the juggler story is (a) Italian. (b) English. (c) Spanish. (d) French. 1. ____

2. The juggler had (a) an accident. (b) a breakdown. (c) his car stolen. (d) an unexpected delay. 2. ____

3. The juggler wore what color turtleneck? (a) green (b) red (c) brown (d) yellow 3. ____

4. What is the limit for the very best juggler? (a) 8 balls (b) 7 balls (c) 6 balls (d) 5 balls 4. ____

5. The author mentions (a) "We Wish You a Merry Christmas." (b) "Away in a Manger." (c) "Silent Night." (d) "It Came Upon the Midnight Clear." 5. ____

GETTING THE MEANING

6. This is mainly to show the (a) juggler's skill. (b) gift of imagination. (c) power of silence. (d) the importance of humor. 6. ____

7. You would infer from the opening allusion to "friend Willy" that Willy (a) appeared in an earlier story. (b) was the juggler's age. (c) was a preacher. (d) needed a refuge. 7. ____

8. The primary purpose was to (a) describe. (b) inspire. (c) inform. (d) amuse. 8. ____

9. In style this is best described as (a) witty. (b) conversational. (c) literary. (d) polished. 9. ____

10. You would infer that the rector author (a) is new. (b) has been rector for some time. (c) is a visiting rector. (d) is actually a layman. 10. ____

Check your answers with the Key on p. 452. Give yourself 10 points for each one right and enter your comprehension score on p. 414.

Comprehension Score: ________

NAME ______________ CLASS ______________ DATE ______________

24 Father and the Tommyknockers

WORD POWER WORKOUT

A. LEANING ON CONTEXT

In each of the blanks provided, place the letter that precedes the best definition of the underlined word in context to the left.

Words in Context	**Definitions**
1. _____ its noble <u>profile</u>	a. side view
2. _____ who asked <u>testily</u>	b. irritating
3. _____ some <u>astrological</u> explanation	c. destroyer of property
4. _____ are the <u>imps</u>	d. irritably
5. _____ trifling, <u>exasperating</u> things	e. brink
6. _____ <u>camouflaged</u> against the hearthrug	f. disguised
7. _____ it was <u>intact</u>	g. will of heaven
8. _____ the young <u>vandal</u>	h. young demons
9. _____ a masked <u>intruder</u>	i. left whole
10. _____ <u>verge</u> of tears	j. trespasser

Check your answers with the Key on p. 442 before going on. Give yourself 10 points for each one right and enter your score on the chart under A on p. 420. Review any that you have missed.

A Score: _______

Pronunciation aids: **3. AS-truh-loj-ih-kal**
5. ig-ZAS-per-ayt-ing

B. LEANING ON PARTS

With a few prefixes the final letter often changes in spelling to blend with the letter that follows. To understand such changes, spell the following combinations of *com-*, noting what happens and asking why.

1. com + nect = ____________ (fasten together)
2. com + lect = ____________ (bring together)
3. com + respond = ____________ (write together)
4. com + flict = ____________ (fight together)
5. com + operate = ____________ (work together)

C. MAKING THE WORDS YOURS

In each blank below, enter the most appropriate word from the ten words in context in the first exercise, substituting it for the word(s) in parentheses. Use these words: *astrological, camouflaged, exasperating, imps, intact, intruder, profile, testily, vandal, verge.*

1. The prisoner was on the (brink) ____________ of confessing to the crime.
2. The ancient mosaics that they discovered were virtually (left whole) ____________.
3. The teacher's (side view) ____________ seemed quite flattering.
4. The (destroyer of property) ____________ was caught in the act of breaking a window.
5. The campaigner believed in (will of heaven) ____________ explanations for his success.
6. They spoke (irritably) ____________ about having to give up their plans.
7. The guards who were on duty easily captured the (trespasser) ____________.
8. The important storage buildings were all (disguised) ____________ to avoid being bombed.
9. Whenever I write I blame the (young demons) ____________ for making me misspell words.
10. It was most (irritating) ____________ to wait for hours to be fed.

Check your answers with the Key on p. 446.

B Score: ________

C Score: ________

Enter your scores on p. 420.

24

Father and the Tommyknockers

RUTH WOODMAN

How do you explain the inexplicable? You may have to resort to tommyknockers. A teacher friend of mine at a teacher's convention saw a totally unknown woman in the balcony, sporting a red hat. He nudged his friend and pointed, saying, "I'm going to marry that woman." And he did! Now explain that! If you have a nose for news, don't turn up your nose at this story—another that's hard to explain.

BEGIN TIMING

Halloween had a special connotation in our family. It was the date on which Father always broke his nose.

The first time it happened, we were giving a party in our home in Rye, New York. Just before the guests arrived, Father and I went down into the cellar to tap the cider, made from our own apples. This particular lot must have been working overtime there in the dark because when Father bent over and began tapping briskly on the side of the barrel, the bung catapulted out with terrific force and caught him smack on the bridge of the nose. Cider poured out of the bunghole. Blood gushed from Father's nose. I didn't know whether to hold the jug under the cider or under his nose.

We went upstairs, where Mother was arranging doughnuts and cookies to go with the cider.

"Bessie, I've broken my nose!" groaned Father.

"Nonsense, George," said Mother. "You always dramatize things." But when he wiggled and creaked the cartilage to prove it, she turned pale and told Patrick, our coachman, to drive Father to Dr. Bassett. He was home again in less than an hour, with his nose neatly wedged between splints. And that was that.

By the time another October 31 rolled around, we'd all but forgotten the incident. Father's nose was the Roman type, and the break had made no noticeable difference in its noble profile.

There was nothing very original about our Halloween parties. We bobbed for apples, ate marshmallows off strings, dived for pennies in a pan of flour. On this occasion Father couldn't resist joining in the apple-bobbing. He knelt beside the tub, hands clasped behind his back, and pounced on a beautiful red Winesap. But a little boy on the opposite side of the tub had the same idea. There was a resounding *cr-r-r-ack!* and when Father's bald head emerged from the tub, blood was streaming all over the apple, which he held firmly clenched in his teeth.

This time Father went to the telephone and called Dr. Bassett, who asked testily, "Why do you always choose to break your nose on Halloween?"

That was the first it had occurred to any of us that this was the anniversary of the other fracture. Mother wondered if there was some astrological explanation. Father snorted—as best he could, under the circumstances. This had nothing to do with the stars; it was the work of the tommyknockers.

"What are tommyknockers?" we asked.

"Tommyknockers," he explained, "are the imps who haunt mines. Whenever anything goes wrong underground—not big disasters but trifling, exasperating things—it's the tommyknockers who are responsible. They're like gremlins."

Father was a mining engineer. Right after his graduation from the Columbia School of Mines in 1876, he went out to Colorado, where a brisk silver rush was under way, and cleaned up.

"Now," he declared solemnly, "these creatures are getting even with me for invading their haunts and stealing their treasure."

When we asked why the revenge took this particular form, he grinned and said, "My nose for ore, of course."

The next Halloween, Father announced that we needn't expect him to take part in any of the games at the party. He'd give a hand decorating the sun parlor, but that was all. It was enough.

He was standing on a stepladder, tacking up orange-and-black crepe-paper streamers, when the ladder tipped, just as if an unseen hand had pushed it, and Father plunged downward. As he fell, he struck his nose against one of the open French doors leading into the sun parlor. We could all hear the crack.

This third experience took the zest out of Halloween parties in our family. Of course, people said that things always go by threes, so there was no chance of its happening again. But these same people said that lightning never strikes twice in the same place.

So, the fourth year, we let somebody else give the party. Father and Mother stayed quietly at home alone. After dinner Father settled himself in his Morris chair to read while Mother crocheted and Prince, our black cocker spaniel, snoozed on the black bearskin hearthrug in front of the fire. It was all very peaceful, not a bit like Halloween.

A log burned through and fell with a shower of sparks. Father got up and took another log out of the woodbox. As he crossed to the fireplace, he didn't see Prince, camouflaged against the hearthrug. He tripped over the dog and pitched headlong against the brass fender.

Mother and Prince yelped in unison.

"Damn that dog!" Father bellowed. "Nearly broke my neck!"

"Never mind your neck," said Mother. "How about your nose?"

Miraculously, it was intact. It had missed one of the brass knobs on the fender by a nostril.

Around nine o'clock there was a sound of scampering feet on the front porch. Father got up to lock the front door. But just then it flew open and in swarmed a bunch of masked children carrying brown paper bags filled with dried beans and flour, which they proceeded to scatter around the front hall with great abandon.

One figure in a sheet and pillowcase slipped into the music room and hurled a handful of the stuff into Mother's new Steinway baby grand. If Mother herself had been assaulted, Father could not have been more outraged. He pounced on the young vandal, who wriggled out of his clutches and made a beeline for the open front door. Father followed. On the porch he grabbed the pillowcase and was about to rip it off, when the child dived down the porch steps. At the same time her foot kicked Father square in the face. It was a kick that would have done a mule proud.

Father came back into the house with his nose lying over on one cheek, and it was several days before the swelling and discoloration subsided enough so that he could go back to work. Ashamed to tell anyone that a little girl had kicked him in the face, he made up a story about a masked intruder he'd surprised and overpowered in a hand-to-hand struggle. The girls in Father's office thought he was terribly brave.

Mother suggested that Father take out accident insurance on his nose, the way dancers insure their legs. This was the first time anyone had come right out and admitted that maybe the end was not yet. Father bristled.

"What makes you think it could happen again?" he demanded.

"How many times do the tommyknockers knock?" I chanted.

I meant it harmlessly, but it had the most devastating effect upon Father. He began muttering about "that superstitious idiot." Mother thought he meant her, and was on the verge of tears. Father said quickly, no, he was talking about an old prospector he'd known in Colorado, by the name of Rocky Mountain Pete, who claimed the tommyknockers always struck a victim five times running. Of course, Father didn't believe it for a minute; he didn't even believe in tommyknockers, for that matter. Nobody of intelligence did. Nevertheless, this five-times-in-a-row superstition preyed on all our minds.

October 31 was a Wednesday that fifth year. Wednesday was the day our floors were always waxed, but when Patrick rolled the rugs back Mother stopped him.

"Not this week, Patrick," she said. "Halloween, you know. . . ."

Patrick nodded understandingly and rolled the rugs down again. The bearskin rug was taken out of the house, presumably to be aired and beaten. Prince was taken to the vet's. Mother inspected the stair carpet to make sure it hadn't worked loose on any of the treads. My brother offered to lend Father his catcher's mask.

"Can you picture me going to New York wearing a catcher's mask?" demanded Father.

"You're not *going* to New York, George," announced Mother quietly. "You're going to spend the day right here at home."

When Father called his office to say he had a cold and wouldn't be in, his partner laughed and said, "Well, that changes the odds."

Father turned from the telephone, livid with indignation. "Bessie, they're laying bets! Bets on my *nose!*" He banged his fist on the desk so hard that the brass inkwell jumped and nearly hit him. Mother removed the inkwell and asked Father what the odds were. Father said he didn't know, and couldn't care less. But he found an excuse to call his secretary a little later and learned that the odds were 7 to 5.

We had invitations to Halloween parties that evening, but we declined them. We wanted to be home, in case anything happened. I couldn't decide whether I hoped it *would* or it *wouldn't.*

After dinner when the family repaired to the living room Father remained at the table, moodily nursing a glass of brandy and a cigar. Suddenly, from the dining room, came the sound of a sharp *cr-r-r-ack!* As one person we leaped to our feet and rushed in—to find Father at the sideboard, picking the meat out of a walnut he'd just cracked.

"Well?" he inquired.

Without a word we slunk away.

By ten o'clock we'd all gone to bed; around eleven, Father switched off the light and settled down for the night. Mother, beside him, heard the clock in the downstairs hall chime the half hour and relaxed. Halloween was nearly over.

"You see?" said Father, who was thinking the same thing. "That idea of five-in-a-row was all superstitious bunk." He kissed her good-night. "The jinx is broken," he said. Mother breathed a little prayer of thanks.

A few minutes before midnight the telephone rang. Father jumped out of bed and started into the hall to answer it. But the door leading into the hall had blown partly open, and Father, still half asleep, ran slam into it. Anyone else would have stubbed his toe. But not Father. For the fifth and last time, he paid through the nose.

Length: 1660 words.
Reading Time: ________
See Conversion Table, p. 421.
Enter WPM Rate on p. 416.

24 Father and the Tommyknockers

COMPREHENSION CHECK

GETTING THE FACTS

1. The family lived in (a) New Jersey. (b) Massachusetts. (c) New York. (d) Maine. — 1. ____

2. Tommyknockers are (a) imps. (b) goblins. (c) ghosts. (d) dwarfs. — 2. ____

3. The family dog, Prince, was a black (a) poodle. (b) dachshund. (c) bull dog. (d) cocker spaniel. — 3. ____

4. Who said that tommyknockers' revenge came in 5's? Rocky Mountain (a) Bud (b) Jake (c) Bill (d) Pete — 4. ____

5. What triggered the last break? (a) a rock against the window (b) the doorbell (c) a scream (d) a telephone ring — 5. ____

GETTING THE MEANING

6. This selection is mainly to (a) inform. (b) entertain. (c) warn. (d) raise questions. — 6. ____

7. What word best describes the author's attitude toward tommyknockers? (a) accepting (b) pessimistic (c) serious (d) fearful — 7. ____

8. The style is best described as (a) witty. (b) literary. (c) conversational. (d) dramatic. — 8. ____

9. You would infer that Father is essentially (a) superstitious. (b) scientific. (c) uncertain. (d) positive. — 9. ____

10. The author's attitude toward her father is (a) critical. (b) puzzled. (c) proud. d) sympathetic. — 10. ____

Check your answers with the Key on p. 452. Give yourself 10 points for each one right and enter your comprehension score on p. 414.

Comprehension Score: ________

B. VOCABULARY REVIEW QUIZ

This quiz contains ten words from the Word Power Workouts, but with other possible meanings of the word. The focus is on words with important prefixes so as to reinforce your awareness of prefixes as aids to meaning.

1. extensions (a) additions (b) traditions (c)tendencies (d) summons (e) complications 1. ____
   Extensions contains the prefix ______, meaning _____.

2. deception (a) exception (b) looking out (c) capturing (d) attempting (e) covering up 2. ____
   Deception contains the prefix ______, meaning _____.

3. reiterates (a) repeats (b) makes younger (c) treats (d) fills (e) purchases 3. ____
   Reiterates contains the prefix ______, meaning _____.

4. debilitating (a) cursing (b) inflating (c) welcoming (d) weakening (e) telling 4. ____
   Debilitating contains the prefix ______, meaning _____.

5. retrieve (a) trace (b) fall in (c) get back (d) expect (e) bury 5. ____
   Retrieve contains the prefix ______, meaning _____.

6. elusive (a) submit (b) hard to grasp (c) limit (d) reserve (e) bind together 6. ____
   Elusive contains the prefix ______, meaning _____.

7. immobilized (a) held firm (b) managed (c) struck against (d) mobbed (e) criticized 7. ____
   Immobilized contains the prefix ______, meaning _____.

8. indifferent (a)not very good (b) sad (c) active (d) tired (e) plain 8. ____
   Indifferent contains the prefix ______, meaning _____.

9. subtle (a) outstanding (b) without blame (c) hopeless (d) rare (e) terrifying 9. ____
   Subtle contains the prefix ______, meaning _____.

10. intact (a) rude (b) polite (c) natural (d) aimless (e) complete 10. ____

Intact contains the prefix ______, meaning _____.

10 points for each correct answer.

See Key on p. 441.

Vocabulary Review Score: ______

NAME ______________ CLASS ______________ DATE ______________

25 Reading Words More Effectively

WORD POWER WORKOUT

A. LEANING ON CONTEXT

In each of the blanks provided, place the letter that precedes the best definition of the underlined word in context to the left.

Words in Context	Definitions
1. ____ an allied plane	a. concealed, hidden
2. ____ figures are conservative	b. difference
3. ____ a convenient substitute	c. visual
4. ____ that latent potential	d. moderate
5. ____ more complicated than usual	e. removing
6. ____ play havoc with reading	f. further, encourage to flourish
7. ____ in dramatic contrast	g. involved
8. ____ improved perceptual skill	h. associated
9. ____ in eliminating regression	i. easy
10. ____ promote effective word grouping	j. confusion

Check your answers with the Key on p. 442 before going on. Give yourself 10 points for each one right and enter your score on the chart under A on p. 420. Review any that you have missed.

A Score: ________

Pronunciation aids: **4. LAY-tunt**
6. HAV-uk
8. pur-SEP-choo-ul

B. LEANING ON PARTS

The prefix *sub-* also has different spellings, the *b* changing to blend with the next letter. Spell the following combinations, observing the changes.

1. sub + port = ____________
2. sub + fix = ____________
3. sub + ceed = ____________
4. sub + gest = ____________
5. sub + pect = ____________

C. MAKING THE WORDS YOURS

In each blank below, enter the most appropriate word from the ten words in context in the first exercise, substituting it for the word(s) in parentheses. Use these words: *allied, complicated, conservative, contrast, convenient, eliminated, havoc, latent, perceptual, promote.*

1. The (moderate) ____________ politician was liked by the older citizens.
2. Students with (visual) ____________ problems tend to read more slowly.
3. The troublemaker was (removed) ____________ from the game.
4. He joined an organization to (further) ____________ world peace.
5. Her (hidden) ____________ interest in acting began to develop in college.
6. In a story, a more (involved) ____________ plot demands more careful reading.
7. Making a cake from a cake mix is quite (easy) ____________.
8. There is a marked (difference) ____________ between the two brothers.
9. The cry of "Fire" created (confusion) ____________ in the crowded theater.
10. During wartime (associated) ____________ forces teamed up to defeat a common enemy.

Check your answers with the Key on p. 447.

B Score: ________

C Score: ________

Enter your scores on p. 420.

25

Reading Words More Effectively

BEGIN TIMING

We're back to words again. But not to vocabulary building. That's already been covered. This chapter focuses on mastering other special problems with words.

WORDS! If you can't see 'em, you can't read 'em. That's a reminder that in dealing with words you need *two* sets of skills. One set brings words from the printed page into your mind. The other set attaches meaning to them, when they arrive. Context, word parts, and dictionary are used here.

What can you do to speed the accurate flow of words from page to brain? That's a whole new area of concern. Fortunately, research has some answers.

Developing Perceptual Skill

As early as World War II, Dr. Samuel Renshaw, psychologist, was able to set up a perceptual training program of amazing effectiveness. With it, over 385,000 men were trained in aircraft recognition. One officer, so trained, paid it the highest tribute. After a year and a half in the thick of the Pacific fighting his crew never once fired on an allied plane and never failed to fire on an enemy one. That's the visual wizardry you want for reading words.

How much improvement can you expect? According to Renshaw, proper perceiving is a learned skill, just like playing the piano or learning French. If you're average, Renshaw's research indicates that you're using your eyes at only about 20 percent efficiency. In short, you should perceive five times better than you do.

Such training is ordinarily given with a tachistoscope. That's a projector with a cameralike shutter. It flashes numbers, words, or phrases on a screen at split-second speeds. Such training helps you (1) see more, (2) see more accurately, and (3) see more quickly.

Actually, classroom results suggest that Renshaw's figures are conservative. You should be able to increase the flow of words from page to brain to ten times your present efficiency, not five.

In our reading classes, we include about twenty ten-minute practice periods. Initial training is at 1/10th of a second. By the end of the course, students perceive as much as 58 percent more accurately *and* ten times faster—1/100th of a second.

To be sure, you probably don't have a tachistoscope handy. You do, however, have a convenient substitute—your hand and something to read. To practice, cover part of a line of print with your hand. Quickly pull your hand down and back to get a split-second look at the words revealed. Repeat that in a reading-like pattern, phrase after phrase. Two minutes a day of such practice will do wonders. In two minutes, you should soon manage from twenty to forty split-second looks. Twenty days of that regimen and you'll have more practice than our usual students. That's the way you develop that latent potential of yours.

Minimizing Regressions

In reading words, you should know what's meant by regressing. That's looking back at a word or words you have already read. It's like stepping backwards every few yards as you walk—hardly the way to move ahead in a hurry. Notice what regressing does to a complex complex sentence like this, like this, making it seem even more complicated than complicated than usual with its regressive rereading of rereading of words. Confusing, isn't it? Regressing does indeed play havoc with both reading speed and comprehension.

Eye movement photographs of some 12,000 readers show that college students regress an average of 15 times in reading only 100 words. That would work out to 150 regressions in reading this one article. No wonder you should get rid of them. They slow you down tremendously.

Faster-than-comfortable reading is the best way to eliminate them. You can soon reduce the number of regressions by as much as 80 percent, judging from class results. And you're still reading every word. You just aren't reading them twice!

Developing Word Grouping Habits

As he reads, the average college or adult reader takes in only 1.1 words at a glance. Make that 2.2, and he's *doubled* his reading rate. Try it. Superior readers, with speeds of 900 to 1,000 wpm, can manage four words per eye-stop. Out of 30,000 cases photographed, however, with an eye-movement camera, only three have read at rates above 1,000 wpm, a relatively rare achievement.

The eye-movement motion-picture camera reveals the possibilities. It records one reader making nine stops or fixations in reading nine words—

an exact word-by-word pattern. In dramatic contrast, it records a highly skilled reader making only three stops in reading those same words.

As in eliminating regressions, practice faster-than-comfortable reading. It's your best move. It forces you to take in more words at a glance.

Noting Key Words

Another special word-reading skill is that of identifying key words. This is part of the skimming technique. But it should also be part of your normal reading. Research shows rather wide variations. Some readers, for example, when asked to list key words in a paragraph with over fifty nouns denoting place, selected only prepositions—*beyond, in, at.* Others were determined by personal concerns. One student, worried about getting a ticket during the experiment, listed *car* and *parking lot.*

The best readers selected nouns almost 90 percent of the time. It makes sense. Take this sentence: "The big ____________ from the ____________ to the ____________." Not very clear, is it? Yet it's 70 percent complete. Let's try the nouns: *book . . . shelf . . . floor.* That's better. Yet that's only 30 percent of the sentence, not 70 percent. Now add the verb—*fell: book fell . . . shelf . . . floor.* That's the best 40 percent. Right?

Other things being equal, then, look for the nouns—the names of persons, places, things, qualities, actions, or ideas. Next, note verbs. By so doing, you'll make sure of focusing your attention on the important things.

Now you know how to read words with enviable skill. Develop improved perceptual skill, minimize regression, promote effective word grouping habits, and zero in on key words—when you do, you'll find added pleasure, ease, and interest in reading.

Length: 1000 words.
Reading Time: ____________
See Conversion Table, p. 421.
Enter WPM Rate on p. 416.

25 Reading Words More Effectively

COMPREHENSION CHECK

GETTING THE FACTS

1. What is specifically mentioned? (a) World War II (b) Hitler (c) the Luftwaffe (d) Eisenhower — 1. ____

2. A tachistoscope has a (a) stroboscopic shutter. (b) reflective device. (c) cameralike shutter. (d) filmstrip attachment. — 2. ____

3. College students regress on an average of how many times in reading 100 words? (a) 4 (b) 7 (c) 11 (d) 15. — 3. ____

4. Eye-movement camera findings show that reading speeds above 1,000 wpm (a) have never been recorded. (b) are frequent. (c) are relatively rare. (d) are quite common. — 4. ____

5. The ability to identify key words is said to (a) be easier for girls. (b) show wide variations. (c) come automatically with age. (d) improve in college. — 5. ____

GETTING THE MEANING

6. The main idea of the selection is how to (a) speed the flow of words. (b) build a vocabulary. (c) spot key words. (d) minimize regressions. — 6. ____

7. You would infer that the chief reason for regressing is (a) lack of training. (b) lack of interest. (c) poor study habits. (d) vocabulary weakness. — 7. ____

8. The average reader, you would infer, is (a) quite inefficient. (b) quite efficient. (c) tireless. (d) casual. — 8. ____

9. Figures on eye-movement cameras show how (a) rapidly gains are made. (b) common the 1,000 wpm rate is. (c) improvement varies. (d) inefficient adults are. — 9. ____

10. The illustrative sentence beginning, "The big . . . from . . ." is to point up the importance of (a) connectives. (b) verbs. (c) nouns. (d) skipping. — 10. ____

Check your answers with the Key on p. 452. Give yourself 10 points for each one right and enter your comprehension score on p. 414.

Comprehension Score: ________

MAKING THE APPLICATION

As a warming-up exercise, every now and then run through these three columns, using a 3 × 5 card. Cover the phrase with the card but leave the dot above it uncovered, to keep your eyes on target. Quickly pull the card down and back, uncovering the phrase below the dot for a fraction of a second. See if you perceived the entire phrase accurately in that split second. Go from dot to dot, through all three columns.

2-word phrase	**3-word phrase**	**4-word phrase**
•	•	•
You should	Did you know	But that is only
•	•	•
try to	that Abraham Lincoln	when we can choose
•	•	•
ead by	got most of	the exact right word.
•	•	•
the grouping	his fine education	When you say that
•	•	•
of words.	from the reading	words win friends and
•	•	•
Your skill	he did when	influence people, can you
•	•	•
as a	he was little?	think of an example?
•	•	•
reader is	It is said	Can you think of
•	•	•
very valuable.	that the pen	some jobs where people
•	•	•
Practice it	is far mightier	make a living by
•	•	•
every day.	than the sword.	the words they use?

For additional practice, draw two light pencil lines down one of the full pages in this or another textbook. Space the lines evenly so as to divide the line into three equal parts. Then, by using your hand or a 3 × 5 card, see if you can take in the first third at one glance, then the second, then the third. Two minutes of such practice should be an excellent warm-up exercise.

Now select a paragraph and underline all the key words in the entire paragraph. Underline as few as possible, however, making certain you do select only the most important. What kinds of words did you select? How many nouns? Verbs? Other parts of speech?

NAME ____________ CLASS ____________ DATE ____________

26 Listening

WORD POWER WORKOUT

A. LEANING ON CONTEXT

In each of the blanks provided, place the letter that precedes the best definition of the underlined word in context to the left.

Words in Context	Definitions
1. ____ in the <u>gloaming</u>	a. educated
2. ____ <u>peals</u> of laughter	b. suppress
3. ____ But <u>basically,</u> the world	c. twilight
4. ____ If you listen <u>totally</u>	d. open
5. ____ I had become <u>enlightened</u>	e. shrieks
6. ____ but <u>simultaneously</u> listen	f. ingrained
7. ____ Listening is <u>receptivity</u>	g. essentially
8. ____ Be <u>submissive</u> to everything	h. completely
9. ____ to <u>repress</u> things	i. open-mindedness
10. ____ forms be <u>imprinted</u> in you	j. at the same time

Check your answers with the Key on p. 442 before going on. Give yourself 10 points for each one right and enter your score on the chart under A on p. 420. Review any that you have missed.

A Score: ________

Pronunciation aids: **6. sy-muhl-TAY-nee-us-lee**
7. ree-sep-TIV-uh-tee

B. LEANING ON PARTS

The prefix *in-* changes its spelling to blend with whatever letter follows. Spell each combination.

1. in + radiate = ____________
2. in + luminate = ____________
3. in + migrant = ____________
4. in + lustrious = ____________
5. in + rigation = ____________

C. MAKING THE WORDS YOURS

In each blank below, enter the most appropriate word from the ten words in context in the first exercise, substituting it for the word(s) in parentheses. Use these words: *basically, enlightened, gloaming, imprinted, peals, receptivity, repress, simultaneously, submissive, totally.*

1. For the first time I begin to feel (educated) ____________ about the causes of the conflict.
2. (Shrieks) ____________ of laughter met my first efforts to paddle a canoe.
3. The shot and the breaking glass came almost (at the same time) ____________.
4. The scene of the bloody accident was indelibly (ingrained) ____________ on my mind.
5. (Essentially) ____________ all you have to do is send in the application form and start work.
6. The newspaper account seemed (completely) ____________ inaccurate.
7. The play program quaintly gave the time of day as in the (twilight) ____________.
8. To get the substance of a lecture you have to develop (open-mindedness) ____________.
9. You may have to (suppress) ____________ your tendency to answer test questions at too great length.
10. In a highly structured regime you have to be (open) ____________ to whatever orders you get.

Check your answers with the Key on p. 447.

B Score: ________

C Score: ________

Enter your scores on p. 420.

26

Listing

NATALIE GOLDBERG

The communication skills of writing, reading, speaking, and listening are all interrelated. Why not capitalize on that fact? As you're told in this selection, writing is "ninety percent listening." How many other things in your life are "ninety percent listening"? Obviously, quite a few. So, for personal improvement, listen—and read!

BEGIN TIMING

At six years old I was sitting at my cousin's piano in Brooklyn making believe I was playing a song and singing along with it: "In the gloaming, oh my darling . . ." My cousin, who was nine years older, sat down beside me on the piano stool and screamed to my mother, "Aunt Sylvia, Natalie is tone-deaf. She can't sing!" From then on, I never sang and I rarely listened to music. When I heard the scores from Broadway shows on radio, I just learned the words and never tried to imitate the melody. As I grew older my friends and I played a game, Name That Tune. I would hum something and they would break into peals of laughter, not possibly believing I was actually humming "Younger Than Springtime" from *South Pacific.* This was a way I received attention, though my young heart secretly longed to be Gypsy Rose Lee. After all, I knew all the words to all the songs. But basically, the world of music was not available to me. I was tone-deaf: I had a physical defect, like a missing foot or finger.

Several years ago I took a singing lesson from a Sufi singing master, and he told me there is no such thing as tone-deafness. "Singing is ninety percent listening. You have to learn to listen." If you listen totally, your body fills with the music, so when you open your mouth the music automatically comes out of you. A few weeks after that, I sang in tune with a friend for the first time in my life and thought for sure I had become enlightened. My individual voice disappeared and our two voices became one.

Writing, too, is ninety percent listening. You listen so deeply to the space around you that if fills you, and when you write, it pours out of you. If you can capture that reality around you, your writing needs nothing else. You don't only listen to the person speaking to you across the table, but simultaneously listen to the air, the chair, and the door. And go beyond the door. Take in the sound of the season, the sound of the color coming in through the windows. Listen to the past, future, and present right where you are. Listen with your whole body, not only with your ears, but with your hands, your face, and the back of your neck.

Listening is receptivity. The deeper you can listen, the better you can write. You take in the way things are without judgment, and the next day you can write the truth about the way things are. Jack Kerouac in his list of prose essentials said, "Be submissive to everything. Open. Listening." He also said, "No time for poetry, but exactly what is." If you can capture the way things are, that's all the poetry you'll ever need.

Rabbi Zalman Schachter once told a group of people at the Lama Foundation that when he was in rabbinical school the students were not allowed to take notes. They had to just listen, and when the lecture was done they were expected to know it. The idea was that we can remember everything. We choose and have trained our minds to repress things.

After something is read in class, I often have the students do a "recall"; "As close as you can to the exact words of what was said or written, repeat anything that was strong for you. Don't step away and say, 'I liked when she talked about the farmland.' Give us exact details: 'Standing in the field, I was lonelier than a crow.'" Besides opening and receiving what was said, this kind of deep, nonevaluative listening awakens stories and images inside you. By listening in this way you become a clear mirror to reflect reality, your reality and the reality around you.

Basically, if you want to become a good writer, you need to do three things. Read a lot, listen well and deeply, and write a lot. And don't think too much. Just enter the heat of words and sounds and colored sensations and keep your pen moving across the page.

If you read good books, when you write, good books will come out of you. Maybe it's not quite that easy, but if you want to learn something, go to the source. Basho, the great seventeenth-century Haiku master, said, "If you want to know about a tree, go to the tree." If you want to know poetry, read it, listen to it. Let those patterns and forms be imprinted in you. Don't step away from poetry to analyze a poem with your logical mind. Enter poetry with your whole body. Dogen, a great Zen master, said, "If you walk in the mist, you get wet." So just listen, read, and write. Little by little, you will come closer to what you need to say and express it through your voice.

Be patient and don't worry about it. Just sing and write in tune.

Length: 840 words.
Reading Time: ________
See Conversion Table, p. 421.
Enter WPM Rate on p. 416.

26 Listening

COMPREHENSION CHECK

GETTING THE FACTS

1. The author's name is (a) Natalie. (b) Sylvia. (c) Rose. (d) Jane. 1. ____

2. Specific mention is made of (a) *My Fair Lady.* (b) *South Pacific.* (c) *The Music Man.* (d) *Camelot.* 2. ____

3. You are specifically told to take in the sound of (a) a mountain stream. (b) the flowers growing. (c) bread baking. (d) the season. 3. ____

4. In rabbinical school students (a) were not allowed to highlight their texts. (b) were not allowed to take notes. (c) had to write poetry. (d) had to note details. 4. ____

5. The author quoted (a) Gypsy Rose Lee. (b) Basho. (c) Haman. (d) Zen. 5. ____

GETTING THE MEANING

6. The central idea is to help you do what better? (a) listen (b) write (c) read poetry (d) sing 6. ____

7. The author uses the word *listening* to mean (a) awareness of everything. (b) noting every sound. (c) focusing on important things. (d) getting central ideas. 7. ____

8. Telling you to go to the tree is to get you to go to (a) a composition text. (b) the dictionary. (c) action. (d) life. 8. ____

9. The primary purpose is to (a) entertain. (b) tell a story. (c) instruct. (d) describe. 9. ____

10. To make her point the author relies largely on (a) contrasts. (b) personal examples. (c) experimental data. (d) opinions of authorities. 10. ____

Check your answers with the Key on p. 452. Give yourself 10 points for each one right and enter your comprehension score on p. 415.

Comprehension Score: ________

NAME ________________ CLASS ________________ DATE ________________

27 How to Remember: Some Fundamental Principles

WORD POWER WORKOUT

A. LEANING ON CONTEXT

In each of the blanks provided, place the letter that precedes the best definition of the underlined word in context to the left.

Words in Context	**Definitions**
1. ____ That's <u>comparable</u> to	a. catch phrases
2. ____ of our <u>inherent</u> memory	b. volley
3. ____ the constant <u>barrage</u>	c. nearness
4. ____ the second <u>prerequisite</u>	d. equivalent
5. ____ Mr. Farley was <u>cited</u>	e. likeness
6. ____ vital that you <u>visualize</u>	f. natural
7. ____ when <u>slogans</u> like these	g. requirement
8. ____ is a cue, a <u>clue</u>	h. picture
9. ____ Law of <u>Resemblance</u>	i. hint
10. ____ Law of <u>Contiguity</u>	j. singled out

Check your answers with the Key on p. 442 before going on. Give yourself 10 points for each one right and enter your score on the chart under A on p. 420. Review any that you have missed.

A Score: ________

Pronunciation aids: **1. KOM-pur-uh-buhl** **2. in-HEER-uhnt** **3. buh-RAHZH** **4. pree-REK-whuh-zit** **10. kon-tuh-GYOO-uh-tee**

B. LEANING ON PARTS

Here are two more quite changeable prefixes: *ad-* and *ob-*. Get better acquainted with them by combining them with the roots given below.

1. ad + cept = ____________
2. ad + low = ____________
3. ob + press = ____________
4. ob + fend = ____________
5. ob + cur = ____________

C. MAKING THE WORDS YOURS

In each blank below, enter the most appropriate word from the ten words in context in the first exercise, substituting it for the word(s) in parentheses. Use these words: *barrage, cited, clue, comparable, contiguity, inherent, prerequisite, resemblance, slogans, visualize.*

1. When wondering about a strange word, be sure to examine context for a (hint) ____________ about meaning.
2. I could see very little (likeness) ____________ between them even though they were twins.
3. "A new word a day keeps the low grades away"—that's one of my (catch phrases) ____________ to motivate vocabulary study.
4. Can you (picture) ____________ the big celebration parade for homecoming?
5. Some people seem born with a strong (natural) ____________ distrust of strangers.
6. The new hospital volunteer was (singled out) ____________ for exceptional service.
7. Do you know the (requirement) ____________ for Chemistry 103?
8. The initial plans placed the two structures in (nearness) ____________.
9. At one time a British pound was (equivalent) ____________ to approximately one dollar and a half.
10. When I returned from vacation, my roommate overwhelmed me with a (volley) ____________ of questions.

Check your answers with the Key on p. 447.

B Score: ________

C Score: ________

Enter your scores on p. 420.

27

How to Remember: Some Fundamental Principles

ROBERT L. MONTGOMERY

Tie a string around your finger! Is that one of the fundamental principles? The great Leonardo da Vinci said, "Iron rusts from disuse . . . even so does inaction sap the vigors of the mind." In short: no one has a bad memory, just an unused or untrained one. Develop your memory now, then use it. Knowing the fundamentals! That's your next step.

BEGIN TIMING

The Prerequisites

Most of us, psychologists say, don't use more than 10 percent of our native ability to remember. That's comparable to running a car on one or two cylinders and just poking along.

Why don't we use more of our inherent memory power? There are several answers. First, because we haven't been trained to. Nowhere in our schooling were we taught how to use our powers of memory. And second, because we often just don't *care.* And that leads me to the three things that I feel are essential to a more powerful memory.

First, you must have a burning *desire* to improve your memory. *You must care about it.* Most people struggle along with poor memories, enduring endless frustrations and embarrassments in their daily lives, because they just don't want to be bothered remembering the constant barrage of names, numbers, facts, and information. What you have to do is remind yourself of the many benefits of a good memory: the increased confidence I promised you, the popularity, the peace of mind. Aren't those three alone enough to stir a desire in you to improve?

The second prerequisite is the ability to *concentrate.* You will be effective in remembering to the degree that you care enough to concentrate. A short period of intense concentration will often enable you to accomplish more than years of dreaming.

The third prerequisite was revealed to me by former Postmaster-General James Farley of New York City. Mr. Farley was cited by associates for having the most remarkable memory in this century. I asked him his secret.

"There's no real secret," he said. "You simply must *love people.* If you do, you won't have any trouble remembering their names, and a lot more about them than that."

And that's the third essential: You must *care about people.* It wasn't long after I talked to Mr. Farley that I came across an interesting line from Alexander Pope. "How vast a memory has love," he wrote. Certainly a deeper interest in people, and in your work as well, should make your desire to remember and your concentration much easier.

The Basic Laws

Visualize

Now you're ready to learn the basic techniques for developing your memory. The first essential is to *visualize.* Picture what you want to remember. Since 85 percent of all you learn and remember in life reaches you through your eyes, it is absolutely vital that you visualize the things you want to recall later. To do that, you must above all become *aware.* And awareness involves becoming both a keen observer and an active listener. You have to see clearly and hear accurately in order to picture vividly what you want to remember. Too many people go through life only partly awake, only partly aware. They don't forget names; they never hear them clearly in the first place. The art of *retention* is the art of *attention.*

Become curious, observant, and sensitive to everything around you. See the roof detail on that old building. Notice the difference between the tree greens of April and of August. Hear the difference between the sirens of an ambulance, a fire truck, a police car. Sharpen your senses of sight and hearing—they're the most important. Together, those two senses account for 95 percent of our memory power. Two ancient sayings highlight the importance of visualizing. "One time seeing is worth a thousand times hearing." And "A picture is worth ten thousand words."

Repeat

If school didn't bother to teach us formal memory work, it did teach us the need for *repeating.* We were taught to memorize by repeating a poem, a date, or the alphabet over and over again. Radio and television commercials rely heavily on repetition to remind listeners to buy, buy, buy.

Is there an American who doesn't recognize "Try it, you'll like it" or "I can't believe I ate the whole thing"? Burger King's famous "Have it your way" moved McDonald's, who got busy and created the line, "You, you're the one." When slogans like these are set to music, people don't just remember them—they even sing them. And there you have the secret of success: repetition.

Associate

Before we get into actual demonstrations of the kinds of memory and the application of techniques, there's one more key to memory, and it's the most important. The one indispensable fundamental is the requirement that you *associate* anything you want to recall later. Association is the natural as well as the easy way to assure instant recall. Your brain is more remarkable than even the most amazing computer in the world. And the principle on which it works is association. The brain is, in fact, an associating machine. To recall a name, date, or fact, what the brain needs is a cue, a clue.

Let's step back into history for a moment. Over 2,000 years ago Aristotle defined what he called the Primary Laws of Association. There is the Law of Resemblance or Similarity, where one impression tends to bring to mind another impression which resembles it in some way. There is the Law of Contrast or Opposites, which says that where there are two or more opposing impressions, the presence of one will tend to recall the others. And finally there is the Law of Contiguity or Togetherness. If two or more impressions occur at the same time, or follow close on one another in either time or space, thinking of one will recall the other.

There are secondary Laws of Association as well, and these are known as Recency, Frequency, and Vividness. *Recency* means we tend to recall associations made recently much better than those made months or years ago. *Frequency* implies that the more often you repeat an association, the easier it will be to recall. And *vividness* means that the more graphic or striking the association is, the quicker you'll be able to recall it.

In summary, the requirements for improving your memory are concentration, a desire to remember, and a love for people.

And the techniques for mastering the art of memory are visualizing, repeating, and associating.

One final note, this time on how to study: Memorizing anything is easier and faster when you practice for a half hour or so, and then go off and forget it for a while. Work again later for another half hour, then take another break. Tests have proved time and again that we learn better and faster when we alternate work and rest in a sort of wave pattern. The rest period actually reinforces the learning.

Now then, can you remember all that?

Length: 1110 words.
Reading Time: ________
See Conversion Table, p. 421.
Enter WPM Rate on p. 416.

27 How to Remember: Some Fundamental Principles

COMPREHENSION CHECK

GETTING THE FACTS

1. How many prerequisites are discussed? (a) only one (b) two (c) three (d) four — 1. ____

2. Specific mention is made of (a) Plato. (b) Alexander Pope. (c) Rockefeller. (d) Henry Ford. — 2. ____

3. What percentage of what you learn and remember do you reach through your eyes? (a) 56 (b) 64 (c) 72 (d) 85 — 3. ____

4. There is specific mention of (a) McDonald's. (b) Whata-burger's. (c) Wendy's. (d) Kentucky Fried Chicken. — 4. ____

5. Your brain is called (a) a computer powerhouse. (b) a bulging storeroom. (c) an associating machine. (d) a memory bank. — 5. ____

GETTING THE MEANING

6. This selection is primarily to do what for memory improvement? (a) explain key techniques (b) stress the importance of visualizing (c) show where the Laws of Association came from (d) provide a solid first step — 6. ____

7. You would infer that the author thinks (a) most people have good memory potential. (b) memory depends on IQ. (c) concentration is the key. (d) age affects memory. — 7. ____

8. This selection is best described as (a) inspirational. (b) entertaining. (c) practical. (d) stimulating. — 8. ____

9. The reference to Aristotle is to (a) indicate the source of certain basic laws. (b) suggest how long memory has had attention. (c) reveal Aristotle's great wisdom. (d) show the value of old ideas. — 9. ____

10. The discussion of slogans shows what as a memory aid? (a) music (b) repetition (c) clever phrasing (d) association — 10. ____

Check your answers with the Key on p. 452. Give yourself 10 points for each one right and enter your comprehension score on p. 415.

Comprehension Score: ________

NAME ______________ CLASS ______________ DATE ______________

28 Reading Paragraphs More Effectively

WORD POWER WORKOUT

A. LEANING ON CONTEXT

In each of the blanks provided, place the letter that precedes the best definition of the underlined word in context to the left.

Words in Context	Definitions
1. ____ the remotest idea	a. permanent
2. ____ their specialized function	b. center, most important part
3. ____ a transitional paragraph	c. benefit
4. ____ a fixed location	d. deliberate
5. ____ full advantage of all such cues	e. enjoy
6. ____ a directional nudge	f. are plentiful
7. ____ the core of narration	g. most distant
8. ____ pictures to relish	h. change-marking
9. ____ the conscious effort	i. push
10. ____ devices for explaining abound	j. precise, exact

Check your answers with the Key on p. 442 before going on. Give yourself 10 points for each one right and enter your score on the chart under A on p. 420. Review any that you have missed.

A Score: ________

B. LEANING ON PARTS

The prefixes *ex-* and *dis-* are also changeable. It's easier to say *emerge* than *exmerge,* a help in understanding something about English spelling.

1. ex + fect = ____________ (grow out of a cause)
2. ex + centric = ____________ (out of the center)
3. ex + mit = ____________ (to send out)
4. dis + ficult = ____________ (not easy)
5. dis + lapidated = ____________ (not in good shape)

C. MAKING THE WORDS YOURS

In each blank below, enter the most appropriate word from the ten words in context in the first exercise, substituting it for the word(s) in parentheses. Use these words: *abound, advantage, conscious, core, fixed, nudge, relish, remotest, specialized, transitional.*

1. You will (enjoy) ____________ being chair of the committee.
2. Hunters know that in the woods up north deer (are plentiful) ____________.
3. To write clearly, one must use proper (change-marking) ____________ words.
4. A reader should try to find the (most important part) ____________ of the article.
5. A (deliberate) ____________ understanding of one's abilities is particularly important.
6. Medicine is a very (exact) ____________ field.
7. There are few hiking trails in the (most distant) ____________ forest areas.
8. Persons with (permanent) ____________ opinions about politics seem narrow-minded.
9. A lazy person needs an occasional (push) ____________.
10. Knowing how to read is a real (benefit) ____________.

Check your answers with the Key on p. 447.

B Score: ________

C Score: ________

Enter your scores on p. 420.

28

Reading Paragraphs More Effectively

BEGIN TIMING

How do you get more out of a paragraph? It's like getting food out of a container. With some you need a can opener. With others you just unscrew a lid. Sometimes you use a key to remove a metal strip or pull on a tab. It depends on the container. There's no point trying to unscrew a pry-off lid. So it is in reading paragraphs. How you do it depends on the paragraph.

Special Paragraph Functions

And so, to summarize, be sure to remember those three structurally oriented kinds of paragraphs just discussed.

Are you confused? You're supposed to be. That paragraph lets you see for yourself how important it is to fit a paragraph into a proper frame of reference.

Imagine a major league baseball game. Suppose the catcher never had the remotest idea what kind of pitch he was about to catch. Curve? Sinker? Slider? Change-up? What problems he'd have! Think of the ones he'd miss. That's one very good reason for signals. The catcher *has* to know, if he's to play his position well.

And so does the reader of paragraphs. He has to know what kind of paragraphs he's dealing with. Otherwise, he can't read them effectively.

Let's look at one important way to classify paragraphs. According to their specialized function, they're either introductory, transitional, or concluding. And you read each in a very special way.

Take introductory paragraphs. They usually have two special functions: they arouse interest; they suggest direction and content. It's as if the author shone a flashlight in your face to attract attention, then turned the beam down a path to indicate where he's going. As a reader, you must take full advantage of all such cues. If you don't, you may lose your way before you're well started in the article.

The second kind of paragraph is called transitional. The writer has your attention and has pointed the way; you start along the path indicated. When he wants to make an important change of direction, he must let you know. Otherwise he may lose you. That calls for a transitional paragraph. Its sole function is to shine a flashlight off on a different path.

Transitional paragraphs are usually short—sometimes only one sentence. After all, they're like a one-word traffic sign—TURN or STOP. You don't need details—just a directional nudge. "Turning now to . . ." or "Still another aspect . . ." are typical signposts.

Finally, alert yourself to concluding paragraphs. Introductory and concluding paragraphs have a fixed location—an expected place. Always read the concluding paragraph slowly and carefully. It probably summarizes the most important points or reexpresses the main idea. It flashes the beam back in the path just traveled. Phrases such as "In conclusion . . . ," "Finally . . . ," or "In closing . . ." label this type of paragraph.

So much for the special paragraphs. What about all the others? Let's try another vantage point and classification.

Types of Paragraphs

You can fit any paragraph into one of four categories—*expository, narrative, descriptive,* and *persuasive.* Each demands somewhat different treatment from you the reader.

Take expository paragraphs. About 55 to 85 percent of those you read fit that category. They explain—explain how to read paragraphs, how an electric motor works, or how clouds can be classified.

Devices for explaining abound. The phrase *for example* reminds you of one good way. An example is like a picture—"worth more than ten thousand words," so the proverb goes. The phrase *in detail* suggests another way. Don't overlook *repeat* or *restate,* other ways to insure clear exposition. The phrases *by comparison* or *by contrast* open up still other ways to explain. Black seems even blacker when contrasted with white.

An analogy is a special kind of comparison, one between two quite unlike things that still have similarities. By analogy, for example, life is like a river. It really isn't. But a river begins, runs its course, and ends, sometimes flowing quietly and slowly, sometimes tumbling over rocks with difficulty. Just like life!

Once you become aware of such road signs, following the author's train of thought is simplified. Often one word or phrase fits a whole paragraph into a clear frame of meaning. You comprehend almost without reading further.

In addition to expository paragraphs, you'll find narrative ones. Here the emphasis is not on explaining, but on telling a story. Explaining how to drive is not the same as telling about getting a traffic ticket for speeding! Action is the core of narration. Focus centers on what happened next. Such words as *then, later, soon* suggest an unfolding of events in time.

The descriptive paragraphs—not nearly so common—give you a picture of something, with emphasis on the five senses. As a reader, savor each detail of taste, smell, sound, sight, and touch. These are word-pictures to relish, not skip.

Finally, persuasive paragraphs are designed to get you to *do* something or believe something—a step beyond pure explanation. Someone may explain the issues. Or he may explain with the intention of getting you to vote a certain way or believe a certain thing.

An awareness of both of those paragraph classifications will help. You do anything better when you know what you're dealing with.

The Main Idea

One last tip. No matter what kind of paragraph, remember it's about one thing. Discover what that one thing is. If you get the main idea, you can make some amazing inferences about details you never even read.

Now you should be able to read paragraphs more easily. You recognize the functions of introductory, transitional, and concluding paragraphs. You know the four types, plus some subvarieties of expository paragraphs. You are reminded to lean on main ideas.

To be sure, you can say these things are commonly known. They may be. *But*—how many readers actually take the next step—*apply* what they know? That's the payoff step. Why not make the conscious effort required?

Length: 1000 words.
Reading Time: ________
See Conversion Table, p. 421.
Enter WPM Rate on p. 416.

28 Reading Paragraphs More Effectively

COMPREHENSION CHECK

GETTING THE FACTS

1. Getting meaning from a paragraph is likened to getting (a) food from a container. (b) meat off a bone. (c) water from a sponge. (d) fruit from a tree. 1. ____

2. Normally, introductory paragraphs are said to have how many functions? (a) one (b) two (c) three (d) four 2. ____

3. Expository paragraphs are said to (a) expose. (b) suggest. (c) explain. (d) summarize. 3. ____

4. Life is likened to a (a) tree. (b) storm. (c) river.(d) seed. 4. ____

5. Such words as *then, later, soon* are typical of what kind of paragraph? (a) expository (b) narrative (c) persuasive (d) descriptive 5. ____

GETTING THE MEANING

6. The main focus is on how (a) to get main paragraph ideas. (b) to deal with paragraphs more effectively. (c) paragraphs develop ideas. (d) to classify paragraphs. 6. ____

7. The sensation of falling suggests what kind of paragraph? (a) expository (b) persuasive (c) narrative (d) descriptive 7. ____

8. Which kind of special paragraph is probably most difficult to spot? (a) introductory (b) concluding (c) transitional (d) all equally so 8. ____

9. Most emphasis is placed on what kind of paragraph? (a) persuasive (b) expository (c) descriptive (d) narrative 9. ____

10. Mention of analogy is to show one way of (a) describing. (b) telling. (c) explaining. (d) persuading. 10. ____

Check your answers with the Key on p. 452. Give yourself 10 points for each one right and enter your comprehension score on p. 415.

Comprehension Score: ________

MAKING THE APPLICATION

As a means of getting a clearer picture of the four types of paragraphs, reread carefully the characteristics of each. With that fourfold classification in mind, turn to the paragraphs indicated below. Read each one and then label each properly, as *expository, narrative, descriptive,* or *persuasive.* No two paragraphs should have the same label. Each is a different type.

Turn to the following paragraphs in selection 23, "The Juggler," beginning on page 185.

1. The paragraph beginning, "My friend . . ." is primarily of what type? ____________
2. The paragraph beginning, "The story . . ." is primarily of what type? ____________
3. The paragraph beginning, "And the juggler . . ." is primarily of what type? ____________
4. The paragraph beginning, "We stood looking . . ." is primarily of what type? ____________

To get additional practice in discovering the essence or main idea of a paragraph, turn to selection 17, page 137. Try to state the idea of each of the five paragraphs indicated below using fewer than ten words. Start with the paragraph beginning, "Not much, . . ." calling that paragraph 1. Take that one and the next four to analyze below.

1. ____

____

2. ____

____

3. ____

____

4. ____

____

5. ____

____

PREFIX MINI-REVIEW

Here's a mini-review of the twenty prefixes, the most important shortcuts in the English language. They're so important you should know them all perfectly. And here's the review to ensure that kind of mastery. Use it from time to time, as needed, to keep top-level performance. Try all three review patterns.

1. Cover the right-hand column with a 3 × 5 card. Try to supply the common meaning for each prefix, moving the card down for an immediate check of your answer. This is the easiest pattern.
2. Cover both the middle and right-hand columns for a more difficult check. See if you can supply both mnemonic and common meaning.
3. For the most difficult review, cover both the middle and left-hand columns and try to supply both mnemonic and prefix to fit each meaning, again checking your answers immediately.

Prefix	Suggested Mnemonic	Common Meaning
1. *pre-*	preview	before
2. *re-*	refund, reread	back, again
3. *pro-*	progress, prolabor	forward, for
4. *inter-*	intermission, interspersed	between, among
5. *non-*	nonresident	not
6. *de-*	depress, depart, defrost	down, away, reverse
7. *un-*	untidy	not
8. *trans-*	transport, transcend	across, beyond
9. *over-*	overpass, overseer	above, beyond
10. *mono-*	monopoly	one
11. *epi-*	epidemic, epidermis	upon, above
12. *mis-*	misspell	wrong, wrongly
13. *com-*	companion, connect	with, together
14. *in-*	insecure	not
15. *ex-*	exit	out
16. *dis-*	dissect, dispatch	apart, away
17. *ad-*	advance	to, toward
18. *ob-*	obstinate, objective	against, to
19. *in-*	inhale	in, into
20. *sub-*	submerge	under

NAME ______________________ CLASS ______________________ DATE ______________

29 How to Work for a Rotten Boss

WORD POWER WORKOUT

A. LEANING ON CONTEXT

In each of the blanks provided, place the letter that precedes the best definition of the underlined word in context to the left.

Words in Context

1. ____ on the agenda
2. ____ at the least provocation
3. ____ cited as bonuses
4. ____ responsible for how you react
5. ____ is culled from 14 years
6. ____ contend on equal terms
7. ____ bullying usually elicits
8. ____ cowering, back-pedaling response
9. ____ prone to mood swings
10. ____ boss must be flawless

Definitions

a. cringing, shrinking
b. brings out
c. perfect
d. order of business
e. extras
f. drawn
g. respond
h. cause
i. struggle
j. disposed

Check your answers with the Key on p. 442 before going on. Give yourself 10 points for each one right and enter your score on the chart under A on p. 420. Review any that you have missed.

A Score: ________

Pronunciation aids: **1. uh-JEN-duh** **7. ih-LIS-its**
2. prov-uh-KAY-shun **8. KOW-ur-ing**

B. LEANING ON PARTS

The Latin root *ducere* means "to lead." Whenever you see a *duc(e), duct,* or *duit,* look for the meaning "lead." Now complete the following.

1. The passage through which air is led is called a ___________.
2. An article usually leads into the main part with an intro___________.
3. To lead yourself back to your slender self, you have to re___________.
4. To lead finished goods out of a factory, you must pro___________ them.
5. A tube leading electric wires around a house is called a con__________.

C. MAKING THE WORDS YOURS

In each blank below, enter the most appropriate word from the ten words in context in the first exercise, substituting it for the word(s) in parentheses. Use these words: *agenda, bonuses, contend, cowering, culled, elicits, flawless, prone, provocation, react.*

1. How did you (respond) ___________ to the changes you had to make?
2. The employees had no (cause) ___________ for criticizing their supervisor so harshly.
3. On our last camping trip we had to (struggle) ___________ with some terrible weather.
4. What's the (order of business) ___________ for today's meeting?
5. The violin soloist gave a (perfect) ___________ performance of a most difficult passage.
6. The police found two people (cringing, shrinking) ___________ in the night shadows after the nearby gun battle.
7. Are there any (extras) ___________ in connection with this position?
8. Some students are (disposed) ___________ to put off writing their term papers until the last minute.
9. The information for my term paper was (drawn) ___________ from several different sources.
10. The unexpected announcement of a quiz usually (brings out) ___________ sighs of unhappiness from some class members.

Check your answers with the Key on p. 447.

B Score: ________

C Score: ________

Enter your scores on p. 420.

29

How to Work for a Rotten Boss

DR. JOYCE BROTHERS

Problems! We all have them. Whatever your problem, you need a solution—sometimes desperately. That's where reading comes in. Someone, sometime, has probably written an article or book providing a solution to any problem you may have. Take the following article, for example. Sometime, unfortunately, you'll probably have to deal with a rotten boss. See how reading can help. You'll even find mention of a book, in case you need additional help.

BEGIN TIMING

Want to send silent party guests rushing into riproaring conversation? Well, toss out the topic of rotten bosses, sit back and watch the sparks fly.

Do you have an impossible boss? One who can't be pleased, no matter what you do? With whom it's useless to try to reason? Who's never satisfied? Who takes all the credit for your work and gives you nothing but grief? Is your boss vague about what she or he wants done yet fires people who don't do it?

If you have a boss who's sending you up in smoke every day, you're probably not smiling often or sleeping much. You're not alone, but you need to develop ways to cope with it all.

There really are such "killer" bosses—too many of them, of both sexes. If you're stuck with one of these daily nightmares, you might: A) Get a new boss (not likely). B) Get a new job (not easy). Or C) Get a new attitude that will allow you to cope, so you can manage your boss—and your reactions to the boss—in the most effective and satisfying manner possible. (Get the message?)

In the '80s, at the Center for Creative Leadership in Greensboro, N.C., the behavioral researchers Michael Lombardo, Morgan McCall, Jr., and Ann Morrison listened to executives' stories about their bosses. These recollections showed that most successful executives had at one time or another suffered under an "impossible" boss and—believe it or not—profited from it.

A good way to start is to learn about the demands your boss has to meet: In addition to you, how many people report to him or her? How many pressures are put on your boss by his or her bosses? Does your boss just want to get the job done, or is gaining greater power also on the agenda? How can you help?

Above all, learn your boss' schedule and rhythms: What time of day is he or she least pressed and most likely to be relaxed enough to help you with a problem? When is the boss most pressed—and best left alone?

Some bosses are more difficult than others. Here are a few types:

The Bulldog He not only takes responsibility, he sinks his teeth into it. He barks commands, won't admit to making a mistake and won't delegate. Since he's overworked from doing everything himself, it's a quality he will appreciate in you (although he probably never will tell you so). To cope, you must find ways to prove to him that you too are responsible. You also must learn to stand your ground—without losing your cool.

The Overbearing Blowhard This boss is on a constant ego trip. If you do very well, he takes all the credit; if you do badly, he shouts out the blame.

The Heel-Grinder This one likes to bully and humiliate. At the least provocation, she grinds you into the ground. In such an extreme case, endure till you can quit conveniently.

The successful executives and near-perfect bosses interviewed by Lombardo, McCall, and Morrison said that coping with bad bosses had helped them form their own best-management approaches. They also cited as bonuses learning to have patience and to deal with conflicts constructively, instead of destroying the troublesome relationship.

Those are hard lessons to master while trying to survive and get ahead, yet most of the successful executives interviewed had managed it. Even so, a few did quit—but only after realizing they couldn't find it rewarding enough to continue working with a very difficult boss.

Before you quit or your rotten boss retires, here are tips from Lombardo, McCall, and Morrison to help you cope:

- *Never forget—he or she is your boss.* It's your job to do the work the way the boss wants it done. You are paid to do your job in a way that makes the boss's job easier. You are there to remove obstacles for the boss—not to be one.
- *Management will judge you by how well you get along with your boss.* And that judgment will affect your progress. Working with—or around—a rotten boss teaches you how to set priorities, neutralize potentially explosive situations and choose your moments.
- *Don't try to change the boss.* There is only one person in this world you should attempt to control, and that person is you. Instead of trying to change the boss, try adjusting your *own* behavior.

The boss may be 100 percent to blame for the conditions under which you struggle. All the same, you are 100 percent responsible for how you react to that boss and for where you go from where you are.

Rotten bosses come in an infinite number of varieties—most of them known to Robert Bramson, a management consultant in Oakland, Calif., and an author. His latest book, *Coping with Difficult Bosses* (Birch Lane Press), is culled from fourteen years of interviews and consulting work. In it, Bramson says "to cope" means "to contend on equal terms." He also says bad bosses have learned through difficult behavior to take advantage of others: Experience shows that bullying usually elicits either a cowering, back-pedaling response or an angry, explosive one. Either response plays into the hands of the difficult boss who wants to be in control.

Bramson adds that the bullying boss learns better behavior once it's clear that you respect him or her as the boss and that *you* have self-respect too. He also advises:

- *Stand your ground.* If the boss cuts in on you while you are speaking, cope by calmly saying: "I'm sorry, Sam, but you interrupted me." Then resume talking.
- *Don't argue, but do disagree.* Catch the boss in an error? Don't say, "You're wrong!" Say something like, "I think that at this point I may disagree with you, Sam, but tell me more about what you're thinking." This way, you are neither argumentative nor afraid.

"Attack" type bosses include:

The Ogre This boss likes to yell and to appear powerful. Often a quick thinker (though not always right), Ogres are unsure of their own value. They need to feel power over others, and they admire strength in those who don't threaten them. When an Ogre starts to bully you, if you can literally stand tall without declaring war (you can't win), he or she usually will back down.

The Fire Eater This boss seems emotionally uneven—prone to mood swings that may begin with grumblings and end with eruptions. When you see a storm is brewing, try to take a breather. Later, try to get the boss's attention, say you value his or her opinion and get back to basics. Be observant—try to chart those bad moods to avoid confrontations.

Then there are those bosses who just "aren't there" for you. They include:

The Super-Delegator This type seems to give you lots of responsibility, but, even when pressed, he or she won't say what's expected of you. Later, this boss might fire you—for not measuring up to expectations! To cope, involve this boss in all you do; give reports on progress and results; get constant feedback, coaxing out his or her guidelines. Give good-boss training!

The Staller This one is so afraid of stress—anybody's—that he or she puts off telling others anything they might find stressful. If the Staller's boss says *you* should be told to improve, you might never hear it. Distressing you would simply make the Staller too tense. (Some way to lose your job!) To cope with the Staller, be reassuring. With questions, get The Staller to tell you how you can improve your work. Then act as if the advice is a calming gift.

Last but not least are the types of bosses who hold the reins too tightly. Here's one:

The Perfectionist This boss *must* be flawless and sees mistakes everywhere. To cope, admit a mistake and tell the Perfectionist what you've learned from it—several times, if necessary. Show the boss that you want to be tops too.

To cope, learn to follow and to lead; let your relationship work for you.

Length: 1350 words.
Reading Time: ________
See Conversion Table, p. 421.
Enter WPM Rate on p. 416.

29 How to Work for a Rotten Boss

COMPREHENSION CHECK

GETTING THE FACTS

1. If you have a rotten boss, you're probably not often (a) singing. (b) relaxing. (c) eating well. (d) smiling. — 1. ____

2. The Center for Creative Leadership is in (a) Greensboro. (b) Georgetown. (c) Memphis. (d) Geneva. — 2. ____

3. You're expressly advised to learn your boss's (a) hobbies. (b) sports interests. (c) schedule and rhythms. (d) family situation and members. — 3. ____

4. *Coping with Difficult Bosses* was written by (a) Michael Lombardo. (b) Robert Bramson. (c) Ann Morrison. (d) William Moore. — 4. ____

5. The Staller is said to be afraid of (a) change. (b) failure. (c) stress. (d) his or her boss. — 5. ____

GETTING THE MEANING

6. The main focus is on (a) working. (b) manipulating. (c) coping. (d) producing. — 6. ____

7. This selection is addressed primarily to (a) job-holders. (b) job-seekers. (c) executives. (d) the general public. — 7. ____

8. The author apparently draws chiefly from (a) her work experience. (b) logic. (c) popular opinion. (d) authorities. — 8. ____

9. The eight types of bosses discussed are arranged (a) from least to most common. (b) in several categories. (c) according to sex. (d) from least to most difficult to work for. — 9. ____

10. You would infer the author would consider which rule to be most helpful? (a) be patient (b) understand your boss (c) never disagree with your boss (d) control your boss — 10. ____

Check your answers with the Key on p. 452. Give yourself 10 points for each one right and enter your comprehension score on p. 415.

Comprehension Score: ________

NAME ______________ CLASS ______________ DATE ______________

30 The Joy of Quitting

WORD POWER WORKOUT

A. LEANING ON CONTEXT

In each of the blanks provided, place the letter that precedes the best definition of the underlined word in context to the left.

Words in Context	**Definitions**
1. ____ least obnoxious way	a. false
2. ____ to be inoffensive	b. flash of insight
3. ____ a serial quitter	c. summary
4. ____ might have been blacklisted	d. hateful
5. ____ as a disloyal employee	e. not disgusting
6. ____ tenure has declined	f. mark of disgrace
7. ____ had an epiphany	g. systematic
8. ____ used to be guidelines	h. standards of action
9. ____ a reverse stigma	i. refused employment
10. ____ compendium of quitting styles	j. position-holding rights

Check your answers with the Key on p. 442 before going on. Give yourself 10 points for each one right and enter your score on the chart under A on p. 420. Review any that you have missed.

A Score: ________

Pronunciation aids: **7. uh-PIF-uh-nee**
10. kom-PEN-dee-um

B. LEANING ON PARTS

Scribere means "to write." Whenever you see a *scrib(e)* or *scrip(t)* in a word, look for the meaning "write." Fill in the following blanks.

1. You fill a doctor's pre____________ at a drug store.
2. A handwritten paper is rightly called a manu____________.
3. The radio announcer read the statement from a typed ____________.
4. I have sub____________ to that magazine for three years.
5. To write down details about someone's appearance is to de____________ her.

C. MAKING THE WORDS YOURS

In each blank below, enter the most appropriate word from the ten words in context in the first exercise, substituting it for the word(s) in parentheses. Use these words: *blacklisted, compendium, disloyal, epiphany, guidelines, inoffensive, obnoxious, serial, stigma, tenure.*

1. It would be (false) ______________ of you not to vote along straight party lines.
2. Suddenly, thanks to the (flash of insight) ______________ the general knew exactly what to do.
3. That (hateful) ______________ rumor should be stopped immediately.
4. I need a (summary) ______________ of all the actions taken this year.
5. That's the third murder by strangulation; there must be a (systematic) ______________ murderer on the loose.
6. That one small misstep left a (mark of disgrace) ______________ that followed her the rest of her life.
7. What the speaker meant was (not disgusting) ______________ and should never be misinterpreted.
8. The worker was (refused employment) ______________ because of his negative attitude.
9. Are any (standards of action) ______________ available for handling this procedure?
10. The university regulations regarding (position-holding rights) ______________ are complex.

Check your answers with the Key on p. 447.

B Score: ________

C Score: ________

Enter your scores on p. 420.

30

The Joy of Quitting

CORA DANIELS AND CAROL VINZANT

If you need encouragement to quit, get Johnny Paycheck's famous worker's anthem. The title? "Take This Job and Shove It." But if you don't like that idea, read **Take This Job and Love It.** ***Remember, however, that people who look ahead tend to get ahead. Even if you haven't yet developed sufficient know-how to be in demand, look ahead to the time when you will have. It's a welcome change from working for a rotten boss. Read on for the details.***

BEGIN TIMING

Jonathan M. spent all morning trying to come up with the least obnoxious way to quit his job at a major advertising agency—a job that had nearly doubled his pay and came with a big window office. But there was really no graceful way to quit on the third day, especially after he had insisted that the company buy him over $2,000 worth of art supplies. So he gave up trying to be inoffensive and simply left a Post-it note on his door for his boss: "Dave—I've walked out. I'm going back to freelancing. Don't bother calling. Jonathan."

Jonathan, who has quit three jobs in two years, is a serial quitter. Once he might have been blacklisted as a disloyal employee. Not anymore. Jonathan, you see, has no trouble finding new jobs to quit.

In this prosperous age, changing jobs is as easy—and requires about as much emotional investment—as shedding an old pair of shoes. It can even be entertaining. Recruiters tell tales of quitters who gave the news with singing telegrams, in a cake with a resignation letter inside, and by writing I QUIT in the snow on the boss' windshield. It's no secret that Americans don't expect enduring loyalty of any kind these days. Marriages end. Companies lay off longtime workers. People don Yankees hats whenever they have a winning season. And in this rip-roaring economy—unemployment at a 30-year low!—workers find the strength to quit over and over again.

Thanks to the workers' market, the National Quit Rate—the percentage of people currently unemployed who left their job voluntarily—is now at 14.7%, the highest in almost ten years. The average worker goes through about nine jobs by age 32, according to the Bureau of Labor Statistics. For workers in some industries, notably tech, quitting is literally an annual event. The *average job tenure in* IT has shrunk to about 13 months, down from about 18 months two years ago, says Ilya Talman, a headhunter with Roy Talman & Associates.

Gen Xers quit often, *but* job *tenure has declined* among both younger and older workers. In 1983 younger workers (we'll look at men aged 25 to 34) averaged 3.4 years on the job, according to the Employee Benefit Research Institute. Today they are gone in three. At the same time, the average tenure among older workers (men 55 to 64) has plunged from 17 years to 12 years.

"People quit the minute any kind of unhappiness creeps into their job," says Amy Fried, a new-media recruiter with Roz Goldfarb Associates. "And it's the smart thing to do. In this economy there's no need to be unhappy."

Take Robert. He had complained to his bosses at a Philadelphia homebuilder that his salary and job title didn't reflect the new tasks he was asked to take on, but to no avail. One morning after he'd worked there for 13 months, he had an epiphany: "I just sat there and thought, 'I don't have to do this anymore.'" He immediately started packing his pictures and personal things into his car. Two months later he was working at another builder in a job with more responsibility, but also more money.

Simply stated, being a quitter is no longer a career killer. "There used to be guidelines that said if a person had more than five jobs in a career or more than three jobs in ten years, they were a job hopper," says Patrick S. Pittard, CEO of Heidrick & Struggles International, an executive search firm. "Those days are over."

In fact, loyal workers may face a reverse stigma in these swinging times, say recruiters and corporate human resources people. Gordon Miller is the author of the subtly titled *Quit Your Job Often and Get Big Raises!* and runs a career-coaching firm in Denver called the Career Edge. Miller says that the person who has been with the same company for 15 years has a harder time getting a new job than the one who has had a half-dozen jobs during that time. That's especially true in the fast-changing tech world, where potential employers sometimes view long-timers as having out-of-date skills, says Reginna Burns, an HR executive for AT&T Global.

So don't just quit for the fun of telling the boss off—quit for profit. Miller's strategy: Quit while you're ahead, and quit often. That's what he did, leaving four jobs in five years. Quitting just after you've closed a major deal or gotten that corner office can increase your salary by about 20% with each jump, he claims.

Evan Harris, who wrote *The Quit,* a compendium of quitting styles and techniques, would call Miller's method the "Achieve and Vanish." For those who need a little help to take the plunge, a veritable quitting industry has sprung up. Now you can read any number of self-help quitting books or go to a Website (www.Iquit.org) that will e-mail your resignation to your boss.

Then, of course, there are quitting professionals to help you get up the nerve. Denise Rene runs I Quit, a weekly seminar in which she leads a following of a dozen or so pre- and post-quitters in chanting and meditation on their spiritual journey to "break the pattern" of working. (Did we mention this is in L.A.?) A typical exercise she recommends: Sit with your legs crossed, cup your hands together, and picture your boss as a tiny holograph. Close your eyes and speak to your boss. Then blow him or her away as you would a speck of dust. Repeat two to three times. "Quitting is a process," says Rene. "Right now I'm quitting sugar."

That some people might have trouble quitting is understandable, even in a great economy. It's hard to walk out the door when your company is desperately clinging to you. All HR people know that it's much less expensive to keep an employee than to hire a new one, so they'll try anything. In one instance, a client of recruiter Fried had a $100,000-a-year job at a Website developer that was bleeding employees. When she resigned, the boss offered her $100,000 to stay for another three months. It turned out to be an offer she couldn't refuse (and then, after cashing in, she left). Or take the case of one software engineer who was trying to move from a Web portal to Netscape. At first his bosses made the customary offer of more money. Then things got weird: His bosses called his wife. They wrote a letter for his signature stating that he preferred to stay at his old job and helpfully volunteered to fax it to Netscape. He quit anyway.

That's generally the right decision once you've announced a departure, says recruiter Talman. Last-minute offers of more cash or other compensation tend to be temporary solutions that don't address the deeper reasons for dissatisfaction. "It tends to postpone the inevitable," he says.

But rest assured, quitting gets easier the more you do it. Some might call it addictive. "It's much easier to recruit someone from their employer the second time," says recruiter Pittard. "When you find out the world doesn't come crashing down when you change employers, you wonder if there's something even better out there."

So what makes people start looking in the first place? The short answer is bad management. "People don't quit because of money," says Bev Kaye, a retention expert and co-author of *Love 'Em or Lose 'Em.* "People leave bad bosses."

Luckily for those out there working for idiotic or lazy or psychotic bosses, demographics are on your side. This rash of quitting will not quit, human resources experts say, even in a recession. As baby-boomers start to retire, the positions they vacate will create an employee vacuum, says John Putzier, president of FirStep, an HR consulting firm. So are you ready to quit yet? We are.

Length: 1310 words.
Reading Time: __________
See Conversion Table, p. 421.
Enter WPM Rate on p. 416.

30 The Joy of Quitting

COMPREHENSION CHECK

GETTING THE FACTS

1. Jonathan had a job at a major (a) advertising agency. (b) brokerage firm. (c) publishing company. (d) insurance company. 1. ____

2. The average worker goes through about how many jobs by age 32? (a) 7 (b) 8 (c) 9 (d) 10 2. ____

3. Loyal workers are said to (a) have an advantage. (b) make added money. (c) be at a disadvantage. (d) receive additional benefits. 3. ____

4. Specific mention is made of (a) e-mail. (b) seminars on quitting. (c) books about quitting. (d) all of the preceding. 4. ____

5. Quitting comes about primarily from (a) poor pay. (b) bad working conditions. (c) lack of responsibility. (d) bad management. 5. ____

GETTING THE MEANING

6. The main idea is to get you to (a) know how to quit. (b) see when you should quit. (c) see why you should quit. (d) accept the idea of quitting. 6. ____

7. The opening episode about Jonathan primarily points up (a) the desirability of quitting. (b) the difficulty of quitting. (c) the reason for quitting. (d) how to quit. 7. ____

8. To convince us, the authors rely largely on (a) opinions of authorities. (b) comparison. (c) reason. (d) examples. 8. ____

9. What word best describes this selection? (a) inspirational (b) dramatic (c) instructive (d) stimulating 9. ____

10. The tone of this selection is primarily (a) sarcastic. (b) forceful. (c) humorous. (d) matter-of-fact. 10. ____

Check your answers with the Key on p. 452. Give yourself 10 points for each one right and enter your comprehension score on p. 415.

Comprehension Score: ________

NAME ____________ CLASS ____________ DATE ____________

31 Reading Entire Selections More Effectively

WORD POWER WORKOUT

A. LEANING ON CONTEXT

In each of the blanks provided, place the letter that precedes the best definition of the underlined word in context to the left.

Words in Context	**Definitions**
1. _____ main and <u>subordinate</u> points	a. depend
2. _____ facts and <u>supporting</u> material	b. stylistic
3. _____ that word <u>captures</u> the primary role	c. minor
4. _____ to <u>extract</u> it	d. assist, help
5. _____ their <u>chief</u> function	e. substantiating
6. _____ <u>lean</u> heavily on paragraphing	f. seizes
7. _____ the <u>rhetorical</u> device of balance	g. remove
8. _____ from the <u>obscure</u> into the obvious	h. little known, vague
9. _____ will <u>facilitate</u> progress	i. main
10. _____ a split-second <u>glance</u> at an outline	j. brief look

Check your answers with the Key on p. 442 before going on. Give yourself 10 points for each one right and enter your score on the chart under A on p. 420. Review any that you have missed.

A Score: ________

Pronunciation aids: 7. rih-TOR-ih-cul

B. LEANING ON PARTS

Ponere means "put" or "place." Whenever you see *pon, posit,* or *pos(t)* in a word, look for that meaning. Supply a form of *ponere* in each blank below.

1. When a notice is placed on a bulletin board, it is ____________ there.
2. If you'd put your shoulders back, you'd have better ____________.
3. The meeting was post____________, putting it a week later.
4. Take this money to the bank and de____________ it in your account.
5. You'll need more ____________ stamps to send your letters overseas.

C. MAKING THE WORDS YOURS

In each blank below, enter the most appropriate word from the ten words in context in the first exercise, substituting it for the word(s) in parentheses. Use these words: *captured, chief, extracted, facilitates, glance, lean, obscure, rhetorical, subordinate, supporting.*

1. A small child will (depend) ____________ on his parents for help.
2. A telephone (assists) ____________ speech communication.
3. She took a (brief look) ____________ at the magazine before discarding it.
4. Teachers often use (stylistic) ____________ devices when lecturing.
5. An answer that is (vague) ____________ can cause misunderstandings.
6. Smoking is a (main) ____________ cause of lung cancer.
7. The dentist (removed) ____________ the man's wisdom tooth.
8. The police (seized) ____________ the criminal.
9. The officials discussed the (minor) ____________ issues first.
10. She did not give any (substantiating) ____________ evidence for her opinion.

Check your answers with the Key on p. 448.

B Score: ________

C Score: ________

Enter your scores on p. 420.

31

Reading Entire Selections More Effectively

BEGIN TIMING

FIDENITY. What does that mean? You don't know! Well, don't reach for your dictionary. You won't find it there. That word captures in a nutshell the primary role of organization. But you have to reorganize those letters. Rearrange them into IDENTIFY. Yes, the role of organization is to help you identify the essentials. It should help you spot all-important ideas, facts, and supporting material for an entire article, chapter, or unit.

But to identify is not enough. Visualize if you will a thousand pounds of crushed ore. It's not enough to identify the presence of gold in that ore. You need to extract it. After all, it's not the thousand pounds of ore that are important. It's the seventy ounces of gold it contains. But, can you imagine trying to extract something you don't even know is there? No. Keep both in mind. First, identify. Next, extract, the second of the two roles of organization.

What is the role of outlining? It's to make organization clear—to help you identify and extract essentials. The outline form sets major points out and shrinks supporting material into a clearly visible subordinate position. Take a split-second glance at an outline. You can determine the main points in no time.

Furthermore, notice what making an outline does. It forces you to think in terms of main and subordinate points. It forces you to go through the mental gymnastics needed to discover and identify the author's plan. Writing the outline proves how skillfully you can extract the essentials. Such a combination of reading and thinking contributes much to comprehension.

How is organization revealed? As you read, what signs or special devices mark the writer's plan? Reading is just the reverse of writing. The author sends; the reader receives. The author uses certain devices to help the reader. Just looking at them more closely will facilitate progress. There are three kinds of devices: *typographical, rhetorical,* and *verbal.*

Take typographical devices. Think what can be done with type. You can put an important point in CAPITAL LETTERS. See how they stand out on the page. Something a bit less important can be set in **boldface** type. This too stands out. Even *italics* differ enough from regular type to be spotted easily on the page.

Now for rhetorical devices, turn instead to *repetition, parallelism,* or *balance.*

Repeating a word or phrase helps the reader fit what is said into a more orderly, easily remembered pattern. Here's an illustration. Do you know the three secrets of a successful speech? Stand up! Speak up! Shut up! The repetition of *s*'s in *stand, speak,* and *shut* puts this device into neat, orderly form.

Lincoln's government, "of the people, by the people, and for the people," relies on parallelism as well as on repetition. Each of these phrases is in parallel form—preposition-article-noun—to accent the threefold pattern he had in mind. Repetition of "the people" helps still further to make the phrase unforgettable.

With the rhetorical device of balance, think of the old-fashioned scales or balance. Or just think of what you do to balance a pencil across your finger. It has to be placed right in the middle in order to balance. Similarly, balance in a sentence has to have an exact middle spot, both sides equal. Patrick Henry did it nicely. Listen to him. "Give me liberty or give me death!"

That word *or* marks the middle, or fulcrum. And on either side exactly three words to balance three words. Furthermore, the repetition of "give me . . . give me" makes it even stronger. You know he's talking about two alternatives.

Verbal devices make up the third and last of these special road signs. Dozens of English words have the following as their chief function: marking transitions, indicating methods of development, or noting outline form. The word *another,* for example, moves the reader easily from one point to the next, a real help in outlining. *Consequently* suggests a cause-effect development. And such words as *first, next,* and *finally* strongly indicate outline form.

All these devices—typographical, rhetorical, and verbal—function as highway signs to a driver. They keep us on the road.

Still another major way to determine organization is through paragraph structure. In each paragraph look for (1) a topic sentence or idea and (2) supporting details. Don't look for two main points in one paragraph. Look for them in two. And if a writer mentions three reasons, expect three paragraphs, if the reasons are important. If one reason is complex or multisided, look for two or more paragraphs to suggest subdivisions of that major point. In short, lean heavily on paragraphing as you outline.

What does organization contribute? Why bother with it, anyway? Well, you get two sets of benefits. For one, you open the way to capturing main ideas and relationships between parts. For another, you gain improved aids to both understanding and remembering.

When you complete your outline, getting the main ideas is no longer a problem. You've reduced the 1,000-word chapter to a mere handful of essentials—the gold.

And the outline lets you see the relationship between parts very clearly. Subordinate parts are in subordinate position in outline form.

Finally, outlining does amazing things for understanding and remembering. Getting details and understanding them are not the same. Organization adds understanding to details. Furthermore, you will remember CAPITALS, **boldface type,** and *italics* better because they are grouped in orderly fashion under the heading *typographical.* If Patrick Henry had not used balance, think of the added difficulty of remembering exactly what he said. Suppose he said, "Give me liberty, or I'd just as soon be killed." That rephrasing doesn't remember itself. The other does.

So, to summarize, make outlining your follow-up for reading. It will help you identify and extract the essentials. It will help you understand and remember them much better. It will turn NEMAGIN into MEANING, the obscure into the obvious.

Length: 1000 words.
Reading Time: __________
See Conversion Table, p. 421.
Enter WPM Rate on p. 416.

31 Reading Entire Selections More Effectively

▶ COMPREHENSION CHECK

GETTING THE FACTS

1. You are told that the role of organization is to help you (a) identify the essentials. (b) note interrelationships. (c) speed your reading. (d) write better. 1. ____

2. Reading is referred to as (a) the be-all and end-all. (b) the reverse of writing. (c) drinking in information. (d) a mental adventure. 2. ____

3. Capital letters belong under the heading (a) typographical. (b) rhetorical. (c) verbal. (d) personal. 3. ____

4. Devices to reveal organization are likened to (a) code signals. (b) highway signs. (c) radar images. (d) recipes. 4. ____

5. Outlining is said to turn the obscure into the (a) obvious. (b) clear. (c) commonplace. (d) plain. 5. ____

GETTING THE MEANING

6. The main focus of the article is on (a) what organization contributes to reading. (b) how organization is revealed. (c) outlining techniques. (d) the role of rhetorical devices. 6. ____

7. The FIDENITY paragraph primarily shows (a) one purpose of organization. (b) how to organize. (c) the simplicity of good organization. (d) the importance of organization. 7. ____

8. Apparently Lincoln was a master in the use of (a) outlining. (b) parallelism. (c) balance. (d) personal appeal. 8. ____

9. The word *because* suggests what kinds of development? (a) logical (b) personal (c) factual (d) detailed 9. ____

10. To remember something it should help particularly to (a) outline it. (b) write it. (c) reread it. (d) recite it aloud. 10. ____

Check your answers with the Key on p. 452. Give yourself 10 points for each one right and enter your comprehension score on p. 415.

Comprehension Score: ________

MAKING THE APPLICATION

To practice applying what you learned about organization in this selection, fill in the blank outline of the selection, looking back as often as you like to clarify your thinking.

I. ______________________________

A. ______________________________

B. ______________________________

II. ______________________________

III. ______________________________

A. ______________________________

1. ______________________________

a. ______________________________

b. ______________________________

c. ______________________________

2. ______________________________

a. ______________________________

b. ______________________________

c. ______________________________

3. ______________________________

a. ______________________________

b. ______________________________

c. ______________________________

B. ______________________________

1. ______________________________

2. ______________________________

IV. ______________________________

A. ______________________________

1. ______________________________

2. ______________________________

B. ______________________________

1. ______________________________

2. ______________________________

V. ______________________________

Outline answers are on page 439.

NAME ____________ CLASS ____________ DATE ____________

32 He Survived His Own Funeral

WORD POWER WORKOUT

A. LEANING ON CONTEXT

In each of the blanks provided, place the letter that precedes the best definition of the underlined word in context to the left.

Words in Context	Definitions
1. ____ embarked on a fishing trip	a. took turns
2. ____ capsized their boat	b. set out
3. ____ waves had subsided	c. twinge
4. ____ drifted aimlessly	d. making sore by rubbing
5. ____ the teenager alternated	e. upset
6. ____ massive sea beast	f. kind
7. ____ performing benevolent acts	g. become less violent
8. ____ pang of regret	h. bulky
9. ____ some dehydration	i. without purpose
10. ____ chafing against his life jacket	j. water loss

Check your answers with the Key on p. 442 before going on. Give yourself 10 points for each one right and enter your score on the chart under A on p. 420. Review any that you have missed.

A Score: ________

Pronunciation aids: 7. be-NEV-uh-lent

B. LEANING ON PARTS

Mittere means "send." When you see *mit(t)* or *mis(s)* in a word, look for that meaning. Fill in the following blanks with forms of *mittere.*

1. When you send in a formal report, you are said to sub____________ it.
2. The __________ sent toward the armed camp was launched from a sub.
3. Our minister was sent to Africa as a ____________.
4. Money sent to pay a bill is called a re____________.
5. Smoke sent out of a car exhaust is e____________ from it.

C. MAKING THE WORDS YOURS

In each blank below, enter the most appropriate word from the ten words in context in the first exercise, substituting it for the word(s) in parentheses. Use these words: *aimlessly, alternated, benevolent, capsized, chafing, dehydration, embarked, massive, pang, subsided.*

1. When the hurricane wind had (become less active) ____________, we went out to see the damage.
2. The nurse (took turns) ____________ in coming to the two schools.
3. We soon (set out) ____________ on our new enterprise.
4. My poorly fitting shoes started (making sore by rubbing) ____________ my feet.
5. After walking for several hours, I felt a sharp (twinge) ____________ of hunger.
6. When the wind (upset) ____________ our boat, we lost all our fishing gear.
7. We were afraid she was (without purpose) ____________ walking around the town.
8. For years a (bulky) ____________ wall separated the two parts of Berlin.
9. Walking in the desert will soon bring on symptoms of (water loss) ____________.
10. The candidate tried to build an image of being a (kind) ____________ office-seeker.

Check your answers with the Key on p. 448.

B Score: ________

C Score: ________

Enter your scores on p. 420.

32

He Survived His Own Funeral

BRAD STEIGER AND SHERRY HANSON-STEIGER

This selection is from the book* Animal Miracles, *a series of true stories in which an animal always provides the miracle. The stories are not told by professional writers but by the very people who lived through the experience. Miracles are unbelievable. If they weren't, they wouldn't be miracles.

BEGIN TIMING

On January 15, 1990, eighteen-year-old Lotty Stevens and a friend embarked on a fishing trip from Port Vila, Vanuatu, an island in the South Pacific. Although both young men were experienced fishermen, they were caught off guard by a sudden storm that capsized their boat.

Helplessly, Lotty and his friend were tossed about by waves as they desperately sought to stay above the water. Fortunately for Lotty, it was his habit always to slip on a life jacket when fishing in the ocean.

Later, when the sea was calmer and the waves had subsided, he looked around the wreckage of their boat for his friend. After calling his name for several minutes, Lotty was forced to conclude that his companion had drowned during the storm.

For three days, Lotty clung to the overturned boat, bobbing lazily up and down as the wreckage drifted aimlessly. Then, with only his life jacket for support, he decided to swim in the direction in which he felt Port Vila lay.

For two days, the teenager alternated swimming as hard as he could, then floating and resting, praying all the while for a miracle. If only some fishing boats would come upon him and rescue him.

He tried hard to fight against despair. He knew that even a large ship could pass relatively close by and not be able to see his head bobbing in the vast ocean.

Toward the end of the fifth day after the raging storm had sent him into the sea, Lotty Stevens got his miracle. He had been floating with his eyes closed when he felt something big lift him from the water. There beneath him was a giant stingray, at least eleven feet long—including its six-foot poisonous tail. And the massive sea beast was taking him for a ride.

At first Lotty was frightened. Stingrays were not known for performing benevolent acts.

But soon, he later told journalists, he began to think of the giant sea creature as his friend. He would pat it as if it were a dog. A big, slimy dog with a hard and strong body.

One afternoon, after several days as a grateful hitchhiker, Lotty suddenly found himself dumped in the water as the stingray dove and disappeared. Lotty shook his head to clear the sea from his eyes—then wished that he hadn't. An enormous shark was heading straight for him.

Dear Lord, he silently screamed, why had his friend left him now? Was the stingray afraid of the killer beast coming toward him?

Then the teenager saw a second shark—and a third. Suddenly Lotty's angel of the sea reappeared, swimming in a fast circle around him. Amazingly, the three sharks turned fin and swam away. Apparently they feared the stingray's long, poisonous tail more than they felt the desire to feed on a human.

Lotty gave his thanks to God and the stingray that had once again saved his life. The great sea creature came alongside Lotty and nudged him, so he climbed back on board its strong back.

Until the joyous morning when he at last sighted land, the teenager survived for eight more days by catching fish from atop his seaborne savior. The stingray also spotted the beach, for it headed for the shallow water and slid Lotty off near the shoreline.

Lotty remembered staggering like a drunken man, then collapsing on the sandy beach. The next morning he was awakened by a fisherman.

It took the teenager several moments to realize that he was not dreaming and that he was actually once again on solid land. As he slowly came to appreciate the fact that he was no longer in danger of drowning or of being eaten by sharks, he also realized with a sudden pang of regret that he hadn't had a chance to thank his remarkable friend from the ocean for saving his life.

The fisherman helped Lotty to a doctor, and later, a hospital on the main island pronounced the teenager in good shape except for some dehydration and a few sores from saltwater and chafing against his life jacket. When he telephoned his family, their grief turned to joy beyond understanding, for they had already held a funeral service for him. It had been twenty-one days since Lotty and his friend had disappeared in the ocean storm.

Lotty does not argue with those who would seek to disbelieve the facts of his remarkable rescue. He is living proof that somehow he survived twenty-one boatless days adrift in the ocean. In the opinion of Lotty Stevens and his family, that most certainly qualifies as a miracle.

Length: 770 words.

Reading Time: __________

See Conversion Table, p. 421.

Enter WPM Rate on p. 416.

32 He Survived His Own Funeral

COMPREHENSION CHECK

GETTING THE FACTS

1. Lotty was how old at this time? (a) 16 (b) 17 (c) 18 (d) 19 — 1. ____

2. The stingray was at least how may feet long? (a) 8 (b) 9 (c) 10 (d) 11 — 2. ____

3. Lotty soon began to think of the stingray as a (a) helper. (b) friend. (c) pet. (d) life-saver. — 3. ____

4. Lotty was awakened on the beach by a (a) beach-comber. (b) hiker. (c) fisherman. (d) boy. — 4. ____

5. How many days did Lotty survive on the ocean? (a) 20 (b) 21 (c) 22 (d) 23 — 5. ____

GETTING THE MEANING

6. This selection is mainly to (a) describe Lotty's life-saver. (b) describe the miracle. (c) show Lotty's resourceful-ness. (d) point up Lotty's amazing health. — 6. ____

7. This selection is primarily to (a) entertain. (b) make clear. (c) convince. (d) teach. — 7. ____

8. This selection is organized (a) on a general-to-specific basis. (b) chronologically. (c) logically. (d) on a problem-solution basis. — 8. ____

9. You would infer Lotty's own attitude is best described as (a) pessimistic. (b) proud. (c) uncertain. (d) optimistic. — 9. ____

10. The style of this selection is best described as (a) lively. (b) dramatic. (c) friendly. (d) straightforward. — 10. ____

Check your answers with the Key on p. 452. Give yourself 10 points for each one right and enter your comprehension score on p. 415.

Comprehension Score: ________

NAME ______________ CLASS ______________ DATE ______________

33 Ten Football Stars and Yours Truly

WORD POWER WORKOUT

A. LEANING ON CONTEXT

In each of the blanks provided, place the letter that precedes the best definition of the underlined word in context to the left.

Words in Context	Definitions
1. _____ expression was quizzical	a. dedicated
2. _____ I feigned sleep	b. wildly insane
3. _____ I was a devoted athlete	c. indicate
4. _____ I felt novocained	d. questioning
5. _____ These shirts would designate	e. made numb
6. _____ I mustered up the courage	f. drugged
7. _____ I was petrified with fright	g. pretended
8. _____ I was in a kind of trance	h. specialized vocabulary
9. _____ My maniacal rompings had	i. daze, stupor
10. _____ and football jargon	j. summoned

Check your answers with the Key on p. 442 before going on. Give yourself 10 points for each one right and enter your score on the chart under A on p. 420. Review any that you have missed.

A Score: ________

Pronunciation aids: 2. FAYN'D
9. muh-NY-uh-cul

B. LEANING ON PARTS

Ferre means "bear" or "carry." When you see *fer* or *lat* in a word, look for those meanings. Fill in the blanks below with a form of *ferre.*

1. If you bear or endure pain, you can be said to suf_____________.
2. If a company moves you from one city to another, it trans_________ you.
3. A boat carrying passengers from shore to shore is a _____________ boat.
4. Rich soil that bears abundantly is known as _____________ soil.
5. For this job you must be able to trans_____________ from French to English.

C. MAKING THE WORDS YOURS

In each blank below, enter the most appropriate word from the ten words in context in the first exercise, substituting it for the word(s) in parentheses. Use these words: *designate, devoted, feigned, jargon, maniacal, mustered, novocained, petrified, quizzical, trance.*

1. He's a (dedicated) __________ follower of his home town football team.
2. One employee (pretended) _____________ sickness so often that she was finally fired.
3. On the insurance application form you need to (indicate) _____________ your beneficiary.
4. When the tornado funnel cloud touched down, some people were (made numb) _____________ with fright.
5. Understanding medical (specialized vocabulary) _____________ is a real problem for most people.
6. After being awake for twenty hours straight I felt (drugged) __________.
7. The (questioning) _____________ look on the driver's face told me she wondered why she was being stopped.
8. After suffering a bad accident you may well feel in a kind of (daze, stupor) _____________.
9. The demonstrator's (wildly insane) _____________ outburst attracted immediate attention from the police.
10. In the large class one shy student finally (summoned) _____________ up enough confidence to raise a question.

Check your answers with the Key on p. 448.

B Score: ________

C Score: ________

Enter your scores on p. 420.

33

Ten Football Stars and Yours Truly

WARREN ROBERTSON

Chief Justice Earl Warren once said, "I always turn to the sports pages first, which record people's accomplishments. The front page has nothing but man's failures." Here's some sport-page reading about an unusual, unbelievable accomplishment! Perhaps it's really true that thinking you can means you can. Just think you're a star. Ready for the kick-off?

BEGIN TIMING

Even now I have the vague feeling that it was just a dream. Sometimes I dig out my photo album to reassure myself. And, sure enough, there's that picture of a football squad sitting before a background of Mount Fuji. Among its members were All-Americans, professionals, college stars—and me.

Who I am? Well, I can tell you I'm not who they thought I was. Two weeks before that picture was taken, I was just a dogface private finishing basic training. The nearest I had been to a college football game was Row 28 of Section E in the bleachers. Then, just like that, there I was in Japan as a halfback on a leading Far East Army football team, being treated like a king.

It all began in 1955 in the drizzling rain of Fort Lewis, Washington, where I was one of two thousand soldiers going through troop processing. I finally came to the last desk in the last wooden building. Here presided a second lieutenant who seemed particularly interested in our personal-information forms. He noticed my name and college, the University of Texas, and asked, "Did you play pro football?" His expression was quizzical, no doubt from observing my 160-pound frame. My expression was quizzical, too, because I didn't know what he was talking about. I answered, "No." to this he replied, "Oh, just college ball, eh?" I decided not to play his silly game, so I said nothing at all. He must have mistaken my silence for modesty because he came back with an emphatic "Oh, yeah, sure. Now I remember you. Sure."

With that the lieutenant arose from his desk and headed for the colonel's office. I heard him mutter something like "Boy, can we use him!"

When the colonel stuck his head around the corner of the door and smiled at me, I realized someone was making a big mistake.

The lieutenant hurried back to his desk, and he was smiling, too—a rare sight for a private. "Soldier," he said, "report for immediate flight to Japan."

By nine o'clock next morning I was aboard an airplane bound for Tokyo. The passengers were twenty-six officers, a six-foot-four-inch, 225-pound All-American from Notre Dame named Art Hunter, and me. And since Superman Hunter and I were privates, you can guess who sat together. Fortunately, he was the strong, silent type and didn't once mention his favorite subject, football.

In Tokyo we were taken directly to the commanding officer of Camp Zama, U.S. Army Forces Far East. He sat behind a big desk, and he was a stern-looking, cigar-smoking colonel. He stayed stern for a minute and then he smiled. "Boys," he said, "it's good to have you with us." Looking Hunter up and down like a rancher judging a prize bull, he added, "You look in great shape, boy." He turned to me and hesitated a minute. "Must be pretty fast, eh?" he said. He then instructed a corporal to drive us to his pet project, the new post football field.

Thirty or forty of the biggest giants I have ever seen were at one end of the field doing little things like knocking the hell out of one another with paralyzing lunges. We followed the colonel toward these Gargantuas, and the coach halted their activity long enough for our introduction. Superman and I shook hands with each player. Since I was already shaking from such a fear as few men have known, all I had to do was hold my hand out.

The next step was the barracks reserved for football players. There were Japanese houseboys to do the house cleaning, make up the beds, and shine the shoes. For this it might be worth risking a few bones.

I had just settled down on my bunk when my two roommates came in. I feigned sleep. From their conversation I learned that I was being confused with a halfback named George Robinson from the University of Texas, and that the team was sure looking forward to my services. The fact that my name was Robertson, Warren, seemed not to make a bit of difference; I was here, so I had to be a football player, and I was "Robbie" from there on in.

I shall never forget putting on the football pads and uniform for that first practice. The shoes were the only thing I was sure of. I watched the man suiting up next to me, with all the concentrated attention of a first-year medical student attending a demonstration in anatomy. Needless to say, I was the last man out of the dressing room. As I jogged toward the practice field I felt like the driver of an old and much-used Model T Ford: something, I was sure, would drop off any minute.

Once on the field I just kept running around and around it. Laps, they call them. I was afraid to stop. I had to exercise utmost restraint to keep from running right across the street, out the gate and down the road. Every time I ran by the coach I panted, "Gettin' in shape." My crimson face and frightful respiration left him with no questions. He must have thought I was a devoted athlete. When practice ended that day, I was still going around.

Next morning it took me about fifteen minutes just to get up from my bunk. From neck to toes I felt novocained. When the coach shouted, "Okay, boys. It's time for morning workout!" the announcement of Judgment Day could not have affected me more. I was almost ready to confess the Army's error and plead insanity.

Then the coach began to call out various players' names, and hand them green undershirts to slip on over their shoulder pads. These shirts would designate the "starting eleven," or first team. As you may guess, I got a green undershirt. The first team was to take the football and run offensive plays against the second-team defense. And, as the devil would have it, the honor of carrying the ball first was awarded to none other than the newly arrived scatback—me!

As the team went into formation I found myself standing about four feet behind and staring directly into the hindquarters of my former traveling companion. When the ball was snapped to the quarterback, I just aimed at that target, shut my eyes and ran. About three feet forward I felt something slap me in the pit of my stomach. I had no choice but to grab my arms to my midsection. And to my amazement, I was locked around the football, still going forward. I must have advanced eight or ten yards before I fell headlong over a prone body on the ground. That was the longest distance I had ever run with my eyes closed.

When I returned to our huddle, the backslaps from my teammates were almost enough to exhaust the little energy I had left. Our quarterback again favored me with the ball-carrying honors. This time I mustered up the courage to try it with eyes open. When I lunged toward the hindquarter target, I realized the cause of the previous ten-yard advance. Big Art Hunter had blasted an opening in the line that even Grandma Frickett could have made a ten-yard run through. But just the same, when we huddled again the backslaps were for me.

The rest of the afternoon, when I stumbled, fumbled, or goofed, everyone marked it up to my being out of shape or to my unique style. They wouldn't allow me to be less than the football player they thought I was. That night in the barracks I was actually beginning to feel like one of the boys.

The big game with Navy came two days later. As we sat in the locker room, all dressed in our brand-new playing uniforms, preparing to charge out onto the field, I was petrified with fright. The practice sessions had been an ordeal by fire, but a real, live game was much more than I could face up to.

The coach and the post commander gave us a pep talk. The team was enthusiastic and ready. The Army band was blazing away with a spirited march, and nearly two thousand eager fans were cheering.

When the official's whistle blew to signal the opening kickoff, quiet fell on the field and bleachers. The ball was booted into the air, and of course it began falling toward me. All I could think was, "Don't drop it, don't *drop* it!" The ball came banging into my chest and, believe me, no mother ever clung to her child in greater desperation than I clung to that football. When I started moving forward, it was the progress of a man mad with fear, and no madman ever moved faster. The coach later remarked that it was the fastest movement for a short distance he had ever witnessed. When the opposition finally got its hands on me I was halfway up the field. I think I got up running after they had tackled me. The rest of the game I was in a kind of trance. I did everything a man would do to survive. When the game ended, I was one of the leading ground-gainers, having used only my favorite straight-ahead play. My maniacal rompings had scored one touchdown and helped with another.

As we journeyed back to our post that evening, I felt as much a combat veteran as any man who had ever served in the U.S. Army. And if Purple Hearts were awarded for this kind of service, I would certainly have qualified. I was one big wound.

As the football season progressed, my fear of being found out as a counterfeit lessened. My confidence and football jargon were increasing by leaps and bounds. I remained in Japan for two seasons, playing on the Camp Zama team. If the officer responsible for mistaking my identity was ever aware of the error, he never made it known. And when my two-year military obligation came to an end I felt saddened to go back to being just me.

Sometime later when I turned on my TV set to watch the National Football League All-Star Pro Bowl game, there was Art Hunter at the starting center position. I tried to visualize myself out there on the field with him. A flood of memories compelled me to dig out my Japan photo album just to assure myself, once again, that it had really happened. It had.

Length: 1760 words.
Reading Time: ________
See Conversion Table, p. 421.
Enter WPM Rate on p. 416.

33 Ten Football Stars and Yours Truly

▶ COMPREHENSION CHECK

GETTING THE FACTS

1. The author's troop processing was done at Fort (a) Sam Houston. (b) Klamath. (c) Snelling. (d) Lewis. 1. ____

2. The author attended the University of (a) Kansas. (b) Texas. (c) Iowa. (d) Notre Dame. 2. ____

3. The author was being confused with a halfback named (a) William Robson. (b) Richard Roberts. (c) George Robinson. (d) Warren Robertson. 3. ____

4. The first team got what color undershirts? (a) green (b) red (c) blue (d) yellow 4. ____

5. In the big Navy game the author got how many touchdowns? (a) none (b) one (c) two (d) three 5. ____

GETTING THE MEANING

6. The main idea is to tell how (a) completely he fooled everyone. (b) well he played. (c) fast he could run. (d) quickly he learned. 6. ____

7. In purpose, this selection is primarily to (a) inform. (b) make clear. (c) describe. (d) entertain. 7. ____

8. As inference, the author tends to credit his success mostly to (a) himself. (b) the coach. (c) Hunter. (d) his speed. 8. ____

9. His attitude toward the military is best described as (a) disapproving. (b) amused. (c) hostile. (d) uncertain. 9. ____

10. He looks back on his football experience with (a) regret. (b) affection. (c) disbelief. (d) bewilderment. 10. ____

Check your answers with the Key on p. 452. Give yourself 10 points for each one right and enter your comprehension score on p. 415.

Comprehension Score: ________

C. VOCABULARY REVIEW QUIZ

This quiz contains ten words from preceding Word Power Workouts, but with other possible meanings of the word. The focus is on words with important prefixes so as to reinforce your awareness of prefixes as aids to meaning.

1. complicated (a) teased (b) captured (c) entangled (d) honored (e) pleased
   Complicated contains the prefix ______, meaning ______. 1. ____

2. submissive (a) accurate (b) threatening (c) humble (d) wealthy (e) effective
   Submissive contains the prefix ______, meaning ______. 2. ____

3. comparable (a) similar (b) well trained (c) calm (d) eager (e) pleasant
   Comparable contains the prefix ______, meaning ______. 3. ____

4. transitional (a) informed (b) moving (c) conservative (d) radical (e) clever
   Transitional contains the prefix ______, meaning ______. 4. ____

5. elicit (a) command (b) listen (c) mix (d) perform (e) get out
   Elicit contains the prefix ______, meaning ______. 5. ____

6. compendium (a) text (b) delay (c) start (d) short version (e) practice
   Compendium contains the prefix ______, meaning ______. 6. ____

7. obscure (a) blur (b) train (c) desire (d) find (e) present
   Obscure contains the prefix ______, meaning ______. 7. ____

8. dehydration (a) opening (b) nozzle (c) mist (d) water removal (e) flood
   Dehydration contains the prefix ______, meaning ______. 8. ____

9. devoted (a) elected (b) faithful (c) valued (d) helped (e) found 9. ______
Devoted contains the prefix ______, meaning ______.

10. immerse (a) mention (b) dip into (c) manage (d) suffer (e) trade 10. ______
Immerse contains the prefix ______, meaning ______.

10 points for each correct answer.

See Key on p. 441.

Vocabulary Review Score: ______

NAME ________________ CLASS ________________ DATE ________________

34 Literature: Nothing to Be Afraid Of

WORD POWER WORKOUT

A. LEANING ON CONTEXT

In each of the blanks provided, place the letter that precedes the best definition of the underlined word in context to the left.

Words in Context

1. _____ an <u>arduous</u> task
2. _____ approaching the assignment <u>apprehensively</u>
3. _____ <u>vicarious</u> experiences
4. _____ <u>immerse</u> themselves
5. _____ <u>calculatingly</u> ready the environment
6. _____ <u>fashion</u> for the reading experience
7. _____ will be <u>consequential</u>
8. _____ <u>elucidations</u> lead to life-lessons
9. _____ <u>temporal</u>, and psychological environment
10. _____ <u>absolute</u> comprehension

Definitions

a. imaginative participation
b. clarifications
c. create
d. difficult
e. deliberately
f. plunge
g. complete
h. important
i. hesitantly
j. time

Check your answers with the Key on p. 442 before going on. Give yourself 10 points for each one right and enter your score on the chart under A on p. 420. Review any that you have missed.

A Score: ________

Pronunciation aids:
1. AR-joo-us
3. vi-KER-ee-us
5. CAL-kyoo-lat-ing-ly
7. kon-si-KWEN-shul
8. e-loo-suh-DAY-shuns
9. TEM-puh-rel

B. LEANING ON PARTS

Stare means "stand." When you see *sist, sta(t),* or *sti,* look for that meaning. Fill in each blank below with some form of *stare.*

1. The bronze equestrian __________ of the captain stood in the plaza.
2. To stand firmly on a point you've made is to in__________ on it.
3. If the car stands perfectly still, it is __________.
4. All hostilities ended when the armi__________ was signed.
5. If you can't do that by yourself, get an as__________.

C. MAKING THE WORDS YOURS

In each blank below, enter the most appropriate word from the ten words in context in the first exercise, substituting it for the word(s) in parentheses. Use these words: *absolute, apprehensively, arduous, calculatingly, consequential, elucidations, fashion, immerse, temporal, vicarious.*

1. The IMAX Theater provides an environment for (imaginative participation) __________ travel through the Grand Canyon.
2. Firefighters (deliberately) __________ advanced through the burning forest.
3. Thanksgiving and Christmas have a closer (time) __________ relationship than do the Fourth of July and Labor Day.
4. His paintings are (clarifications) __________ of his early childhood memories.
5. To remove the label, (plunge)__________ the bottle in hot water.
6. Using this as a model, (create) __________ the chest to accommodate one adult's clothing for a week.
7. After hearing the loud explosion, Chris opened the door, (hesitantly) __________.
8. Removing the injured from the crumpled vehicle was a dangerous and (difficult) __________ assignment.
9. The speaker insisted upon (complete)__________ attention.
10. A miscalculation of $.11 on your monthly budget is not (important) __________.

Check your answers with the Key on p. 448.

B Score: ________

C Score: ________

Enter your scores on p. 420.

34

Literature: Nothing to Be Afraid Of

BEGIN TIMING

Many students delay taking Composition II or other literature-based courses because they fear not being able to read and understand the content of the course. Others are sure they will "hate it," be bored, or have to sacrifice endless hours to get the job done. If you sometimes struggle with literature assignments, try the following strategies to make an arduous task manageable.

Adopt a Receptive Attitude

The person who said, "Ninety percent of success is in the attitude" was wise. To succeed at reading literature, begin with a positive attitude toward the task. Rather than approaching the assignment apprehensively, look at it as an opportunity to enhance your knowledge through vicarious experiences. A successful strategy for developing a receptive attitude is to view reading literature as a sensory adventure, allowing authors to transport you into other worlds. Efficient readers immerse themselves in the writer's world and make every effort to experience the content through the author's eyes.

Create a Conducive Study Environment

You should calculatingly ready the environment where you plan to study literature. Just as setting is important to the literature you read, it is also important to the frame of mind you fashion for the reading experience. Find a spot where you will be free of most distractions: a library reading room, a learning center, a secure park or other public space, or on public transit during your commute. If you must study in a busy household, request that those who share the space with you respect your need for privacy and give them a schedule of times when you will be available for other activities.

Before beginning, make sure you are in good physical condition: not sleepy, tired, hungry, or ill. Then organize all of the tools you will need, such as your texts, pens, paper, a dictionary and thesaurus, and comfortable lighting. Ensure that the study environment is adequately ventilated and between 70 and 75 degrees Fahrenheit. An uncomfortable space will interfere with your concentration.

Study the Selection, Don't Just *Read* It

Unfortunately, many students reserve only a few minutes to "quickly read" a literature assignment. Not surprisingly, many of these same students derive only a vague idea of what the selection is about.

Successful readers know that reading and studying are not the same. Reading is an essential step in the study process, but simply reading the text does not ensure comprehension. A proven approach is to begin by reading the title and speculating about the author's message. Next, note who the author is and reflect on other pieces she or he has written.

Then, preview the selection by reading the introduction, reviewing discussion questions that often follow the selection, and considering the tips and challenges your instructor set forth in the assignment.

Finally, actively study the selection. That means visualizing the setting and action, hearing the dialogue, experiencing the sensory references, feeling the emotions of the characters, and anticipating what will happen next. If you have time, *read* the entire piece, quickly, for a first impression. Then *study* the text by doing the following: (1) read with deliberation, making notations in the margins about your impressions; (2) question the characters and the author's interpretation of actions and dialogue; (3) test the developments against your own experiences and against logic; (4) highlight new vocabulary, using context, where possible, to approximate meaning; (5) note actions or circumstances that you believe will be consequential to the development of the piece; (6) mark any portions of the text that are difficult for you to understand; and (7) when finished, write a 100-word summary of the piece in your own words. If you are unable to do step seven so that a person who has not studied the selection would understand it, repeat the steps in the process and/or seek assistance from your instructor or the staff in your learning center.

Assess the Elements of Literature

Authors develop the following literary features to reveal their message: plot, characters, theme, setting, and point of view. Students who fail to evaluate these components and determine their interdependency fail to reap the full benefit of the selection. Successful students analyze the following:

Plot: What is happening (has or will happen)? What is the pattern of the action? Is there a relationship between events? How do the events lead to conflict and resolution?

Characterization: Who are the characters? What are they like? What are their traits? What are their relationships to one another? Which characters, if any, undergo change? Why do they change? How does the change affect events? How do events affect character change? What problems do the characters have? How do characters solve their problems? Do the elucidations lead to life-lessons? Do some characters share similar or conflicting traits, mannerisms, and/or beliefs? If so, what are the resulting dynamics?

Theme: What is the work's central idea? What comment is the author making about life? To identify theme, ask "What is the subject of this piece? What does this author want the reader to understand about the subject?"

Setting: What is the physical, social, temporal, and psychological environment of the work? Where and when does the work take place? What does the environment look, sound, feel, and smell like? What is the relationship of setting to characters and theme? How does the social and psychological environment affect characters?

Point of View: From what perspective does the author present the action? What voice does the author allow characters to use? Who is telling the story and why? Why did the author choose this point of view? What effect does point of view have on theme, setting, and characterization? What effect does the author's point of view have on your interpretation? How does the author want readers to see the world on this subject?

This plan does not guarantee absolute comprehension, but it does provide you reasonable access to authors' story-telling techniques. It also helps to read literary criticisms (essays that analyze literature) of the piece you are studying and discuss your discoveries with others.

Length: 1000 words.
Reading Time: ___________
See Conversion Table, p. 421.
Enter WPM Rate on p. 416.

34 Literature: Nothing to Be Afraid Of

COMPREHENSION CHECK

GETTING THE FACTS

1. Many students avoid literature courses because they're (a) too busy. (b) afraid. (c) not curious. (d) negligent. 1. ____

2. To do well in literature classes, you must have (a) been a writer. (b) taken a writing course. (c) a positive attitude. (d) a literary background. 2. ____

3. Your study space should be between (a) 60°–65°. (b) 65°–70°. (c) 70°–72°. (d) 70°–75°. 3. ____

4. When studying literature, make notations in the margins about (a) your impressions. (b) test questions. (c) lecture notes. (d) other works by the author. 4. ____

5. Criticisms are (a) synopses. (b) analyses. (c) rejections. (d) characterizations. 5. ____

GETTING THE MEANING

6. The purpose of this piece is to show you how to (a) read literature. (b) write literature. (c) study literature. (d) critique literature. 6. ____

7. Emphasis is on (a) choosing the right author. (b) preparing to succeed. (c) memorizing text. (d) reading quickly. 7. ____

8. Where you study literature is (a) very important. (b) mildly important. (c) inconsequential. (d) non-negotiable. 8. ____

9. Summarizing a piece of literature tests (a) previewing skills. (b) objectivity. (c) imagination. (d) comprehension. 9. ____

10. This selection is primarily (a) entertaining. (b) argumentative. (c) condescending. (d) instructional. 10. ____

Check your answers with the Key on p. 452. Give yourself 10 points for each one right and enter your comprehension score on p. 415.

Comprehension Score: ________

NAME ______________ CLASS ______________ DATE ______________

35 The Open Window

WORD POWER WORKOUT

A. LEANING ON CONTEXT

In each of the blanks provided, place the letter that precedes the best definition of the underlined word in context to the left.

Words in Context	Definitions
1. _____ endeavoured to say	a. swamp
2. _____ unduly discounting	b. birds
3. _____ migrate to this rural retreat	c. improperly
4. _____ an undefinable something	d. fantasy
5. _____ a treacherous piece	e. tried
6. _____ piece of bog	f. outcast
7. _____ falteringly human	g. dangerous
8. _____ snipe in the marshes	h. unsteadily
9. _____ widespread delusion	i. move
10. _____ pariah dogs	j. vague

Check your answers with the Key on p. 442 before going on. Give yourself 10 points for each one right and enter your score on the chart under A on p. 420. Review any that you have missed.

A Score: ________

Pronunciation aids: **1. en-DEV-urd** **2. un-DU-ly** **5. TREACH-er-us** **7. FALT-er-ing-ly** **10. pa-RI-ah**

B. LEANING ON PARTS

Tendere means "stretch." When you see *tent, tend,* or *tens* in a word, look for those meanings. Use forms of *tendere* to fill the blanks below.

1. If it's interesting, it's bound to hold your at____________.
2. When you take care of a certain matter, you at____________ to it.
3. In a dangerous situation you are likely to feel ____________.
4. Comets are regarded by many as a por____________ of evil.
5. If you're too in____________ on talking, your driving may suffer.

C. MAKING THE WORDS YOURS

In each blank below, enter the most appropriate word from the ten words in context in the first exercise, substituting it for the word(s) in parentheses. Use these words: *bog, delusion, endeavoured, falteringly, migrate, pariah, snipe, treacherous, undefinable, unduly.*

1. Sheila is (improperly) ____________ burdened by the irresponsibility of her staff.
2. If we cannot have (birds) ____________ for the main course, fish is our second choice.
3. The boundaries of their property were (vague) ____________.
4. During playoffs, the Bulldogs (tried) ____________ to dominate the court early in the game.
5. The (swamp) ____________ is home to wildlife that need a wet and humid environment.
6. Many displaced workers (move) ____________ to far-away places in search of good-paying jobs.
7. The unpaved road from Prescott to Crown King is (dangerous) ____________.
8. Believing she won the lottery was certainly a (fantasy) ____________ since she had not bought a ticket.
9. The sex offender was a (outcast) ____________ in the neighborhood.
10. The toddler moved (unsteadily) ____________ along the edge of the sidewalk.

Check your answers with the Key on p. 448.

B Score: ________

C Score: ________

Enter your scores on p. 420.

35

The Open Window

SAKI

When emotions are running amuck and life becomes a confusing mess, it's difficult to tell whether the dream is the reality or the "reality" is the dream. Mrs. Sappleton's life-altering trauma left her and those around her groping for ways to make some sense of what was left of their lives. Do dreams really come true if one believes strongly enough?

BEGIN TIMING

"My aunt will be down presently, Mr. Nuttel," said a very self-possessed young lady of fifteen; "in the meantime you must try and put up with me."

Framton Nuttel endeavoured to say the correct something which should duly flatter the niece of the moment without unduly discounting the aunt that was to come. Privately he doubted more than ever whether these formal visits on a succession of total strangers would do much towards helping the nerve cure which he was supposed to be undergoing.

"I know how it will be," his sister had said when he was preparing to migrate to this rural retreat; "you will bury yourself down there and not speak to a living soul, and your nerves will be worse than ever from moping. I shall just give you letters of introduction to all the people I know there. Some of them, as far as I can remember, were quite nice."

Framton wondered whether Mrs. Sappleton, the lady to whom he was presenting one of the letters of introduction, came into the nice division.

"Do you know many of the people round here?" asked the niece, when she judged that they had sufficient silent communion.

"Hardly a soul," said Framton. "My sister was staying here, at the rectory, you know, some four years ago, and she gave me letters of introduction to some of the people here."

He made the last statement in a tone of distinct regret.

"Then you know practically nothing about my aunt?" pursued the self-possessed young lady.

"Only her name and address," admitted the caller. He was wondering whether Mrs. Sappleton was in the married or widowed state. An undefinable something about the room seemed to suggest masculine habitation.

"Her great tragedy happened just three years ago," said the child; "that would be since your sister's time."

"Her tragedy?" asked Framton; somehow in this restful country spot tragedies seemed out of place.

"You may wonder why we keep that window wide open on an October afternoon," said the niece, indicating a large French window that opened on to a lawn.

"It is quite warm for the time of the year," said Framton; "but has that window got anything to do with the tragedy?"

"Out through that window, three years ago to a day, her husband and her two young brothers went off for their day's shooting. They never came back. In crossing the moor to their favourite snipe-shooting ground they were all three engulfed in a treacherous piece of bog. It had been that dreadful wet summer, you know, and places that were safe in other years gave way suddenly without warning. Their bodies were never recovered. That was the dreadful part of it." Here the child's voice lost its self-possessed note and became falteringly human. "Poor aunt always thinks that they will come back some day, they and the little brown spaniel that was lost with them, and walk in at that window just as they used to do. That is why the window is kept open every evening till it is quite dusk. Poor dear aunt, she has often told me how they went out, her husband with his white waterproof coat over his arm, and Ronnie, her youngest brother, singing, 'Bertie, why do you bound?' as he always did to tease her, because she said it got on her nerves. Do you know, sometimes on still, quiet evenings like this, I almost get a creepy feeling that they will all walk in through that window—"

She broke off with a little shudder. It was a relief to Framton when the aunt bustled into the room with a whirl of apologies for being late in making her appearance.

"I hope Vera has been amusing you?" she said.

"She has been very interesting," said Framton.

"I hope you don't mind the open window," said Mrs. Sappleton briskly; "my husband and brothers will be home directly from shooting, and they always come in this way. They've been out for snipe in the marshes today, so they'll make a fine mess over my poor carpets. So like you men-folk, isn't it?"

She rattled on cheerfully about the shooting and the scarcity of birds, and the prospects for duck in the winter. To Framton it was all purely horrible. He made a desperate but only partially successful effort to turn the talk on to a less ghastly topic; he was conscious that his hostess was giving him only a fragment of her attention, and her eyes were constantly straying past him to the open window and the lawn beyond. It was certainly an unfortunate coincidence that he should have paid his visit on this tragic anniversary.

"The doctors agree in ordering me complete rest, an absence of mental excitement, and avoidance of anything in the nature of violent physical exercise," announced Framton, who laboured under the tolerably widespread delusion that total strangers and chance acquaintances are hungry for the least detail of one's ailments and infirmities, their cause and cure. "On the matter of diet they are not so much in agreement," he continued.

"No?" said Mrs. Sappleton, in a voice which only replaced a yawn at the last moment. Then she suddenly brightened into alert attention—but not to what Framton was saying.

"Here they are at last!" she cried. "Just in time for tea, and don't they look as if they were muddy up to the eyes!"

Framton shivered slightly and turned towards the niece with a look intended to convey sympathetic comprehension. The child was staring out through the open window with dazed horror in her eyes. In a chill shock of nameless fear Framton swung round in his seat and looked in the same direction.

In the deepening twilight three figures were walking across the lawn towards the window; they all carried guns under their arms, and one of them was additionally burdened with a white coat hung over his shoulders. A tired brown spaniel kept close at their heels. Noiselessly they neared the house, and then a hoarse young voice chanted out of the dusk: "I said, Bertie, why do you bound?"

Framton grabbed wildly at his stick and hat; the halldoor, the gravel-drive, and the front gate were dimly noted stages in his headlong retreat. A cyclist coming along the road had to run into the hedge to avoid imminent collision.

"Here we are, my dear," said the bearer of the white mackintosh, coming in through the window; "fairly muddy, but most of it's dry. Who was that who bolted out as we came up?"

"A most extraordinary man, a Mr. Nuttel," said Mrs. Sappleton; "could only talk about his illness, and dashed off without a word of good-bye or apology when you arrived. One would think he had seen a ghost."

"I expect it was the spaniel," said the niece calmly; "he told me he had a horror of dogs. He was once hunted into a cemetery somewhere on the banks of the Ganges by a pack of pariah dogs, and had to spend the night in a newly dug grave with the creatures snarling and grinning and foaming just above him. Enough to make any one lose their nerve."

Romance at short notice was her specialty.

Length: 1210 words.
Reading Time: ________
See Conversion Table, p. 421.
Enter WPM Rate on p. 416.

35 The Open Window

COMPREHENSION CHECK

GETTING THE FACTS

1. Framton Nuttel's visit was (a) casual. (b) unexpected. (c) formal. (d) informal. 1. ____

2. Mr. Nuttel had letters of introduction from his (a) sister. (b) niece. (c) aunt. (d) brother. 2. ____

3. Mrs. Sappleton's husband had been away for (a) a year. (b) three months. (c) thirty hours. (d) three years. 3. ____

4. When Mr. Sappleton left, he carried (a) a map. (b) an umbrella. (c) a stick. (d) a coat. 4. ____

5. The visitor talked incessantly about (a) war. (b) his illnesses. (c) his family. (d) hunting. 5. ____

GETTING THE MEANING

6. Which best expresses the central idea of the story? (a) Seeing is believing. (b) Reality is in the mind's eye. (c) Doubt nothing. (d) Doubt everything. 6. ____

7. Mr. Nuttel found the conversation (a) uninteresting. (b) distasteful. (c) humorous. (d) confusing. 7. ____

8. Letters of introduction vouched for the character of (a) community residents. (b) friends. (c) newcomers. (d) adversaries. 8. ____

9. Framton's departure was motivated by (a) curiosity. (b) anger. (c) illness. (d) fear. 9. ____

10. Vera felt a need to (a) insult. (b) be alone. (c) make excuses. (d) be rude to guests. 10. ____

Check your answers with the Key on p. 452. Give yourself 10 points for each one right and enter your comprehension score on p. 415.

Comprehension Score: ________

NAME ____________ CLASS ____________ DATE ____________

36 The Gun

WORD POWER WORKOUT

A. LEANING ON CONTEXT

In each of the blanks provided, place the letter that precedes the best definition of the underlined word in context to the left.

Words in Context	Definitions
1. _____ quick and agile	a. secure
2. _____ finished his commentary	b. remarks
3. _____ drizzly March day	c. assembly
4. _____ out for a stroll	d. shudder
5. _____ almost conversational	e. supple
6. _____ on the little gathering	f. ingenious
7. _____ strong and confident	g. saunter
8. _____ knees wouldn't quiver	h. misty
9. _____ Very clever	i. unattached
10. _____ a stray bullet	j. casual

Check your answers with the Key on p. 442 before going on. Give yourself 10 points for each one right and enter your score on the chart under A on p. 420. Review any that you have missed.

A Score: ________

Pronunciation aids: 1. AJ-il

B. LEANING ON PARTS

Specere means "see" or "look." When you see *spec(t)* or *spic* in a word, look for those meanings. Enter a form of *specere* in each blank below.

1. A person looking at a sporting event is called a ___________.
2. To look on someone with honor and esteem is to show re___________.
3. To see better, the teacher got a new pair of ___________.
4. You must look into all a___________ of the situation before acting.
5. On such an au___________ occasion, everyone seemed overjoyed.

C. MAKING THE WORDS YOURS

In each blank below, enter the most appropriate word from the ten words in context in the first exercise, substituting it for the word(s) in parentheses. Use these words: *agile, clever, commentary, confident, conversational, drizzly, gathering, quiver, stray, stroll.*

1. Temperatures of 10°F–15°F caused his voice to (shudder) ___________.
2. Jennifer had no time for a (saunter) ___________ along the edge of Lake Michigan.
3. Thursday turned into a (misty) ___________ fall day.
4. Earning an *A* on her precalculus exam helped Kim feel (secure) ___________.
5. The (assembly) ___________ provided an opportunity for the family to get to know the bride.
6. The police officer's voice was more (casual) ___________ when she spoke with people who lived in her own neighborhood.
7. Being (supple) ___________ allowed my grandmother to crawl into my daughter's playhouse.
8. The sports announcer provided enthusiastic (remarks) ___________ about the event.
9. Using aluminum foil as giftwrap was a (ingenious) ___________ idea.
10. A steak left on the patio table attracted the (unattached) ___________ dogs.

Check your answers with the Key on p. 448.

B Score: ________

C Score: ________

Enter your scores on p. 420.

36

The Gun

ANN CAROL

"Losers weepers, finders keepers," kids used to say. This short story suggests that finders might end up being weepers, too. Learn how innocent curiosity turned into a disaster of monumental proportions, wrecking several people's lives.

BEGIN TIMING

"He runs!" Derek said, dribbling the basketball down the cracked cement of the empty school yard. "He jumps!" Quick and agile, he sidestepped his friend Jerry and leaped into the air. "He shoots, and—" he watched as the ball dropped through the hoop, then finished his commentary with a grin "—nothing but net!"

"Nothing but trouble, you mean." Jerry grabbed the ball and tucked it under his arm. "Look over there."

Turning, Derek saw two men coming through the gate of the school yard. It was a drizzly March day and both of them wore trench coats. Their faces were calm, and they walked casually, like maybe they were out for a stroll. But Derek knew they weren't. Even before the taller one reached into his pocket, he knew they were cops.

It was about the gun, Derek thought. It had to be. He felt panicky for a second, and had to remind himself that he'd thrown it away.

"Derek Robinson?" the tall one said.

"Yeah?"

"Detectives Kramer and Reed." His hand came all the way out of his pocket and he flashed his badge. "Can we talk to you for a minute? We have a few questions."

"What about?"

"Why don't you step into our office?" Reed motioned to a bench on the other side of the school yard.

Derek's heart sped up. *Definitely the gun,* he thought. With a quick glance at Jerry, he followed the officers across the yard and sat down on the bench. Kramer sat next to him. Reed stayed on his feet, looking around.

Kramer came right to the point. “It’s about the gun, Derek.”

Derek felt his face get hot, but he asked, “What gun?”

Kramer sighed. “The one you were flashing around in school yesterday.”

His eyes on the building across the street, Reed said, “And before that, the one Max Cooper saw you stuffing under your jacket.”

Max Cooper owned the deli that Derek passed every day on his way to school. *Great,* Derek thought. *The guy had seen him.*

“Plenty of people saw you with it,” Kramer said. “And we’ll find it, Derek, you can count on that. So do yourself a favor and cooperate.”

“OK . . . OK,” Derek said. “I had a gun.”

“Right. Where’d you get it?”

“I found it. In a lot.” Derek shook his head, remembering the fear and excitement he’d felt when he saw it. “I couldn’t believe it. A .38, just lying there!”

“You knew the caliber?” Kramer raised an eyebrow. “Where’d you learn about guns?”

“Where do you think? It’s not the first gun I’ve seen in this neighborhood.”

“Just the first one you found lying in a vacant lot.”

“Yeah.”

Kramer raised his eyebrow again. “So you took it to school?”

“Yeah. Look,” Derek said, sitting up straighter on the hard bench. “It was dumb, OK? I know it. That’s why I got rid of it. I dumped it on my way home, right back where I found it.”

“Where’s this lot?” Reed asked, getting out a notebook.

“Corner of Fourth and Cooper,” Derek said. “Nothing there but weeds. That’s where I picked it up and that’s where I put it back. All you have to do is look and you’ll find it.”

“We’ll find it, all right,” Kramer said. “but let’s back up a little. You still had the gun with you after school. That’s what . . . three, three-thirty?”

Derek nodded. “Three.”

“So you left school. Then what’d you do?”

“Shot some hoops. Had some pizza,” Derek said. “The usual stuff.”

Reed slipped the notebook back in his pocket. “Does the usual stuff include holding up a hardware store at four-thirty?” His voice was quiet, almost conversational. But his eyes were as gray and chilly as the sky.

Derek’s face got hot again and his heart started hammering. He wanted to stand but he was afraid his legs might shake. “That’s crazy!” He wanted to sound cool, but he knew he sounded scared. “I never held up any hardware store! That’s crazy,” he said again.

“Seventeen or eighteen. Brown hair.” Kramer was reading from a little notepad. “About five-eleven, approximately a hundred and fifty pounds. Wearing jeans and a hooded, black-and-red Bulls jacket.” He stopped and eyed Derek's jacket. "Black-and-white high-tops." He glanced down at Derek's shoes, then closed the notepad. "And carrying a .38 caliber revolver."

"It fits pretty well," Reed commented quietly. "Don't you think, Derek?"

Derek knew he didn't have any reason to be so scared, but when he spoke, his voice shook. He couldn't help it. "Yeah, it fits. But it wasn't me. I had nothing to do with any robbery."

"Maybe you didn't," Kramer admitted. "So let's go back over what you did after school, OK?"

"I told you." Derek looked at Jerry standing on the other side of the yard, shooting hoops and missing them all because he was keeping one eye on the little gathering by the bench. Suddenly, Derek's fear left him. When he spoke again, his voice was strong and confident because he was telling the truth. "We left school at three," he said. "We shot a few hoops, then we had some pizza."

"We?"

"Me and Jerry." Derek nodded toward his friend. "We had some pizza at Luigi's, you can ask Jerry. That was about four." He stood up now, knowing that his knees wouldn't quiver like an old man's. "And then we went down by the train tracks."

There was a pause as the two detectives eyed each other. Then Reed asked, "With the gun?" His voice was quieter than ever.

Derek nodded.

"And what were you doing there?"

"Shooting at tin cans," Derek said. He hadn't told them before because he didn't want to admit any more about the gun than he had to. But it didn't matter now. They were after a hold-up guy; they wouldn't care about a little target practice. Especially since Derek didn't have the gun anymore.

"Let's see if I've got this straight," Kramer said. "You left Luigi's and went to the train tracks and shot at tin cans with the .38 you found."

"Yeah, it was about four-thirty, quarter to five," Derek said.

"Did you shoot at anything besides tin cans?"

"Bottles and cans. That's all."

"Weren't you afraid somebody would hear the gunshots?" Kramer asked.

Derek shook his head. "We waited for the trains to pass through."

Kramer nodded. "Very clever. Did Jerry fire the gun, too?"

"No. Only me."

"And then what?" Reed asked.

"When the gun was empty, we split. Jerry went home and so did I," Derek told him. "And I threw the gun back in the lot where I found it." He shoved his hands in his pockets. "Look, ask Jerry. He was with me at Luigi's. Plenty of other people saw me there, too. And Jerry was with me at the tracks."

"About four-thirty, quarter to five?" Kramer asked.

"Yeah."

As Kramer got up from the bench and headed over to Jerry, Derek took a deep breath and let it out. He might still be in trouble about the gun. But no way could they pin the robbery on him. He hadn't done it and he'd just proved it.

When Kramer came back, he nodded at Reed. "It checks out," he said.

Derek let out a sigh of relief. "OK if I go now?"

"I don't think so," Reed said.

"But I told you what happened and you said it checked out!" Derek cried. "I didn't rob anyone!"

"No, we know you didn't," Reed said.

"So?"

"So at four-forty yesterday afternoon, a stray bullet from a .38 caliber revolver smashed through the window of the D train and into the head of a young woman." Reed looked at Derek with cold eyes. "You didn't rob anyone, Derek," he said. "You killed someone."

Length: 1300 words.
Reading Time: __________
See Conversion Table, p. 421.
Enter WPM Rate on p. 416.

36 The Gun

COMPREHENSION CHECK

GETTING THE FACTS

1. Derek found the gun (a) in a box. (b) in a lot. (c) at school. (d) at the deli. 1. ____

2. Derek disposed of the gun by (a) selling it. (b) giving it away. (c) throwing it away. (d) hiding it. 2. ____

3. There was a holdup at (a) a grocery store. (b) an appliance store. (c) a fast food store. (d) a hardware store. 3. ____

4. Jerry and Derek were eating pizza at (a) 3:00 p.m. (b) 3:30 p.m. (c) 4:00 p.m. (d) 4:30 p.m. 4. ____

5. Derek shot the gun (a) during the holdup. (b) during target practice. (c) after basketball practice. (d) before eating at Luigi's. 5. ____

GETTING THE MEANING

6. This selection is primarily to warn the reader about the (a) cleverness of police officers. (b) value of friendship. (c) availability of guns. (d) deadliness of guns. 6. ____

7. As they approached the teenagers, the police officers were (a) aggressive. (b) confident. (c) edgy. (d) hyped. 7. ____

8. Reed's office was (a) a bench. (b) an alley. (c) a railroad car. (d) the squad car. 8. ____

9. The murder was (a) deliberate. (b) premeditated. (c) accidental. (d) circumstantial. 9. ____

10. Jerry was (a) an innocent bystander. (b) an accomplice. (c) a victim. (d) a hero. 10. ____

Check your answers with the Key on p. 452. Give yourself 10 points for each one right and enter your comprehension score on p. 415.

Comprehension Score: ________

NAME ______________________ CLASS ______________________ DATE ______________

37 Getting Better Grades

WORD POWER WORKOUT

A. LEANING ON CONTEXT

In each of the blanks provided, place the letter that precedes the best definition of the underlined word in context to the left.

Words in Context

1. ____ your academic success
2. ____ will pose no problem
3. ____ this ensures personal involvement
4. ____ the fearful toll of forgetting
5. ____ slightly modified form
6. ____ culmination of your efforts
7. ____ frantic all-night cramming
8. ____ reading and listening endeavors
9. ____ the utmost importance
10. ____ it releases all information

Definitions

a. cost, extent of damage
b. school
c. efforts
d. highest point
e. cause, create
f. changed, altered
g. guarantees
h. primary, highest degree of
i. makes known
j. desperate, frenzied

Check your answers with the Key on p. 442 before going on. Give yourself 10 points for each one right and enter your score on the chart under A on p. 420. Review any that you have missed.

A Score: ________

B. LEANING ON PARTS

Plicare means "fold." When you see *plic, plex, ply,* or *ploy* in a word, look for that meaning. Fill in the following with forms of *plicare.*

1. To state clearly or unfold meaning is to be ex__________.
2. It's not what you say but what you fold in or im__________.
3. To fold troops into position is to de__________ them.
4. There are two families in the big du__________ next door.
5. How would you re__________ to that question?

C. MAKING THE WORDS YOURS

In each blank below, enter the most appropriate word from the ten words in context in the first exercise, substituting it for the word(s) in parentheses. Use these words: *academic, culmination, endeavors, frantic, ensures, modified, pose, released, toll, utmost.*

1. The (cost) __________ was 300 persons dead or missing.
2. The new product was (made known) __________ to the public.
3. The (highest point) __________ of the actor's success was reached in his last performance.
4. Her (efforts) __________ to acquire a high-paying job were successful.
5. My (school) __________ interests conflicted with my interest in sports.
6. The track star's ability to throw the javelin (guarantees) __________ his success.
7. The drama critic soon (changed) __________ her ideas about the play.
8. The meeting between the heads of states was a matter of the (highest degree of) __________ secrecy.
9. Last-minute cramming for an exam can be a (desperate) __________ experience.
10. If a young couple wants to get married, the parents may (cause) __________ a problem.

Check your answers with the Key on p. 449.

B Score: ________

C Score: ________

Enter your scores on p. 420.

37

Getting Better Grades

BEGIN TIMING

Did you hear about the student in the bookstore? He was failing and asked the clerk if there was a book to help him get better grades. The clerk picked up a how-to-study guide and said, "Here's one that will do half your work for you." The student brightened up immediately. "Fine!" A pause while he did some mental arithmetic. "Fine! I'll take *two.*"

Sounds like another musical, doesn't it—*How to Succeed in College without Really Trying!* Well, if it weren't for all those quizzes, midterms, and finals, it might be that easy. Even those, however, with the right approach, will pose no problem.

Requirements

But what *is* the right approach? You want a substitute for that common frantic all-night cramming, that washing down of chapter after chapter with strong black coffee. By exam time that regimen means bleary eyes and fuzzy mind—means unwanted *D*'s instead of hoped-for *B*'s.

As a substitute, you need an approach that is comprehensive, simple, appealing, and, above all, effective.

1. *Comprehensive.* It must cover everything—lectures as well as reading.
2. *Simple.* A complex system may work well, judging from research. But if it's too complex, it just won't be used. Those good grades will be as elusive as ever.
3. *Appealing.* It must have sufficient appeal to be actually used. Take the SQ3R system, for example. Three weeks after its presentation in detail to one of our classes, the students were asked what SQ3R stood for. Only 3 percent knew exactly. Obviously, no more than that number could possibly be applying the system. Insufficient appeal.
4. *Effective.* It *must* work—and work better than other approaches. That's of the utmost important, of course.

The Natural Approach

Actually every single chapter in this book contributes significantly to your academic success. Better readers *are* better grade-getters, other things being equal. And this book focuses on developing and refining a wide variety of reading and vocabulary-building skills.

Now is the time to fit parts together into a special grade-getting approach. Look on it as either a capstone or culmination of your efforts. Here it is.

Identify. This is a natural first move, lying at the very heart of all your reading and listening endeavors. You can't remember everything you read and hear. As mentioned earlier, you must learn to identify essentials and note meaningful relationships. This you should already know how to do efficiently.

Extract. This second step does involve something new. Mark each notebook page by drawing a line down the left side about two inches from the edge. When you finish reading a few pages, enter your summary of essential material on the right-hand portion of the page. Make your notes complete enough so you'll be able to understand them later. Continue in this way until you have finished your reading. Take lecture notes the same way, using the right-hand side.

Speaking of lectures, someone once described the lecture system as a way of getting information from the notes of the teacher to the notes of the student, without affecting the minds of either. This mustn't happen with you. Be sure, as you listen or read, to take notes in your own words. This ensures personal involvement. This runs ideas through your mind and into your notes, putting your own mark upon them.

Label. After completing your notes, master the material. Go back to the beginning and write down a word or phrase in the left-hand margin opposite each idea or point in your notes. Use words that will best help you recall the full information. Think in terms of a computer. You feed it a key word. It releases all information it has on that point. Your key entries in the left-hand narrow margin will function the same way, providing a convenient handle for picking up the information. Treat lecture notes as you do your reading notes. After class, look them over, supplying key words in the left margin.

Recite. Here's where you can appreciate the full advantage of this approach. You see, it's not enough to read and comprehend. You must also remember. This above all! Research indicates that after two weeks, without recitation, you'll remember only about 20 percent. With recitation, however, that figure becomes 80 percent—*four times more.*

The review is simplicity itself. Just cover the notes on the right side of your notebook. Then start down, looking at each key word or phrase on the left. With that as a clue, recite aloud the full information on the right for which it stands. Uncover, then, to check how accurately and fully you know the material. Continue through in this way. Correct any mistakes. Add any omissions. Restudy any points not remembered.

Recognize this as a fact of life. Suppose that key word doesn't now trigger the information covered on the right. Don't expect that on an exam something—perhaps the same key word in one of the questions—will, like magic, bring the information flooding into your mind. It just doesn't work that way. If it works for your review, fine. You can expect it to work also during the exam. During review, restudy, if you can't recall the material on the right. That's your true, natural test of mastery—being able to recite your notes completely when seeing the key word.

Cautions

Don't use a formal outline as you take notes. Concentrate on content. Some things just don't lend themselves easily to outline form.

Don't misschedule your review-recite sessions. Remember—you forget most right after you've learned or reviewed something. For that reason, schedule your review immediately before the examination. At least minimize the time between review and exam to minimize the fearful toll of forgetting.

As you can see, this approach is indeed an easy, natural approach. It is a slightly modified form of one described and advocated by Dr. Walter Pauk. He says that "over 98 percent of the students instructed in this approach continue to use it and report unusual success." Why not join the ranks? Enjoy similar success yourself.

Length: 1000 words.
Reading Time: __________
See Conversion Table, p. 421.
Enter WPM Rate on p. 416.

37 Getting Better Grades

▶ COMPREHENSION CHECK

GETTING THE FACTS

1. How many copies of the how-to-study book did the student decide to buy? (a) one (b) two (c) three (d) four — 1. ____

2. Specific mention was made of what system? (a) PQRST (b) OARWET (c) SQ3R (d) SPD4 — 2. ____

3. You were asked to think of the approach advocated here as a (a) capstone. (b) shortcut. (c) cure-all. (d) study-substitute. — 3. ____

4. You are cautioned not to use (a) ink. (b) shorthand. (c) a formal outline. (d) a typewriter. — 4. ____

5. About what percentage of the students taught this approach continued to use it? (a) 13 percent (b) 36 percent (c) 46 percent (d) 98 percent — 5. ____

GETTING THE MEANING

6. The main focus is on (a) taking notes. (b) improving study techniques. (c) taking tests. (d) using recitation. — 6. ____

7. Most emphasis is on (a) the simple. (b) the appealing. (c) the effective. (d) the comprehensive. — 7. ____

8. What was the point of the lecture system definition? To make sure that notes are (a) complete. (b) not busy work. (c) translated into sounds. (d) not too detailed. — 8. ____

9. Apparently it is most important to (a) involve yourself. (b) be efficient. (c) plan carefully. (d) practice often. — 9. ____

10. Figures as to the numbers of students using this program were to show (a) its effectiveness. (b) the degree of interest. (c) its simplicity. (d) the degree of need. — 10. ____

Check your answers with the Key on p. 452. Give yourself 10 points for each one right and enter your comprehension score on p. 420.

Comprehension Score: ________

MAKING THE APPLICATION

To learn how to do anything, even some very simple things, you have to try them yourself. Try this new system on the first page only of selection 37, using the space marked off below.

Word or phrase labels	Fairly complete summary of essentials

Establish this as your system for both lectures and textbook reading. It works if you'll form the habit right now and put it to weekly use.

MAKING THE APPLICATION

THE SSQ FORMULA

Before a new pitcher heads for the mound, he takes time to warm up. Before you begin reading, you too should do some waming up—some preparing.

When you sit down to study, those first few minutes are not too productive. Interest and concentration cannot be switched on and **off**, as a light switch. **Unrelated thoughts** have to be **pushed out gradually**, as you begin a new activity. Can you **shorten this** warm-up process? **Yes**—by the following formula.

Survey: This first step gives you the best possible overview in the shortest possible time. To survey an article or chapter, **read** the **title**, the **first paragraph**, **all headings, italicized words**, and the **last paragraph**. You should then have the bare essentials.

To illustrate, note the underlined parts here. They are **what** you would **read in** your **survey. If** you can **read** the entire 500-word **selection in two minutes,** it will take only **twelve seconds to survey** it. Or take a **longer chapter** from an anthropology text. **Surveying** the 7,650-word chapter means reading only 350 words—**over twenty-one times faster** than normal reading. This diving in headfirst **forces** almost immediate **concentration.**

Skim: Skimming builds up an even stronger foundation. For this, **read** the **title** and **first paragraph,** as in survey. **Then** read the first sentence and **key words in** all the **following paragraphs, plus** any **headings, boldfaced type** or **italicized words.** When you reach the **last paragraph, read it** completely. This means rereading all parts covered in the survey, but taking an important next step. **This** selective **reading,** of from 20 to 40 percent of the material, **takes** only **about** a **fifth to** a **third** your usual reading time. **Note** the **parts** in **bold type** on this page. It **marks what** you would **cover in skimming.** Instead of two minutes, it should take only fifty-two seconds.

Questions: Generally, a faster-than-comfortable reading speed means better-than-usual concentration. One **student,** however, slipped into an **unfortunate habit,** while trying to develop added concentration. He **tried** so hard to **finish** a certain number of pages **in** a **limited time** that he was **not actually reading**—just **going through** the **motions. To break himself** of this habit, he used this third step—**raising questions.**

More than anything else, a question is likely to drive unwanted thoughts out of mind. This tends to **shorten** the needed **warm-up** period. **Raise questions** both after surveying and after skimming the material. For example, the reader who reads the title and consciously asks, "What does SSQ stand for?" will obviously **read with** much **more purpose** than one who has not evidenced such curiosity. **When** you **survey** and **skim, much** is **missed.** In a sense, however, this **tends** to **encourage** more **questions** than in normal reading, making this dynamic third step an almost automatic consequence of the first two.

So—use these prereading steps. Survey the material. Skim it rapidly. Then raise questions—ideal preparation for the reading to follow.

NAME ________________ CLASS ________________ DATE ____________

38 The Dividends for Quitters

WORD POWER WORKOUT

A. LEANING ON CONTEXT

In each of the blanks provided, place the letter that precedes the best definition of the underlined word in context to the left.

Words in Context

1. ____ dividends for quitters
2. ____ aggressive efforts
3. ____ disability leave
4. ____ why shouldn't publishers . . . decree
5. ____ luxury cruise
6. ____ glamorize smoking
7. ____ leaving market shares essentially frozen
8. ____ merely to persuade
9. ____ it's ironic
10. ____ Tobacco is unique.

Definitions

a. make very appealing
b. practically
c. profits
d. contradictory
e. determined
f. incapacity
g. proclaim
h. just
i. extravagant
j. atypical

Check your answers with the Key on p. 442 before going on. Give yourself 10 points for each one right and enter your score on the chart under A on p. 420. Review any that you have missed.

A Score: ________

Pronunciation aids: **9. eye-RON-ik**
10. yoo-NEEK

B. LEANING ON PARTS

Facere means "make" or "do." When you see *fac(t), fec, fic, fas,* or *fea* in a word, look for those meanings. Use a form of *facere* in each blank below.

1. The washer still won't work; I think the motor is de____________.
2. They had suf____________ help to finish the project on time.
3. The tennis team was not de____________ even once all season long.
4. The artist ____________ a beautiful sculptured figure of Venus.
5. To do a task with ease is to do it with great ____________.

C. MAKING THE WORDS YOURS

In each blank below, enter the most appropriate word from the ten words in context in the first exercise, substituting it for the word(s) in parentheses. Use these words: *aggressive, decree, disability, dividends, essentially, glamorize, ironic, luxury, merely, unique.*

1. Few people are able to afford (extravagant) ____________ items.
2. The driver suffered some (incapacity) ____________ after the accident.
3. The (profits) ____________ are far greater than the effort.
4. Because of their (determined) ____________ struggle, the team won.
5. The newly formed government will (proclaim) ____________ this date "Founders Day."
6. The earthquake left the town (practically) ____________ unharmed.
7. People use cosmetics in an attempt to (make very appealing) ____________ themselves.
8. All of the artist's original works are (atypical) ____________.
9. It is (contradictory) ____________ that many people who are very thin perceive themselves to be overweight.
10. They wanted (just) ____________ to introduce the concept to the planning committee.

Check your answers with the Key on p. 449.

B Score: ________

C Score: ________

Enter your scores on p. 420.

38

The Dividends for Quitters

ANDREW TOBIAS

Every day, many smokers ask, "Why should I quit?" They rationalize their habit by saying that they derive enough pleasure to justify ignoring the health risks that smoking imposes. But there are mounting reasons why smoking could be hazardous to more than your health. Learn why quitting could provide dividends you can bank on.

BEGIN TIMING

New Yorker Joseph Scott quit smoking and put the money he would have spent on cigarettes into a cookie jar. Seeing the money mount, he says, helped reinforce his resolve. Now, two years later, Scott has amassed $3,285, and he's taking a luxury cruise.

Forget health; let's talk money.

Consider a teenage girl, eager to be attractive and confronted constantly with images of healthy, Virginia-slim tobacco models. Like about 1 in 5 teenage girls today, she gets hooked. Taking into account FICA and income taxes, she could see $1,500 in pretax earnings each year go up in smoke—$1,500 that could otherwise be put toward her kids' education, a first home, equity in a small business, or an IRA.

Nor are cigarettes the only cost.

- Smokers spend more on cold remedies and health care. (A division of Dow Chemical found that smokers averaged 5.5 more days of absence each year and took eight more days of disability leave.)
- And they spend more for life insurance. (The Tobacco Institute may not be convinced that smoking kills, but the three life insurers *owned* by tobacco companies certainly are. CNA is owned by Lorillard parent Loews, the Franklin Life and American Tobacco are owned by American Brands, and Farmers Group and British-American Tobacco are owned by B.A.T. Industries. All three charge smokers nearly double for term insurance. Why? Because at any age, a smoker is about twice as likely to die as a nonsmoker.)

In short, tobacco addiction is a major economic handicap. A child who can avoid it has a far better shot at lifelong financial health than one who gets hooked.

The tobacco industry professes not to want children to smoke. It points to a free pamphlet it distributes called *Tobacco: Helping Youth Say No.* But the pamphlet never once mentions the word cancer, never once mentions addiction. (Nicotine is as addictive as heroin, says the Surgeon General.) Instead, the reason given is that kids aren't old enough. Smoking—like driving and sex—is for adults. Of course, it's hard to imagine a message that would make smoking more attractive.

The tobacco industry says its advertising is designed merely to persuade existing smokers to switch brands, not to encourage nonsmokers to start. If so, why not simply ban *all* tobacco advertising and promotion? Surely Congress would agree to do so if the industry asked it to. And look what would happen: brand switching would largely stop, leaving market shares essentially "frozen." And the $4 billion the industry currently spends on U.S. advertising would fall straight to the bottom line! Pure profit! You'd think the tobacco industry would be begging for this.

Instead, of course, it's crucial to keep that lovable Camel cartoon character in front of children, and to fly Newport banners up and down the beach, because if we don't hook the kids, how are we to replace all the customers who quit or die each year? Most smokers start between the ages of 8 and 18—thousands of them a day in the U.S. (and, thanks in part to aggressive efforts by the first Bush Administration, many more abroad).

More than 800,000 Americans derive their livelihood from tobacco-related jobs—almost double the 435,000 that the Surgeon General estimates die each year from tobacco-caused disease. A ban on promotion would cost some of those jobs. Still, it's ironic that, as a society, we spend billions to keep people from breathing asbestos—the EPA estimates 17 nonoccupational asbestos-related deaths a year—but billions more to *promote* smoking.

Limiting the industry's right to glamorize smoking raises obvious First Amendment questions. But even if Congress hasn't the power to ban tobacco promotion—and it well may—what of private restrictions? Why shouldn't publishers, including Time Inc., decree that they will no longer push tobacco? When is *TV Guide* owner Rupert Murdoch (a Philip Morris board member) going to announce that since cigarette ads are inappropriate on TV, they're also wrong for *TV Guide,* which has a huge readership among kids? Is it appropriate that seven pages of a recent issue of *Self* magazine, with all its articles on fitness and health, were devoted to making smoking look healthy, sexy, and fun? How about *Rolling Stone?* Any kids read that? It's been estimated that fully one-third of all U.S. hospital beds are devoted to tobacco-caused disease. Many magazines, including the nation's largest, *Modern Maturity* and the *Reader's Digest,* already reject tobacco ads.

Tobacco is unique. It's the only legal product that's highly addictive and that, when used *exactly as intended,* causes great harm.

Obviously, smoking should be legal. Obviously, smokers are fine people. But should we actively *promote* America's leading cause of preventable death?

Forget about health. Think about the money!

Length: 790 words.
Reading Time: __________
See Conversion Table, p. 421.
Enter WPM Rate on p. 416.

38 The Dividends for Quitters

COMPREHENSION CHECK

GETTING THE FACTS

1. What ratio of teenage girls gets hooked on cigarettes? (a) 3 in 5 (b) 2 in 5 (c) 1 in 5 (d) 3 in 10 — 1. ____

2. According to the tobacco industry, advertisement is targeted at (a) nonsmokers. (b) former smokers. (c) young adults. (d) current smokers. — 2. ____

3. The approximate number of Americans who derive their living from tobacco-related jobs is (a) 800,000. (b) 80,000. (c) 18,000. (d) 8,000. — 3. ____

4. Tobacco is (a) highly addictive. (b) illegal. (c) inexpensive. (d) a low-profit product. — 4. ____

5. Smoking is the leading cause of (a) asbestos-related illnesses. (b) all deaths. (c) unemployment. (d) preventable death. — 5. ____

GETTING THE MEANING

6. This selection is mainly about the (a) benefits of the tobacco industry. (b) benefits of being a nonsmoker. (c) glamor of smoking. (d) legalization of tobacco. — 6. ____

7. The Surgeon General's comment that "nicotine is as addictive as heroin" is meant to (a) condone. (b) flatter. (c) reprimand. (d) warn. — 7. ____

8. The most effective way to get people to quit smoking is to emphasize (a) how much it costs. (b) health benefits. (c) how unattractive it is. (d) how many people have quit successfully. — 8. ____

9. The author implies that tobacco advertisement is (a) infrequent. (b) unique. (c) profitable. (d) ineffective. — 9. ____

10. The primary purpose is to (a) question. (b) entertain. (c) influence. (d) instruct. — 10. ____

Check your answers with the Key on p. 452. Give yourself 10 points for each one right and enter your comprehension score on p. 415.

Comprehension Score: ______

NAME ______________ CLASS ______________ DATE ______________

39 The Road to Wellville

WORD POWER WORKOUT

A. LEANING ON CONTEXT

In each of the blanks provided, place the letter that precedes the best definition of the underlined word in context to the left.

Words in Context	Definitions
1. _____ plaguing American health care	a. looking into
2. _____ insurance premiums	b. vexing
3. _____ investigating the influence	c. compelling
4. _____ significantly lower	d. accompanying matters
5. _____ implications are enormous	e. meaningfully
6. _____ gross domestic product	f. amount paid
7. _____ extrapolate our data	g. life span
8. _____ benefit substantially	h. draw inferences on
9. _____ fitness on longevity	i. entire, complete
10. _____ it's imperative	j. noticeably

Check your answers with the Key on p. 442 before going on. Give yourself 10 points for each one right and enter your score on the chart under A on p. 420. Review any that you have missed.

A Score: _________

Pronunciation aids: **1. PLAG-ing** **9. lahn-JEV-uh-tee** **7. ek-STRAP-uh-lat** **10. im-PER-uh-tiv**

B. LEANING ON PARTS

Legein means "speak" or "study of." When you see *logue, log,* or *loq* in a word, look for those meanings. Use a form of *legein* in each blank below.

1. Talk between two or more is known as a dia__________.
2. A person who gives a powerful speech is an e__________ speaker.
3. The study of myths is mytho__________.
4. A speech coming before a dramatic performance is called a pro__________.
5. Bio__________ is the study of the life processes of plants and animals.

C. MAKING THE WORDS YOURS

In each blank below, enter the most appropriate word from the ten words in context in the first exercise, substituting it for the word(s) in parentheses. Use these words: *extrapolate, gross, imperative, implications, investigating, longevity, plaguing, premiums, significantly, substantially.*

1. The survey showed a (meaningfully) __________ lower inflation rate.
2. The accountant needed the (entire, complete) __________ income figures for the year.
3. It is (compelling) __________ that you catch the very next plane to New York.
4. It's (vexing) __________ us to find a place where we can park the car.
5. Most people I know hope for good (life span) __________.
6. The (amount paid) __________ come due at the first of every month.
7. You will benefit (noticeably) __________ if you invest in that company.
8. Based on the data you have, can you now (draw inferences) __________ for the entire year?
9. The (accompanying matters) __________ were that I was the guilty party.
10. The police were busy (looking into) __________ the latest robbery.

Check your answers with the Key on p. 449.

B Score: __________

C Score: __________

Enter your scores on p. 420.

39

The Road to Wellville

TODD MITCHELL

Money talks about health as well as about cigarette smoking, as you'll soon see. Would you like to live longer? Would you like to enjoy a better quality of life? Who wouldn't! That's why you'll want to read on to find out just how to manage. Wellville—here you come!

BEGIN TIMING

You probably already know that the single most important thing you can do for your health is to exercise regularly. Currently, only 20–30% of Americans engage in regular physical activity. But did you know exercise also could be the solution to the cost crisis plaguing American health care?

If you're like the average American, you spent more than $4,000 on health care in 1998, between co-payments for doctor's visits, medical-insurance premiums and other costs. (Figures for last year aren't yet available.) And those costs have been rising dramatically. According to the journal *Health Affairs,* private health-insurance premiums jumped 8.2% in 1998, more than twice as much as in each of the previous three years (2.8% in 1995, 3.3% in 1996, 3.5% in 1997).

As medical professionals, the federal government, insurance companies and others continue to debate the best way to lower the skyrocketing costs of health care, they're overlooking one simple solution: exercise.

In a study just completed at the Cooper Clinic in Dallas, where I am a staff physician, we have been investigating the influence of physical fitness on the need for health care. The results show fit people require fewer visits to their physicians as well as fewer hospital stays, which translates into significantly lower health-care costs.

On the face of it, our findings may seem obvious: Exercise more and you need to see the doctor less. But the implications are enormous. Medicare costs jumped from $37.5 billion in 1980 to $216.6 billion in 1998. Medicare expenditures as a percentage of the gross domestic product more than tripled from 1970 to 1998 (the most recent year for which data are available). If you extrapolate our data to the 97.8 million adult men living in the United States today, the least fit 25% of those men spend $4.1

billion more every year on hospitalization and doctor's visits than the most fit—twice as much. That's money that could be saved if they improved their physical fitness by even a small degree.

Our study followed 6,679 apparently healthy men who came to the Cooper Clinic for checkups over a 20-year period. Each patient was given at least two complete physicals approximately five years apart, and each filled out a 20-page questionnaire detailing a number of lifestyle factors, including how often he had been to the doctor or been hospitalized every year.

We found that the least fit group (judging by a treadmill test and physical exam) spent almost 63% more on overnight hospitalization costs and 25% more on doctor visits each year. The extra costs for hospitalization alone for the least fit group were close to $250,000 a year—and we used extremely conservative numbers in estimating those costs ($500 a night for a hospital stay, $50 for an office visit). The actual costs were probably even higher.

One of the most encouraging findings of our study and others at the Cooper Clinic is that you don't need high levels of physical activity to benefit substantially from being more fit. The men in our study who were in the best shape were not elite athletes. Of course, they weren't just "weekend athletes," either. They were men from all walks of life who exercised 20–30 minutes a day, four or five days a week.

Quality vs. Quantity of Life

Exercise regularly and you'll save money. But you'll also be in better condition to enjoy spending the money you save, especially as you age. By 2010, more than 97 million Americans will be age 50 or older. Still, as the nation's population ages, most of us want to live longer only as long as we are healthy. Lifestyle factors such as exercise powerfully influence not only *quantity* of life, but *quality* of life as well.

At Cooper's research institute, Dr. Steven N. Blair has followed our patient population for more than 20 years to study the effects of physical fitness on longevity. In a landmark study first published in the *Journal of the American Medical Association* in 1989, Blair found that fit men and women were 65% less likely to die during the nine years of the study period than were their unfit peers. More important, even those who were only moderately fit were less likely to die.

In another study, Blair then followed patients to see what would happen if their level of fitness *changed* over time. He found that physically unfit people who then started to exercise also were likely to live longer.

Is it really worth it to live a few years longer if you have to spend the extra time exercising? This gets back to quantity vs. quality. When you exercise regularly and lead a healthy lifestyle, you don't just prolong life. You also delay disability. This is a key issue. Because America's population is growing older, it's imperative that we remain healthy so we don't exhaust the limited resources available for health care and human services to the elderly.

To sum it all up, these studies reveal two key points: First, regular exercise improves your odds of living longer and, more important, living healthy until the very end of your life. Second, regular exercise reduces health-care costs dramatically.

I hope the federal government, corporate heads and others will pay attention to our study results. Think of the billions of dollars that could be saved each year in healthcare costs and lost work time if more people were fit. I'd like to see more corporations institute onsite wellness programs, including incentives such as paying bonuses to employees if they don't smoke, if they work out a certain number of times a week or if they attend health seminars. I'd like the government to consider giving a tax break to non-smokers and regular exercisers.

There you have it. As we enter the new millennium, the availability of modern medicine, food, clothing and shelter has given us advantages our grandparents never had. It's up to us to make the best of those advances.

Length: 890 words.
Reading Time: __________
See Conversion Table, p. 421.
Enter WPM Rate on p. 416.

39 The Road to Wellville

COMPREHENSION CHECK

GETTING THE FACTS

1. Currently, how many Americans exercise regularly? (a) 10–20% (b) 20–30% (c) 30–40% (d) 40–50% 1. ____

2. This was written by a (a) doctor. (b) research assistant. (c) journalist. (d) clinic supervisor. 2. ____

3. The Cooper Clinic is in (a) Faribault. (b) San Antonio. (c) Dallas. (d) New Orleans. 3. ____

4. The study conducted by Dr. Blair covered how many years? (a) 10 (b) 15 (c) 20 (d) 25 4. ____

5. The selection mentions giving a tax break to (a) non-smokers. (b) athletes. (c) dieters. (d) runners. 5. ____

GETTING THE MEANING

6. This selection is mainly to get us to (a) escape rising medical costs. (b) exercise regularly. (c) stop overeating. (d) live longer. 6. ____

7. If you were to illustrate this selection most appropriately, what would you show on the road? (a) motorcyle (b) bicycle (c) station wagon (d) small car 7. ____

8. In the title the author uses the word *road* to suggest the (a) way. (b) distances. (c) destination. (d) mode of travel. 8. ____

9. The development is primarily dependent on (a) expert opinion. (b) individual examples. (c) details. (d) repetition. 9. ____

10. In style this selection is best described as (a) conversational. (b) literary. (c) dramatic. (d) sparkling. 10. ____

Check your answers with the Key on p. 452. Give yourself 10 points for each one right and enter your comprehension score on p. 415.

Comprehension Score: ______

NAME ______________ CLASS ______________ DATE ______________

40 Generating New and Wider Interests

WORD POWER WORKOUT

A. LEANING ON CONTEXT

In each of the blanks provided, place the letter that precedes the best definition of the underlined word in context to the left.

Words in Context	Definitions
1. _____ a colleague of mine	a. fame
2. _____ never yet voluntarily read a book	b. associate
3. _____ smiled condescendingly at his roommate	c. remarkable
4. _____ a genuinely interested student	d. unreasonable
5. _____ of world renown	e. sincerely
6. _____ impersonal objectivity	f. inefficiency
7. _____ killed by academic restraint	g. willingly
8. _____ showing off his ineptitude	h. disinterested
9. _____ almost irrational enthusiasm	i. control
10. _____ to bring outstanding achievement	j. with an air of superiority

Check your answers with the Key on p. 442 before going on. Give yourself 10 points for each one right and enter your score on the chart under A on p. 420. Review any that you have missed.

A Score: ________

Pronunciation aids: **1. KOL-eeg** **5. rih-NOWN** **3. kon-dih-SEND-ing-lee** **8. in-EP-tuh-tood**

B. LEANING ON PARTS

Tenere means "have" or "hold." When you see *ten(t), tend, tain,* or *tin,* look for those meanings. Fill in the blanks below with a form of *tenere.*

1. Some people observe total abs__________ to control a drinking problem.
2. A person who rents real estate or property is a __________.
3. To hold someone from going is to de__________ the person.
4. To hold firmly to something is to hold on __________.
5. The star's discon__________ lessened everyone else's pleasure.

C. MAKING THE WORDS YOURS

In each blank below, enter the most appropriate word from the ten words in context in the first exercise, substituting it for the word(s) in parentheses. Use these words: *colleague, condescendingly, genuinely, impersonal, ineptitude, irrational, outstanding, renown, restraint, voluntarily.*

1. His (unreasonable) __________ plan lost the battle.
2. A parent must sometimes be (disinterested) __________ when disciplining a child.
3. His (inefficiency) __________ at typing lost him the job.
4. A person's (control) __________ may disappear when he is being teased.
5. My hope was to achieve (fame) __________ in major league baseball.
6. The nurse was (sincerely) __________ interested in helping disabled children.
7. She (willingly) __________ accepted her responsibilities.
8. The baseball player's (remarkable) __________ success got him into the Hall of Fame.
9. My (associate) __________ was known for her humorous remarks.
10. The students asked only a few questions because the teacher answered (with an air of superiority) __________.

Check your answers with the Key on p. 449.

B Score: __________

C Score: __________

Enter your scores on p. 420.

40

Generating New and Wider Interests

BEGIN TIMING

Why do some people reach their goals so quickly? What's their secret? That is, indeed, knowledge most worth knowing.

The Driving Force of Interest

The best car ever made still needs fuel to get you anywhere. Similarly, the best of minds needs a strong interest to bring outstanding achievement.

Interest led Napoleon to become a military leader of world renown. Interest led Charles Darwin to discover the origin of species. Interest led Glenn Cunningham to overcome a major physical handicap and become a record-breaking mile runner.

Interest led Thomas Edison to try 6,000 different substances in his attempt to find a suitable electric light filament. How many people do you know who would have sufficient interest to try even 1,000 substances? No wonder he is known the world over. Interest is the secret. Just as gunpowder speeds a bullet toward its mark, so interest can speed you toward any and every goal you have in mind.

Turn to reading. A comprehensive survey of over 400 colleges and universities disclosed that an estimated 64 to 95 percent of all freshmen are handicapped by reading deficiencies.

Get the implication? Probably 64 to 95 percent are not as interested in reading as in other things. Put it another way: It also suggests that unless reading is the most interesting thing you ever do, you're not reading up to your full potential.

The Need to Enlist Interest

Let's have a closer look. You've noticed that people like to do those things that they do fairly well. A terrible swimmer doesn't really look forward to a swim. Who enjoys showing off his or her inepitude?

It's equally true with reading. The better you read, the stronger your interest. *And*—the stronger your interest, the more you read. But there's the other side, the vicious circle side. The poorer you read, the less your interest. *And*—the less your interest, the less you read.

Take the 64 to 95 percent who don't real well. For them, the secret of improvement lies in enlisting the powerful force of interest.

The normal academic climate isn't always too helpful. To develop interest, you need almost irrational enthusiasm. And that kind of enthusiasm is all too often killed by academic restraint, cold reason, and impersonal objectivity. Together they may dampen completely the little spark of interest an individual has in developing desired skills. What's needed is sufficient enthusiasm to fan that spark into brilliant fame. Then you'll get results. Interest is your assurance.

Build Interest by Personalizing

As a first move, ask yourself this question: What can reading do for me, personally?

Specifically, list your present most important four or five goals. Next, find specific articles or books to help you reach each one. For example, one goal might be to improve your reading. List this book. It will help you attain that goal.

You'll find articles or books help you do anything better. Yes, *anything.* A colleague of mine beat me at handball. How? Reading a book on how to play winning handball tipped the close rivalry in his favor. You can get help from reading even if the goal is to play better handball. Once you connect reading to an important personal goal, that interest actively promotes your reading progress.

Build on Present Interests

As a second move, tap your current interests. Let them lead you to improved reading ability.

What three things are *you* most interested in? Whatever you put down—say, hunting, money, nutrition, scuba diving—be sure they reflect really strong interest. Suppose you have never yet voluntarily read an entire book. Only those required. But, there's a book about one of your strongest interests. That will be the easiest book of all to read.

Take such books as *Hunter* or *I Married a Hunter.* You'll find them fascinating reading. Why? Because of your strong interest in hunting. Or take Mark Skousen's practical book *High Finance on a Low Budget,* or *Jane Fonda's Workout Book,* or *Jane Brody's Nutrition Book* or *Coping with Difficult People.* Such books focus on your strongest interests, making them much easier to read. Furthermore, each book you complete makes the next one that much easier.

Building New Interests

At this point, you're ready for the much more difficult problem—reading a book in a subject area where you have little or no interest. How do you manage that? Let's say you're required to take chemistry, whether you're interested or not. And that means reading the chemistry text.

Here are four suggestions.

First, cultivate the acquaintance of a genuinely interested student. In the chemistry course, for example, listen for a student who's talking with some enthusiasm about a point raised in class. Fall into step with him or her. Suggest a cup of coffee. You'll find that genuine enthusiasm rubs off on you. One student drew a bird-watcher for a roommate. At first he smiled condescendingly at his roommate's talk about birds. In two months, however, sufficient enthusiasm had rubbed off to make him buy binoculars and bird books and go on early morning bird-watching trips. Interest is contagious.

Second, read a popular book on the subject. To generate interest in painting or art, read Stone's book *Lust for Life,* a biography of Vincent Van Gogh. Stefansson, the arctic explorer, traced his lifelong interest in exploring to the reading of one book. Henri Fabre, the famous French entomologist, said the same thing happened to him. One book generated a lifelong interest.

Third, spend extra time on your dullest and most difficult subject. The more you know about any field, the stronger your interest. If you know nothing about football, you're not likely to watch any games.

Fourth, watch for educational TV shows or movies touching areas of your low interest. A movie about Pasteur should stimulate added interest in chemistry.

Now, get busy! Tap interests already present. Develop new ones. Let deepened interest turn study from work to pleasure, and turn a potential *D* into a *B.*

Length: 1000 words.
Reading Time: ______
See Conversion Table, p. 421.
Enter WPM Rate on p. 416.

40 Generating New and Wider Interests

COMPREHENSION CHECK

GETTING THE FACTS

1. Which person is mentioned? (a) Napoleon (b) Darwin (c) Glenn Cunningham (d) all of the preceding — 1. ____

2. What percentage do not read too well? (a) up to 30% (b) up to 65% (c) up to 80% (d) up to 95% — 2. ____

3. One book title mentioned is (a) *Hunter.* (b) *Call of the Wild.* (c) *Into the Silk.* (d) *Between the Elephant's Eyes.* — 3. ____

4. What subject is mentioned? (a) physics (b) chemistry (c) zoology (d) biology — 4. ____

5. Fabre was (a) an entomologist. (b) an ecologist. (c) a painter. (d) a sculptor. — 5. ____

GETTING THE MEANING

6. The selection's main focus is on (a) how to develop interest. (b) the uses of interest. (c) the personal factor in interest. (d) variations in interest. — 6. ____

7. The reference to well-known individuals is to show (a) how to develop interest. (b) how important interest is. (c) the different areas of interest. (d) the varying degrees of interest. — 7. ____

8. Mention of the normal academic environment is made to show (a) the importance of the right setting. (b) the way to fan a spark into a flame. (c) the way to supplement reason. (d) the need to add to the normal academic setting. — 8. ____

9. The handball illustration shows (a) the importance of experience. (b) the importance of reading. (c) the value of experience and reading. (d) the limitations of reading. — 9. ____

10. The bird-watching story shows (a) how interests are developed. (b) what strange interests we have. (c) the importance of interest. (d) how fast interest can be developed. — 10. ____

Check your answers with the Key on p. 452. Give yourself 10 points for each one right and enter your comprehension score on p. 415.

Comprehension Score: ________

MAKING THE APPLICATION

Interests—your own—deserve a close, careful scrutiny. Start by listing the five things you are presently most interested in. List them in order of interest—the most interesting first, the next most interesting second, and so on.

1. ______________________________

2. ______________________________

3. ______________________________

4. ______________________________

5. ______________________________

Now list two things you think it would be most important to have as interests, in place of two in your first listing. Think in terms of your next five years and your personal growth and development. If your original five still seem most important for the next five years, just leave these spaces blank.

1. ______________________________

2. ______________________________

In terms of reading interest, what are the two most interesting books you have read recently?

1. ______________________________

2. ______________________________

What magazines do you usually read?

1. ______________________________

2. ______________________________

3. ______________________________

Do you (a) read a news magazine, (b) read a newspaper, or (c) listen to the radio or TV for most of your news? a ____ b ____ c ____

Estimate the total time spent daily in reading, including required reading. ________________

How many books, generally speaking, do you have of your own? ________________

How many books do you think you read in a year, excluding required textbooks? ______________

Which two selections in this book have you found most interesting reading?

(titles)

1. ____

2. ____

You don't have to eat an entire cake to know whether or not you like it. No, you just need a sample. A single bite should answer your question. That's so with books also. You don't have to read an entire book to know if it's interesting. All you need is a taste.

That's the beauty of short samples, such as the twenty in this book. If you like the sample, you'll want to read more. That's exactly why samples were included—to help you discover really enjoyable reading.

For example, if you liked selection 21, "Watching a Surgeon at Work," because you're considering surgery as a career, you'll probably want to read the full-length book, *Making of a Surgeon,* from which this episode was taken. Only one brief glimpse into the life of a surgeon is hardly enough to help you decide whether that career is for you. The whole book will be much more helpful. In addition, that examination will remind you that whatever your career choice, it would pay you to find a book dealing with the normal activities of that career.

If you found selection 14, "The First Rule of Conversation," interesting reading, you should find the full-length book, *How to Talk to Anyone, Anytime, Anywhere,* equally so. The book jacket reminds you that you'll discover how to start a conversation, how to give speeches, and how to overcome shyness and put people at ease.

Again, if you liked selection 17, "Two Ways of Looking at Life," you'll want to read the full-length book from which this was taken, *Learned Optimism,* for help in determining where you stand and how best to design your life for optimal living—a truly life-changing book.

And if you found selection 23, "The Juggler," interesting, you should then find Fulghum's whole book, *Uh-Oh,* equally so. The author began his writing career by having *two* books on the bestseller list at the same time—a very rare occurrence. *Uh-Oh* makes his third bestseller. Obviously, if you want interesting reading, turn to any of them: *All I Really Need to Know I Learned in Kindergarten, It Was on Fire When I Lay Down on It,* or *Uh-Oh.*

NAME ________ CLASS ________ DATE ________

41 America Won't Win 'Till It Reads More

WORD POWER WORKOUT

A. LEANING ON CONTEXT

In each of the blanks provided, place the letter that precedes the best definition of the underlined word in context to the left.

Words in Context	Definitions
1. ____ that aptitude	a. humdrum
2. ____ steadily corrode	b. storage place
3. ____ Reading transcends	c. talent
4. ____ unrelated events	d. wear away
5. ____ is so portable	e. please greatly
6. ____ the biggest predictor	f. standard
7. ____ became the norm	g. forecaster
8. ____ capacity to enthrall	h. goes beyond
9. ____ foremost repository	i. easily carried around
10. ____ from the mundane	j. separate

Check your answers with the Key on p. 442 before going on. Give yourself 10 points for each one right and enter your score on the chart under A on p. 420. Review any that you have missed.

A Score: ________

B. LEANING ON PARTS

The Greek root *graphein,* which appears in English as *graph,* means "to write." Fill in each of the following blanks, using that root.

1. A written account of your own life is an autobio____________.
2. A list of source books at the end of an article is a biblio____________.
3. A device to wire written messages is called a tele____________.
4. A piece of writing treating a single subject is a mono____________.
5. A vivid written description of an event provides a ____________ account.

C. MAKING THE WORDS YOURS

In each blank below, enter the most appropriate word from the ten words in context in the first exercise, substituting it for the word(s) in parentheses. Use these words: *aptitude, enthrall, erode, mundane, norm, predictor, portable, repository, transcends, unrelated.*

1. That kind of window has been the (standard) ____________ for several years in construction.
2. Early in life some people discover an inborn (talent) ____________ for playing the violin.
3. For the entire evening the conversation focused on (humdrum) ____________ subjects.
4. Their continual lying tended to (wear away) ____________ any confidence in their honesty.
5. Where is the (storage place) ____________ for the exposed x-ray plates?
6. The return on that stock investment (goes beyond) ____________ my expectations.
7. The new detective series on TV tends to (please greatly) __________ me.
8. This new reading test is the best (forecaster) ____________ yet of academic success.
9. You don't need a big moving van to move your (easily carried around) ____________ TV set.
10. As they debated the arms agreement, one raised a totally (separate) ____________ issue.

Check your answers with the Key on p. 449.

B Score: ________

C Score: ________

Enter your scores on p. 420.

41

America Won't Win 'Till It Reads More

STRATFORD P. SHERMAN

What country is the world's greatest power? And why? Does the best-informed country stand at the very top? And is it true that every country is competing with every other country in the world? Does all that explain the title of this next selection?

BEGIN TIMING

If you can understand this article, odds are you read at the level of a college freshman or better. In the U.S., which has produced more high school dropouts than college grads, that aptitude pushes you well outside the mainstream of society. This fact should worry you—for while the statistics on basic literacy look encouraging, they mask trends that, left to continue, will steadily corrode American competitiveness.

Once defined as the ability merely to sign one's name, basic literacy now implies at least a fourth-grade education, enough, say, to read a McDonald's menu. About 90% of U.S. adults have reached such a level, according to the Education Department. Yet experts on international competition think this is far from good enough if the U.S. wants to prosper in an information-based global economy. Work tasks in coming years will be more complex, not less, and understanding them will require better reading skills.

Perhaps more worrisome is that Americans who can read, don't. The buzzword is "aliteracy." Beckoned by countless alternatives—notably work and TV—Americans seem ever less willing to devote their time and attention to page after page of silent black type. John P. Robinson, a sociology professor at the University of Maryland, has collected some of the best available data on how people spend their time, and his surveys show that the average adult American reads just 24 minutes a day. That represents a one-quarter decline since 1965. Newspaper sales per household have been plunging for years, and today roughly half of American adults almost never read books or magazines. Leonard Riggio, CEO of Barnes & Noble, the largest U.S. book retailer, guesses that half the books his customers buy—some as gifts, some perhaps just for display—go unread.

This phenomenon has spread even among the highly educated. Ask yourself how many books you've read recently. Now that we have our MTV—and our VCR and Nintendo and Walkman—the prospect of plowing through a book doesn't seem as easy as it did in simpler times. Consider Robert Lichter, 43, a Harvard Ph.D. who runs the nonprofit Center for Media and Public Affairs, which analyzes the content of television news broadcasts. Says he: "Now, when I come home tired from a long day, I turn on the TV instead of picking up a book. It's easier." Ain't that the truth.

Should anyone care? After all, people get information from television, radio, videocassettes, and audio tapes. Workers can learn their jobs by attending a class or putting a tape in the VCR. Computer databases give you more facts than you'll ever need, and CNN tells you what's happening in the world. Who needs to read?

The answer is everyone who hopes to be productive or successful. Reading turns out to be strongly connected to many of the most important skills in business—among them speech and writing, the primary forms of human communication. Management experts say that communicating often and clearly with workers will be among every manager's key skills in coming years, while in an interconnected world, skillful communication outside one's company becomes steadily more important. Yet just as these trends take hold, many managers are becoming worse communicators. If you doubt it, a look at the standard of memo writing around your shop will probably persuade you.

Reading transcends the mere transmission of information: It fosters an imaginative dialogue between the text and the reader's mind that actually helps people think. Monsanto CEO Richard Mahoney, a devoted reader, regards reading skill as essential for success: "People who read more seem to have that marvelous ability to see linkages between unrelated events. That's the most important quality an executive can have." Research backs up Mahoney's point: In general, the higher a person's reading skills, the higher his professional achievement.

Many media compete with print; none can replace it. No other information technology packs as much data into as few widely comprehensible symbols as the written word. None is so portable or so suited to self-pacing by users. Nor can any other medium economically distribute the depth and breadth of instantly usable information that print does. A publisher can turn a profit on a book that sells just 10,000 copies, whereas films, TV shows, and even most computer databases require much larger audiences.

Through a short chain of causality, America's aliteracy could lead to declining competitiveness vs. other nations. A study by the National

Center on Education and the Economy—a nonprofit policy analysis group chaired by Ira Magaziner, a brilliant, woolly-haired consultant to such corporations as GE—argues persuasively that the skills of U.S. workers are and may continue to be well matched to the available jobs. According to the report, that's because 95% of American companies still cling to turn-of-the-century methods of organizing work that do not require highly skilled workers. Demand for janitors, salesclerks, and bolt tighteners hasn't abated.

Magaziner's report says that American business can compete successfully in world markets in either of two ways. It can pay workers lower wages than prevail abroad, or reorganize in ways that enable workers to produce more. Reorganizing, the more attractive choice, requires changes that most managers can recite by heart: eliminating layers in the organization and pushing authority down into the hands of front-line workers. But giving workers more power and responsibility is another way of saying that they'll be thinking, judging, and deciding more. Magaziner worries that workers who don't read well, and therefore don't think well, may not be able to handle the added responsibility. And the less they read, the worse their chances grow.

Many large companies know they've got a problem and are trying to address it. Motorola is preparing to invest $5 million in teaching production workers basic skills such as reading. Since 1982, Ford Motor has sent some 32,000 workers through a skills program that includes reading. Of course every problem is someone's opportunity: Simon & Schuster foresees a $500-million-a-year market selling remedial reading and other basic skills programs to corporations.

Practically no one disputes the surest way to produce skillful readers. Educators and informed students of education—such as the Committee for Economic Development, sponsored by 200 blue-chip corporations, including Procter & Gamble and Ford—agree that aptitude for reading depends largely on the foundation parents provide their children. Most crucial: reading aloud to preschoolers and setting an example of adult reading at home. Even a spokesman for the National Association of Broadcasters acknowledges that "the biggest predictor of scholastic success is the time parents spend reading to their children."

By that criterion, the outlook is not bright. While no one has reliable figures on time spent reading aloud, it's clear that harried Americans aren't spending much time on their kids. More than two-thirds of mothers of school-age children work. Having showered, worked, eaten, and watched three to four hours of TV each day, the typical American mother devotes less than an hour and a half a day to child care; fathers spend less than half an hour, according to the University of Maryland's Robinson. Quality time, perhaps, but what about reading *Goodnight Moon* to dear little Kimberly and Max?

Blaming TV is easy—and in large part justified. Since 1980, when the two-TV household became the norm, that second set has assumed a growing role in child care. John MacDonald, an Assistant Secretary of Education, points out that "children are spending more time in front of the television set than in school." Daniel Burke, CEO of Capital Cities/ABC, concedes that much of kids' TV is junk. His analysis is depressing: "Television's capacity to enthrall and distract children has probably been helpful to parents in the short run but destructive to children's tendencies to read and imagine."

Despite the ascendancy of moving images and recorded sound in American life, the printed word will likely remain for centuries the foremost repository of mankind's accumulated knowledge—not just a database but also a vessel for history and culture and all the lessons wrung from thousands of years of human experience. If Americans increasingly disregard it, the effects may touch our ability to think and imagine at all levels, from the mundane to the largest and most sweeping. As the philosopher Ludwig Wittgenstein said, the limits of our language are the limits of our world.

If so, our world could someday collapse like matter into a black hole. Brad Leithauser, a poet and novelist, argues that Americans who don't read once popular fiction by Jane Austen or Charles Dickens—and who don't engage their minds as such books require—are losing patience even with the widely enjoyed black and white movies of just 30 years ago. Reason: Black and white requires the viewer to imagine too much. Yes, inadequate reading skills are hurting U.S. business right now. But unless Americans start reading more, they may someday lose their ability to imagine much of anything for themselves—including a world different from the one they see on the screen.

Length: 1500 words.
Reading Time: __________
See Conversion Table, p. 421.
Enter WPM Rate on p. 416.

41 America Won't Win 'Till It Reads More

COMPREHENSION CHECK

GETTING THE FACTS

1. The average American reads how many minutes a day? (a) 22 (b) 24 (c) 26 (d) 28 — 1. ____

2. Specific mention is made of (a) NBC. (b) A&E. (c) CNN. (d) TV Digest. — 2. ____

3. How many successful ways to compete in a world market are mentioned? (a) only one (b) two (c) three (d) four — 3. ____

4. What company is said to teach reading to its employees? (a) Motorola (b) Monsanto (c) Procter & Gamble (d) Simon & Schuster — 4. ____

5. Specific mention is made of (a) Mark Twain. (b) Victor Hugo. (c) Rudyard Kipling. (d) Charles Dickens. — 5. ____

GETTING THE MEANING

6. The main idea is to show (a) why we're reading less. (b) ways to encourage skillful reading. (c) the growing illiteracy in America. (d) the result of reading less on competition. — 6. ____

7. This selection is organized on what basis? (a) problem-solution (b) problem-result (c) general to specific (d) chronologically — 7. ____

8. Most emphasis is on (a) individual success. (b) American competitiveness. (c) relationship between TV viewing and reading. (d) management and reading. — 8. ____

9. The writer's attitude toward his subject is (a) puzzled. (b) pessimistic. (c) concerned. (d) optimistic. — 9. ____

10. To make his point, the writer depends primarily on (a) specific examples. (b) opinions of experts. (c) comparisons. (d) factual information. — 10. ____

Check your answers with the Key on p. 452. Give yourself 10 points for each one right and enter your comprehension score on p. 415.

Comprehension Score: ________

NAME ____________ CLASS ____________ DATE ____________

42 My Alma Mater

WORD POWER WORKOUT

A. LEANING ON CONTEXT

In each of the blanks provided, place the letter that precedes the best definition of the underlined word in context to the left.

Words in Context	**Definitions**
1. ____ license plate quota	a. thumbing through
2. ____ expounded upon him	b. portion
3. ____ he was gruff	c. inactive
4. ____ told me flatly	d. explained
5. ____ tried to emulate him	e. absorbing
6. ____ riffling uncertainly	f. grouchy
7. ____ I was so fascinated	g. restoration
8. ____ emphasis on rehabilitation	h. plainly
9. ____ of something engrossing	i. copy
10. ____ long dormant craving	j. attracted

Check your answers with the Key on p. 442 before going on. Give yourself 10 points for each one right and enter your score on the chart under A on p. 420. Review any that you have missed.

A Score: ________

Pronunciation aids: **5. EM-yoo-layt**
8. re-ha-bil-ih-TA-shun
10. DOR-munt

B. LEANING ON PARTS

Capere means "take" or "seize." When you see *cept, cap, cip,* or *ceiv* in a word, look for that meaning. Use forms of *capere* in the blanks below.

1. A person seized by the police is their ___________.
2. The executive was the re___________ of an honorary degree.
3. When you take your choice, you ___________ what you've chosen.
4. Seizing your opponent's forward pass is inter___________ it.
5. A slave taken out of bondage was said to be eman___________.

C. MAKING THE WORDS YOURS

In each blank below, enter the most appropriate word from the ten words in context in the first exercise, substituting it for the word(s) in parentheses. Use these words: *dormant, emulate, engrossing, expounded, fascinated, flatly, gruff, quota, rehabilitation, riffling.*

1. The child tried to (copy) ___________ the actions of her friends.
2. He (plainly) ___________ refused to give out any more information about the accident.
3. Each member has a (portion) ___________ based on shares owned.
4. The grizzly bears in Yellowstone are (inactive) ___________ during the winter.
5. The lecturer (explained) ___________ at great length on everything about the excavation.
6. The student found the new novel the most (absorbing) ___________ she had ever read.
7. The engineer was idly (thumbing through) ___________ the pages of the big dictionary.
8. I'm not working any longer for anyone so (grouchy) ___________.
9. They were (attracted) ___________ by the performance of the new computer model.
10. That is the agency concerned with the (restoration) ___________ of young criminals.

Check your answers with the Key on p. 449.

B Score: ________

C Score: ________

Enter your scores on p. 420.

42

My Alma Mater

MALCOLM X

You know America won't win 'till it reads more. Well, the same for everyone in America. An individual won't win 'till he or she reads more. Here's an individual in jail for trying without success to win. But his reading and writing program turned things around. His dictionary-based, self-help program is without parallel.

BEGIN TIMING

The first man I met in prison who made any positive impression on me whatever was a fellow inmate, "Bimbi." I met him in 1947, at Charlestown. He was a light, kind of red-complexioned Negro, as I was; about my height, and he had freckles. Bimbi, an old-time burglar, had been in many prisons. In the license plate shop where our gang worked he operated the machine that stamped out the numbers. I was along the conveyor belt where the numbers were painted.

Bimbi was the first Negro convict I'd known who didn't respond to "What'cha know, Daddy?" Often, after we had done our day's license plate quota, we would sit around, perhaps fifteen of us, and listen to Bimbi. Normally, white prisoners wouldn't think of listening to Negro prisoners' opinions on anything, but guards, even, would wander over close to hear Bimbi on any subject.

He would have a cluster of people riveted, often on odd subjects you never would think of. He would prove to us, dipping into the science of human behavior, that the only difference between us and outside people was that we had been caught. He liked to talk about historical events and figures. When he talked about the history of Concord, where I was to be transferred later, you would have thought he was hired by the Chamber of Commerce, and I wasn't the first inmate who had never heard of Thoreau until Bimbi expounded upon him. Bimbi was known as the library's best customer. What fascinated me with him most of all was that he was the first man I had ever seen command total respect . . . with his words.

Bimbi seldom said much to me; he was gruff to individuals, but I sensed he liked me. What made me seek his friendship was when I heard him discuss religion. I considered myself beyond atheism—I was Satan.

But Bimbi put the atheist philosophy in a framework, so to speak. That ended my vicious cursing attacks. My approach sounded so weak alongside his, and he never used a foul word.

Out of the blue one day, Bimbi told me flatly, as was his way, that I had some brains, if I'd use them. I had wanted his friendship, not that kind of advice. I might have cursed another convict, but nobody cursed Bimbi. He told me I should take advantage of the prison correspondence courses and the library.

When I finished the eighth grade back in Mason, Michigan, that was the last time I'd thought of studying anything that didn't have some hustle purpose. And the streets had erased everything I'd ever learned in school; I didn't know a verb from a house. . . .

Many who today hear me somewhere in person, or on television, or those who read something I've said, will think I went to school far beyond the eighth grade. This impression is due entirely to my prison studies.

It had really begun back in the Charlestown Prison, when Bimbi first made me feel envy of his stock of knowledge. Bimbi had always taken charge of any conversation he was in, and I had tried to emulate him. But every book I picked up had few sentences which didn't contain anywhere from one to nearly all of the words that might as well have been in Chinese. When I just skipped those words, of course, I really ended up with little idea of what the book said. So I had come to the Norfolk Prison Colony still going through only book-reading motions. Pretty soon, I would have quit even these motions, unless I had received the motivation that I did.

I saw that the best thing I could do was get hold of a dictionary—to study, to learn some words. I was lucky enough to reason also that I should try to improve my penmanship. It was sad. I couldn't even write in a straight line. It was both ideas together that moved me to request a dictionary along with some tablets and pencils from the Norfolk Prison Colony school.

I spent two days just riffling uncertainly through the dictionary's pages. I'd never realized so many words existed! I didn't know which words I needed to learn. Finally, to start some kind of action, I began copying.

In my slow, painstaking, ragged handwriting, I copied into my tablet everything printed on that first page, down to the punctuation marks.

I believe it took me a day. Then, aloud, I read back, to myself, everything I'd written on the tablet. Over and over, aloud, to myself, I read my own handwriting.

I woke up the next morning, thinking about those words—immensely proud to realize that not only had I written so much at one time, but I'd written words that I never knew were in the world. Moreover, with a little effort, I also could remember what many of these words meant. I reviewed the words whose meanings I didn't remember. Funny thing, from the dictionary first page right now, that "aardvark" springs to my mind. The dictionary had a picture of it, a long-tailed, long-eared, burrowing African mammal, which lives off termites caught by sticking out its tongue as an anteater does for ants.

I was so fascinated that I went on—I copied the dictionary's next page. And the same experience came when I studied that. With every succeeding page, I also learned of people and places and events from history. Actually the dictionary is like a miniature encyclopedia. Finally the dictionary's A section had filled a whole tablet—and I went on into the B's. That was the way I started copying what eventually became the entire dictionary. It went a lot faster after so much practice helped me to pick up handwriting speed. Between what I wrote in my tablet, and writing letters, during the rest of my time in prison I would guess I wrote a million words.

I suppose it was inevitable that as my word-base broadened, I could for the first time pick up a book and read and now begin to understand what the book was saying. Anyone who has read a great deal can imagine the new world that opened. Let me tell you something; from then until I left that prison, in every free moment I had, if I was not reading in the library, I was reading on my bunk. You couldn't have gotten me out of books with a wedge. Between Mr. Muhammad's teachings, my correspondence, my visitors—usually Ella and Reginald—and my reading of books, months passed without my even thinking about being imprisoned. In fact, up to then, I never had been so truly free in my life. . . .

As you can imagine, especially in a prison where there was heavy emphasis on rehabilitation, an inmate was smiled upon if he demonstrated an unusually intense interest in books. There was a sizable number of well-read inmates, especially the popular debaters. Some were said by many to be practically walking encyclopedias. They were almost celebrities. No university would ask any student to devour literature as I did when this new world opened to me, of being able to read and *understand.*

I read more in my room than in the library itself. An inmate who was known to read a lot could check out more than the permitted maximum number of books. I preferred reading in the total isolation of my own room.

When I had progressed to really serious reading, every night about ten P.M. I would be outraged with the "lights out." It always seemed to catch me right in the middle of something engrossing.

Fortunately, right outside my door was a corridor light that cast a glow into my room. The glow was enough to read by, once my eyes adjusted to it. So when "lights out" came, I would sit on the floor where I could continue reading in that glow.

At one-hour intervals the night guards paced past every room. Each time I heard the approaching foot-steps, I jumped into bed and feigned sleep. And as soon as the guard passed, I got back out of bed onto the floor area of that light-glow, where I would read for another fifty-eight minutes—until the guard approached again. That went on until three or four every morning. Three or four hours of sleep a night was enough for me. Often in the years in the streets I had slept less than that.

I have often reflected upon the new vistas that reading opened to me. I knew right there in prison that reading had changed forever the course of my life. As I see it today, the ability to read awoke inside me some long dormant craving to be mentally alive. I certainly wasn't seeking any degree, the way a college confers a status symbol upon its students. My homemade education gave me, with every additional book that I read, a little bit more sensitivity to the deafness, dumbness, and blindness that was afflicting the black race in America. Not long ago, an English writer telephoned me from London, asking questions. One was, "What's your alma mater?" I told him, "Books." You will never catch me with a free fifteen minutes in which I'm not studying something I feel might be able to help the black man. . . .

Every time I catch a plane, I have with me a book that I want to read—and that's a lot of books these days. If I weren't out here every day battling the white man, I could spend the rest of my life reading, just satisfying my curiosity—because you can hardly mention anything I'm not curious about. I don't think anybody ever got more out of going to prison than I did. In fact, prison enabled me to study far more intensively than I would have if my life had gone differently and I had attended some college. I imagine that one of the biggest troubles with colleges is there are too many distractions, too much panty-raiding, fraternities, and boola-boola and all of that. Where else but in prison could I have attacked my ignorance by being able to study intensely sometimes as much as fifteen hours a day?

Length: 1720 words.
Reading Time: ________
See Conversion Table, p. 421.
Enter WPM Rate on p. 416.

42 My Alma Mater

COMPREHENSION CHECK

GETTING THE FACTS

1. Bimbi is spoken of as (a) a safe blower. (b) an old-time burglar. (c) a second-story man. (d) a dope pusher. 1. ____

2. The author says he didn't know a verb from a (a) noun. (b) book. (c) hole in the ground. (d) house. 2. ____

3. The author felt he should improve his (a) speech. (b) arithmetic. (c) grammar. (d) penmanship. 3. ____

4. How many words does Malcolm X think he wrote while in prison? (a) two million (b) a million (c) half a million (d) amount not specified. 4. ____

5. Lights out came at what time? (a) nine P.M. (b) ten P.M. (c) eleven P.M. (d) no exact time given. 5. ____

GETTING THE MEANING

6. The main focus is on how (a) Bimbi inspired Malcolm X. (b) Malcolm X developed his reading abilities and interests. (c) Malcolm X developed his vocabulary. (d) strongly Malcolm X was motivated. 6. ____

7. Malcolm X felt that Bimbi was respected for his (a) age. (b) experience. (c) words. (d) personality. 7. ____

8. What subject of discussion attracted Malcolm X most strongly to Bimbi? (a) the science of human behavior (b) Thoreau (c) religion (d) historical events and figures 8. ____

9. Copying the dictionary seemed to please Malcolm X primarily because he (a) could remember the words easily. (b) improved his handwriting greatly. (c) learned words he didn't know existed. (d) found he could use the words frequently. 9. ____

10. Of the following words, which best characterizes Malcolm X? (a) tough (b) clever (c) persistent (d) sociable 10. ____

Check your answers with the Key on p. 452. Give yourself 10 points for each one right and enter your comprehension score on p. 415.

Comprehension Score: ________

D. VOCABULARY REVIEW QUIZ

This quiz contains ten words taken from preceding Word Power Workouts, but with other possible meanings of the word. The focus is on words with important prefixes so as to reinforce your awareness of prefixes as aids to word meaning.

1. undefinable (a) fair (b) vague (c) safe (d) sad (e) decent 1. _____
Undefinable contains the prefixes _____ and _____, meaning _____ and _____.

2. conversational (a) clever (b) well-dressed (c) clear (d) friendly (e) talkative 2. _____
Conversational contains the prefix _____, meaning _____.

3. releases (a) lets go (b) provides (c) rents (d) admits (e) closes 3. _____
Releases contains the prefix _____, meaning _____.

4. disability (a) handicap (b) threat (c) failure (d) demand (e) mistake 4. _____
Disability contains the prefix _____, meaning _____.

5. substantially (a) fairly (b) gladly (c) solidly (d) clearly (e) handsomely 5. _____
Substantially contains the prefix _____, meaning _____.

6. colleague (a) player (b) trainer (c) umpire (d) coworker (e) fielder 6. _____
Colleague contains the prefix _____, meaning _____.

7. corrode (a) wear away (b) ride (e) open (d) combine (e) suffer 7. _____
Corrode contains the prefix _____, meaning _____.

8. expounded (a) beat (b) explained (c) prepared (d) accepted (e) heard 8. _____
Expounded contains the prefix _____, meaning _____.

9. assurance

(a) fee (b) outlook (c) sense (d) promise (e) range
Assurance contains the prefix _____, meaning, _____.

9. ____

10. deviations

(a) examples (b) varieties (c) values (d) digressions (e) discoveries
Deviations contains the prefix _____, meaning _____.

10. ____

10 points for each correct answer.
See Key on p. 441.
Vocabulary Review Score: _______

PART V

The Round-up

NAME ____________ CLASS ____________ DATE ____________

43 Reading for School and Life

WORD POWER WORKOUT

A. LEANING ON CONTEXT

In each of the blanks provided, place the letter that precedes the best definition of the underlined word in context to the left.

Words in Context	Definitions
1. ____ the <u>boundaries</u> of the human mind	a. attic
2. ____ a poor man in a <u>garret</u>	b. search
3. ____ your most important <u>quest</u>	c. occupation
4. ____ those about your <u>vocation</u>	d. tasted
5. ____ <u>surplus</u> of approximately two million schoolteachers	e. limits
6. ____ they supply <u>assurance</u>	f. confidence
7. ____ the <u>ideal</u> supplement	g. shock
8. ____ before being properly <u>savored</u>	h. excess
9. ____ Greeks <u>epitomized</u> that problem	i. perfect
10. ____ avoid the <u>trauma</u>	j. typified

Check your answers with the Key on p. 442 before going on. Give yourself 10 points for each one right and enter your score on the chart under A on p. 420. Review any that you have missed.

A Score: ________

Pronunciation aids: **8. SA-vur'd**
9. ih-PIT-uh-myz'd
10. TRAW-muh

B. LEANING ON PARTS

Take another look at the root *facere,* meaning "make" or "do." It comes over into English with so many different spellings. Fill in each of the following blanks, using that root.

1. If some style is found everywhere, we say it's stylish or __________able.
2. If you show real speed and skill at your work, you're a __________ile worker.
3. You can call a blemish or flaw in a gem an imper__________tion.
4. If you accomplish something of an unusual nature, it deserves to be called a __________.
5. If someone does well for you, it's a real bene__________.

C. MAKING THE WORDS YOURS

In each blank below, enter the most appropriate word from the ten words in context in the first exercise, substituting it for the word(s) in parentheses. Use these words: *assurance, boundaries, epitomized, garret, ideal, quest, savored, surplus, trauma, vocation.*

1. The damp (attic) __________ made the clothes mildew.
2. A dry, warm day is (perfect) __________ for a car race.
3. His actions (typified) __________ those of a jealous husband.
4. The U.S. no longer has (excess) __________ grain to give away.
5. Because of her interest in helping others, she chose social work as her (occupation) __________.
6. The boy's (search) __________ for his dog led him into the woods.
7. To write an appealing ad, a person must set (limits) __________ on what to include.
8. After you have studied a word carefully, you can then use it with real (confidence) __________.
9. The artist finally (tasted) __________ the rewards of success.
10. The father's death put his daughter into a state of (shock) __________.

Check your answers with the Key on p. 450.

B Score: ________

C Score: ________

Enter your scores on p. 420.

43

Reading for School and Life

Round-up time! Only it's not for cattle—it's for all the things you've learned so far to improve your reading and vocabulary. Now's the time to put your personal touch on everything you've covered. The next eight readings after this one come from textbooks—school reading—essential reading. They make perfect additional practice. And, as you well know, without practice you don't get any nearer to perfection. So, round up all you've learned. Put your brand on it, apply it, then enjoy to the full the satisfaction that successful progress brings.

BEGIN TIMING

Today is the first day of the rest of your life. How can reading fill it to overflowing with adventures, richness, and fullness?

Your Pleasure-Giving Skill

Skills are skills. Pleasures are pleasures. *But,* some skills are lasting pleasures. Such is reading. Listen to Hazlitt: "The greatest pleasure in life is that of reading." Or Macaulay: "I would rather be a poor man in a garret with plenty of books than a king who did not love reading." To them and countless others all over the world, reading is a source of deepest and fullest enjoyment. That's true from early school days to days of leisure and retirement.

Your Fountain of Youth

Reading is more than that. It can be your fountain of youth. Virginia Woolf said, "The true reader is essentially young." One of your major problems is how to stay alive as long as you live. Some die at 30 but are not buried until they're 70. With some, youth slips away before being properly savored. Reading provides a spring of living water, refreshing and life-giving. Stay young for life with reading.

Your Dream-Fulfillment Aid

Part of youth lies in dreaming—dreaming impossible dreams that you can sometimes make possible. Robert F. Kennedy said this: "Some men see things as they are and say 'Why?' I dream things that never were and say 'Why not?'" Certain books push the boundaries of the human mind out beyond belief. After all, a little bit of greatness hides in everyone. Let books bring it into full bloom.

Your Know-Thyself Aid

What's your most important quest? Finding yourself. Finding your own identity. The Greeks epitomized that problem in two words: Know thyself. Well, articles and books help in that all-important search. They supply assurance of the power and worth of your own life, a measure of your possibilities.

To see yourself in proper perspective, you need detailed pictures of real people in real situations. We need to see three-dimensional characters, with all the typical human fears and limitations. Then, and only then, can you begin to see and know yourself as you should.

Your Vocational Counselor and Consultant

What about practical questions, such as those about your vocation? Will reading help you decide more intelligently (1) what to do, (2) how to prepare yourself, and (3) how to succeed on the job?

To answer the first question, you have to know your own talents, abilities, and interests well. You must also, however, know the opportunities in the world around you. Some Bureau of Labor statistics, for example, predicted a surplus of approximately two million schoolteachers. Still another source indicated that right now "the health fields are the only fields in which we have shortages." Balance such information with self-knowledge and you have some of the ingredients needed to make intelligent, perceptive choices.

Second. You've decided on a career. How and where do you get the required preparation? Again, turn to reading. You'll probably find a listing of school programs to choose from. You may even find them rated. If so, you'll know exactly where to go for the best possible preparation.

Third. Don't stop yet. You've selected a career and trained yourself. Lean on reading now to help you succeed on the job. A variety of magazines and books will provide guidance and help.

But that's not all. The days of only one lifetime career may be almost over. All too often, change throws hundreds out of work. Change hit the aircraft industry, for example. Result? Hundreds of well-qualified engineers suddenly out on the street.

If you manage things well, keeping a close eye on changing conditions, you can avoid the trauma of waking up to find yourself out of a job. Through reading develop some new skills and interests. Then if conditions change, you can slip with comparative ease from one field into another, hardly breaking stride.

Most of the things taught in school—typing, computer programming, languages, farming, business management—are readily available in interesting self-help articles and books. Let them smooth your path in any new direction you decide to take.

Your Experience Extender

What's the best teacher? Experience, of course! It's priceless. It comes from what you yourself have seen, heard, tasted, smelled, and felt—what you yourself have lived through.

Take a closer look. Look at our limitations. No wonder experience is so precious. We can't begin to get enough of it. We can't even experience again what we just lived through. We're not born with instant replay. We can't actually relive any moment. And, obviously, we're limited to one lifetime.

Space and time! How they limit us. Who has a time machine to carry him back into history? No one. It's the same with space. We can't literally be in two places at the same time. Right now you can't be sitting where you are and at the same time be strolling down the famed Champs Elysées in Paris.

And there's so much experience we need. What's it really like to work on an assembly line? What's it really like to be an administrator?

Here's where reading fits. It can bring us, personally, almost unlimited additional experience. To be sure, it's secondhand experience. But it's often so vivid it seems firsthand, just as if we're living through it ourselves, being moved to tears, laughter, or suspense. That rich range of experience provides the ideal supplement to our own limited experience. In this way, reading becomes one of our most profound mind-shaping activities.

Furthermore, all this experience is available when we want it. Books never impose on us. When we want them, we reach out and pull them off the shelf or table. At our convenience we invite them to share their unbelievable wealth with us.

Carlyle sums this all up nicely. "All that mankind has done, thought, gained, or been; it is lying as in magic preservation in the pages of books." Help yourself! Make reading your experience extender for the rest of your life.

Length: 1000 words.
Reading Time: ________
See Conversion Table, p. 421.
Enter WPM Rate on p. 416.

43 Reading for School and Life

COMPREHENSION CHECK

GETTING THE FACTS

1. One quotation is from (a) the Bible. (b) Hazlitt. (c) Shakespeare. (d) Alexander Pope. 1. ____

2. Complete this quotation: "The true reader is essentially . . ." (a) busy. (b) wise. (c) young. (d) alive. 2. ____

3. Specific mention is made of the (a) aircraft industry. (b) automotive industry. (c) electronic industry. (d) plastic industry. 3. ____

4. The best teacher is said to be (a) experience. (b) books. (c) friends. (d) TV. 4. ____

5. What place is mentioned? (a) Madison Avenue (b) Champs Elysées (c) State Street (d) Main Street, U.S.A. 5. ____

GETTING THE MEANING

6. This article is mainly about how to make reading (a) a normal habit. (b) contribute to living. (c) fulfill your dreams. (d) stimulate thought. 6. ____

7. To die at thirty but be buried at seventy uses the word *die* in the sense of to (a) lose purpose. (b) lose incentive. (c) stop growing. (d) die spiritually. 7. ____

8. Kennedy's quote implies that we (a) all do less than we could. (b) need prodding to act. (c) need interest to get us going. (d) need frequent stimulus for a response. 8. ____

9. The talk about several careers is to show (a) the need for variety. (b) how uncertain life is. (c) the need for stability. (d) the need for broad planning. 9. ____

10. The talk about limitations of time and space is intended to point up the need (a) to do different things. (b) to do a few things well. (c) for thorough training. (d) to supplement our experience with that of others. 10. ____

Check your answers with the Key on p. 452. Give yourself 10 points for each one right and enter your comprehension score on p. 415.

Comprehension Score: ________

MAKING THE APPLICATION

A carefully planned reading program can help you reach about any personal goal you can think of. Try your hand at drawing up a specific reading plan for the next year to help with the following two goals:

1. Describe a specific plan for continuing your improvement in reading, in rate, comprehension, and development of broader interests.

2. Describe a specific plan for continuing your vocabulary development. It might be a word-a-day plan, words drawn from your reading. It might be a prefix-a-day plan, or a dictionary-study plan.

Now, set down a purpose of your own choice. List the books and articles that will help you reach this goal.

Finding Just the Right Word, Electronically

Ever get "word stuck"? You know; that's when you use the same word over and over again when composing an *essay.* It seems that as soon as you sit down to write, your mind goes blank except for a few words that just seem to pop into your *essay* despite your wanting to use others. When you finally read the *essay* you have worked so hard to write, you are shocked to see one or two words repeated throughout the *essay.* Writing instructors expect you to include vocabulary in your *essays* that hold the reader's interest and paint a vivid picture. If you don't, readers are likely to be bored when your *essay* is dominated by the repetition of a few words.

As you read the paragraph above, did you notice anything monotonous? Well, I certainly did. In a 128-word paragraph, I used the word *essay* six times—that's approximately once every 21 words! Few readers would find reading that paragraph an interesting experience, and even though the paragraph is not about the latest movie or most popular vocalist, I could have enlivened it by adding variety—using synonyms for the word *essay* some of the time. To prove my point, reread the first paragraph and substitute any of the following words for *essay: paper, composition, piece, writing, article,* or *theme.* Wasn't that more interesting?

I have to admit; I had a little help. I found the synonyms for *essay* in a thesaurus. If you create your compositions using a word processor, stopping to use a book every time you need a new word would slow you down. Don't worry! Most word processing programs have a built-in thesaurus. I used the thesaurus in Microsoft Word to generate the substitution list above. All you have to do is highlight the word you would like to replace, click on Tools on the Tool bar, click on Language, then click on Thesaurus. The word you have highlighted will appear in a box, and synonyms—words that have a similar meaning—will appear in a column for you to select. If you have difficulty using this feature of your word processing program, seek assistance from the staff in your learning center, writing center, or library. If you do not use a word processor, looking up an overused word in a print thesaurus takes only a few minutes.

No matter how busy you are, spice up your writing with words that clearly convey the meaning you want to share, and use an electronic thesaurus to make it fast and easy.

MAKING THE APPLICATION

It pays to make the dictionary your friend. But, you need more than one friend when you're dealing with words.

Let me tell you about the foreign student who was frantically trying to build up his vocabulary. As he was thumbing through the dictionary, he saw the word *skinny,* which he had never seen before. It means "very thin." Well, he thought, that good-looking girl I sit next to in my English class is thin. I'll compliment her tomorrow and show off my new word. And he did. He said, "My, but you're skinny!" Instead of smiling at the compliment, she glared at him and turned away. He came up to the instructor after class and told him what had happened and asked why.

The instructor explained that words can have two sides—denotative and connotative. The denotation of words is what you find in the dictionary—the definition or meaning of the word. Finding the connotative side can be a problem—the problem the foreign student just discovered. Words can express favor or disfavor. Word connotation grows gradually from how the word is normally used. If *skinny* is used generally to suggest disfavor, then using it communicates disfavor in the thinness. That's exactly what *skinny* does. It denotes "thin" but connotes displeasure at that thinness.

One writer became poetic about such differences:

Call a woman a lamb, but never a sheep;
Economic she likes, but you can't call her cheap.
You can say she's a vision, can't say she's a sight;
And no woman is skinny, she's slender or slight;
If she burns you up, say she sets you on fire,
And you'll always be welcome, you tricky old liar.

And that's where the thesaurus helps. How many synonyms can you think of for the word *thin?* List as many as you can on the line below.

____

Now look up *thin* in a thesaurus. You'll find several different categories. But look under *slender* and list below some of the synonyms you find. That foreign student could have used any of those words as real compliments and gotten a smile, not a frown.

____

____

Now look under *lean* and you'll find *skinny.* List some of the synonym choices you find there. Connotatively, beware of those.

___

Now you're acquainted with the reference that will help you find the right words for your ideas. Just look up the idea word and then choose the exact word in the listing for the meaning you want to express.

Try this exercise in word choice to indicate different connotations. Follow this example.

Observation	**Favorable Connotation**	**Unfavorable Connotation**
Example: She's *thin*	slender	skinny
He's *fat*	___	___
What a *long* speech	___	___
She *spends carefully*	___	___
His shirt was *different*	___	___

Discuss differences in class to point up connotative word values and how the thesaurus can help.

Overcoming "Textbook Blues"

Homework. Ugh!

Most students find reading textbooks a very challenging and daunting responsibility. Often, new college students just can't find ways to motivate themselves to study material that does not interest them or is too difficult for quick comprehension. Textbooks are so overwhelming to some students that they put off doing homework assignments until the last minute, if they do them at all. The result is that these students forego the benefits of one of the most valuable educational tools—textbooks—and are forced to rely on classroom lectures and discussion to learn course content. Besides that, students who don't use their textbooks waste money, reaping little more from their books than the muscle power gained from carrying them around in a backpack for a whole semester.

It's Hard to Develop Interest

Most college students, especially in the first two years, take required courses whose content is of little interest to them. If it's hard for you to become interested in your homework, go on the Internet, to an online encyclopedia, or read about the topic in a general reference book in your library. Or you might ask an instructor at your college who is an expert in the subject for suggestions to heighten your interest. *Wanting to know* is an incredible interest-builder and will help you to store and retain knowledge more efficiently.

Why We Chose the Following Selections

To help students leap over this hurdle, we increased the number of text selections in this edition at the request of instructors and students who have used *Reading Power* previously. Excerpts on the following pages come from introductory college texts, typical of the ones students like you use in colleges across the country. A single college reading assignment averages 2,500–5,000 words, but space prohibits our including pieces that long. So, we have chosen eight selections, ranging in length from 920–1,650 words, that typify the structure, layout, vocabulary, and syntax of college texts. You will notice that the design of the textbook selections is different from other selections in the book. We have reproduced the original text as accurately as possible so you can learn to use the structural elements of textbooks to your advantage.

These text selections are available for you and your instructor to use in a variety of ways. Your instructor may illustrate how authors organize ideas for effective textbooks and how to use the helpful tools authors infuse throughout the text. Your instructor may also use the text selection to teach study techniques such as SQ3R, mapping, summarizing, or note taking. Or your class may choose to study text excerpts, discuss the concepts in class, and share strategies for mastering difficult content. Though we do not advise that you speed read while studying textbook material, we have included the word count for each selection in case you want to study it and then speed read the piece for practice.

No matter how you use the textbook selections, the mere focus on the subject, structure, vocabulary, and concepts will enhance your ability to read and comprehend academic materials. The more you refine these skills, the better you will become at apprehending information germane to your college pursuits and get over "textbook blues."

NAME ______________ CLASS ______________ DATE ______________

44 Good Health for Sale

WORD POWER WORKOUT

A. LEANING ON CONTEXT

In each of the blanks provided, place the letter that precedes the best definition of the underlined word in context to the left.

Words in Context	Definitions
1. _____ the <u>transcendent</u> calm	a. outdated
2. _____ rushed and <u>harried</u> bunch	b. certainly
3. _____ the <u>archaic</u> term	c. extraordinary
4. _____ a little <u>vial</u>	d. exhausted
5. _____ an <u>inexcusable</u> shakedown	e. weakness
6. _____ will <u>inevitably</u> grow	f. container
7. _____ indefinable <u>malaise</u>	g. speech style
8. _____ <u>unimpeded</u> by the need	h. indefensible
9. _____ neighborly <u>locution</u>	i. departures
10. _____ <u>deviations</u> from "cost effectiveness"	j. unrestricted

Check your answers with the Key on p. 442 before going on. Give yourself 10 points for each one right and enter your score on the chart under A on p. 420. Review any that you have missed.

A Score: _______

Pronunciation aids: **2. HAR-eed** **3. ar-KAY-ik** **5. in-ek-SKYOO-zuh-bu** **6. in-EV-i-tuh-bul-ee** **7. ma-LAZ** **9. lo-KYOO-shun**

B. LEANING ON PARTS

Now for some suffixes, those useful parts you fit on the end of words. Take *describe.* How do you turn it into "one who describes"? Just add an *-er* to make *describer.* In each blank below, add the required suffix.

1. One who helps is a help__________.
2. One who is young is youth__________.
3. If you work without tiring, you are a tire__________ worker.
4. A female lion is a lion__________.
5. Of or pertaining to an infant is infant__________.

C. MAKING THE WORDS YOURS

In each blank below, enter the most appropriate word from the ten words in context in the first exercise, substituting it for the word(s) in parentheses. Use these words: *archaic, deviations, harried, inevitably, inexcusable, locution, malaise, transcendent, unimpeded, vial.*

1. That approach to the problem is (outdated) __________.
2. The parents of active twins seemed (exhausted) __________ at the end of their trip.
3. The tour group's (weakness) __________ was a result of the 16-hour trip.
4. Entrance to the south parking lot was (unrestricted) __________.
5. She kept her favorite perfumes in an airtight (container) __________.
6. Each of the (departures) __________ from the procedure cost him time and money.
7. The angry ballplayer's outbursts were (indefensible) __________.
8. Their family is (certainly) __________ polite.
9. The (speech style) __________ of the professor forced the students to stay awake.
10. Their experience was more (extraordinary) __________ than frightening.

Check your answers with the Key on p. 450.

B Score: ________

C Score: ________

Enter your scores on p. 420.

44

Good Health for Sale

BARBARA EHRENREICH

Do advertisements make you do things that you didn't think you wanted to do, buy things that you never thought you needed, and go places that had never interested you in the least? Well, persuasive ads may now entice you to self-diagnose and demand the drug de jour at your next visit to the doctor. Patients, beware!

BEGIN TIMING

You're feeling a little peckish perhaps, some indefinable malaise of the intestinal tract or maybe it's the thyroid gland. So you're surfing around for distraction and, suddenly there it is—Claritin! The commercial doesn't say what it does, but you sense, somehow, that whatever it does is going to work for you. The transcendent calm of those clear blue skies! The cool triumph of that goddess-like face! Rush out to the nearest physician, is the message, and get yourself a little of this!

Time was when the pharmaceutical companies were content to market to the physicians themselves—hosting them, for example, at free weekend-long "seminars" at important margarita-producing sites. But doctors are a rushed and harried bunch these days, struggling to survive in their HMOs. Only the consumers—still known in the medical business by the archaic term "patients"—have the time to savor a well-crafted commercial and decide whether it suits their needs.

Hence the sudden expansion of "direct-to-consumer" prescription drug advertising, which began, innocently enough, with Rogaine, and extends now to remedies for everything from high blood pressure and prostate problems to fungus and migraines. Pharmaceutical companies spent $35 million on it in 1987 and almost ten times more—$308 million—in '94. And whatever the pills do, at least the advertising works: In 1989, 45% of doctors said they had patients who were able to specify, by brand name, exactly what they wanted prescribed. By 1995, 93% of doctors were encountering such medically gifted patients.

But why go to a doctor if you already know what you need? When an ad works, when it touches you in that deep subconscious layer of the brain where the ad-receptors are located, you don't want to diddle around with appointments and insurance forms and long waits on cold plastic seats. It gets irritating, in fact, that you have to go through this odd ritual—undressing in front of strangers, answering personal questions—just to get hold of some product that a nice voice on TV has already told you that you need.

Then there's the cost. Drug prices, already giddily high, are rising at more than twice the rate of inflation. This makes sense when you realize that pharmaceutical companies, just like presidential candidates and breakfast cereals, have to spend hundreds of millions a year on high-concept prime-time commercials. But when you're already facing $90 or more for a little vial of chemical comfort, that $50 surcharge for a doctor's prescription begins to look like an inexcusable shakedown.

So the pressure will inevitably grow to cut the doctors out of the loop. We're already being groomed by the medical companies in the skills of kitchen-table diagnosis. Take that indefinable malaise you were feeling: Now you can go to a drug store and, without any prescription at all, pick up a testing kit that will allow you to determine whether the problem is pregnancy or diabetes or possibly AIDS. So what are you paying the doctor for—$50 worth of bedside manner?

Think of it as the ultimate market-based health reform: A system in which consumers will decide what they need and then go out and get it, unimpeded by the need to support some gray-templed fellow with a serious golf habit. Americans currently spend billions a year on visits to physicians, and, despite the nice neighborly locution, most of these "visits" are purely bureaucratic formalities required to renew our antihistamine prescriptions. Why not go the way of Mexico and so much of the Third World and let consumers fill their shopping carts with beta-blockers and serotonin-uptake inhibitors as impulse demands? We don't, after all, require anyone to have a note from a fashion consultant before going home with a salmon-colored leisure ensemble.

There is of course the issue of safety. The drug with the most appealing packaging or cunning commercial could conceivably put an end to one's entire medical shopping career. But the truth is we're not doing so well on the safety front now, even with doctors manning the medical checkpoints. About 2 million people are hospitalized each year, and 140,000 actually die, as a result of dire reactions to drugs that were duly prescribed. Besides, if prescriptions are such an indispensable safeguard, why are the drug companies rushing to make their antacids and analgesics available over the counter, where we can O.D. on them to our hearts content?

Sadly, in a health system dominated by mega-corporations, the physician is fast becoming an evolutionary throwback. Today, the insurance companies that manage "managed care" don't even trust a doctor to monitor a routine blood pressure problem without some low-level bureaucrat looking over his or her shoulder for deviations from "cost effectiveness." And any loyalty the medical profession may have had from the long-suffering public evaporated last year when the AMA made a deal to let the Republicans cut Medicare without cutting doctors' fees. As for threatening us with serious trouble if we don't stop smoking and take off 15 pounds—well, what are spouses for?

So, Physician, heal thyself—is the message from Madison Avenue—and patients, heal thyselves too. Health reformers used to fantasize about networks of neighborhood clinics filled with nurturing, culturally sensitive, holistic providers. But in a health system ruled increasingly from Wall Street, where the only vital signs of interest are profits and market-share, doctor-free drug shopping may be the best we can hope for.

Length: 920 words.
Reading Time: __________
See Conversion Table, p. 421.
Enter WPM Rate on p. 416.

44 Good Health for Sale

▶ COMPREHENSION CHECK

GETTING THE FACTS

1. Pharmaceutial companies market commercials to (a) researchers. (b) doctors. (c) patients. (d) pharmacists. 1. ____

2. According to the author, a more appropriate 21st-century term for patients is (a) consumers. (b) interns. (c) customers. (d) clients. 2. ____

3. Drug prices are rising more than (a) 45% a year. (b) 93% a year. (c) ten times the rate of inflation. (d) twice the rate of inflation. 3. ____

4. Each year, Americans spend how much on doctor visits? (a) thousands (b) millions (c) billions (d) trillions 4. ____

5. About 140,000 people die each year because of (a) misdiagnosis. (b) lack of prescriptions. (c) prescription reactions. (d) serotonin-uptake inhibitors. 5. ____

GETTING THE MEANING

6. This selection is mainly about the commercialization of the (a) medical profession. (b) television industry. (c) pharmaceutical companies. (d) local pharmacies. 6. ____

7. The author implies that future patients will need doctors (a) more. (b) less. (c) about the same. (d) not at all. 7. ____

8. Ehrenreich asserts that "medically gifted patients" are those who know what they want and (a) negotiate for it. (b) deny it. (c) research it. (d) ask for it. 8. ____

9. The author believes "patients" will pressure pharmaceuticals to sell drugs (a) directly to them. (b) directly to doctors. (c) to HMOs. (d) to researchers. 9. ____

10. Drugs commercials suggest that patients should determine which (a) doctor to use. (b) drugs to take. (c) dosage to use. (d) drugs to avoid. 10. ____

Check your answers with the Key on p. 452. Give yourself 10 points for each one right and enter your comprehension score on p. 415.

Comprehension Score: ________

NAME ______________ CLASS ______________ DATE ______________

45 Challenges to Racial and Sexual Discrimination

WORD POWER WORKOUT

A. LEANING ON CONTEXT

In each of the blanks provided, place the letter that precedes the best definition of the underlined word in context to the left.

Words in Context	Definitions
1. ____ assertion rang true	a. correct
2. ____ treatment and degradation	b. blending
3. ____ to pursue assimilation	c. movingly
4. ____ intellectual vanguard	d. claim
5. ____ voiced these doubts poignantly	e. requirement
6. ____ attempts to redress	f. exciting
7. ____ ardently opposed	g. motivation
8. ____ the best criterion	h. forefront
9. ____ to rousing meetings	i. strongly
10. ____ the final impetus	j. poverty

Check your answers with the Key on p. 443 before going on. Give yourself 10 points for each one right and enter your score on the chart under A on p. 420. Review any that you have missed.

A Score: ________

Pronunciation aids: **2. de-gruh-DAY-shun**
5. POIN-yuhtn-lee
10. IM-puh-tus

B. LEANING ON PARTS

Try getting acquainted with a few more suffixes. In the following, fill in each blank with the suffix that provides the right meaning.

1. A very small glob of water would be a glob__________.
2. If it happens every hour, it's an hour__________ occurrence.
3. If the bottles can be returned, they are return__________.
4. Someone with the qualities of a child is child__________.
5. To make a room dark is to dark__________ it.

C. MAKING THE WORDS YOURS

In each blank below, enter the most appropriate word from the ten words in context in the first exercise, substituting it for the word(s) in parentheses. Use these words: *ardently, assertion, assimilation, criterion, degradation, impetus, poignantly, redress, rousing, vanguard.*

1. Your supervisor will (correct) __________ this situation soon.
2. Because of the skill and talent of the people involved, this company's dynamic leaders are in the (forefront) __________.
3. Hundreds of students attended a (exciting) __________ pep rally.
4. Heavy indebtedness is the (motivation) __________ for Joyce's working three jobs.
5. The rescue team fought (strongly) __________ to keep inexperienced climbers from joining the venture.
6. Hal suffered inescapable (poverty) __________ in the 1980s.
7. A large kitchen was their first (requirement) __________.
8. The (claim) __________ that the team shaved points was never proven.
9. Many freshmen find (blending) __________ into college life very difficult.
10. The seventh grader surprised the crowd as she read the poem (movingly) __________.

Check your answers with the Key on p. 450.

B Score: ________

C Score: ________

Enter your scores on p. 420.

45

Challenges to Racial and Sexual Discrimination

MARY BETH NORTON, ET AL.

Our Constitution has not always guaranteed all of its citizens equal protection under the law. Therefore, over the course of our country's short history, disenfranchised groups have fought for rights afforded to those of prestige and power. Learn how some of the rights and recognition Americans take for granted were won.

BEGIN TIMING

W. E. B. Du Bois, a forceful black scholar and writer, ended an essay in The Souls of Black Folk (1903) with a blunt prediction for American society. "The problem of the Twentieth Century," he wrote, "is the problem of the color line." Du Bois's assertion rang true; people of color continued to endure violent treatment and degradation. But at the same time, women of all races also suffered from an underprivileged status.

For both African-Americans and women, the Progressive challenge to entrenched ideas and customs gave impetus to their struggles for equal rights, but it also posed a dilemma. Should women and people of color strive to become just like white men, with white men's values as well as their rights? Or was there something unique about racial and sexual cultures that should be preserved at the risk of sacrificing some gains?

African-American leaders differed sharply over how—and whether—to pursue assimilation. In the wake of emancipation, ex-slave Frederick Douglass urged "ultimate assimilation through self-assertion, and on no other terms." Those who favored separation from white society supported migration to Africa or the establishment of all-black communities in Oklahoma Territory and Kansas. Others advocated violence.

Most blacks, however, could neither escape nor conquer white society. They had to find other routes to economic and social improvement. Self-help, a strategy articulated by educator Booker T. Washington, was one popular alternative. Born to slave parents in 1856, Washington worked his way through school and in 1881 founded Tuskegee Institute in Alabama, a vocational school for blacks. There he developed the philosophy that blacks' best hopes for assimilation lay in at least temporarily accommodating to whites. Rather than fighting for political rights,

Washington said, blacks should work hard, acquire property, and prove they were worthy of rights.

Washington voiced his views in a widely acclaimed speech at the Atlanta Exposition in 1895. In this speech, which became known as the Atlanta Compromise, Washington observed that "in all things that are purely social we can be as separate as the fingers, yet one as the hand in all matters essential to mutual progress." Whites welcomed Washington's accommodation policy because it urged patience and reminded black people to stay in their place.

Some blacks thought that Booker T. Washington seemed to favor a degrading second-class citizenship. In 1905 a group of "anti-Bookerites" convened near Niagara Falls and pledged a militant pursuit of rights such as unrestricted voting, economic opportunity, integration, and equality before the law. Spokesperson for the Niagara movement was W. E. B. Du Bois, an outspoken critic of the Atlanta Compromise.

A New Englander with a Ph.D. from Harvard, Du Bois was both a Progressive and a member of the black elite. He held an undergraduate degree from all-black Fisk University and had studied in Germany, where he learned about scientific investigation. Du Bois had compiled fact-filled sociological studies of black ghetto dwellers and had written poetically in support of civil rights. He treated Washington politely but could not accept white domination.

Du Bois demonstrated that accommodation was an unrealistic strategy, but his solution had its own drawbacks. A blunt elitist, Du Bois believed that an intellectual vanguard of cultured, highly trained blacks, the "Talented Tenth," would save the race by setting an example to whites and uplifting other blacks. Such sentiment had more appeal for middle-class white liberals than for African-American share-croppers. Thus in 1909 when Du Bois and his allies formed the National Association for the Advancement of Colored People (NAACP), which aimed to end racial discrimination by pursuing legal redress in the courts, the leadership consisted chiefly of white Progressives.

Whatever their views, African-Americans faced continued oppression. Those who managed to acquire property and education encountered bitter resentment, especially when they fought for civil rights. The federal government only aggravated biases. During Woodrow Wilson's presidency, discrimination within the federal government expanded: southern cabinet members supported racial separation in restrooms, restaurants, and government office buildings and balked at hiring black workers.

Disfranchisement, instituted by southern states in the late nineteenth century, still prevented blacks from becoming full American citizens. Washington seemed to accept disfranchisement; Du Bois believed suffrage was essential to protect social and economic rights.

African-Americans still sought to fulfill the American dream, but many wondered whether their goals should include membership in a corrupt white society. Du Bois voiced these doubts poignantly, observing that "one ever feels his twoness—an American, a Negro, two souls, two thoughts, two unreconciled strivings, two warring ideals in one dark body."

. . . In 1911 educated, middle-class Indian men and women formed their own association, the Society of American Indians (SAI), which worked for better education, civil rights, and healthcare. It also sponsored "American Indian Days" to cultivate pride.

The SAI's emphasis on racial pride, however, was squeezed between pressures for assimilation from one side and tribal allegiance on the other. Its small membership did not genuinely represent the diverse and unconnected Indian nations, and its attempt to establish a governing body faltered. At the same time, the goal of achieving acceptance in white society proved elusive, and attempts to redress grievances through legal action bogged down for lack of funds. Ultimately, the SAI had to rely on rhetoric and moral exhortation, which had little effect on poor and powerless Indians. Torn by internal disputes, the association folded in the early 1920s.

What tactics should women use to achieve equality? What should be their role in society? Could women achieve equality with men and at the same time change male-dominated society? The answers that women found involved a subtle but important shift in women's politics. Before about 1910, those engaged in the quest for women's rights referred to themselves as "the woman movement." This label was given to middle-class women striving to move beyond the home into social welfare activities, higher education, and paid labor. They argued that legal and voting rights were indispensable to such moves. These women's rights advocates based their claims on the theory that women's special, even superior, traits as guardians of family and morality would humanize all of society.

The women's club movement represented a unique dimension of Progressive era reform. . . . Because female activists were excluded from holding office, they were drawn less to government reform than to drives for social betterment. Women reformers tended to work for factory inspection, regulation of children's and women's labor, housing improvement, upgrading of education, and consumer protection. Such efforts were not confined to white women. The National Association of Colored Women, founded in 1895, was the nation's first African-American social service organization; it concentrated on establishing nurseries, kindergartens, and retirement homes.

Around 1910 some people concerned with women's place in society began using a new term, feminism. Whereas members of the woman movement spoke generally of duty and moral purity, feminists—more explicitly conscious of their identity as women—emphasized rights and self-development. Feminism focused primarily on economic and sexual independence. Charlotte Perkins Gilman articulated feminist goals in Women and Economics (1898), declaring that domesticity and female innocence were obsolete and attacked the male monopoly on economic opportunity.

Feminists also supported "sex rights"—a single standard of behavior for men and women—and a number of feminists joined the birth-control movement led by Margaret Sanger. As a visiting nurse in New York's immigrant neighborhoods, Sanger distributed information about contraception, in hopes of helping poor women prevent unwanted pregnancies. Her crusade won support from middle-class women who wanted both to limit their own families and to control the growth of the immigrant masses. It also aroused opposition from those who saw birth control as a threat to family and morality.

In 1914, Sanger's opponents caused her to be indicted for defying an 1873 law that prohibited the sending of obscene literature (articles on contraception) through the mails, and she fled the country for a year. Sanger persevered and in 1921 formed the American Birth Control League, which enlisted physicians and social workers to convince judges to allow distribution of birth-control information.

Feminists achieved an important victory in 1920 when enough states ratified the Nineteenth Amendment to give women the vote in federal elections. Until the 1890s, the suffrage crusade was led by elite women who believed that the political system needed more participation by refined and educated people like themselves, and that working-class women would defer to better educated women on political matters.

The younger generation of feminists ardently opposed this logic. To them, achievement rather than wealth and refinement was the best criterion for public influence. Thus women should exercise the vote not to enhance the power of elites in public life but to promote and protect women's economic roles.

Despite internal differences, suffragists achieved some successes. Nine states, all in the West, allowed women to vote in state and local elections by 1912, and women continued to press for national suffrage. Their tactics ranged from the moderate but persistent propaganda campaigns of the National American Woman Suffrage Association, led by Carrie Chapman Catt, to rousing meetings and marches of the National Woman's Party, led by feminist Alice Paul. All these activities heightened public awareness. The First World War contributions of women as factory workers, medical volunteers, and municipal workers served as the final impetus to secure political support for the suffrage amendment.

Length: 1510 words.

Reading Time: __________

See Conversion Table, p. 431.

Enter WPM Rate on p. 418.

45 Challenges to Racial and Sexual Discrimination

COMPREHENSION CHECK

GETTING THE FACTS

1. Booker T. Washington espoused (a) aggressive behavior. (b) all-black communities. (c) militant pursuits. (d) acquiring property. 1. ____

2. The SAI emphasized (a) economic development. (b) segregation. (c) tribal isolation. (d) racial pride. 2. ____

3. W. E. B. Du Bois believed blacks should uplift other blacks and (a) ignore whites. (b) set an example for whites. (c) include whites. (d) try to understand whites. 3. ____

4. The "women's club movement" primarily focused on (a) improving the family. (b) helping immigrants. (c) legal and voting rights. (d) women's labor issues. 4. ____

5. The Nineteenth Amendment passed in (a) 1900. (b) 1910. (c) 1920. (d) 1930. 5. ____

GETTING THE MEANING

6. This piece is mostly about (a) economic issues. (b) equal opportunities. (c) social issues. (d) political issues. 6. ____

7. Washington and Du Bois (a) used the same strategies. (b) were from similar backgrounds. (c) were from New England. (d) were architects of social revolution. 7. ____

8. Birth control information has been available in the United States for about (a) 60 years. (b) 70 years. (c) 80 years. (d) 100 years. 8. ____

9. African Americans, Native Americans, and women in the early 20th century struggled for (a) equal rights. (b) women's values. (c) political equity. (d) privileged status. 9. ____

10. Racial and sexual discrimination at the end of the 19th century was (a) pervasive. (b) regional. (c) covert. (d) erratic. 10. ____

Check your answers with the Key on p. 452. Give yourself 10 points for each one right and enter your comprehension score on p. 415.

Comprehension Score: ________

ROOT MINI-REVIEW

Here's your speed review for the fourteen roots you are studying. Use your 3 × 5 card as before. Remember the three review patterns: cover the right-hand column first; then cover the middle and right-hand columns; finally, cover the middle and left-hand columns to ensure perfect mastery.

Root	Suggested Mnemonic	Common Meaning
1. ducere	duct	lead
2. scribere	inscribe	write
3. ponere	deposit	put, place
4. mittere	missile	send
5. capere	capture	take, seize
6. plicare	reply	fold
7. graphein	autograph	write
8. legein, logos	geology, travelogue	study of, speech
9. tenere	tenant	have, hold
10. ferre	ferry	bear, carry
11. facere	manufacture	make, do
12. specere	inspect	see
13. tendere	distend	stretch
14. stare	stationary	stand

NAME ______ CLASS ______ DATE ______

46 Short Stories

WORD POWER WORKOUT

A. LEANING ON CONTEXT

In each of the blanks provided, place the letter that precedes the best definition of the underlined word in context to the left.

Words in Context	Definitions
1. ____ longer than an <u>anecdote</u>	a. columns
2. ____ <u>plumes</u> of radiance	b. illustrate
3. ____ <u>fierce</u> subjectivity	c. cruel
4. ____ thoughts <u>exemplify</u> a type	d. type
5. ____ diverse <u>perspectives</u>	e. story
6. ____ a powerful <u>mode</u>	f. defines
7. ____ <u>manipulating</u> the point	g. disaster
8. ____ stern and <u>repressive</u> nun	h. strong
9. ____ the dialogue <u>crystallizes</u>	i. altering
10. ____ danger and <u>doom</u>	j. outlooks

Check your answers with the Key on p. 443 before going on. Give yourself 10 points for each one right and enter your score on the chart under A on p. 420. Review any that you have missed.

A Score: ______

Pronunciation aid: 1. AN-ik-dote

B. LEANING ON PARTS

Try working with a few more suffixes. In the following sentences, fill in the blanks with the suffixes that provide the right meaning.

1. A scheme full of grandeur is grandi__________.
2. If it's worth commending, it's commend__________.
3. If the action tends to remedy the situation, it's remed__________.
4. If it's like a picture, it's pictur__________.
5. If you show affection, you're affection__________.

C. MAKING THE WORDS YOURS

In each blank below, enter the most appropriate word from the ten words in context in the first exercise, substituting it for the word(s) in parentheses. Use these words: *anecdote, crystallizes, doom, exemplify, fierce, manipulating, mode, perspectives, plumes, repressive.*

1. (Columns) __________ of steam bellowed from the boiling pot of pasta.
2. (Disaster) __________ hovered above them when they admitted they were lost.
3. Visiting urban areas and farm communities gave candidates new (outlooks) __________ on their campaigns.
4. In the playoffs, teams demonstrate (strong) __________ competition.
5. The weather reporter shared an (story) __________ with viewers every evening.
6. Forcing tired and hungry travelers to sit three to a seat for the one-hour trip was (cruel) __________.
7. The prosecutor accused the suspect of (altering) __________ the records to hide the theft.
8. Convection cooking is the (type) __________ he will use.
9. The video will (illustrate) __________ the talent this team has.
10. This new information (defines) __________ the course of action we will pursue.

Check your answers with the Key on p. 450.

B Score: ________

C Score: ________

Enter your scores on p. 420.

46

Short Stories

JOHN E. SCHWIEBERT

Some readers are baffled when they pick up a book, read all of the words on the page, and still fail to comprehend the story. However, successful readers know that reading short stories effectively requires them to understand the elements of prose. If you can't tell point of view from plot and theme from setting, information in this selection should help you make sense of literature assignments.

BEGIN TIMING

A **short story** is a brief work of prose fiction, shorter than a novel or novella and longer than an anecdote. All short stories include such elements as point of view, characters, plot, theme, and setting that are found in longer works of fiction.

Point of View

Point of view refers to the perspective from which a story is told. The two basic types of point of view are first-person and third-person.

In the **first-person** point of view the storyteller or **narrator** is a major or minor character within the story who uses the pronoun "I." . . . When the youth, naiveté, limited intelligence, or extreme subjectivity of a first-person narrator leads us to question the accuracy of his or her version of characters and events, he or she is called a **naive** or **unreliable** narrator. An example is Marie Lazarre, the Native American narrator of Louise Erdrich's "Saint Marie." Marie is about to enter a convent school, where she will end up in an almost deadly struggle with her teacher, Sister Leopolda. The story begins:

> So when I went there, I knew the dark fish must rise. Plumes of radiance had soldered on me. No reservation girl had ever prayed so hard. There was no use in trying to ignore me any longer. I was going up there on the hill with the black robe women. . . . I was going up there to pray as good as they could. Because I don't have that much Indian blood. And they never thought they'd have a girl from this reservation as a saint they'd have to kneel to. But they'd have me.

Marie's declared aim of making the nuns (i.e., "the black robe women") "kneel to" her is an example of her fierce subjectivity and alerts us to read and interpret what follows with caution.

In the **third-person** point of view the narrator is outside the story and refers to characters as "he," "she," or "they," or by their proper names. A third-person **omniscient** narrator functions as an all-knowing presence who has access to the thoughts, feelings, and actions of any and all of the characters. An **intrusive** omniscient narrator evaluates the actions and motives of characters and inserts other of his/her personal views into a story. An **objective** narrator, on the other hand, merely shows or reports actions and characters without evaluating them. . . .

Rather than seeing everything, a narrator in a **third-person limited** point of view relates events from the perspective of one of the characters within the story. . . .

Writers sometimes *mix* various points of view in a single story. For instance, William Faulkner's "Barn Burning" is told, for the most part, from a third-person limited point of view (by a narrator who perceives events through the consciousness of the boy Sarty). At times, however, Faulkner shifts the point of view to first-person and writes as Sarty, as in the italicized portions of the following passage:

> They were running a middle buster now, his brother holding the plow straight while he handled the reins, and walking beside the straining mule, the rich black soil shearing cool and damp against his bare ankles, he thought *Maybe this is the end of it. Maybe even that twenty bushels that seems hard to have to pay for just a rug will be a cheap price for him to stop forever and always from being what he used to be;* thinking, dreaming now, so that his brother had to speak sharply to him to mind the mule: *Maybe he even won't collect the twenty bushels. Maybe it will all add up and balance and vanish—corn, rug, fire; the terror and grief, the being pulled two ways like between two teams of horses—gone, done with for ever and ever.*

Sarty's thoughts exemplify a type of narrative technique called stream of consciousness. In stream of consciousness a writer seeks to reproduce, without a narrator's intervention, the exact flow of thoughts, feelings, and associations that go through a character's mind as that character moves in the "stream" of time.

Point of view in a story is important for at least two major reasons. . . . A writer's choice of point of view profoundly affects every other aspect of the story, from its themes and plot structure to its characters and style. . . .

Playing with point of view helps a writer understand things (self, culture, life, the world, etc.) *better* or *differently* by knowing them from diverse perspectives. In addition, the possibility of alternative points of view provides a writer with a powerful mode of invention. If the stories you write in your notebook lack vitality, you can bring them to life by manipulating the point of view. You can rewrite your dull first-person narrative about "growing up in the eighties" as a third-person narrative or relate the first-person story that "isn't quite working" from the first-person perspective of a different character in the same story.

Characters

Characters are the imaginary persons who appear in fictional narratives or dramatic works, and characterization is achieved through the depiction of action, description, and/or dialogue. A **flat character** is one who remains essentially unchanged throughout the story and tends to be less an individual than a type. Akin to flat characters are the merely undeveloped minor characters who appear in many stories and plays. A **round character**, on the other hand, evolves or undergoes change in the course of the story and is more individualized and complex. . . .

The main character around whom a narrative or dramatic work centers is called the **protagonist** or **hero/heroine.** The protagonist's main opponent, if any, is the **antagonist.** In Louise Erdrich's "Saint Marie," the protagonist is Marie, a Native American girl who goes to a convent school to be "educated"; the antagonist is Sister Leopolda, the stern and repressive nun who seeks to transform her. . . .

Dialogue

Dialogue is the spoken conversation that occurs in a story and is a major means both of characterization and of advancing the story's plot. Consider the wife/protagonist in Charlotte Perkins Gilman's "The Yellow Wallpaper." The wife's illness has prompted her physician husband to take her to a house in the country for a complete "rest" cure. From the wife's point of view, however, the cure is not working, and, in the following dialogue, she approaches her husband about leaving the house:

> I thought it was a good time to talk, so I told him that I really was not gaining here, and that I wished he would take me away.
>
> "Why, darling!" said he. "Our lease will be up in three weeks, and I can't see how to leave before.
>
> "The repairs are not done at home, and I cannot possibly leave town just now. Of course if you were in any danger, I could and would, but you really are better, dear, whether you can see it or not. I am a doctor, dear, and I know. You are gaining flesh and color, your appetite is better, I feel really much easier about you."
>
> "I don't weigh a bit more," said I, "nor as much; and my appetite may be better in the evening when you are here but it is worse in the morning when you are away!"
>
> "Bless her little heart!" said he with a big hug. "She shall be as sick as she pleases! But now let's improve the shining hours by going to sleep, and talk about it in the morning!"

"And you won't go away?" I asked gloomily.

"Why, how can I, dear? It is only three weeks more and then we will take a nice little trip of a few days while Jennie is getting the house ready. Really, dear, you are better!"

"Better in body perhaps—" I began, and stopped short, for he sat up straight and looked at me with such a stern, reproachful look that I could not say another word.

"My darling," said he, "I beg of you, for my sake and for our child's sake, as well as for your own, that you will never for one instant let that idea enter your mind! There is nothing so dangerous, so fascinating, to a temperament like yours. It is a false and foolish fancy. Can you not trust me as a physician when I tell you so?"

So of course I said no more on that score, and we went to sleep before long.

This bit of dialogue speaks volumes about the two characters and their relationship. . . . The dialogue crystallizes the fundamental conflicts and differences between wife and husband; it shows us wife and husband with far more suggestiveness and precision than could any comparably short passage that might merely tell us about that relationship.

Plot

Point of view, character, and dialogue interconnect with plot and other features to create a story. The **plot** of a story refers to the pattern of actions and events that combine to produce a total effect in readers. . . . Traditional plots have a beginning, a middle, and an end and move chronologically. Some critics divide plots into a **rising action,** which introduces the characters and establishes the conflict; a **climax** in which the conflict reaches its height in the form of some decisive action or decision; a **falling action,** in which the conflict moves toward **resolution;** and a resolution, in which the conflicts are resolved. This is only a basic pattern for plot, however, and story writers often generate suspense and surprise by upsetting our conventional expectations about how a story should begin, proceed, and end.

One common departure from straightforward chronology is **flashback.** In a flashback a narrator interrupts the narrative to present or relate some event(s) that occurred at a time chronologically prior to the events of the story itself. . . .

Theme and Setting

Theme is the basic idea advanced (or implied) in the text. Of course, any group of readers coming from diverse situations and backgrounds will perceive different nuances of theme in the same text, and the more complex and interesting the story, the more diverse the articulations of theme are likely to be. . . .

Setting refers to the place, time, and social context in which a story or other narrative takes place. In some stories setting is extremely important. . . . Edgar Allan Poe's "The Masque of the Red Death" is about a plague that has "long devastated the country" of the arrogant Prince Prospero. Poe devotes long paragraphs . . . to describing the environs and interior of the "castellated" abbey where Prospero and "a thousand light-hearted friends" think to insulate themselves from the Red Death. Evoking feelings of horror and the macabre, place becomes a major part of our experience of the story; on the other hand, Poe's nonspecificity about the historical time in which the events are supposed to occur makes the sense of danger and doom even greater by rendering the "Red Death" suggestively timeless.

Length: 1650 words.
Reading Time: __________
See Conversion Table, p. 431.
Enter WPM Rate on p. 418.

46 Short Stories

COMPREHENSION CHECK

GETTING THE FACTS

1. The short story is a brief work of (a) poetry. (b) prose fiction. (c) summaries. (d) biographies. 1. ____

2. Point of view is (a) characterization. (b) development. (c) conflict/resolution. (d) perspective. 2. ____

3. A flat character in a short story (a) evolves. (b) remains the same. (c) is unimportant. (d) is underdeveloped. 3. ____

4. In fiction, characters are (a) real. (b) imaginary. (c) limited. (d) predictable. 4. ____

5. A story's theme is its (a) expanded idea. (b) competing idea. (c) implied idea. (d) central idea. 5. ____

GETTING THE MEANING

6. This selection mainly focuses on (a) writing short stories. (b) the elements of short stories. (c) the importance of plot and theme. (d) the interrelationships of theme and setting. 6. ____

7. Understanding the plot of a story is most essential to (a) good comprehension. (b) vocabulary development. (c) character development. (d) reading rate. 7. ____

8. A flashback (a) provides background. (b) predicts the future. (c) explains the theme. (d) simplifies the plot. 8. ____

9. A story's protagonist is (a) obscure. (b) prominent. (c) the author. (d) the reader. 9. ____

10. A short story is (a) detailed. (b) complicated. (c) elaborate. (d) compact. 10. ____

Check your answers with the Key on p. 452. Give yourself 10 points for each one right and enter your comprehension score on p. 415.

Comprehension Score: ________

NAME ____________ CLASS ____________ DATE ____________

47 Bureaucratic "Pathologies"

WORD POWER WORKOUT

A. LEANING ON CONTEXT

In each of the blanks provided, place the letter that precedes the best definition of the underlined word in context to the left.

Words in Context	Definitions
1. ____ the <u>enormous</u> variety	a. enticements
2. ____ to <u>intercept</u> illegal drugs	b. distant control
3. ____ encounter <u>cumbersome</u> rules	c. last
4. ____ weak <u>incentives</u>	d. embellishments
5. ____ <u>exaggerations</u> or unusual occurrences	e. current
6. ____ the <u>latter</u> charge	f. undivided
7. ____ the "<u>prevailing</u>" wage	g. exactly
8. ____ To check <u>imperialism</u>	h. complicated
9. ____ <u>precisely</u> those goals	i. colossal
10. ____ <u>inseparable</u> from the problem	j. capture

Check your answers with the Key on p. 443 before going on. Give yourself 10 points for each one right and enter your score on the chart under A on p. 420. Review any that you have missed.

A Score: ________

Pronunciation aid: 5. eg-zaj-uhr-RAY-shunz

B. LEANING ON PARTS

Try this new kind of review exercise. Fit the appropriate word into each of the numbered blanks below. Select from the following list of words derived from *stare,* meaning "to stand": *exist, restate, persist, constant, obstacles, constitute, stationary, assistance, substantial, establishing, circumstance.*

If, despite (1) ______________, you (2) ______________ in your efforts, you'll soon see (3) ______________ gains. These exercises provide positive (4) ______________ in (5) ______________ improved word power habits.

C. MAKING THE WORDS YOURS

In each blank below, enter the most appropriate word from the ten words in context in the first exercise, substituting it for the word(s) in parentheses. Use these words: *cumbersome, enormous, exaggerations, imperialism, incentives, inseparable, intercept, latter, precisely, prevailing.*

1. All of the choices are attractive, but I prefer the (last) ______________.
2. Since they met at college two years ago, those two have become (undivided) ______________.
3. This job is (exactly) ______________ what I hoped to find.
4. Rebates of $5–$10 are great (enticements) ______________ to purchase the camping equipment we need.
5. The process for returning merchandise is (complicated) ______________.
6. Everything the opponents have published about us has been (embellishments) ______________.
7. During war, battles have been won when one side was able to (capture) ______________ messages intended for the opponent.
8. (Distant control) ______________ is an oppressive form of government.
9. The tourists' gambling losses were (colossal) ______________.
10. The (current) ______________ opinions differ dramatically from surveys conducted last year.

Check your answers with the Key on p. 450.

B Score: ________

C Score: ________

Enter your scores on p. 420.

47

Bureaucratic "Pathologies"

JAMES Q. WILSON AND JOHN J. DILULIO

If you have always heard negative comments about the bureaucracy of governments, have you ever wondered why governments are bureaucratic? Well, bureaucracies are natural results of the way our culture does business. Bureaucracies are inevitable, but they may have a redeeming feature or two. In fact, most may be more benign than they seem. Understanding bureaucratic "pathologies" will give you a better appreciation for how things work in agencies that impact our lives.

BEGIN TIMING

Bureaucratic "Pathologies"

Everyone complains about bureaucracy in general (though rarely about bureaucratic agencies that everyone believes are desirable). This chapter should persuade you that it is difficult to say anything about bureaucracy "in general"; there are too many different kinds of agencies, kinds of bureaucrats, and kinds of programs to label the entire enterprise with some single adjective. Nevertheless, many people who recognize the enormous variety among government agencies still believe that they all have some general features in common and suffer from certain shared problems or pathologies.

This is true enough, but the reasons for it—and the solutions, if any—are not often understood. There are five major (or at least frequently mentioned) problems with bureaucracies: red tape, conflict, duplication, imperialism, and waste. **Red tape** refers to the complex rules and procedures that must be followed to get something done. **Conflict** exists because some agencies seem to be working at cross-purposes with other agencies. (For example, the Agricultural Research Service tells farmers how to grow crops more efficiently, while the Agricultural Stabilization and Conservation Service pays farmers to grow fewer crops or to produce less.) **Duplication** (usually called "wasteful duplication") occurs when two government agencies seem to be doing the same thing, as when the Customs Service and the Drug Enforcement Administration both attempt to intercept illegal drugs being smuggled into the country. **Imperialism** refers to the tendency of agencies to grow without regard to the benefits that their programs confer or the costs that they entail. **Waste** means spending more than is necessary to buy some product or service.

These problems all exist, but they do not necessarily exist because bureaucrats are incompetent or power-hungry. Most exist because of the very nature of government itself. Take red tape: partly we encounter cumbersome rules and procedures because any large organization, governmental or not, must have some way of ensuring that one part of the organization does not operate out of step with another. Business corporations have red tape also; it is to a certain extent a consequence of bigness. But a great amount of governmental red tape is also the result of the need to satisfy legal and political requirements. Government agencies must hire on the basis of "merit," must observe strict accounting rules, must supply Congress with detailed information on their programs, and must allow for citizen access in countless ways. Meeting each need requires rules; enforcing the rules requires forms.

Or take conflict and duplication: they do not occur because bureaucrats enjoy conflict or duplication. (Quite the contrary!) They exist because Congress, in setting up agencies and programs, often wants to achieve a number of different, partially inconsistent goals or finds that it cannot decide which goal it values the most. Congress has 535 members and little strong leadership; it should not be surprising that 535 people will want different things and will sometimes succeed in getting them.

Imperialism results in large measure from government agencies' seeking goals that are so vague and so difficult to measure that it is hard to tell when they have been attained. When Congress is unclear as to exactly what an agency is supposed to do, the agency will often convert that legislative vagueness into bureaucratic imperialism by taking the largest possible view of its powers. It may do this on its own; more often it does so because interest groups and judges rush in to fill the vacuum left by Congress. . . . The 1973 Rehabilitation Act was passed with a provision barring discrimination against the disabled in any program receiving federal aid. Under pressure from the disabled, that lofty but vague goal was converted by the Department of Transportation into a requirement that virtually every big-city bus have a device installed to lift people in wheelchairs on board.

Waste is probably the biggest criticism that people have of the bureaucracy. Everybody has heard stories of the Pentagon's paying $91 for screws that cost 3 cents in the hardware store. President Reagan's "Private Sector Survey on Cost Control," generally known as the Grace Commission (after its chairman, J. Peter Grace), publicized these and other tales in a 1984 report.

No doubt there is waste in government. After all, unlike a business firm worried about maximizing profits, in a government agency there are only weak incentives to keep costs down. If a business employee cuts costs, he or she often receives a bonus or raise, and the firm gets to add the savings to its profits. If a government official cuts costs, he or she receives no reward, and the agency cannot keep the savings—they go back to the Treasury.

But many of the horror stories are either exaggerations or unusual occurrences. Most of the screws, hammers, and light bulbs purchased by the government are obtained at low cost by means of competitive bidding among several suppliers. When the government does pay outlandish amounts, the reason typically is that it is purchasing a new or one-of-a-kind item not available at your neighborhood hardware store—for example, a new bomber or missile.

Even when the government is not overcharged, it still may spend more money than a private firm in buying what it needs. The reason is red tape—the rules and procedures designed to ensure that when the government buys something, it will do so in a way that serves the interests of many groups. For example, it must often buy from American rather than foreign suppliers, even if the latter charge a lower price; it must make use of contractors that employ minorities; it must hire only union laborers and pay them the "prevailing" (that is, the highest) wage; it must allow public inspection of its records; it frequently is required to choose contractors favored by influential members of Congress; and so on. Private firms do not have to comply with all these rules and thus can buy for less.

From this discussion it should be easy to see why these five basic bureaucratic problems are so hard to correct. To end conflicts and duplication, Congress would have to make some policy choices and set some clear priorities, but with all the competing demands that it faces, Congress finds it difficult to do that. You make more friends by helping people than by hurting them, and so Congress is more inclined to add new programs than to cut old ones, whether or not the new programs are in conflict with existing ones. To check imperialism, some way would have to be found to measure the benefits of government, but that is often impossible; government exists in part to achieve precisely those goals—such as national defense—that are least measurable. Furthermore, what might be done to remedy some problems would make other problems worse: if you simplify rules and procedures to cut red tape, you are likely also to reduce the coordination among agencies and thus to increase the extent to which there is duplication or conflict. If you want to reduce waste, you will have to have more rules and inspectors—in short, more red tape. The problem of bureaucracy is inseparable from the problem of government generally.

Just as people are likely to say that they dislike Congress but like their own member of Congress, they are also inclined to express hostility toward "the bureaucracy" but goodwill for that part of the bureaucracy with which they have dealt personally. In 1973 a survey of Americans found that over half had had some contact with one or more kinds of government agencies, most of which were either run directly or funded indirectly by the federal government. The great majority of people were satisfied with these contacts and felt that they had been treated fairly and given useful assistance. When these people were asked their feelings about government officials in general, however, they expressed much less favorable attitudes. Whereas about 80 percent liked the officials with whom they had dealt, only 42 percent liked officials in general. This finding helps explain why government agencies are rarely reduced in size or budget: whatever the popular feelings about the bureaucracy, any given agency tends to have many friends.

Length: 894 words.
Reading Time: __________
See Conversion Table, p. 431.
Enter WPM Rate on p. 418.

47 Bureaucratic "Pathologies"

COMPREHENSION CHECK

GETTING THE FACTS

1. Bureaucracies are plagued with red tape, imperialism, waste, duplication, and (a) exclusion. (b) conflict. (c) interception. (d) enterprise. 1. ____

2. Red tape results from the need to satisfy (a) customers. (b) bureaucrats. (c) requirements. (d) proposals. 2. ____

3. The authors contend that imperialism results because agencies pursue goals that are (a) hard to achieve. (b) poorly defined. (c) short lived. (d) inappropriate. 3. ____

4. The biggest criticism of bureaucracy is (a) cost. (b) secrecy. (c) inconsistency. (d) waste. 4. ____

5. Most bureaucratic problems exist because of the very nature of (a) politics. (b) management. (c) downsizing. (d) government. 5. ____

GETTING THE MEANING

6. Many people feel bureaucracies are (a) undesirable. (b) ethical. (c) attentive. (d) satisfactory. 6. ____

7. Compared to government agencies, private firms are (a) more bureaucratic. (b) less bureaucratic. (c) friendlier. (d) less creative. 7. ____

8. Bureaucracies have no (a) characteristics. (b) pathologies. (c) profile. (d) value. 8. ____

9. Government agency employees are not aggressive about efficiency because there are few (a) examples. (b) parallels. (c) monitors. (d) incentives. 9. ____

10. One cause of bureaucracy is (a) business. (b) Congress. (c) families. (d) private industry. 10. ____

Check your answers with the Key on p. 452. Give yourself 10 points for each one right and enter your comprehension score on p. 415.

Comprehension Score: ________

NAME ____________ CLASS ____________ DATE ____________

48 The Nature and Importance of Effective Listening

WORD POWER WORKOUT

A. LEANING ON CONTEXT

In each of the blanks provided, place the letter that precedes the best definition of the underlined word in context to the left.

Words in Context	Definitions
1. ____ a judicious follower	a. taxing
2. ____ a tedious interruption	b. aggressive bargainers
3. ____ a dynamic activity	c. fluency
4. ____ business derived from	d. project
5. ____ eloquence of a speaker's voice	e. conservative
6. ____ scantily clad	f. resulted
7. ____ political hucksters	g. barely
8. ____ convey your support	h. invigorating
9. ____ dour and inattentive	i. severe
10. ____ an exhilarating experience	j. unstable

Check your answers with the Key on p. 443 before going on. Give yourself 10 points for each one right and enter your score on the chart under A on p. 420. Review any that you have missed.

A Score: ________

Pronunciation aids: **1. ju-DISH-us**
6. SKANT-i-lee
10. eg-ZIL-uh-rate-ng

B. LEANING ON PARTS

Here's another context-root review exercise—over *tendere,* meaning "to stretch." Fit the appropriate word into each of the numbered blanks below. Select from the following list of words derived from *tendere: tent, tends, extend, tension, pretend, portent, extensive, intention, attention, superintend.*

Anything that makes words more interesting (1) ____________ to (2) ____________ your vocabulary. (3) ____________ to derivation has that effect. So your present (4) ____________ efforts with derivation are a (5) ____________ of increased interest and better results.

C. MAKING THE WORDS YOURS

In each blank below, enter the most appropriate word from the ten words in context in the first exercise, substituting it for the word(s) in parentheses. Use these words: *convey, derived, dour, dynamic, eloquence, exhilarating, hucksters, judicious, scantily, tedious.*

1. The community concert was (invigorating) ____________.
2. They seem charming, but are really (aggressive bargainers) ____________.
3. Be (conservative) ____________ in distributing the remaining water.
4. We are not sure what will happen after the press conference, because this situation is (unstable) ____________.
5. People thought he was never happy because of his (severe) ____________ appearance.
6. Corey (barely) ____________ sprinkled the grass with water.
7. Navigating through traffic on I-5 can be (taxing) ____________.
8. She delivered the commencement address with great (fluency) ____________.
9. Profits (resulted) ____________ from his clever investments.
10. Barry White's music in the background will (project) ____________ a romantic mood.

Check your answers with the Key on p. 443.

B Score: ________

C Score: ________

Enter your scores on p. 420.

48

The Nature and Importance of Effective Listening

MICHAEL OSBORN AND SUZANNE OSBORN

"Oh, I'm sorry; I wasn't listening." If more people were honest, you'd hear that retort more often. The truth is that most people find paying careful attention and working to understand what someone else is saying a difficult thing to do. Just a few adjustments in the way you respond to speakers can increase the value of the experience. Give effective listening a try.

BEGIN TIMING

Although we spend the greatest amount of our communication time listening, we receive less formal training in listening than we do in speaking, writing, or reading. Why is this so? Perhaps educators assume that we know by nature how to listen well, despite a great deal of evidence to the contrary. They may undervalue listening because they associate it with following, whereas they associate speaking with leading. In the dominant American culture, leadership is admired more than "followership," even though being a judicious follower is one definition of a good citizen. As S. I. Hayakawa once commented, "Living in a competitive culture, most of us are . . . chiefly concerned with getting our own view across, and we . . . find other people's speeches a tedious interruption of our own ideas." . . . Finally, in a society that admires being "on the move," we may think of speaking as an active and listening as a passive behavior. This ignores the fact that effective listening is a dynamic activity that

- Seeks out the meaning intended in messages
- Considers apparent and not-so-apparent motivations
- Evaluates the soundness of the reasoning and the reliability of supporting materials
- Calculates the value and risk of accepting recommendations
- Integrates them creatively into the world of the listener

Other cultures place a higher premium on good listening behaviors. Some Native American tribes, for example, have a far better appreciation of their importance. The council system of the Ojai Foundation has three main rules for conducting business derived from tribal custom: "Speak honestly, be brief, and listen from the heart." The Lakota also recognize the value of listening. In their culture:

> **Conversation was never begun at once, nor in a hurried manner. No one was quick with a question, no matter how important, and no one was pressed for an answer. A pause giving time for thought was the truly courteous way of beginning and conducting a conversation. Silence was meaningful with the Lakota, and his granting a space of silence to the speech-maker and his own moment of silence before talking was done in the practice of true politeness and regard for the rule that, "thought comes before speech."**

We shall apply these lessons from the Ojai and Lakota people and regard listening as vital to successful communication.

The Ladder of Listening

The Chinese symbol for the verb "to listen" has four basic elements: undivided attention, ears, eyes, and heart. This symbol suggests some of the basic differences between simply hearing and actually listening. *Hearing* is an automatic process in which sound waves stimulate nerve impulses to the brain. We may call it the **discriminative phase,** in which we detect the vital sounds of spoken communication. While it is a necessary condition to the listening experience, it is only the first step up the ladder that rises over communication barriers. *Listening* is a voluntary activity that goes beyond the mere physical reaction to sounds. At the very least, listening involves focusing, understanding, and interpreting:

- You must focus on the message and block out factors that compete for your attention.
- You must understand the speaker's verbal and nonverbal language.
- You must interpret what you hear in light of your own knowledge and experiences.

These elements make up the **comprehensive phase,** the next rung of the ladder. Beyond these basic processes is the **empathic phase,** which emphasizes the heart in the Chinese symbol. When we are empathic, we encourage speakers by suspending judgment and allowing them to be heard. We try to see things from their point of view, even though we may not agree with them. Our next step up the ladder of listening is to the **appreciative phase,** in which we respond to beauty in the message. For example, we may enjoy the simplicity, balance, and proportion of a speech structure, or the eloquence of a speaker's words.

Critical listening represents another step up the ladder. Critical listeners analyze and evaluate the content of a message. They factor into the analysis their assessment of the speaker's motives and feelings. This step adds the element "mind" to the Chinese symbol for listening. Critical listeners also provide appropriate feedback to the speaker. As you evaluate, you may offer visual cues such as smiles or frowns, puzzled looks, or nods of agreement that let a speaker know how you are responding.

The final rung on the ladder of listening is **constructive listening.** Constructive listening involves seeking in messages their value for our lives. . . . Constructive listeners add to a message, finding in it special applications to their lives. As they listen to a speech on the importance of air bags in automobiles, they may question whether there are differences in the quality of air bags from one automobile to another. They may wonder if there are any drawbacks to air bags and, if so, how they might avoid them. If they don't hear the answers they seek in the speech itself, these listeners may question the speaker afterwards, creating a dialogue that extends the meaning of the speech. Such dialogues often produce discoveries, better realizations of values, and better answers to public questions. . . .

Benefits of Effective Listening

Effective listening benefits both listeners and speakers.

Benefits to the Listener

Charlatans often try to cover up a lack of substance or reasoning with a glib presentation or with irrelevant appeals. How many times have you seen attractive, scantily clad young men and women appearing in ads to sell everything from soft drinks to automatic transmission repair services? Or consider ads that rely on celebrity endorsements. What are the ads really selling? Ads may also ask you to buy what "doctors" recommend without explaining the credentials of these "doctors"—Ph.D.s in history may know very little about vitamins! Finally, political hucksters may hope that you won't notice their substitution of assertion for evidence, their appeals to prejudice in the place of good reasons. Effective listening skills may help ward off such deception.

Listening skills also have broad application to your academic and professional life. Students who listen effectively earn better grades and achieve beyond expectation. The reasons would seem obvious: Effective listeners learn to concentrate on what is being said and to identify what is important. They motivate themselves to learn by exploring the value of information for their lives. The most effective student listeners read assignments ahead of time to familiarize themselves with the language and to provide a foundation for understanding. . . .

At work, improved listening skills can mean the difference between success and failure—both for individuals and for companies. A Department of Labor report emphasized the value of learning how to listen effectively. A survey of over 400 top-level personnel directors suggested that the two most important factors in helping graduates find jobs are speaking and listening ability. Another survey of major American corporations reported that poor listening is "one of [the companies'] most important problems" and that "ineffective listening leads to ineffective performance." If you listen effectively on the job, you will improve your chances for advancement. . . .

Benefits to the Speaker

Speakers obviously benefit from an audience of good listeners. When audiences don't listen well, they can't provide useful feedback. Moreover, a good audience can help alleviate communication apprehension by creating a supportive classroom environment. Speakers need to realize that their listeners want them to succeed. You can convey your support by being a pleasant and responsive listener rather than dour and inattentive. Give speakers your undivided attention. Take an occasional note at appropriate moments—this suggests to them that you think their ideas are important. Nod occasionally in response to what they say. Show respect for them as people, even when you disagree with their ideas. Look for value in what they say.

An audience of effective listeners also can boost a speaker's self-esteem and make speaking an exhilarating experience. How many times have you had people really listen to you? How often have you had an opportunity to educate others? How frequently have your ideas and recommendations been taken seriously? If your answer is "seldom" or "never," you may be in for a pleasant surprise when you make your presentations. You will soon discover that there are few things quite as rewarding as having people really listen to you and respect what you say. . . . Negative evidence of the importance of this factor is provided by the difficulty many women executives have in American business. Often they hold an organizational title, but are not regarded as company "insiders." Consequently, they are sometimes not taken seriously when they speak. They suffer, and the company suffers from the loss of their ideas.

Length: 1420 words.
Reading Time: __________
See Conversion Table, p. 431.
Enter WPM Rate on p. 418.

48 The Nature and Importance of Effective Listening

COMPREHENSION CHECK

GETTING THE FACTS

1. According to the text, humans receive more formal training in reading, writing, and speaking than in (a) concentration. (b) English. (c) math. (d) listening. 1. ____

2. Effective listening seeks out the (a) intended meaning. (b) intended receiver. (c) origin of the idea. (d) impact of the message. 2. ____

3. Effective listening requires good skills in (a) speaking. (b) presentation. (c) notetaking. (d) concentration. 3. ____

4. The Chinese symbol for the verb "to listen" has four basic elements: undivided attention, eyes, ears, hands, and (a) soul. (b) conscience. (c) guilt. (d) heart. 4. ____

5. The text specifically says students who listen effectively (a) work faster. (b) graduate sooner. (c) earn better grades. (d) get better interviews. 5. ____

GETTING THE MEANING

6. The main idea is effective listening contributes to better (a) consuming. (b) selling. (c) recreation. (d) living. 6. ____

7. Effective listening skills are (a) learned. (b) costly. (c) impossible to improve. (d) accidental. 7. ____

8. A speaker's effectiveness is influenced by listeners' (a) eloquence. (b) presentation. (c) attentiveness. (d) position in the audience. 8. ____

9. The author implies that sometimes when women executives speak, listeners (a) question them. (b) ignore them. (c) revere them. (d) rebuke them. 9. ____

10. Effective listeners (a) apply what they learn. (b) scrutinize the message. (c) reject the facts. (d) contradict the facts. 10. ____

Check your answers with the Key on p. 452. Give yourself 10 points for each one right and enter your comprehension score on p. 415.

Comprehension Score: ________

NAME ____________ CLASS ____________ DATE ____________

49 Matter and Energy

WORD POWER WORKOUT

A. LEANING ON CONTEXT

In each of the blanks provided, place the letter that precedes the best definition of the underlined word in context to the left.

Words in Context	Definitions
1. ____ researchers adhere	a. transformed
2. ____ researcher seeks regularities	b. stick
3. ____ a hypothesis expresses	c. widespread
4. ____ no detectable difference	d. expectations
5. ____ extensive experimentation	e. shapeless
6. ____ the heat ignites	f. extraterrestrial
7. ____ energy is converted to	g. crash
8. ____ amorphous solids	h. starts
9. ____ collide with the walls	i. belief
10. ____ celestial bodies	j. apparent

Check your answers with the Key on p. 443 before going on. Give yourself 10 points for each one right and enter your score on the chart under A on p. 420. Review any that you have missed.

A Score: ________

Pronunciation aids: **3. hi-PAWTH-uh-sis**
8. uh-MOR-fuhs
10. suh-LES-chul

B. LEANING ON PARTS

This context-root review exercise focuses on *ducere,* meaning "to lead." Fit the appropriate word into each of the numbered blanks below. Select from the following list of words derived from *ducere: reduce, deduct, conduct, produce, educated, conducive, reproduce, introduce, abduct, productiveness.*

When you (1) ____________ your learning effectively, you (2) ____________ the time needed to (3) ____________ results. By now you should be well (4) ____________ in the managing of prefix, root, and suffix elements. Such an accomplishment is (5) ____________ to further progress.

C. MAKING THE WORDS YOURS

In each blank below, enter the most appropriate word from the ten words in context in the first exercise, substituting it for the word(s) in parentheses. Use these words: *adhere, amorphous, celestial, collide, converted, detectable, extensive, hypothesis, ignites, regularities.*

1. The whistles of trains passing through are comforting (expectations) ____________ in Flagstaff, AZ.
2. The melted snowman is now (shapeless) ____________.
3. He has had (widespread) ____________ travel opportunities.
4. This kind of music (starts) ____________ a fire in the marching band.
5. What (belief) ____________ is the researcher attempting to test?
6. In banking, (stick) ____________ to the rules or face a stiff penalty.
7. It is difficult not to (crash) ____________ with carts in these narrow aisles.
8. The group believes there are (extraterrestrial) ____________ beings on this planet.
9. A hint of vanilla was (apparent) ____________ in the air as we entered the kitchen.
10. They (transformed) ____________ their garage into a workshop.

Check your answers with the Key on p. 451.

B Score: ________

C Score: ________

Enter your scores on p. 420.

49

Matter and Energy

SHARON SHERMAN AND ALAN SHERMAN

To learn more about our universe, scientists use the scientific method to examine phenomena. This selection, taken from a chemistry textbook, explains two basic and essential things that describe the whole universe—matter and energy. See how much you know about the "stuff" everything's made of.

BEGIN TIMING

The Scientific Method

Chemistry is an experimental science that is concerned with the behavior of matter. Much of the body of chemical knowledge consists of abstract concepts and ideas. Without application, these concepts and ideas would have little impact on society. Chemical principles are applied for the benefit of society through technology. Useful products are developed by the union of basic science and applied technology.

Over the past 200 years, science and technology have moved forward at a rapid pace. Ideas and applications of these ideas are developed through carefully planned experimentation, in which researchers adhere to what is called the **scientific method.** The scientific method is composed of a series of logical steps that allow researchers to approach a problem and try to come up with solutions in the most effective way possible. It is generally thought of as having four parts:

1. *Observation and classification.* Scientists begin their research by carefully observing natural phenomena. They carry out experiments, which are observations of natural events in a controlled setting. This allows results to be duplicated and rational conclusions to be reached. The data the scientists collect are analyzed, and the facts that emerge are classified.
2. *Generalization.* Once observations are made and experiments carried out, the researcher seeks regularities or patterns in the results that can lead to a generalization. If this generalization is basic and can be communicated in a concise statement or a mathematical equation, the statement or equation is called a law.
3. *Hypothesis.* Researchers try to find reasons and explanations for the generalizations, patterns, and regularities they discover. A hypothesis expresses a tentative

explanation of a generalization that has been stated. Further experiments then test the validity of the hypothesis.

4. *Theory*. The new experiments are carried out to test the hypothesis. If they support it without exception, the hypothesis becomes a theory. A theory is a tested model that explains some basic phenomenon of nature. It cannot be proven to be absolutely correct. As further research is performed to test the theory, it may be modified or a better theory may be developed.

The scientific method represents a systematic means of doing research. There are times when discoveries are made by accident, but most knowledge has been gained via careful, planned experimentation. . . .

Matter and Energy

We begin with the two things that describe the entire universe: *matter* and *energy*. **Matter** is *anything that occupies space and has mass.* That includes trees, clothing, water, air, people, minerals, and many other things. . . .

Energy is the *ability to perform work.* Like matter, energy is found in a number of forms. Heat is one form of energy, and light is another. There are also chemical, electrical, and mechanical forms of energy. And energy can change from one form to another. In fact, matter can also change form or change into energy, and energy can change into matter, but not easily.

Law of Conservation of Mass and Energy

The **Law of Conservation of Mass** tells us that when a chemical change takes place, no detectable difference in the mass of the substances is observed. In other words, mass is neither created nor destroyed in an ordinary chemical reaction. This law has been tested by extensive experimentation in the laboratory, and the work of the brilliant French chemist-physicist Antoine Lavoisier provides evidence for this conclusion. Lavoisier performed many experiments involving matter. In one instance he heated a measured amount of tin and found that part of it changed to a powder. He also found that the *product* (powder plus tin) weighed *more* than the original piece of tin. To find out more about the added weight, he heated metals in sealed jars, which, of course, contained air. He measured the mass of his starting materials (*reactants*), and when the reaction concluded and the metal no longer changed to powder, he measured the mass of the products. In every such reaction, the mass of the reactants (oxygen from the air in the jar plus the original metal) equaled the mass of the products (the remaining metal plus the powder). Today we know that the reaction actually stopped when all of the oxygen in the sealed jar combined with the metal to form the powder. Lavoisier concluded that when a chemical change occurs, *matter is neither created nor destroyed, it just changes from one form to another,* which is a statement of the Law of Conservation of Mass.

. . . The **Law of Conservation of Energy** tells us that *in any chemical or physical change, energy is neither created nor destroyed, it is simply converted from one form to another.*

An auto engine provides a good example of how one form of energy is converted to a different form. *Electrical* energy from the battery generates a spark that contains *heat* energy. The heat ignites the gasoline–air mixture, which explodes, transforming chemical energy into heat and *mechanical* energy. The mechanical energy causes the pistons to rise and fall, rotating the engine crankshaft and moving the car.

At the same time, in the same engine, matter is changing from one form to another. When the gasoline explodes and burns, it combines with oxygen in the cylinders to form carbon dioxide and water vapor. (Unfortunately, carbon monoxide and other dangerous gases may also be formed. This is one of the major causes of air pollution.)

. . . Matter is always changing from one form to another, and so is energy. Besides that, matter is changing to energy and energy to matter. But *the sum of all the matter (or mass) and energy in the universe always remains the same.* This repeated observation is called the **Law of Conservation of Mass and Energy.**

Potential Energy and Kinetic Energy

Which do you think has more energy, a metal cylinder held 1 foot above the ground or an identical cylinder held 5 feet above the ground? If you dropped them on your foot, you would know immediately that the cylinder with more energy was the one that was 5 feet above the ground. But where does this energy come from?

Work had to be done to raise the two cylinders to their respective heights—to draw them up against the pull of gravity. And energy was needed to do that work. The energy used to lift each cylinder was "stored" in each cylinder. The higher the cylinder was lifted, the more energy was stored in it—due to its position. *Energy that is stored in an object by virtue of its position* is called **potential energy.**

If we drop the cylinders, they fall toward the ground. As they do so, they lose potential energy because they lose height. But now they are moving: their potential energy is converted to "energy of motion." The more potential energy they lose, the more energy of motion they acquire. *The energy that an object possesses by virtue of its motion* is called **kinetic energy.** The conversion of potential energy to kinetic energy is a very common phenomenon. It is observed in a wide variety of processes, from downhill skiing to the generation of hydroelectric power.

The States of Matter

Matter may exist in any of the three physical states: solid, liquid, and gas.

A **solid** has a definite shape and volume that it tends to maintain under normal conditions. The particles composing a solid stick rigidly to one another. Solids most commonly occur in the **crystalline** form, which means they have a fixed, regularly repeating, symmetrical internal structure. Diamonds, salt, and quartz are examples of crystalline solids. A few solids, such as glass and paraffin, do not have a well-defined crystalline structure, although they do have a definite shape and volume. Such solids are called **amorphous solids,** which means they have no definite internal structure or form.

A **liquid** has a definite volume but does not have its own shape since it takes the shape of the container in which it is placed. Its particles cohere firmly, but not rigidly, so the particles of a liquid have a great deal of mobility while maintaining close contact with one another.

A **gas** has no fixed shape or volume and eventually spreads out to fill its container. As the gas particles move about they collide with the walls of their container causing pressure, which is a force exerted over an area. Gas particles move independently of one another. Compared with those of a liquid or solid, gas particles are quite far apart. Unlike solids and liquids, which cannot be compressed very much at all, gases can be both compressed and expanded.

Often referred to as the fourth state of matter, **plasma** is *a form of matter composed of electrically charged atomic particles.* Many objects found in the earth's outer atmosphere, as well as many celestial bodies found in space (such as the sun and stars), consist of plasma. A plasma can be created by heating a gas to extremely high temperatures or by passing a current through it. A plasma responds to a magnetic field and conducts electricity well.

Length: 1330 words.
Reading Time: ___________
See Conversion Table, p. 434.
Enter WPM Rate on p. 418.

49 Matter and Energy

COMPREHENSION CHECK

GETTING THE FACTS

1. Chemistry is (a) a biological science. (b) an exact science. (c) an experimental science. (d) an absolute science. 1. ____

2. The scientific method uses (a) logical steps. (b) random application. (c) alternating methods. (d) arbitrary selection. 2. ____

3. Matter is anything that occurs in space and has (a) depth. (b) breadth. (c) mass. (d) height. 3. ____

4. In chemical changes, mass is neither created nor (a) changed. (b) attached. (c) moved. (d) destroyed. 4. ____

5. Stored energy is called (a) kinetic energy. (b) crystallized energy. (c) complex energy. (d) potential energy. 5. ____

GETTING THE MEANING

6. This selection illustrates that chemistry is an essential (a) element of science. (b) force of nature. (c) influence in our lives. (d) collection of elements. 6. ____

7. "The more potential energy they lose, the more energy of motion they acquire," explains how (a) birds fly. (b) trains move. (c) ice melts. (d) the sun warms. 7. ____

8. Gases are (a) farther apart. (b) closer together. (c) more volatile. (d) more docile. 8. ____

9. Lavoisier proved that there is as much matter in the universe as there was (a) 100 years ago. (b) 100,000 years ago. (c) a million years ago. (d) in the beginning. 9. ____

10. Gas particles are (a) liquid. (b) mobile. (c) fixed. (d) solid. 10. ____

Check your answers with the Key on p. 452. Give yourself 10 points for each one right and enter your comprehension score on p. 415.

Comprehension Score: ________

NAME ______________ CLASS ______________ DATE ______________

50 The Organization's Culture

WORD POWER WORKOUT

A. LEANING ON CONTEXT

In each of the blanks provided, place the letter that precedes the best definition of the underlined word in context to the left.

Words in Context	Definitions
1. ____ building that fosters informality	a. elusive
2. ____ converge for lunch-time conversation	b. outfits
3. ____ The stereotypic image	c. promoting
4. ____ business attire	d. generalized
5. ____ of paramount importance	e. casualness
6. ____ incur bank debt	f. commandeer
7. ____ intangible nature	g. primary
8. ____ by articulating the culture	h. fancy
9. ____ an elaborate display	i. congregate
10. ____ to usurp power	j. experience

Check your answers with the Key on p. 443 before going on. Give yourself 10 points for each one right and enter your score on the chart under A on p. 420. Review any that you have missed.

A Score: ________

Pronunciation aids: **3. ster-ee-oh-TIP-ik**
7. in-TAN-juh-bul
10. yoo-ZURP

B. LEANING ON PARTS

This context-root review exercise focuses on *specere,* meaning "to see or look." Fit the appropriate word into each of the numbered blanks below. Select from the following incomplete list of words derived from *specere: spy, expect, specify, special, prospect, specimens, spectacles, inspecting, circumspect, perspicacity.*

These exercises will help you develop (1) __________ (2) __________ with words. You can (3) __________ to use prefix and root knowledge with increasing skill, a (4) __________ to be welcomed. You're establishing that all-important habit of (5) __________ words carefully to discover known parts.

C. MAKING THE WORDS YOURS

In each blank below, enter the most appropriate word from the ten words in context in the first exercise, substituting it for the word(s) in parentheses. Use these words: *articulating, attire, converge, elaborate, incur, informality, intangible, paramount, stereotypic, usurp.*

1. These tedious projects (commandeer) __________ my time and money.
2. An (elusive) __________ feeling warns me that something is wrong.
3. The tourists will (experience) __________ the cost of the side trip to San Francisco.
4. Assuming all doctors have poor penmanship is a (generalized) __________ perception.
5. The President's daily (outfits) __________ will probably change when he leaves office.
6. Let's not all (congregate) __________ on the same beach at once.
7. Finishing my Ph.D. is my (primary) __________ concern.
8. The team has purchased (fancy) __________ uniforms for this special occasion.
9. We are adept at (promoting) __________ our candidates' beliefs.
10. The evening's (casualness) __________ led to wonderful conversation and laughter.

Check your answers with the Key on p. 443.

B Score: __________

C Score: __________

Enter your scores on p. 420.

50

The Organization's Culture

RICKY GRIFFIN

Just what makes one organization different from another? Why are some environments great places to work and others more like battlefields? A primary reason is organizational culture. But what, exactly, is that? Knowing could influence you to accept a job in an organization perfectly suited for you, and not knowing may permit you to make the mistake of a lifetime.

BEGIN TIMING

Culture is an amorphous concept that defies objective measurement or observation. Nevertheless, because it is the foundation of the organization's internal environment, it plays a major role in shaping managerial behavior.

The Importance of Organizational Culture

Several years ago, executives at Levi Strauss believed that the company had outgrown its sixty-eight-year-old building. Even though everyone enjoyed its casual and relaxed atmosphere, the company needed more space. So Levi Strauss moved into a modern office building in downtown San Francisco where its new headquarters spread over twelve floors in a skyscraper. It quickly became apparent that the change was affecting the corporate culture—and that people did not like it. Executives felt isolated, and other managers missed the informal chance meetings in the halls. Within just a few years, Strauss moved out of the skyscraper and back into a building that fosters informality. This new site is adjacent to a park area where employees converge for lunch-time conversation. Clearly, Levi Strauss has a culture that is important to the people who work there.

Culture determines the "feel" of the organization. The stereotypic image of Microsoft, for example, is a workplace where people dress very casually and work very long hours. In contrast, the image of Bank of America for some observers is a formal setting with rigid work rules and people dressed in conservative business attire. And Texas Instruments likes to talk about its "shirt sleeve" culture in which ties are avoided and few managers ever wear jackets. Southwest Airlines maintains a culture that stresses fun and excitement. The firm's CEO, Herb Kelleher, explains the company's emphasis on fun in an orientation video set to rap music.

Of course, the same culture is not necessarily found throughout an entire organization. For example, the sales and marketing department may have a culture quite different from that of the operations and manufacturing department. Regardless of its nature, however, culture is a powerful force in organizations, one that can shape the firm's overall effectiveness and long-term success. . . .

■ Determinants of Organizational Culture

Where does an organization's culture come from? Typically it develops and blossoms over a long period of time. Its starting point is often the organization's founder. For example, James Cash Penney believed in treating employees and customers with respect and dignity. Employees at J. C. Penney are still called associates rather than employees (to reflect partnership), and customer satisfaction is of paramount importance. The impact of Sam Walton, Ross Perot, and Walt Disney is still felt in the organizations they founded. As an organization grows, its culture is modified, shaped, and refined by symbols, stories, heroes, slogans, and ceremonies. For example, an important value at Hewlett-Packard Co. is the avoidance of bank debt. A popular story still told at the company involves a new project being considered for several years. All objective criteria indicated that Hewlett-Packard Co. should incur bank debt to finance it, yet Bill Hewlett and David Packard rejected the project out of hand simply because "HP avoids bank debt." This story, involving two corporate heroes and based on a slogan, dictates corporate culture today. And many decisions at Walt Disney Company today are still framed by asking, "What would Walt have done?"

Corporate success and shared experiences also shape culture. For example, Hallmark Cards has a strong culture derived from its years of success in the greeting card industry. Employees speak of the Hallmark family and care deeply about the company; many of them have worked at the company for years. At Kmart, in contrast, the culture is quite weak, the management team changes rapidly, and few people sense any direction or purpose in the company. The differences in culture at Hallmark and Kmart are in part attributable to past successes and shared experiences.

■ Managing Organizational Culture

How can managers deal with culture, given its clear importance but intangible nature? Essentially, the manager must understand the current culture and then decide whether it should be maintained or changed. By understanding the organization's current culture, managers can take appropriate actions. At

Hewlett-Packard Co. the values represented by "the HP way" still exist. Moreover, they guide and direct most important activities that the firm undertakes. Culture can also be maintained by rewarding and promoting people whose behaviors are consistent with the existing culture and by articulating the culture through slogans, ceremonies, and so forth. "The World of Management" describes how Merrill Lynch is working to extend its famed organizational culture into its foreign offices.

But managers must walk a fine line between maintaining a culture that still works effectively versus changing a culture that has become dysfunctional. Many of the firms already noted, as well as numerous others, take pride in perpetuating their cultures. Shell Oil Company, for example, has an elaborate display in the lobby of its Houston headquarters building that tells the story of the firm's past. But other companies may face situations in which their culture is no longer a strength. For example, some critics feel that Ford's culture places too much emphasis on product development and not enough on marketing. This culture sometimes results in new products that fail to live up to expectations.

Culture problems sometimes arise from mergers or the growth of rival factions within an organization. For example, Wells Fargo and Company, which relies heavily on snazzy technology and automated banking services, recently acquired another large bank, First Interstate, which had focused more attention on personal services and customer satisfaction. Blending the two disparate organizational cultures has been difficult for the firm as managers have argued over how best to serve customers and operate the new enterprise. Arthur Andersen, one of the Big Six accounting firms, faces a different type of cultural problem. Its relatively new Andersen Consulting Group has grown in size and importance to the point where it threatens to usurp power from the original accounting group. Differences in culture between the two groups makes reconciling their goals and agendas difficult. Indeed, plans are currently being developed to split the organization into two companies. And the primary reason is cultural incompatibility.

To change culture, managers must have a clear idea of what they want to create. Schwinn Bicycle Co. has tried to redefine itself to be more competitive and to break free of its old approaches to doing business. The firm's new motto—"Established 1895. Re-established 1994"—represents an effort to create a new culture that more accurately reflects today's competitive environment in the bicycle market. Likewise, when Continental Airlines reinvented itself a few years ago, employees were invited outside the corporate headquarters building in Houston to watch as the firm's old policies and procedures manuals were set afire. The firm's new strategic direction is known throughout Continental Airlines as the "Go Forward" plan, intentionally named so as to avoid reminding people about the firm's troubled past and to, instead, focus on the future.

One major way to shape culture is by bringing outsiders into important managerial positions. The choice of a new CEO from outside the organization is often a clear signal that things will be changing. Indeed, new CEOs were the catalyst for the changes at Schwinn Bicycle and Continental Airlines noted above. Adopting new slogans, telling new stories, staging new ceremonies, and breaking with tradition can also alter culture.

Length: 1000 words.
Reading Time: __________
See Conversion Table, p. 434.
Enter WPM Rate on p. 418.

50 The Organization's Culture

COMPREHENSION CHECK

GETTING THE FACTS

1. The culture of an organization's divisions (a) is unimportant. (b) may vary. (c) should be the same. (d) should be obscured. 1. ____

2. The most significant factor in organizational culture is (a) customers. (b) leadership. (c) time. (d) personnel. 2. ____

3. One major way to shape cultures is to bring outsiders into (a) human relations. (b) production. (c) advertisement. (d) management. 3. ____

4. According to the text, when companies merge, cultures often (a) collide. (b) determine cost. (c) undermine cost. (d) influence management. 4. ____

5. Managerial behavior is shaped mostly by company (a) location. (b) culture. (c) politics. (d) sales. 5. ____

GETTING THE MEANING

6. The main idea is that organizational culture is (a) tangible. (b) measurable. (c) static. (d) defining. 6. ____

7. The Levi Strauss example illustrates that companies should (a) change their organizational culture. (b) value their organizational culture. (c) discourage informality. (d) support lunch-time interaction. 7. ____

8. Management's understanding of a company's culture is most essential to the company's (a) stability. (b) image. (c) management. (d) consumers. 8. ____

9. An organization's culture is the organization's (a) profit. (b) reputation. (c) context. (d) product. 9. ____

10. A strong influence on an organization's culture is its (a) early leadership. (b) industry ranking. (c) diversity. (d) size. 10. ____

Check your answers with the Key on p. 452. Give yourself 10 points for each one right and enter your comprehension score on p. 415.

Comprehension Score: ________

NAME ______________ CLASS ______________ DATE ______________

51 The Nature of Social Responsibility

WORD POWER WORKOUT

A. LEANING ON CONTEXT

In each of the blanks provided, place the letter that precedes the best definition of the underlined word in context to the left.

Words in Context

1. ____ social responsibility thus deals with
2. ____ legal repercussions
3. ____ successful transition
4. ____ in their vicinity
5. ____ engage in litigation
6. ____ philanthropic activities
7. ____ beyond these dimensions
8. ____ codified as laws
9. ____ decisions foster trust
10. ____ drugs to eradicate

Definitions

a. lawsuit
b. designated
c. hence
d. consequences
e. promote
f. surroundings
g. conversion
h. benevolent
i. obliterate
j. scope

Check your answers with the Key on p. 443 before going on. Give yourself 10 points for each one right and enter your score on the chart under A, on p. 420. Review any that you have missed.

A Score: ________

Pronunciation aids: **2. ree-puhr-KUSH-uhnz**
6. fil-uhn-THRAWP-ik
10. ee-RAD-i-kate

B. LEANING ON PARTS

This context-root review exercise focuses on *ferre,* meaning "to bear or carry." Fit the appropriate word into each of the numbered blanks below. Select from the following incomplete list of words derived from *ferre: infer, defer, ferry, suffer, offered, different, inference, reference, coniferous, preference.*

It's easy to remember that *ferre* means to bear or carry. Just think of a (1) ____________ boat carrying people over a body of water. If a (2) ____________ mnemonic works better for you, fine. Use your own (3) ____________ rather than the one (4) ____________ above. The important thing is not to (5) ____________ making a useful connection to help you remember.

C. MAKING THE WORDS YOURS

In each blank below, enter the most appropriate word from the ten words in context in the first exercise, substituting it for the word(s) in parentheses. Use these words: *codified, dimensions, eradicate, foster, litigation, philanthropic, repercussions, thus, transition, vicinity.*

1. Most people in our society avoid (a lawsuit) ____________ if possible.
2. Since we have never backed out of a real estate contract, I am not sure what the (consequences) ____________ will be.
3. Regulations for Internet use at most libraries and colleges have been (designated) ____________ as institutional policy.
4. In an effort to (promote) ____________ cooperation, the mayors of the two cities met.
5. Aggressive research is one attempt to (obliterate) ____________ cancer.
6. Bill and Camille Cosby are known for their (benevolent) ____________ acts.
7. The (conversion) ____________ from city to rural life was difficult for the whole family.
8. This information provides broader (scope) ____________.
9. The (surroundings) ____________ had been plagued with red ants.
10. She loved jazz; (hence) ____________ the presence of jazz memorabilia.

Check your answers with the Key on p. 451.

B Score: ________

C Score: ________

Enter your scores on p. 420.

51

The Nature of Social Responsibility

WILLIAM PRIDE AND O. C. FERRELL

Organizations that reside in communities and do business there have an impact on the environment and the lifestyles of its neighbors. Most believe organizations should be good citizens and contribute rather than detract from their surroundings. Assess the social responsibility index of your community's businesses against the recommendations provided in this selection. Do the organizations you do business with make the grade?

BEGIN TIMING

In marketing, **social responsibility** refers to an organization's obligation to maximize its positive impact and minimize its negative impact on society. Social responsibility thus deals with the total effect of all marketing decisions on society. There is ample evidence to demonstrate that ignoring society's demands for responsible marketing can destroy customers' trust and even prompt government regulations. Irresponsible actions that anger customers, employees, or competitors may not only jeopardize a marketer's financial standing, but have legal repercussions as well. For instance, many insurance companies, such as Prudential and MetLife, have been fined and experienced negative publicity for misrepresenting their products in sales presentations. In contrast, socially responsible activities can generate positive publicity and boost sales. The Breast Cancer Awareness Crusade sponsored by Avon Products, for example, has raised over $25 million to help fund community-based breast cancer education and early detection services. Within the first two years of the Awareness Crusade, more than 400 stories about Avon's efforts appeared in major media, which contributed to an increase in company sales. Avon, a marketer of women's cosmetics, is also known for employing a large number of women and promoting them to top management; the firm has more female top managers (86 percent) than any other Fortune 500 company.

Socially responsible efforts like Avon's have a positive impact on local communities; at the same time, they indirectly help the sponsoring organization by attracting goodwill, publicity, and potential customers and employees. Thus, while social responsibility is certainly a positive concept in itself, most organizations embrace it in the expectation of indirect long-term benefits. . . .

The Dimensions of Social Responsibility

Socially responsible organizations strive for **marketing citizenship** by incorporating economic, legal, ethical, and philanthropic concerns into their marketing strategies. . . . The economic and legal aspects have long been acknowledged, but philanthropic and ethical issues have gained recognition more recently.

At the most basic level, all companies have an economic responsibility to be profitable so they can provide a return on investment to their stockholders, create jobs for the community, and contribute goods and services to the economy. How organizations relate to stockholders, employees, competitors, customers, the community, and the natural environment affects the economy. Marketing Citizenship describes how one company's efforts to improve its performance affected its relationship with stockholders and employees. An organization's sense of economic responsibility is especially significant for employees, raising such issues as equal job opportunities, workplace diversity, job safety, health, and employee privacy. In Germany, BMW is reducing workers' hours from thirty-seven to thirty-one per week while keeping their pay at the original levels. BMW's goal is to introduce a shift system that will keep the plant operating around the clock at double the current productivity level. Sharing the profits with employees assures a more successful transition, as well as employee support of BMW's goals for product quality.

To be socially responsible in their management of employees, companies should address several key issues. They should consider employees' economic security by ensuring that the wage and total compensation package satisfies employees' basic needs. They should attempt to maximize safety in the workplace to minimize employee injuries on the job, which cost companies \$10 billion per year. They should train their employees to improve their skills, motivation, and, potentially, productivity. To foster diversity, companies should consider options (flextime, job-sharing, parental leave, subsidized day care, etc.) that create a family-friendly workplace. Southwest Airlines, for example, offers employees training through its "University for People," and many employees have very flexible work arrangements that include flextime and special work/family programs. . . .

Marketers also have an economic responsibility to compete fairly. Size frequently gives companies an advantage over others. Large firms can often generate economies of scale that allow them to put smaller firms out of business. Consequently, small companies and even whole communities may resist the efforts of firms like Wal-Mart, Home Depot, and Best Buy to open stores in their vicinity. These firms are able to operate at such low costs that small local firms cannot compete. While consumers appreciate lower prices, the failure of small businesses increases unemployment, which places a burden on communities. Such issues create concerns about social responsibility for organizations, communities, and consumers.

Marketers are also expected to obey laws and regulations. The efforts of elected representatives and special interest groups to promote responsible corporate behavior have resulted in laws and regulations designed to keep U.S. companies' actions within the range of acceptable conduct. When customers, interest groups, or businesses become outraged over what they perceive as irresponsibility on the part of a marketing organization, they may urge their legislators to draft new legislation to regulate the behavior, or they may engage in litigation to force an organization to "play by the rules." For example, Teva, which markets a line of popular sport sandals, sued Wal-Mart, accusing the retailer of selling Teva knockoffs for 25 percent less than Teva's sandals. The knockoffs may have been a factor in the decline of Teva's sales by $69 million in two years. Teva won the lawsuit, and Wal-Mart was forced to stop selling the sandals.

Economic and legal responsibilities are the most basic levels of social responsibility for a good reason: failure to consider them may mean that a marketer is not around long enough to engage in ethical or philanthropic activities. Beyond these dimensions is **marketing ethics,** which refers to principles and standards that define acceptable conduct in marketing as determined by various stakeholders, including the public, government regulators, private interest groups, consumers, industry, and the organization itself. The most basic of these principles have been codified as laws and regulations to encourage marketers to conform to society's expectations of conduct. For example, new laws prohibit organizations from collecting information from children 13 and younger on the Internet without specific parental permission. Internet marketers need to be aware of this new law and to inform their employees of its implications. Even though the new law's constitutionality has been questioned, a socially responsible marketer would want to implement its requirements. However, it is important to realize that marketing ethics goes beyond legal issues. Ethical marketing decisions foster trust, which helps to build long-term marketing relationships. . . .

At the top of the pyramid are philanthropic responsibilities. These responsibilities, which go beyond marketing ethics, are not required of a company, but they promote human welfare or goodwill, as do the economic, legal, and ethical dimensions of social responsibility. That many companies have demonstrated philanthropic responsibility is evidenced by over $6 billion in annual donations and contributions to environmental and social causes. Ben & Jerry's, for example, has aggressively supported social causes (children and families, disenfranchised groups, and the environment) with 7.5 percent of its pretax profits. . . . SmithKline Beecham has formed a partnership with the World Health Organization to develop and donate drugs to eradicate Lymphatic Filariasis, a disease affecting 120 million people worldwide. . . .

Many firms link their products to a particular social cause on an ongoing or short-term basis. One of the first companies to apply this practice, known as **cause-related marketing,** was American Express, which donated to the Statue of Liberty restoration fund every time customers used their American Express card. The promotion was extraordinarily successful, generating new customers and increasing the use of charge cards dramatically. Customers tend to like such cause-related programs because they provide an additional reason to "feel good" about a particular purchase. Marketers like the programs because well-designed ones increase sales and create positive feelings of respect and admiration for the companies involved.

Length: 1200 words.
Reading Time: ________
See Conversion Table, p. 434.
Enter WPM Rate on p. 418.

51 The Nature of Social Responsibility

COMPREHENSION CHECK

GETTING THE FACTS

1. Social responsibility refers to an organization's (a) involvement. (b) profit. (c) impact. (d) contributions. 1. ____

2. Ignoring society's demands can erode customers' (a) buying power. (b) trust. (c) access. (d) preference. 2. ____

3. Marketing citizenship involves incorporating economic, legal, philanthropic, and (a) growth opportunities. (b) recreational opportunities. (c) ethical strategies. (d) profit-sharing strategies. 3. ____

4. All companies have an economic responsibility to be (a) socially aware. (b) customer oriented. (c) prudent. (d) profitable. 4. ____

5. Marketing ethics refers to (a) principles and standards. (b) litigation. (c) honesty. (d) profits and losses. 5. ____

GETTING THE MEANING

6. This selection is mainly about organizations' (a)structure. (b) history. (c) obligation to society. (d) obligation to employees. 6. ____

7. A company's social responsibility often benefits the sponsoring organization by promoting (a) competition. (b) collusion. (c) a positive image. (d) a dominant position. 7. ____

8. When organizations give back to communities in which they reside, they satisfy (a) marketing ethics. (b) community expectations. (c) corporate promotions. (d) employee obligations. 8. ____

9. Some purchase products and services to benefit (a) stockholders. (b) employees. (c) the economy. (d) a cause. 9. ____

10. When marketing ethics are not enough to force companies to "play by the rules," society (a) recoils. (b) acts in accordance. (c) complies. (d) passes laws. 10. ____

Check your answers with the Key on p. 452. Give yourself 10 points for each one right and enter your comprehension score on p. 415.

Comprehension Score: ________

E. VOCABULARY REVIEW QUIZ

This quiz contains ten words taken from preceding Word Power Workouts, but with other possible meanings of the word. The focus is on words with important prefix and root elements so as to reinforce your awareness of how those elements aid in arriving at word meanings.

1. affect — (a) rank (b) state (c) combine (d) beg (e) influence — 1. ____
   Affect contains the prefix ______, meaning ______, and the root _________, meaning _________.

2. intercept — (a) cut off (b) call (c) examine (d) send (e) reach — 2. ____
   Intercept contains the prefix ______, meaning ______, and the root _________, meaning _________.

3. explication — (a) clarification (b) application (c) statement (d) call (e) look — 3. ____
   Explication contains the prefix ______, meaning ______, and the root _________, meaning _________.

4. pertinent — (a) in part (b) legal (c) to the point (d) final (e) practical — 4. ____
   Pertinent contains the prefix ______, meaning ______, and the root _________, meaning _________.

5. dismissal — (a) standing (b) going out (c) taking (d) planning (e) attacking — 5. ____
   Dismissal contains the prefix ______, meaning ______, and the root _________, meaning _________.

6. productivity — (a) heaviness (b) opening (c) harvest (d) fruitfulness (e) field — 6. ____
   Productivity contains the prefix ______, meaning ______, and the root _________, meaning _________.

7. imposing — (a) grand (b) new (c) modern (d) imperfect (e) impractical — 7. ____
   Imposing contains the prefix ______, meaning ______, and the root _________, meaning _________.

8. perspective (a) perfection (b) outlook (c) plan (d) condition (e) practice *Perspective* contains the prefix ______, meaning ______, and the root _________, meaning _________. 8. ____

9. extensive (a) large (b) tight (c) awkward (d) slim (e) breakable *Extensive* contains the root ______, meaning ______, and the root_________, meaning_________. 9. ____

10. prefer (a) allow (b) invite (c) return (d) explain (e) want *Prefer* contains the prefix ______, meaning ______, and the root_________, meaning_________. 10. ____

Count 10 points for each correct answer.
Key on page 441.
Vocabulary Review Score: ________

Appendix

Difficulty Rating Index

Selection	Flesch Reading Ease Score
VERY EASY	
8. Short Words Are Words of Might	93
36. The Gun	92
9. The Three Who Found Death	91
EASY	
24. Father and the Tommyknockers	85
FAIRLY EASY	
23. The Juggler	79
26. Listening	79
17. Two Ways of Looking at Life	78
20. Watching a Veterinarian at Work	78
21. Watching a Surgeon at Work	78
29. How to Work for a Rotten Boss	78
32. He Survived His Own Funeral	76
11. The All-Important Question	74
12. Words Can Be Slippery	74
2. Surviving the Information Avalanche	73
14. The First Rule of Conversation	73
15. How to REALLY Talk to Another Person	73
3. How to Read a Difficult Book	72
35. The Open Window	72
6. Words That Laugh and Cry	71
STANDARD	
33. Ten Football Stars and Yours Truly	68
18. Two Words to Avoid, Two to Remember	68
42. My Alma Mater	68
5. The Master-Word Approach	64
30. The Joy of Quitting	64
27. How to Remember: Some Fundamental Principles	62
FAIRLY DIFFICULT	
38. The Dividends for Quitters	58
50. The Organization's Culture	53*
39. The Road to Wellville	52
44. Good Health for Sale	50*
41. America Won't Win 'Till It Reads More	49
46. Short Stories	45*
DIFFICULT	
45. Challenges to Racial and Sexual Discrimination	40*
47. Bureaucratic "Pathologies"	39*
48. The Nature and Importance of Effective Listening	34*
49. Matter and Energy	20*
51. The Nature of Social Responsibility	25*

*These selections were all taken from textbooks.

Progress Record Charts

For each selection enter a dot to indicate your comprehension score and, on the next page, a dot to indicate your wpm (word-per-minute) rate. If you read the selections in the exact order given in the text, the numbers in the Reading Order will be identical with the Selection Numbers. If, however, the third reading you do is not selection #3 but selection #8, enter 8 under 3 to indicate that you read that selection third.

COMPREHENSION SCORE				
Reading Order	**1 2 3 4 5 6 7**	**8 9 10 11 12 13**	**14 15 16 17 18 19**	**20 21 22 23 24 25 26**
Selection #				
Comprehension Score: 100				
90				
80				
70				
60				
50				
40				
30				
20				
10				
0				

	COMPREHENSION SCORE			
Reading Order	**27 28 29 30 31 32**	**33 34 35 36 37 38**	**39 40 41 42 43 44**	**45 46 47 48 49 50 51**
Selection #				
Comprehension Score: 100				
90				
80				
70				
60				
50				
40				
30				
20				
10				
0				

	WPM RATE			
Reading Order	1 2 3 4 5 6 7	8 9 10 11 12 13 14	15 16 17 18 19 20	21 22 23 24 25 26
Selection #				
Word-per-minute Rate: 1200				
1175				
1150				
1125				
1100				
1075				
1050				
1025				
1000				
975				
950				
925				
900				
875				
850				
825				
800				
775				
750				
725				
700				
675				
650				
625				
600				
575				
550				
525				

Reading Order	1 2 3 4 5 6 7	8 9 10 11 12 13 14	15 16 17 18 19 20	21 22 23 24 25 26
Selection #				
Word-per-minute Rate: 500				
475				
450				
425				
400				
375				
350				
325				
300				
275				
250				
225				
200				
175				
150				

WPM RATE				
Reading Order	27 28 29 30 31 32	33 34 35 36 37 38 39	40 41 42 43 44 45	46 47 48 49 50 51
Selection #				
Word-per-minute Rate: 1200				
1175				
1150				
1125				
1100				
1075				
1050				
1025				
1000				
975				
950				
925				
900				
875				
850				
825				
800				
775				
750				
725				
700				
675				
650				
625				
600				
575				
550				

Reading Order	27 28 29 30 31 32	33 34 35 36 37 38 39	40 41 42 43 44 45	46 47 48 49 50 51
Selection #				
Word-per-minute Rate: 525				
500				
475				
450				
425				
400				
375				
350				
325				
300				
275				
250				
225				
200				
175				
150				

Word Power Workout Chart

Enter your scores for each of the three Word Power Workout parts below: 10 for each one right in A, 20 for each one right in B, and 10 for each one right in C. As with the earlier Progress Record Charts, if you change the work order, enter the number of the selection in place of the normal order given. Your scores will uncover problem areas with context, parts, or application.

Reading Order	Sel. #	Context A	Parts B	Application C	Reading Order	Sel. #	Context A	Parts B	Application C
1.					27.				
2.					28.				
3.					29.				
4.					30.				
5.					31.				
6.					32.				
7.					33.				
8.					34.				
9.					35.				
10.					36.				
11.					37.				
12.					38.				
13.					39.				
14.					40.				
15.					41.				
16.					42.				
17.					43.				
18.					44.				
19.					45.				
20.					46.				
21.					47.				
22.					48.				
23.					49.				
24.					50.				
25.					51.				
26.									

Conversion Tables

Determine your exact word-per-minute reading rate by dividing the number of words in a selection by your reading time in seconds, multiplying the resulting figure by 60.

For a time-saving approximation for converting your reading time in minutes and seconds to a wpm rate figure, use the following conversion tables. When you read a selection, look for your closest reading time figure in the column headed *Time.* You'll find your reading rate to the right of that figure under the number of the selection read. For example, if you read selection 1 in 9:10 (9 minutes and 10 seconds), your reading rate would be 150 wpm, the figure under Sel. 1, to the right of 9:10.

If your reading rate for any selection is *less* than one minute (1:00), *double* your reading time figure before using the table. Then double the figure in the table to get your rate. Suppose you read selection 3 in 50 seconds. Double that figure to get 100 seconds, or 1:40, then look for that number in the table. You'll see the figure 660. Double that figure to get your rate—1320 wpm.

CONVERSION TABLES

Time	Sel. 1	Sel. 2	Sel. 3	Sel. 4	Sel. 5	Sel. 6	Sel. 7	Sel. 8	Sel. 9	Sel. 10	Sel. 11	Sel. 12
1:00	1375	2820	1100	1490	1000	1030	1866	1880	1290	1370	2050	2090
1:05	1269	2603	1015	1375	923	951	1722	1735	1191	1265	1892	1929
1:10	1179	2417	943	1277	857	883	1599	1611	1106	1174	1757	1791
1:15	1100	2256	880	1192	800	824	1493	1504	1032	1096	1640	1672
1:20	1031	2115	825	1118	750	773	1400	1410	968	1028	1538	1568
1:25	971	1991	776	1052	706	727	1317	1327	911	967	1447	1475
1:30	917	1880	733	993	667	687	1244	1253	860	913	1367	1393
1:35	868	1781	695	941	632	651	1179	1187	815	865	1295	1320
1:40	825	1692	660	894	600	618	1120	1128	774	822	1230	1254
1:45	786	1611	629	851	571	589	1066	1074	737	783	1171	1194
1:50	750	1538	600	813	545	562	1018	1025	704	747	1118	1140
1:55	717	1471	574	777	522	537	974	981	673	715	1070	1090
2:00	688	1410	550	745	500	515	933	940	645	685	1025	1045
2:05	660	1354	528	715	480	494	896	902	619	658	984	1003
2:10	635	1302	508	688	462	475	861	868	595	632	946	965
2:15	611	1253	489	662	444	458	829	836	573	609	911	929

Time	Sel. 1	Sel. 2	Sel. 3	Sel. 4	Sel. 5	Sel. 6	Sel. 7	Sel. 8	Sel. 9	Sel. 10	Sel. 11	Sel. 12
2:20	589	1209	471	639	429	441	800	806	553	587	879	896
2:25	569	1167	455	617	414	426	772	778	534	567	848	865
2:30	550	1128	440	596	400	412	746	752	516	548	820	836
2:35	532	1092	426	577	387	399	722	728	499	530	794	809
2:40	516	1058	413	559	375	386	700	705	484	514	769	784
2:45	500	1025	400	542	364	375	679	684	469	498	745	760
2:50	485	995	388	526	353	364	659	664	455	484	724	738
2:55	471	967	377	511	343	353	640	645	442	470	703	717
3:00	458	940	367	497	333	343	622	627	430	457	683	697
3:10	434	891	347	471	316	325	589	594	407	433	647	660
3:20	413	846	330	447	300	309	560	564	387	411	615	627
3:30	393	806	314	426	286	294	533	537	369	391	586	597
3:40	375	769	300	406	273	281	509	513	352	374	559	570
3:50	359	736	287	389	261	269	487	490	337	357	535	545
4:00	344	705	275	373	250	258	467	470	323	343	513	523
4:10	330	677	264	358	240	247	448	451	310	329	492	502
4:20	317	651	254	344	231	238	431	434	298	316	473	482
4:30	306	627	244	331	222	229	415	418	287	304	456	464
4:40	295	604	236	319	214	221	400	403	276	294	439	448
4:50	284	583	228	308	207	213	386	389	267	283	424	432
5:00	275	564	220	298	200	206	373	376	258	274	410	418
5:10	266	546	213	288	194	199	361	364	250	265	397	405
5:20	258	529	206	279	188	193	350	353	242	257	384	392
5:30	250	513	200	271	182	187	339	342	235	249	373	380
5:40	243	498	194	263	176	182	329	332	228	242	362	369
5:50	236	483	189	255	171	177	320	322	221	235	351	358
6:00	229	470	183	248	167	172	311	313	215	228	342	348
6:10	223	457	178	242	162	167	303	305	209	222	332	339
6:20	217	445	174	235	158	163	295	297	204	216	324	330
6:30	212	434	169	229	154	158	287	289	198	211	315	322

Time	Sel. 1	Sel. 2	Sel. 3	Sel. 4	Sel. 5	Sel. 6	Sel. 7	Sel. 8	Sel. 9	Sel. 10	Sel. 11	Sel. 12
6:40	206	423	165	224	150	155	280	282	194	206	308	314
6:50	201	413	161	218	146	151	273	275	189	200	300	306
7:00	196	403	157	213	143	147	267	269	184	196	293	299
7:10	192	393	153	208	140	144	260	262	180	191	286	292
7:20	188	385	150	203	136	140	254	256	176	187	280	285
7:30	183	376	147	199	133	137	249	251	172	183	273	279
7:40	179	368	143	194	130	134	243	245	168	179	267	273
7:50	176	360	140	190	128	131	238	240	165	175	262	267
8:00	172	353	138	186	125	129	233	235	161	171	256	261
8:10	168	345	135	182	122	126	228	230	158	168	251	256
8:20	165	338	132	179	120	124	224	226	155	164	246	251
8:30	162	332	129	175	118	121	220	221	152	161	241	246
8:40	159	325	127	172	115	119	215	217	149	158	237	241
8:50	156	319	125	169	113	117	211	213	146	155	232	237
9:00	153	313	122	166	111	114	207	209	143	152	228	232
9:10	150	308	120	163	109	112	204	205	141	149	224	228
9:20	147	302	118	160	107	110	200	201	138	147	220	224
9:30	145	297	116	157	105	108	196	198	136	144	216	220
9:40	142	292	114	154	103	107	193	194	133	142	212	216
9:50	140	287	112	152	102	105	190	191	131	139	208	213
10:00	138	282	110	149	100	103	187	188	129	137	205	209
10:10	135	277	108	147	98	101	184	185	127	135	202	206
10:20	133	273	106	144	97	100	181	182	125	133	198	202
10:30	131	269	105	142	95	98	178	179	123	130	195	199
10:40	129	264	103	140	94	97	175	176	121	128	192	196
10:50	127	260	102	138	92	95	172	174	119	126	189	193
11:00	125	256	100	135	91	94	170	171	117	125	186	190
11:10	123	253	99	133	90	92	167	168	116	123	184	187
11:20	121	249	97	131	88	91	165	166	114	121	181	184
11:30	120	245	96	130	87	90	162	163	112	119	178	182

Time	Sel. 1	Sel. 2	Sel. 3	Sel. 4	Sel. 5	Sel. 6	Sel. 7	Sel. 8	Sel. 9	Sel. 10	Sel. 11	Sel. 12
11:40	118	242	94	128	86	88	160	161	111	117	176	179
11:50	116	238	93	126	85	87	158	159	109	116	173	177
12:00	115	235	92	124	83	86	156	157	108	114	171	174

CONVERSION TABLES

Time	Sel. 13	Sel. 14	Sel. 15	Sel. 16	Sel. 17	Sel. 18	Sel. 19	Sel. 20	Sel. 21	Sel. 22	Sel. 23	Sel. 24
1:00	1734	920	1270	1800	1270	2540	1300	1990	2060	1000	1100	1660
1:05	1601	849	1172	1662	1172	2345	1200	1837	1902	923	1015	1532
1:10	1486	789	1089	1543	1089	2177	1114	1706	1766	857	943	1423
1:15	1387	736	1016	1440	1016	2032	1040	1592	1648	800	880	1328
1:20	1301	690	953	1350	953	1905	975	1493	1545	750	825	1245
1:25	1224	649	896	1271	896	1793	918	1405	1454	706	776	1172
1:30	1156	613	847	1200	847	1693	867	1327	1373	667	733	1107
1:35	1095	581	802	1137	802	1604	821	1257	1301	632	695	1048
1:40	1040	552	762	1080	762	1524	780	1194	1236	600	660	996
1:45	991	526	726	1029	726	1451	743	1137	1177	571	629	949
1:50	946	502	693	982	693	1385	709	1085	1124	545	600	905
1:55	905	480	663	939	663	1325	678	1038	1075	522	574	866
2:00	867	460	635	900	635	1270	650	995	1030	500	550	830
2:05	832	442	610	864	610	1219	624	955	989	480	528	797
2:10	800	425	586	831	586	1172	600	918	951	462	508	766
2:15	771	409	564	800	564	1129	578	884	916	444	489	738
2:20	743	394	544	771	544	1089	557	853	883	429	471	711
2:25	718	381	526	745	526	1051	538	823	852	414	455	687
2:30	694	368	508	720	508	1016	520	796	824	400	440	664
2:35	671	356	492	697	492	983	503	770	797	387	426	643
2:40	650	345	476	675	476	953	488	746	773	375	413	623
2:45	631	335	462	655	462	924	473	724	749	364	400	604
2:50	612	325	448	635	448	896	459	702	727	353	388	586
2:55	595	315	435	617	435	871	446	682	706	343	377	569
3:00	578	307	423	600	423	847	433	663	687	333	367	553
3:10	548	291	401	568	401	802	411	628	651	316	347	524
3:20	520	276	381	540	381	762	390	597	618	300	330	498
3:30	495	263	363	514	363	726	371	569	589	286	314	474
3:40	473	251	346	491	346	693	355	543	562	273	300	453

Time	Sel. 13	Sel. 14	Sel. 15	Sel. 16	Sel. 17	Sel. 18	Sel. 19	Sel. 20	Sel. 21	Sel. 22	Sel. 23	Sel. 24
3:50	452	240	331	470	331	663	339	519	537	261	287	433
4:00	434	230	318	450	318	635	325	498	515	250	275	415
4:10	416	221	305	432	305	610	312	478	494	240	264	398
4:20	400	212	293	415	293	586	300	459	475	231	254	383
4:30	385	204	282	400	282	564	289	442	458	222	244	369
4:40	372	197	272	386	272	544	279	426	441	214	236	356
4:50	359	190	263	372	263	526	269	412	426	207	228	343
5:00	347	184	254	360	254	508	260	398	412	200	220	332
5:10	336	178	246	348	246	492	252	385	399	194	213	321
5:20	325	173	238	338	238	476	244	373	386	188	206	311
5:30	315	167	231	327	231	462	236	362	375	182	200	302
5:40	306	162	224	318	224	448	229	351	364	176	194	293
5:50	297	158	218	309	218	435	223	341	353	171	189	285
6:00	289	153	212	300	212	423	217	332	343	167	183	277
6:10	281	149	206	292	206	412	211	323	334	162	178	269
6:20	274	145	201	284	201	401	205	314	325	158	174	262
6:30	267	142	195	277	195	391	200	306	317	154	169	255
6:40	260	138	191	270	191	381	195	299	309	150	165	249
6:50	254	135	186	263	186	372	190	291	301	146	161	243
7:00	248	131	181	257	181	363	186	284	294	143	157	237
7:10	242	128	177	251	177	354	181	278	287	140	153	232
7:20	236	125	173	245	173	346	177	271	281	136	150	226
7:30	231	123	169	240	169	339	173	265	275	133	147	221
7:40	226	120	166	235	166	331	170	260	269	130	143	217
7:50	221	117	162	230	162	324	166	254	263	128	140	212
8:00	217	115	159	225	159	318	163	249	258	125	138	208
8:10	212	113	156	220	156	311	159	244	252	122	135	203
8:20	208	110	152	216	152	305	156	239	247	120	132	199
8:30	204	108	149	212	149	299	153	234	242	118	129	195
8:40	200	106	147	208	147	293	150	230	238	115	127	192

Time	Sel. 13	Sel. 14	Sel. 15	Sel. 16	Sel. 17	Sel. 18	Sel. 19	Sel. 20	Sel. 21	Sel. 22	Sel. 23	Sel. 24
8:50	196	104	144	204	144	288	147	225	233	113	125	188
9:00	193	102	141	200	141	282	144	221	229	111	122	184
9:10	189	100	139	196	139	277	142	217	225	109	120	181
9:20	186	99	136	193	136	272	139	213	221	107	118	178
9:30	183	97	134	189	134	267	137	209	217	105	116	175
9:40	179	95	131	186	131	263	134	206	213	103	114	172
9:50	176	94	129	183	129	258	132	202	209	102	112	169
10:00	173	92	127	180	127	254	130	199	206	100	110	166
10:10	171	90	125	177	125	250	128	196	203	98	108	163
10:20	168	89	123	174	123	246	126	193	199	97	106	161
10:30	165	88	121	171	121	242	124	190	196	95	105	158
10:40	163	86	119	169	119	238	122	187	193	94	103	156
10:50	160	85	117	166	117	234	120	184	190	92	102	153
11:00	158	84	115	164	115	231	118	181	187	91	100	151
11:10	155	82	114	161	114	227	116	178	184	90	99	149
11:20	153	81	112	159	112	224	115	176	182	88	97	146
11:30	151	80	110	157	110	221	113	173	179	87	96	144
11:40	149	79	109	154	109	218	111	171	177	86	94	142
11:50	147	78	107	152	107	215	110	168	174	85	93	140
12:00	145	77	106	150	106	212	108	166	172	83	92	138

CONVERSION TABLES

Time	Sel. 25	Sel. 26	Sel. 27	Sel. 28	Sel. 29	Sel. 30	Sel. 31	Sel. 32	Sel. 33	Sel. 34	Sel. 35	Sel. 36
1:00	1000	840	1110	1000	1350	1310	1000	770	1720	1000	1210	1300
1:05	923	775	1025	923	1246	1209	923	711	1588	923	1117	1200
1:10	857	720	951	857	1157	1123	857	660	1474	857	1037	1114
1:15	800	672	888	800	1080	1048	800	616	1376	800	968	1040
1:20	750	630	833	750	1013	983	750	578	1290	750	908	975
1:25	706	593	784	706	953	925	706	544	1214	706	854	918
1:30	667	560	740	667	900	873	667	513	1147	667	807	867
1:35	632	531	701	632	853	827	632	486	1086	632	764	821
1:40	600	504	666	600	810	786	600	462	1032	600	726	780
1:45	571	480	634	571	771	749	571	440	983	571	691	743
1:50	545	458	605	545	736	715	545	420	938	545	660	709
1:55	522	438	579	522	704	683	522	402	897	522	631	678
2:00	500	420	555	500	675	655	500	385	860	500	605	650
2:05	480	403	533	480	648	629	480	370	826	480	581	624
2:10	462	388	512	462	623	605	462	355	794	462	558	600
2:15	444	373	493	444	600	582	444	342	764	444	538	578
2:20	429	360	476	429	579	561	429	330	737	429	519	557
2:25	414	348	459	414	559	542	414	319	712	414	501	538
2:30	400	336	444	400	540	524	400	308	688	400	484	520
2:35	387	325	430	387	523	507	387	298	666	387	468	503
2:40	375	315	416	375	506	491	375	289	645	375	454	488
2:45	364	305	404	364	491	476	364	280	625	364	440	473
2:50	353	296	392	353	476	462	353	272	607	353	427	459
2:55	343	288	381	343	463	449	343	264	590	343	415	446
3:00	333	280	370	333	450	437	333	257	573	333	403	433
3:10	316	265	351	316	426	414	316	243	543	316	382	411
3:20	300	252	333	300	405	393	300	231	516	300	363	390
3:30	286	240	317	286	386	374	286	220	491	286	346	371
3:40	273	229	303	273	368	357	273	210	469	273	330	355

Time	Sel. 25	Sel. 26	Sel. 27	Sel. 28	Sel. 29	Sel. 30	Sel. 31	Sel. 32	Sel. 33	Sel. 34	Sel. 35	Sel. 36
3:50	261	219	290	261	352	342	261	201	449	261	316	339
4:00	250	210	278	250	338	328	250	193	430	250	303	325
4:10	240	202	266	240	324	314	240	185	413	240	290	312
4:20	231	194	256	231	312	302	231	178	397	231	279	300
4:30	222	187	247	222	300	291	222	171	382	222	269	289
4:40	214	180	238	214	289	281	214	165	369	214	259	279
4:50	207	174	230	207	279	271	207	159	356	207	250	269
5:00	200	168	222	200	270	262	200	154	344	200	242	260
5:10	194	163	215	194	261	254	194	149	333	194	234	252
5:20	188	158	208	188	253	246	188	144	323	188	227	244
5:30	182	153	202	182	245	238	182	140	313	182	220	236
5:40	176	148	196	176	238	231	176	136	304	176	214	229
5:50	171	144	190	171	231	225	171	132	295	171	207	223
6:00	167	140	185	167	225	218	167	128	287	167	202	217
6:10	162	136	180	162	219	212	162	125	279	162	196	211
6:20	158	133	175	158	213	207	158	122	272	158	191	205
6:30	154	129	171	154	208	202	154	118	265	154	186	200
6:40	150	126	167	150	203	197	150	116	258	150	182	195
6:50	146	123	162	146	198	192	146	113	252	146	177	190
7:00	143	120	159	143	193	187	143	110	246	143	173	186
7:10	140	117	155	140	188	183	140	107	240	140	169	181
7:20	136	115	151	136	184	179	136	105	235	136	165	177
7:30	133	112	148	133	180	175	133	103	229	133	161	173
7:40	130	110	145	130	176	171	130	100	224	130	158	170
7:50	128	107	142	128	172	167	128	98	220	128	154	166
8:00	125	105	139	125	169	164	125	96	215	125	151	163
8:10	122	103	136	122	165	160	122	94	211	122	148	159
8:20	120	101	133	120	162	157	120	92	206	120	145	156
8:30	118	99	131	118	159	154	118	91	202	118	142	153
8:40	115	97	128	115	156	151	115	89	198	115	140	150

Time	Sel. 25	Sel. 26	Sel. 27	Sel. 28	Sel. 29	Sel. 30	Sel. 31	Sel. 32	Sel. 33	Sel. 34	Sel. 35	Sel. 36
8:50	113	95	126	113	153	148	113	87	195	113	137	147
9:00	111	93	123	111	150	146	111	86	191	111	134	144
9:10	109	92	121	109	147	143	109	84	188	109	132	142
9:20	107	90	119	107	145	140	107	83	184	107	130	139
9:30	105	88	117	105	142	138	105	81	181	105	127	137
9:40	103	87	115	103	140	136	103	80	178	103	125	134
9:50	102	85	113	102	137	133	102	78	175	102	123	132
10:00	100	84	111	100	135	131	100	77	172	100	121	130
10:10	98	83	109	98	133	129	98	76	169	98	119	128
10:20	97	81	107	97	131	127	97	75	166	97	117	126
10:30	95	80	106	95	129	125	95	73	164	95	115	124
10:40	94	79	104	94	127	123	94	72	161	94	113	122
10:50	92	78	102	92	125	121	92	71	159	92	112	120
11:00	91	76	101	91	123	119	91	70	156	91	110	118
11:10	90	75	99	90	121	117	90	69	154	90	108	116
11:20	88	74	98	88	119	116	88	68	152	88	107	115
11:30	87	73	97	87	117	114	87	67	150	87	105	113
11:40	86	72	95	86	116	112	86	66	147	86	104	111
11:50	85	71	94	85	114	111	85	65	145	85	102	110
12:00	83	70	93	83	113	109	83	64	143	83	101	108

Time	Sel. 37	Sel. 38	Sel. 39	Sel. 40	Sel. 41	Sel. 42	Sel. 43	Sel. 44	Sel. 45	Sel. 46	Sel. 47	Sel. 48
1:00	1000	790	890	1000	1500	1480	1000	920	1510	1650	890	1420
1:05	923	729	822	923	1385	1366	923	849	1394	1523	822	1311
1:10	857	677	763	857	1286	1269	857	789	1294	1414	763	1217
1:15	800	632	712	800	1200	1184	800	736	1208	1320	712	1136
1:20	750	593	668	750	1125	1110	750	690	1133	1238	668	1065
1:25	706	558	628	706	1059	1045	706	649	1066	1165	628	1002
1:30	667	527	593	667	1000	987	667	613	1007	1100	593	947
1:35	632	499	562	632	947	935	632	581	954	1042	562	897
1:40	600	474	534	600	900	888	600	552	906	990	534	852
1:45	571	451	509	571	857	846	571	526	863	943	509	811
1:50	545	431	485	545	818	807	545	502	824	900	485	775
1:55	522	412	464	522	783	772	522	480	788	861	464	741
2:00	500	395	445	500	750	740	500	460	755	825	445	710
2:05	480	379	427	480	720	710	480	442	725	792	427	682
2:10	462	365	411	462	692	683	462	425	697	762	411	655
2:15	444	351	396	444	667	658	444	409	671	733	396	631
2:20	429	339	381	429	643	634	429	394	647	707	381	609
2:25	414	327	368	414	621	612	414	381	625	683	368	588
2:30	400	316	356	400	600	592	400	368	604	660	356	568
2:35	387	306	345	387	581	573	387	356	585	639	345	550
2:40	375	296	334	375	563	555	375	345	566	619	334	533
2:45	364	287	324	364	545	538	364	335	549	600	324	516
2:50	353	279	314	353	529	522	353	325	533	582	314	501
2:55	343	271	305	343	514	507	343	315	518	566	305	487
3:00	333	263	297	333	500	493	333	307	503	550	297	473
3:10	316	249	281	316	474	467	316	291	477	521	281	448
3:20	300	237	267	300	450	444	300	276	453	495	267	426
3:30	286	226	254	286	429	423	286	263	431	471	254	406
3:40	273	215	243	273	409	404	273	251	412	450	243	387

Time	Sel. 37	Sel. 38	Sel. 39	Sel. 40	Sel. 41	Sel. 42	Sel. 43	Sel. 44	Sel. 45	Sel. 46	Sel. 47	Sel. 48
3:50	261	206	232	261	391	386	261	240	394	430	232	370
4:00	250	198	223	250	375	370	250	230	378	413	223	355
4:10	240	190	214	240	360	355	240	221	362	396	214	341
4:20	231	182	205	231	346	342	231	212	348	381	205	328
4:30	222	176	198	222	333	329	222	204	336	367	198	316
4:40	214	169	191	214	321	317	214	197	324	354	191	304
4:50	207	163	184	207	310	306	207	190	312	341	184	294
5:00	200	158	178	200	300	296	200	184	302	330	178	284
5:10	194	153	172	194	290	286	194	178	292	319	172	275
5:20	188	148	167	188	281	278	188	173	283	309	167	266
5:30	182	144	162	182	273	269	182	167	275	300	162	258
5:40	176	139	157	176	265	261	176	162	266	291	157	251
5:50	171	135	153	171	257	254	171	158	259	283	153	243
6:00	167	132	148	167	250	247	167	153	252	275	148	237
6:10	162	128	144	162	243	240	162	149	245	268	144	230
6:20	158	125	141	158	237	234	158	145	238	261	141	224
6:30	154	122	137	154	231	228	154	142	232	254	137	218
6:40	150	119	134	150	225	222	150	138	227	248	134	213
6:50	146	116	130	146	220	217	146	135	221	241	130	208
7:00	143	113	127	143	214	211	143	131	216	236	127	203
7:10	140	110	124	140	209	207	140	128	211	230	124	198
7:20	136	108	121	136	205	202	136	125	206	225	121	194
7:30	133	105	119	133	200	197	133	123	201	220	119	189
7:40	130	103	116	130	196	193	130	120	197	215	116	185
7:50	128	101	114	128	191	189	128	117	193	211	114	181
8:00	125	99	111	125	188	185	125	115	189	206	111	178
8:10	122	97	109	122	184	181	122	113	185	202	109	174
8:20	120	95	107	120	180	178	120	110	181	198	107	170
8:30	118	93	105	118	176	174	118	108	178	194	105	167
8:40	115	91	103	115	173	171	115	106	174	190	103	164

Time	Sel. 37	Sel. 38	Sel. 39	Sel. 40	Sel. 41	Sel. 42	Sel. 43	Sel. 44	Sel. 45	Sel. 46	Sel. 47	Sel. 48
8:50	113	89	101	113	170	168	113	104	171	187	101	161
9:00	111	88	99	111	167	164	111	102	168	183	99	158
9:10	109	86	97	109	164	161	109	100	165	180	97	155
9:20	107	85	95	107	161	159	107	99	162	177	95	152
9:30	105	83	94	105	158	156	105	97	159	174	94	149
9:40	103	82	92	103	155	153	103	95	156	171	92	147
9:50	102	80	91	102	153	151	102	94	154	168	91	144
10:00	100	79	89	100	150	148	100	92	151	165	89	142
10:10	98	78	88	98	148	146	98	90	149	162	88	140
10:20	97	76	86	97	145	143	97	89	146	160	86	137
10:30	95	75	85	95	143	141	95	88	144	157	85	135
10:40	94	74	83	94	141	139	94	86	142	155	83	133
10:50	92	73	82	92	138	137	92	85	139	152	82	131
11:00	91	72	81	91	136	135	91	84	137	150	81	129
11:10	90	71	80	90	134	133	90	82	135	148	80	127
11:20	88	70	79	88	132	131	88	81	133	146	79	125
11:30	87	69	77	87	130	129	87	80	131	143	77	123
11:40	86	68	76	86	129	127	86	79	129	141	76	122
11:50	85	67	75	85	127	125	85	78	128	139	75	120
12:00	83	66	74	83	125	123	83	77	126	138	74	118

Time	Sel. 49	Sel. 50	Sel. 51
1:00	1330	1000	1200
1:05	1228	923	1108
1:10	1140	857	1029
1:15	1064	800	960
1:20	998	750	900
1:25	939	706	847
1:30	887	667	800
1:35	840	632	758

Time	Sel. 49	Sel. 50	Sel. 51
1:40	798	600	720
1:45	760	571	686
1:50	725	545	655
1:55	694	522	626
2:00	665	500	600
2:05	638	480	576
2:10	614	462	554
2:15	591	444	533
2:20	570	429	514
2:25	550	414	497
2:30	532	400	480
2:35	515	387	465
2:40	499	375	450
2:45	484	364	436
2:50	469	353	424
2:55	456	343	411
3:00	443	333	400
3:10	420	316	379
3:20	399	300	360
3:30	380	286	343
3:40	363	273	327
3:50	347	261	313
4:00	333	250	300
4:10	319	240	288
4:20	307	231	277
4:30	296	222	267
4:40	285	214	257
4:50	275	207	248
5:00	266	200	240
5:10	257	194	232
5:20	249	188	225

Time	Sel. 49	Sel. 50	Sel. 51
5:30	242	182	218
5:40	235	176	212
5:50	228	171	206
6:00	222	167	200
6:10	216	162	195
6:20	210	158	189
6:30	205	154	185
6:40	200	150	180
6:50	195	146	176
7:00	190	143	171
7:10	186	140	167
7:20	181	136	164
7:30	177	133	160
7:40	173	130	157
7:50	170	128	153
8:00	166	125	150
8:10	163	122	147
8:20	160	120	144
8:30	156	118	141
8:40	153	115	138
8:50	151	113	136
9:00	148	111	133
9:10	145	109	131
9:20	143	107	129
9:30	140	105	126
9:40	138	103	124
9:50	135	102	122
10:00	133	100	120
10:10	131	98	118
10:20	129	97	116

Time	Sel. 49	Sel. 50	Sel. 51
10:40	125	94	113
10:50	123	92	111
11:00	121	91	109
11:10	119	90	107
11:20	117	88	106
11:30	116	87	104
11:40	114	86	103
11:50	112	85	101
12:00	111	83	100
10:30	127	95	114

Answer Keys

Outline for Selection 31: Making the Application

I. The role of organization.
   A. To help identify.
   B. To help extract.

II. What is the role of outlining?

III. How is organization revealed?
   A. Through special devices.
      1. Typographical devices.
         a. Capitals.
         b. Boldface type.
         c. Italics.
      2. Rhetorical devices.
         a. Repetition.
         b. Parallelism.
         c. Balance.
      3. Verbal devices.
         a. To mark transitions.
         b. To mark methods of development.
         c. To mark outline form.
   B. Through paragraph structure.
      1. Topic sentences.
      2. Supporting details.

IV. What does organization contribute?
   A. Sharpened awareness.
      1. Of main idea or thesis.
      2. Of interrelationships.
   B. Improved ability.
      1. To understand.
      2. To remember.

V. Summary of purpose or role of organization.

Key for Vocabulary Pre-Tests A and B

PRE-TEST A	PRE-TEST B
1. c	26. b
2. b	27. d
3. d	28. a
4. c	29. c
5. d	30. c
6. b	31. e
7. b	32. e
8. b	33. a
9. c	34. b
10. d	35. a
11. c	36. c
12. d	37. e
13. b	38. e
14. a	39. d
15. b	40. d
16. c	41. a
17. e	42. b
18. e	43. e
19. c	44. c
20. a	45. c
21. c	46. d
22. e	47. c
23. d	48. e
24. d	49. a
25. e	50. a

Key for Context Vocabulary Test

1. c	6. d
2. e	7. c
3. a	8. a
4. b	9. d
5. b	10. b

Key for Master-Word Vocabulary Test

1. d
2. a
3. c
4. b
5. a
6. c
7. a
8. e
9. a
10. b

Key for Vocabulary Review Quizzes

A

1. c (com, "together")
2. a (ex, "out")
3. e (com, "together")
4. b (re, "back, again")
5. d (re, "back, again")
6. e (ad, "to, toward")
7. a (com, "together")
8. c (ad, "to, toward")
9. b (com, "together")
10. a (pre, "before")

B

1. a (ex, "out")
2. e (de, "away, down")
3. a (re, "back, again")
4. d (de, "away, down")
5. c (re, "back, again")
6. b (ex, "out")
7. a (in, "not")
8. a (in, "not")
9. d (sub, "under")
10. e (in, "into")

C

1. c (com, "together")
2. c (sub, "under")
3. a (com, "together")
4. b (trans, "across, beyond")
5. e (ex, "out")
6. d (com, "together")
7. a (ob, "against")
8. d (de, "down, away")
9. b (de, "down, away")
10. b (in, "into")

D

1. b (un, "not"—de, "down, away")
2. e (com, "together")
3. a (re, "back, again")
4. a (dis, "apart from")
5. c (sub, "under")
6. d (com, "together")
7. a (com, "together")
8. b (ex, "out")
9. d (ad, "to, toward")
10. d (de, "down, away")

E

1. e (ad, "to, toward," facere, "make or do")
2. a (inter, "between," capere, "take, seize")
3. a (ex, "out," plicare, "fold")
4. c (per, "through," tenere, "hold, have")
5. b (dis, "apart from," mittere, "send")
6. d (pro, "forward," ducere, "lead")
7. a (in, "into," ponere, "put, place")
8. b (per, "through," specere, "see")
9. a (ex, "out," tendere, "stretch")
10. e (pre, "before," ferre, "bear, carry")

Key for Word Power Workouts, Part A

SELECTION	4	5	6	7	8	9	10	11	12	13	14	15	16	17	18	19	20
1.	i	c	c	g	c	d	b	b	c	c	j	d	b	c	f	e	c
2.	a	e	e	b	e	f	j	d	f	i	i	f	e	e	g	f	d
3.	d	h	h	c	h	c	c	e	h	d	b	h	h	i	e	i	g
4.	e	i	g	a	a	i	d	a	g	e	h	a	f	a	a	g	j
5.	h	j	f	j	i	j	f	f	b	b	f	e	g	j	d	d	h
6.	b	g	a	e	g	a	a	g	i	f	c	j	i	b	c	h	a
7.	j	a	i	d	d	h	g	h	j	h	g	i	j	f	j	b	i
8.	c	d	j	f	j	g	i	c	e	a	e	b	a	d	i	a	e
9.	f	f	d	h	f	b	h	j	a	g	a	g	d	h	b	j	f
10.	g	b	b	i	b	e	e	i	d	j	d	c	c	g	h	c	b

SELECTION	21	22	23	24	25	26	27	28	29	30	31	32	33	34
1.	a	f	d	a	h	c	d	g	d	d	c	b	d	d
2.	e	e	i	d	d	e	f	j	h	e	e	e	g	i
3.	g	h	g	g	i	g	b	h	e	g	f	g	a	a
4.	f	g	h	h	a	h	g	a	g	i	g	i	f	f
5.	h	d	f	b	g	a	j	c	f	a	i	a	c	e
6.	b	c	a	f	j	j	h	i	i	j	a	h	j	c
7.	i	i	j	i	b	i	a	b	b	b	b	f	e	h
8.	d	a	c	c	c	d	i	e	a	h	h	c	i	b
9.	j	b	e	j	e	b	e	d	j	f	d	j	b	j
10.	c	j	b	e	f	f	c	f	c	c	j	d	h	g

SELECTION	35	36	37	38	39	40	41	42	43	44	45	46
1.	e	e	b	c	b	b	c	b	e	c	d	e
2.	c	b	e	e	f	g	d	d	a	d	j	a
3.	i	h	g	f	a	j	h	f	b	a	b	h
4.	j	g	a	g	e	e	j	h	c	f	h	b
5.	g	j	f	i	d	a	i	i	h	h	c	j
6.	a	c	d	a	i	h	g	a	f	b	a	d
7.	h	a	j	b	h	i	f	j	i	e	i	i
8.	b	d	c	h	j	f	e	g	d	j	e	c
9.	d	f	h	d	g	d	b	e	j	g	f	f
10.	f	i	i	j	c	c	a	c	g	i	g	g

SELECTION	47	48	49	50	51
1.	i	e	b	e	c
2.	j	a	d	i	d
3.	h	j	i	d	g
4.	a	f	j	b	f
5.	d	c	c	g	a
6.	c	g	h	j	h
7.	e	b	a	a	j
8.	b	d	e	c	b
9.	g	i	g	h	e
10.	f	h	f	f	i

Key for Word Power Workouts, Parts B and C

Scoring instructions: For Part B questions, give yourself 20 points for each correct answer. For Part C questions, give yourself 10 points for each correct answer.

	SELECTION 4	SELECTION 5	SELECTION 6
B.	1. preheat	1. depart	1. interstate
	2. prepare	2. descend	2. intermission
	3. president	3. deposit	3. intermediator
	4. prefix	4. depressed	4. interrupt
	5. before	5. down	5. between
C.	1. consolidated	1. intricacies	1. mere
	2. hybrid	2. eventually	2. symbols
	3. expedite	3. technique	3. affect
	4. hindered	4. chameleon	4. capacity
	5. corroborated	5. variant	5. facility
	6. predilection	6. explication	6. commit
	7. interplay	7. invaluable	7. competent
	8. tentative	8. maxim	8. copy
	9. discrimination	9. unabridged	9. exhibition
	10. context	10. literally	10. parcel

SELECTION 7

B.
1. object
2. obstacle
3. objections
4. obscure
5. against

C.
1. dominates
2. abysmally
3. maximum
4. prime
5. sensory
6. blurred
7. fallacious
8. appropriate
9. related
10. terminology

SELECTION 8

B.
1. independent
2. incapable
3. informal
4. indirect
5. not

C.
1. heed
2. sham
3. bound
4. naught
5. sires
6. zest
7. wail
8. gild
9. minx
10. freak

SELECTION 9

B.
1. monoplane
2. monosyllable
3. monopoly
4. monotonous
5. one

C.
1. churl
2. knaves
3. brawls
4. flasks
5. knell
6. boon
7. score
8. dirk
9. stark
10. hoard

SELECTION 10

B.
1. epitaph
2. epidermis
3. epilepsy
4. epidemic
5. upon

C.
1. minimize
2. plodded
3. reinforces
4. sliver
5. temporarily
6. relented
7. phenomenon
8. key
9. entry
10. initial

SELECTION 11

B.
1. adheres
2. admit
3. adjacent
4. advanced
5. to

C.
1. convinced
2. loin
3. acronym
4. babble
5. sponsoring
6. attain
7. utter
8. crucial
9. prefer
10. goal

SELECTION 12

B.
1. unusual
2. uncertain
3. unwise
4. unworthy
5. not

C.
1. wallow
2. conned
3. plea
4. connivance
5. negotiated
6. endearment
7. crammed
8. marital
9. sodden
10. tinker's

	SELECTION 13	SELECTION 14	SELECTION 15
B.	1. compact	1. nonessential	1. exhale
	2. companion	2. nonconformist	2. exit
	3. compare	3. nonfiction	3. exhausted
	4. compound	4. nonsense	4. explosion
	5. together	5. not	5. out
C.	1. apportion	1. foremost	1. indifference
	2. zeros in	2. spokesman	2. deceptive
	3. jacket	3. respond	3. resultant
	4. concise	4. accomplishments	4. repercussions
	5. compressed	5. frivolous	5. valid
	6. subsequent	6. peeve	6. arrogantly
	7. obviously	7. extensions	7. clarify
	8. veritable	8. unalterable	8. initiates
	9. capsule	9. regardless	9. vulnerable
	10. pertinent	10. permission	10. recapped

	SELECTION 16	SELECTION 17	SELECTION 18
B.	1. reread	1. procession	1. inside
	2. reappear	2. projector	2. insert
	3. return	3. prolong	3. invest
	4. back	4. propeller	4. include
	5. again	5. forward	5. in
C.	1. cultivated	1. bouts	1. perceptiveness
	2. priority	2. dismissal	2. perverse
	3. repertoire	3. reflex	3. insight
	4. counteract	4. platitudes	4. ruefully
	5. intervening	5. unfazed	5. eminent
	6. superficial	6. ruminating	6. retrieve
	7. productivity	7. reversal	7. berated
	8. reiterate	8. debilitating	8. indestructible
	9. snatched	9. surmountable	9. miscalculations
	10. exceptional	10. isolation	10. audible

SELECTION 19

B.
1. disagree
2. dispatch
3. disperse
4. dismissed
5. away

C.
1. jog
2. surpasses
3. elusive
4. sufficient
5. enviable
6. feasible
7. undigested
8. proverbial
9. versatile
10. relevant

SELECTION 20

1. overprice
2. overweight
3. overcoat
4. overflows
5. above

1. cantankerous
2. purgatory
3. immobilized
4. niggled
5. contortions
6. predatory
7. supplication
8. imposing
9. recital
10. malevolent

SELECTION 21

1. subbasement
2. substandard
3. subsonic
4. subtitle
5. under

1. incision
2. infinitesimal
3. classical
4. inverted
5. equanimity
6. eligibility
7. abnormal
8. reverted
9. scalpel
10. hesitant

SELECTION 22

B.
1. misbehavior
2. mislead
3. mispronounce
4. misdeal
5. wrongdoing

C.
1. subtle
2. conceited
3. emphasis
4. ambiguity
5. in-depth
6. insinuations
7. variety
8. accusation
9. margins
10. mature

SELECTION 23

1. transatlantic
2. transfer
3. transfusion
4. translate
5. beyond

1. jester
2. encore
3. meaningful
4. eloquent
5. refuge
6. absorbed
7. generosity
8. routine
9. ovation
10. compassion

SELECTION 24

1. connect
2. collect
3. correspond
4. conflict
5. cooperate

1. verge
2. intact
3. profile
4. vandal
5. astrological
6. testily
7. intruder
8. camouflaged
9. imps
10. exasperating

SELECTION 25

B.
1. support
2. suffix
3. succeed
4. suggest
5. suspect

C.
1. conservative
2. perceptual
3. eliminated
4. promote
5. latent
6. complicated
7. convenient
8. contrast
9. havoc
10. allied

SELECTION 26

B.
1. irradiate
2. illuminate
3. immigrant
4. illustrious
5. irrigation

C.
1. enlightened
2. peals
3. simultaneously
4. imprinted
5. basically
6. totally
7. gloaming
8. receptivity
9. repress
10. submissive

SELECTION 27

B.
1. accept
2. allow
3. oppress
4. offend
5. occur

C.
1. clue
2. resemblance
3. slogans
4. visualize
5. inherent
6. cited
7. prerequisite
8. contiguity
9. comparable
10. barrage

SELECTION 28

B.
1. effect
2. eccentric
3. emit
4. difficult
5. dilapidated

C.
1. relish
2. abound
3. transitional
4. core
5. conscious
6. specialized
7. remotest
8. fixed
9. nudge
10. advantage

SELECTION 29

B.
1. duct
2. introduction
3. reduce
4. produce
5. conduit

C.
1. react
2. provocation
3. contend
4. agenda
5. flawless
6. cowering
7. bonuses
8. prone
9. culled
10. elicits

SELECTION 30

B.
1. prescription
2. manuscript
3. script
4. subscribed
5. describe

C.
1. disloyal
2. epiphany
3. obnoxious
4. compendium
5. serial
6. stigma
7. inoffensive
8. blacklisted
9. guidelines
10. tenure

SELECTION 31

B.
1. posted
2. posture
3. postponed
4. deposit
5. postage

C.
1. lean
2. facilitates
3. glance
4. rhetorical
5. obscure
6. chief
7. extracted
8. captured
9. subordinate
10. supporting

SELECTION 32

B.
1. submit
2. missile
3. missionary
4. remittance
5. emitted

C.
1. subsided
2. alternated
3. embarked
4. chafing
5. pang
6. capsized
7. aimlessly
8. massive
9. dehydration
10. benevolent

SELECTION 33

B.
1. suffer
2. transfers
3. ferry
4. fertile
5. translate

C.
1. devoted
2. feigned
3. designate
4. petrified
5. jargon
6. novocained
7. quizzical
8. trance
9. maniacal
10. mustered

SELECTION 34

B.
1. statue
2. insist
3. stationary
4. armistice
5. assistant

C.
1. vicarious
2. calculatingly
3. temporal
4. elucidations
5. immerse
6. fashion
7. apprehensively
8. arduous
9. absolute
10. consequential

SELECTION 35

B.
1. attention
2. attend
3. tense
4. portents
5. intent

C.
1. unduly
2. snipe
3. undefinable
4. endeavoured
5. bog
6. migrate
7. treacherous
8. delusion
9. pariah
10. falteringly

SELECTION 36

B.
1. spectator
2. respect
3. spectacles
4. aspects
5. auspicious

C.
1. quiver
2. stroll
3. drizzly
4. confident
5. gathering
6. conversational
7. agile
8. commentary
9. clever
10. stray

	SELECTION 37	SELECTION 38	SELECTION 39
B.	1. explicit	1. defective	1. dialogue
	2. imply	2. sufficient	2. eloquent
	3. deploy	3. defeated	3. mythology
	4. duplex	4. fashioned	4. prologue
	5. reply	5. facility	5. biology
C.	1. toll	1. luxury	1. significantly
	2. released	2. disability	2. gross
	3. culmination	3. dividends	3. imperative
	4. endeavors	4. aggressive	4. plaguing
	5. academic	5. decree	5. longevity
	6. ensures	6. essentially	6. premiums
	7. modified	7. glamorize	7. substantially
	8. unreal	8. unique	8. extrapolate
	9. frantic	9. ironic	9. implications
	10. pose	10. merely	10. investigating

	SELECTION 40	SELECTION 41	SELECTION 42
B.	1. abstinence	1. autobiography	1. captive
	2. tenant	2. bibliography	2. recipient
	3. detain	3. telegraph	3. receive
	4. tenaciously	4. monograph	4. intercepting
	5. discontent	5. graphic	5. emancipated
C.	1. irrational	1. norm	1. emulate
	2. impersonal	2. aptitude	2. flatly
	3. ineptitude	3. mundane	3. quota
	4. restraint	4. erode	4. dormant
	5. renown	5. repository	5. expounded
	6. genuinely	6. transcends	6. engrossing
	7. voluntarily	7. enthrall	7. riffling
	8. outstanding	8. predictor	8. gruff
	9. colleague	9. portable	9. fascinated
	10. condescendingly	10. unrelated	10. rehabilitation

SELECTION 43

B. 1. fashionable
2. facile
3. imperfection
4. feat
5. benefactor

C. 1. garret
2. ideal
3. epitomized
4. surplus
5. vocation
6. quest
7. boundaries
8. assurance
9. savored
10. trauma

SELECTION 44

B. 1. helper
2. youthful
3. tireless
4. lioness
5. infantile

C. 1. archaic
2. harried
3. malaise
4. unimpeded
5. vial
6. deviations
7. inexcusable
8. inevitably
9. locution
10. transcendent

SELECTION 45

B. 1. globule
2. hourly
3. returnable
4. childish
5. darken

C. 1. redress
2. vanguard
3. rousing
4. impetus
5. ardently
6. degradation
7. criterion
8. assertion
9. assimilation
10. poignantly

SELECTION 46

B. 1. grandiose
2. commendatory
3. remedial
4. picturesque
5. affectionate

C. 1. plumes
2. doom
3. perspectives
4. fierce
5. anecdote
6. repressive
7. manipulating
8. mode
9. exemplify
10. crystallizes

SELECTION 47

B. 1. obstacles
2. persist
3. substantial
4. assistance
5. establishing

C. 1. latter
2. inseparable
3. precisely
4. incentives
5. cumbersome
6. exaggerations
7. intercept
8. imperialism
9. enormous
10. prevailing

SELECTION 48

B. 1. tends
2. extend
3. attention
4. extensive
5. portent

C. 1. exhilarating
2. hucksters
3. judicious
4. dynamic
5. dour
6. scantily
7. tedious
8. eloquence
9. derived
10. convey

	SELECTION 49	SELECTION 50	SELECTION 51
B.	1. conduct	1. special	1. ferry
	2. reduce	2. perspicacity	2. different
	3. produce	3. expect	3. preference
	4. educated	4. prospect	4. offered
	5. conducive	5. inspecting	5. defer
C.	1. regularities	1. usurp	1. litigation
	2. amorphous	2. intangible	2. repercussions
	3. extensive	3. incur	3. codified
	4. ignites	4. stereotypic	4. foster
	5. hypothesis	5. attire	5. eradicate
	6. adhere	6. converge	6. philanthropic
	7. collide	7. paramount	7. transition
	8. celestial	8. elaborate	8. dimensions
	9. detectable	9. articulating	9. vicinity
	10. converted	10. informality	10. thus

Key for Comprehension Checks

SELECTION	1	2	3	4	5	6	7	8	9	10	11	12	13	14	15	16	17	18	19	20
1.	b	b	d	d	c	b	b	d	d	c	d	a	c	a	d	a	d	b	a	a
2.	b	d	b	c	d	b	c	a	a	d	a	c	d	b	a	b	d	a	d	b
3.	d	c	a	c	d	c	a	c	c	a	c	c	b	a	c	a	a	c	d	b
4.	a	c	c	d	a	a	b	c	b	b	b	a	d	a	a	b	b	b	c	a
5.	d	b	b	c	b	d	b	c	d	c	c	d	b	c	b	c	b	d	c	a
6.	c	a	a	a	c	d	a	d	b	a	b	a	a	a	b	d	c	b	d	c
7.	b	c	b	a	a	a	c	b	b	d	b	c	b	b	c	b	c	a	c	d
8.	d	c	a	d	c	c	a	d	c	b	a	d	d	c	d	c	a	d	b	c
9.	c	c	b	d	d	b	d	d	a	a	c	a	c	c	b	d	c	b	b	b
10.	b	c	c	b	b	b	c	d	d	c	c	a	c	d	c	d	d	c	a	c

SELECTION	21	22	23	24	25	26	27	28	29	30	31	32	33	34	35	36
1.	b	b	d	c	a	a	c	a	d	a	a	c	d	b	c	b
2.	a	c	c	a	c	b	b	b	a	c	b	d	b	c	a	c
3.	b	c	a	d	d	d	d	c	c	c	a	b	c	d	d	d
4.	c	a	b	d	c	b	a	c	b	d	b	c	a	a	d	c
5.	b	c	c	d	b	b	c	b	c	d	a	b	b	b	b	b
6.	b	b	b	b	a	b	d	b	c	d	a	b	a	c	b	d
7.	a	d	a	c	a	a	a	d	a	a	a	c	d	b	d	b
8.	c	c	b	c	a	d	c	c	d	a	b	b	c	a	c	a
9.	b	b	b	b	d	c	a	b	b	d	a	d	b	d	d	c
10.	d	d	b	d	c	b	b	c	b	b	a	d	c	d	c	b

SELECTION	37	38	39	40	41	42	43	44	45	46	47	48	49	50	51
1.	b	c	b	d	b	b	b	c	d	b	b	d	c	b	c
2.	c	d	a	d	c	d	c	a	d	d	c	a	a	b	b
3.	a	a	c	a	b	d	a	d	b	b	a	d	c	d	c
4.	c	a	c	b	a	b	a	c	c	b	d	d	d	a	d
5.	d	d	a	a	d	b	b	c	c	d	d	c	d	b	a
6.	b	b	d	a	d	b	b	c	c	b	a	d	c	d	c
7.	c	d	b	b	b	c	c	b	d	a	b	a	a	b	c
8.	b	a	a	d	b	c	a	d	c	a	c	c	a	b	a
9.	a	c	c	b	c	c	d	a	d	b	d	b	d	c	d
10.	a	c	a	a	d	c	d	b	a	d	a	a	b	a	b

Ultimate Review

Conversion Table for Ultimate Review Selections

Reading Time in Seconds	WPM Rate	Reading Time	WPM Rate	Reading Time	WPM Rate
25	1200	85	353	145	207
30	1000	90	333	150	200
35	857	95	316	155	193
40	750	100	300	160	188
45	667	105	286	165	182
50	600	110	273	170	176
55	544	115	261	175	171
60	500	120	250	180	167
65	461	125	240	185	162
70	428	130	231	190	158
75	400	135	222	195	154
80	375	140	214	200	150

(To determine your wpm rate for these selections, divide 500 by your reading time in seconds, then multiply the resulting figure by 60.)

■1

Beating Academic Stress

"Oh, you're a college student. That's nice. Beats dealing with the stress of a real job. Wish I could just go to college and live the easy life," he said as he hitched my sixteen-year-old pickup to the truck. "You guys have got it made."

Many people sincerely believe that going to college is "a piece of cake" and have little appreciation for the time school requires or the financial and emotional investments necessary for academic success.

However, even the best students find attending college can be all-consuming and stressful. First, many must compete for space in courses they need to take. Second, a college education can be expensive, so some students make lifestyle sacrifices. Next, academic obligations compete with other interests and responsibilities, forcing students to make choices about how to spend their time. In addition, coursework can be challenging and require many hours of study. Fifth, for students who cannot afford to attend college full-time, maintaining a job that allows for class attendance and study can result in complex scheduling. Finally, securing and sustaining supportive relationships with family and friends requires open communication and heightened sensitivity to the needs of all involved. Any one of the considerations listed above can be stress-producing, but combine two or more and the result is often overwhelming. Knowing what to do when situations become stressful is essential to succeeding in college. The following tips will equip you with academic survival tools.

Plan: Before registering for college courses, work with an academic advisor, plan your schedule carefully, register early, learn the layout of the campus, and locate campus support services.

Attend Class: Unless you face a life or death situation, don't miss class. Keeping up or moving ahead in a class is a sure recipe for academic success, as is getting to know a few of your fellow classmates. Conversely, falling behind and missing essential course content almost guarantees failure.

Make Use of Campus Resources: Most campuses offer academic and student support services without cost or at a minimal charge. *Use these* *services!* They are likely to make your college experience more pleasant and easier than you ever dreamed possible.

Involve the People in Your Life: Let the significant people in your life know the challenges and joys you experience as a student. Doing so will serve two purposes: provide them with information and allow them to be supportive, if they desire.

Use Stress Reducers: Nothing will remove the stress completely, but you can lessen it by doing one or more of the following: (1) at least five times a day, sit quietly and count slowly to 20, breathing deeply and deliberately as you count; (2) periodically listen to soothing music; (3) exercise—ski, walk, run, skateboard, swim, ride a bike, or shoot hoops; (4) keep a diary and write freely about your successes and frustrations; and (5) take mini-vacations—a few hours to a few days—away from your academic pursuits.

Don't let stress prevent you from getting the education you desire.

500 words

NAME ________________ CLASS ________________ DATE ____________

1 Beating Academic Stress

COMPREHENSION CHECK

GETTING THE FACTS

1. The man hitching the pickup to the truck thinks college students (a) have it made. (b) are lazy. (c) are wasting time. (d) have no money. 1. ____

2. Many people do not appreciate college students' (a) freedom. (b) confusion. (c) emotional investment. (d) social investment. 2. ____

3. Academic obligations compete with other (a) interests and jobs. (b) hobbies and responsibilities. (c) responsibilities and jobs. (d) responsibilities and interests. 3. ____

4. Keeping people in your life informed about your college experience will allow them to (a) enroll in courses also. (b) meet with your advisor. (c) be introspective. (d) be supportive. 4. ____

5. According to the text, an effective stress reducer is (a) listening to stimulating music. (b) deep breathing. (c) competitive sports. (d) playing cards. 5. ____

GETTING THE MEANING

6. The main idea is that you can learn to manage (a) schedules. (b) support services. (c) academic advisors. (d) academic stress. 6. ____

7. When going to college becomes stressful, successful students (a) push ahead anyway. (b) know what to do. (c) determine who's at fault. (d) remove all of the stress. 7. ____

8. A successful student (a) misses essential course work. (b) attends class when possible. (c) ignores strategies to manage stress. (d) outwits instructors. 8. ____

9. The author suggests that getting into some courses can be (a) amusing. (b) competitive. (c) automatic. (d) medicinal. 9. ____

10. Campus support services are there to (a) help manage the budget. (b) maintain the facilities. (c) communicate with alumni. (d) help students achieve. 10. ____

WPM Rate for Reading Selection: ________
(See chart on p. 454)

Comprehension Score: ________
(to be filled in by instructor)

2

That All-Important Attitude

When you think about yourself, what is that intangible, invisible, and indefinable something that you must never overlook? It's that elusive thing called attitude—your way of looking at life, your "state of mind," as the dictionary defines it.

Medical doctors are keenly aware of its importance. For example, Dr. Alvarez of the famed Mayo Clinic tells of a woman who for four years ran a fever and suffered severe abdominal pains. Three exploratory operations revealed nothing. When Dr. Alvarez had satisfied himself that there was nothing physically wrong, he talked at some length with her. The information he uncovered finally led the patient to make a difficult personal decision—a decision that brought an immediate cure. Her trouble was psychosomatic.

Attitude is equally important to the student. For centuries thinkers have pondered the mystic relationship between mind and body, attitude and action. In "Proverbs"—that portion of the *Old Testament* written in about the 8th century, B.C.—note this early evidence of insight: "As he thinketh in his heart, so is he."

A little later—about 19 B.C.—Virgil, in his *Aeneid,* wrote, *Possunt quia posse videtur,* which, translated, means "They can because they think they can."

Coming down to more modern times we find Emil Coué, a French doctor, developing in 1922 what became known as Couism, a principle of self-mastery by auto-suggestion. Here is his famous formula: "Every day, in every way, I am getting better and better." Say that five times every morning to start the day and sense the increased confidence which follows.

And now even later, for this idea seems to be one that needs to be reexpressed for every generation, Norman Vincent Peale, in 1952, came out with his best-selling book, *The Power of Positive Thinking.*

At this point we may want to agree with J. Donald Adams that such fundamental truths "are all men's property." He adds, "Whether or not we live by them, we all know them with a deep instinctiveness."

This brings us to the point. Take two students with almost identical intelligence and background. Why will one sometimes make three times the progress of the other in a reading improvement class? Largely because one has discovered and applied the vitality of a positive attitude. As Hazlitt says, "Great thoughts reduced to practice become great acts."

Obviously, if you really think you can't master a subject, develop a skill, or reach a certain goal, you can hardly make an honest, all-out effort in that direction. At best, you will work half-heartedly and ineffectually, inviting failure. Of course, that does not mean you should be unrealistic. But who actually knows his limits until he has put out his best efforts?

So, exactly what is your attitude? Is it the positive dynamic force it should be? If so, congratulations! If not, begin to change it. You cannot afford to disregard a principle that will carry you so effectively toward increased reading efficiency as well as toward your personal vocational and professional goals.

500 words

NAME ____________ CLASS ____________ DATE ____________

2 That All-Important Attitude

COMPREHENSION CHECK

GETTING THE FACTS

1. The patient was cured by (a) an operation. (b) changing her diet. (c) making a decision. (d) shock treatment. 1. ____

2. One quotation is from (a) Shakespeare. (b) Virgil. (c) Petrarch. (d) Confucius. 2. ____

3. Emil Coué was referred to as a (a) lawyer. (b) doctor. (c) psychologist. (d) scientist. 3. ____

4. Mr. Adams is quoted as saying that such fundamental truths (a) are truths we all live by. (b) are discovered by great thinkers. (c) are learned through experience. (d) are all men's property. 4. ____

5. The author of *The Power of Positive Thinking* is (a) Dr. Walter C. Alvarez. (b) Dale Carnegie. (c) Norman Vincent Peale. (d) Joshua Liebman. 5. ____

GETTING THE MEANING

6. This selection is chiefly about the effect of attitude (a) on accomplishment. (b) on character. (c) on school. (d) on reading improvement. 6. ____

7. The importance of attitude is established largely through (a) reliance on authority. (b) use of specific examples. (c) logical evidence. (d) analogy. 7. ____

8. The opening story about the patient was intended primarily to show (a) the importance of attitude. (b) the widespread nature of psychosomatic troubles. (c) the need for careful diagnosis. (d) the need to change your attitude. 8. ____

9. After the opening story the next part is organized (a) around a problem-solution pattern. (b) around a special classification system. (c) based on a chronological order. (d) based on a known-to-unknown sequence. 9. ____

10. The reference to the two students was intended to point up (a) individual differences. (b) maturation differences. (c) differences in outlook. (d) differences in potential. 10. ____

WPM Rate for Reading Selection: ________
(See chart on p. 454)

Comprehension Score: ________
(to be filled in by instructor)

3

Mistakes

Mistakes are as much a part of living as breathing. Unless one is comatose, mistakes are inevitable. However, for many people, making a mistake is a devastating experience because they equate making a mistake with failure. When such people discover that they have not performed up to their own or someone else's expectation, they experience one or more of the following feelings: defensiveness, embarrassment, shame, and/or humiliation. Often these painful feelings are accompanied by physical reactions such as sweating, blushing, rapid speech, excessive speech, and confusion. To cope, some people flee the environment, blame others, divert attention, or lie in an effort to *save face.* This type of behavior is understandable but unproductive and ego-damaging.

Everyone, especially students, could benefit from looking at mistakes from a new perspective: see mistakes as "mis-takes," an inaccurate assessment of a situation. For instance, when one *mistakenly* dials the wrong number, it is usually because the caller confuses, misreads, misdials, or cannot distinguish one or more of the digits in the number. When this happens, most people do not see the incident as a personal failure and become upset about the experience. They simply try the task again after determining what went wrong.

The same attitude would make learning a much easier task for most students. If students looked at each wrong answer on a math problem, each confusing thought during a philosophy lecture, and every incorrect execution of a computer command as a *mis-take* of the situation, they would be in a more receptive frame of mind to remedy the situation and succeed. They would also discover that *mis-takes* present prime opportunities to learn.

When people are learning a new skill, they are vulnerable, and even the best students feel anxious about the unknown. However, most successful students know that no learning takes place without trying new tasks, so they are willing to risk making mistakes to learn. Outstanding students know that each attempt is a step closer to success.

Changing your attitude toward making mistakes is an eight-step process (1) acknowledge the *mis-take,* (2) be positive about the experience, (3) do not personalize the outcomes, (4) think about the *mis-take* as an opportunity to learn, (5) determine what went wrong, (6) assess other ways to respond, (7) try the task again, and (8) seek assistance, when necessary.

Most famous inventors are people who are masters at making mistakes. For instance, Thomas Edison attempted more than one thousand times to make a light bulb before succeeding. He treated each attempt that did not succeed as an approximation of his vision rather than as a failure. Also, he kept careful records of his *mis-takes* and learned that every effort is a step toward success.

Take a careful look at your attitude toward taking risks and making mistakes. If you only try tasks that you are assured to master and see any effort that falls short of your goal as a failure, you are probably limiting how much and how rapidly you will learn.

500 words

NAME ______________ CLASS ______________ DATE ______________

3 Mistakes

COMPREHENSION CHECK

GETTING THE FACTS

1. Mistakes are (a) always negative. (b) usually costly. (c) inevitable. (d) ego-building. 1. ____

2. The text states that when some people make mistakes, they become (a) confused. (b) comatose. (c) unproductive. (d) defensive. 2. ____

3. According to the text, when people are learning new skills, they are (a) vulnerable. (b) violent. (c) vital. (d) vocal. 3. ____

4. Mistakes are (a) failures. (b) disasters. (c) diversions. (d) opportunities. 4. ____

5. The author specifically mentions (a) running a red light. (b) blowing a math test. (c) dialing the wrong number. (d) making the wrong turn. 5. ____

GETTING THE MEANING

6. The main idea is that mistakes can be (a) time consuming. (b) embarrassing. (c) upsetting. (d) beneficial. 6. ____

7. Thinking of mistakes as *mis-takes* means admitting that you (a) failed the task. (b) erred in judgment. (c) weren't paying attention. (d) acted hastily. 7. ____

8. Learning new tasks requires that you (a) question everything. (b) take risks. (c) don't admit you are wrong. (d) personalize the outcomes. 8. ____

9. The statement about Thomas Edison illustrates that he (a) doubted his conviction. (b) considered each attempt a failure. (c) hid his mistakes. (d) profited from his mistakes. 9. ____

10. An approximation is a (a) near hit. (b) duplication. (c) goal. (d) task. 10. ____

WPM Rate for Reading Selection: ________
(See chart on p. 454)

Comprehension Score: ________
(to be filled in by instructor)

4

Getting on Track, Part I—The Value of Academic Advising

Ty stormed out of class after getting another *D* on a test. "This college isn't for me," he complained to Chris. "I've tried to be interested in economics, and I've studied hard. I just can't get it," Ty added. "I'm more interested in drawing stuff."

Chris replied, "What's wrong with you, man? This class is great! The instructor is dynamite and has lots of experience in the real world. I can't wait to complete my A.A. degree and move on for my B.S. in Economics. After that, I'm going for my M.B.A. while I work full time. Look out Bill Gates; here I come!" Chris joked.

Ty shot back, "Chris, you know what you want to do with the rest of your whole life, and I can't even decide what class to take next. How do you do it?"

Chris answered, "Well, I haven't always been this sure. When I first started college, I took any class that fit my schedule or seemed easy. Then I thought, I'm wasting my time and my money because I don't have a clue what I'm trying to achieve."

"Then how'd you get on track?" Ty asked. "I finally gave in and went to see an advisor. That was the smartest thing I could have done," Chris responded. "I took a few interest tests, talked to the advisor about things that I do well, and, before I knew it, I was narrowing in on a career that matches my interests perfectly."

"I think I'm going to drop out, Chris. This has all been a waste of time."

"Hey, Ty, give this advising thing a chance, man. You've got a great future waiting out there."

Ty is like many struggling college students: They don't have goals, so they are aimlessly trying courses, hoping one will hit the *interest* nerve. However, the only way to achieve your goal is to know what your goal is. Henriette Anne Klauser, Ph.D. and President of *Writing Resources*, says, "If you want to achieve your goal, write it down." According to Klauser, when you write down your goals, unconsciously your brain filters incoming information and sends it to the conscious part of your brain. Becoming aware of this information, you can act on data that you would otherwise never have noticed. Writing down your goals primes your mind to recognize the steps you must take and the resources available to help you get where you want to go.

In Ty's case, an advisor would help him assess his interests and skills, then direct him to resources that will help him decide on a direction for his studies and career. Once that is complete, Ty can articulate a specific goal—for example, becoming the lead graphic artist for the St. Louis Cardinal's baseball organization or being the CEO of his own Web page design company.

In most cases, college just won't make sense unless you know how to apply the knowledge that's available. Get the help you need making career choices.

500 words

NAME ____________ CLASS ____________ DATE ____________

4 Getting on Track, Part I—The Value of Academic Advising

COMPREHENSION CHECK

GETTING THE FACTS

1. Ty stormed out of (a) an art class. (b) an economics class. (c) a business class. (d) an M.B.A. seminar. 1. ____

2. Chris planned to major in (a) business. (b) art. (c) engineering. (d) economics. 2. ____

3. Chris credits his setting appropriate goals to working with (a) a professor. (b) fellow students. (c) Ty. (d) an advisor. 3. ____

4. It is impossible to achieve your goals if you (a) enroll late. (b) don't have an advisor. (c) aren't sure what your goals are. (d) change your major. 4. ____

5. Chris took (a) performance tests. (b) aptitude tests. (c) interest tests. (d) placement tests. 5. ____

GETTING THE MEANING

6. The focus of this selection is on (a) making good grades. (b) getting an advisor. (c) confiding in friends. (d) choosing good instructors. 6. ____

7. Chris seems to be (a) on track. (b) floundering. (c) confused. (d) insecure. 7. ____

8. Ty had earned (a) a *D* on only one test. (b) at least two *D*s on tests. (c) outstanding grades in this class. (d) better grades in art. 8. ____

9. According to Klauser, writing down your goals helps you (a) intensify. (b) remain dispassionate. (c) focus. (d) vacillate. 9. ____

10. It is smart to get help establishing your goals (a) in your junior year. (b) in your senior year. (c) before choosing a major. (d) after choosing a major. 10. ____

WPM Rate for Reading Selection: ________
(See chart on p. 454)

Comprehension Score: ________
(to be filled in by instructor)

5

Getting on Track, Part II—Choosing a Major

Deciding on a college major is an important, and sometimes difficult, task. In some cases, parents, counselors, spouses, friends, and teachers impose enormous pressure on students to decide what they want to be "when they grow up." In other cases, students impose undue pressure on themselves to pick a major that is easy, will make them rich, will lead them on exciting adventures, or be the fastest route to the world of work.

Choosing a major does not have to be a stressful chore, however. When students approach the task calmly and with a plan, this phase of post-secondary education can actually be a pleasurable adventure in self-discovery.

First, students, parents, and counselors must acknowledge that not everyone begins college with enough knowledge about themselves, the college curriculum, or the job market to make an immediate and informed decision about an appropriate major. Many students need a period of time in which to explore their own interests, learn about courses of study, assess the job market, and determine which curricula are good matches for their skills and abilities.

Second, when students cannot decide, they should enroll in a college readiness course, take an interest inventory and aptitude test, and talk to students who are enthusiastically pursuing specific courses of study. Some students cannot decide on a major because they do not know enough about any discipline to make a strong and long-term commitment. When this is the case, students should talk to professors who are passionate about their fields of study or interview those outside the academic area to learn how they are applying their major.

Third, if the major is to be a perfect fit, students must take responsibility for making this all-important decision themselves. Others can *help* with this decision by brainstorming, providing additional information, and helping students assess their skills and abilities, but making the decision and commitment is a very individual experience. Through a process of elimination, students can determine which college majors will allow them to pursue careers and maintain the kind of lifestyle that is appealing and rewarding. For instance, Charlie, a college freshman, enjoys science, staying close to home, being with lots of people, a beautifully decorated work space, a cool, dry climate, and working with computers. No matter how much his mother, a supervisor in the Forest Service, wants him to join her in the national forests, Charlie should choose a major that will allow him to be comfortable in his work environment. Perhaps, majoring in science education with the intention of teaching at the middle school level would be a better choice than becoming a Forest Service employee.

Unfortunately, and for a variety of reasons, deciding on a major for some students is a knee-jerk reaction, though it shouldn't be. If you are in the process of determining what field of study will lead you to the career(s) of your dream, take your time, get the facts, and ask advice of those who have made the choice you are considering.

500 words

NAME ____________________ CLASS ____________________ DATE ______________

5 Getting on Track, Part II—Choosing a Major

COMPREHENSION CHECK

GETTING THE FACTS

1. According to the selection, choosing a major can be (a) fulfilling. (b) stressful. (c) complex. (d) comforting. 1. ____

2. The author mentioned students' limited knowledge about (a) databases. (b) curriculum. (c) locations. (d) financial aid. 2. ____

3. When students are undecided, they should enroll in a college (a) psychology course. (b) study skills course. (c) readiness course. (d) self-analysis course. 3. ____

4. Students should talk to professors who are (a) researchers. (b) tenured. (c) popular. (d) passionate. 4. ____

5. Students can learn about fields of study by (a) interviewing. (b) manipulating. (c) conjecturing. (d) hypothesizing. 5. ____

GETTING THE MEANING

6. The focus of the selection is on (a) job hunting. (b) career paths. (c) deciding on an advisor. (d) deciding on a major. 6. ____

7. A "knee-jerk" reaction is (a) thoughtless. (b) thoughtful. (c) committed. (d) calculated. 7. ____

8. You can surmise that some students choose college majors (a) after graduation. (b) for the wrong reasons. (c) once they are on the job. (d) to manage their GPA. 8. ____

9. When choosing a major, you should (a) modify poor choices. (b) investigate poor choices. (c) publicize poor choices. (d) eliminate poor choices. 9. ____

10. People who have majored in the field you are considering are (a) wise. (b) talented. (c) good resources. (d) good alumni. 10. _____

WPM Rate for Reading Selection: ________
(See chart on p. 454)

Comprehension Score: ________
(to be filled in by instructor)

6

Developing Problem-solving Skills

Hot potato is a children's game that has brought pleasure to generations. Players stand in a circle. One player has a "hot potato" which contains a wind-up device that ticks loudly. When the game begins, the person holding the potato must (1) wind the device as tightly as she or he chooses, (2) announce that the game has begun, and (3) toss the "hot potato" to one of the other players while trying to conceal the identity of the intended recipient. The player who catches the "hot potato" must get it airborne to another player before the alarm rings. The objective is not to be left holding the "hot potato."

Hot potato is a great game, but playing hot potato with your problems can lead to trouble. Few people face problems confidently. Most try to *wish* their problems away or run from person to person seeking sympathy. Then, when they are forced to make a decision, they think briefly about the first few solutions that come to mind, treat each thought like a "hot potato," and choose the resolution that appears least stress-producing.

This is not an effective approach to decision making. Tony Robins, author of *Personal Power,* says, on average, people spend 80 percent of their time worrying about the problem and only 20 percent exploring workable solutions. Problem solvers should do just the reverse: spend 20 percent of the time focused on understanding the problem and 80 percent trying to solve it. People who heed Tony's advice are amazed at how much less stressful solving problems can be. The following will help you learn to overcome obstacles without being overwhelmed.

First, stop the moment you suspect a problem and write down the following questions and their answers: (1) What is the problem? (2) Have I experienced similar problems before? (a) If yes, how did I solve them? (b) Were the solutions effective? (c) How could the solutions have been improved? (3) If no, do I know people who have faced similar problems? (a) How did they solve them? (b) Were the solutions effective? (c) How could the solutions have been improved? This procedure eliminates the tendency to "stew"—exist in a state of anxiety—about an impending situation without knowing exactly how simple or complex the predicament actually is. It also allows you to dedicate 20 percent of your concentrated effort to clarify the problem before beginning to tackle its resolution.

Next, spend 80 percent of your effort exploring solutions. Make a list of all of the possible ways the problem could be solved. Identify the resources you will need for each solution, and identify the consequences of each option before making the decision best suited for you.

Third, if time permits, focus your attention on other thoughts for a while before deciding which option you will choose. Taking a break from the task usually brings a clearer perspective.

Finally, examine the issue afresh and choose the solution that best fits your circumstance. Remember, decisions are much easier made if you have a plan and spend quality time focused on the solution(s) rather than lamenting the problem.

500 words

NAME ______________ CLASS ______________ DATE ______________

6 Developing Problem-solving Skills

COMPREHENSION CHECK

GETTING THE FACTS

1. The objective of hot potato is to (a) catch the potato. (b) eat the potato. (c) be left holding the potato. (d) get rid of the potato. 1. ____

2. Adults sometimes play hot potato with their (a) pets. (b) children. (c) problems. (d) colleagues. 2. ____

3. In *Personal Power,* Tony Robins says people should spend what percent of their time working on the solutions to their problems? (a) 20 (b) 40 (c) 60 (d) 80 3. ____

4. When one first suspects a problem, the author suggests (a) writing. (b) reading. (c) talking. (d) reflecting. 4. ____

5. Problem solving is much easier if one has (a) lots of experience. (b) lots of friends. (c) unlimited resources. (d) a plan. 5. ____

GETTING THE MEANING

6. This selection is mainly about (a) asking questions. (b) identifying problems. (c) solving problems. (d) playing games. 6. ____

7. On what should you spend most of your time? (a) the problem (b) the question (c) the resources (d) the solution 7. ____

8. Most who face problems (a) worry less than they should. (b) don't "stew" long enough. (c) look outside themselves for solutions. (d) are advice givers. 8. ____

9. When solving a problem, thinking about something else periodically is (a) helpful. (b) frustrating. (c) a waste of time. (d) nonproductive. 9. ____

10. Effective problem solving is primarily (a) strategy. (b) chance. (c) wishful thinking. (d) problem analysis. 10. ____

WPM Rate for Reading Selection: ________
(See chart on p. 454)

Comprehension Score: ________
(to be filled in by instructor)

7

Why Study Groups Work

Have you heard there is strength in numbers? Do you believe two heads are better than one? If you answered "yes," then why do you study for difficult classes alone? Why don't you routinely pool your intellectual resources with those of others in your class(es) and capitalize on the positives of group learning? The answer probably is you have been conditioned to compete against others in classes and even against yourself. In the business world, this kind of behavior is commonly called "healthy competition," and it has led to new and improved products and procedures. However, unharnessed competition in the classroom may limit learning opportunities for countless numbers of students from preschool through graduate school. Read on to learn how participating in study groups may make a spectacular difference in your study and learning habits.

If you are enrolled in a course that seems particularly difficult, chances are others in the class are struggling also. However, every student may not be having trouble learning the same concepts. Under these circumstances, organizing motivated students into study groups can increase the learning potential for all involved. This is what you do:

1. Ask your instructor to survey the class to determine who might be interested in forming study groups.
2. Ask students who wish to participate to sign up, listing their names, a common time to meet, and their telephone numbers (optional).
3. One student should assume the responsibility for organizing the study group's initial session by selecting a safe and easily accessible study facility,* notifying members, and gathering resource materials necessary for the first meeting.
4. At the first meeting, the "temporary" group leader asks members to identify themselves and give a brief statement that outlines his or her expectation(s). If all agree to work together as a team and contribute unselfishly to the collective learning opportunities of all participants,

*College libraries, learning center conference rooms, unscheduled classrooms, portions of student lounges, outdoor campus sitting areas, etc., are good places for study groups to meet.

the study group is launched. If some have expectations that are not harmonious and complementary to others in the group, those students may find that the study group will not meet their needs.

5. Study groups should have no more than five or six students for maximum effectiveness. If more than six students attend the first session, it is wise to form additional groups.
6. Each study group should have a leader who assigns tasks, acts as the contact person with the professor or other learning resources, and keeps track of the tasks assigned to members.
7. The group should meet at prearranged times when members explore concepts introduced in class, share effective strategies for learning, divide large learning tasks into manageable chunks, and review for exams and oral presentations.

Usually, students who form strong, cohesive, and mutually supportive study groups do better than they would have done had they attempted to master the content alone. Give study groups a try. What do you have to lose?

500 words

NAME ______________ CLASS ______________ DATE ______________

7 Why Study Groups Work

COMPREHENSION CHECK

GETTING THE FACTS

1. For which courses are study groups particularly valuable? (a) all (b) difficult ones (c) upper-division classes (d) major classes — 1. ____

2. Group members must agree to work (a) competitively. (b) individually. (c) defensively. (d) harmoniously. — 2. ____

3. Each group should have a(n) (a) instructor. (b) note taker. (c) leader. (d) researcher. — 3. ____

4. One study group task specifically mentioned is (a) establishing rules. (b) reviewing tests. (c) quizzing members. (d) exploring expectations. — 4. ____

5. Group members must be (a) mutually exclusive. (b) mutually supportive. (c) defensive. (d) complacent. — 5. ____

GETTING THE MEANING

6. The primary purpose of the selection is to promote (a) thinking skills. (b) group study. (c) teacher-student relationships. (d) student determination. — 6. ____

7. Study group members must be (a) reliable. (b) refocused. (c) undisciplined. (d) gregarious. — 7. ____

8. Effective study groups are (a) inclusive. (b) selective. (c) crisis driven. (d) socially focused. — 8. ____

9. Study groups should (a) not apportion the work load. (b) rely on a key member. (c) share work responsibilities. (d) promote competition. — 9. ____

10. Successful study group membership requires (a) faithfulness. (b) apathy. (c) caution. (d) complacency. 10. ____

WPM Rate for Reading Selection: ________
(See chart on p. 454)

Comprehension Score: ________
(to be filled in by instructor)

8

Developing a Study Plan

Many students are notorious liars. They spend hours doing what they tell themselves and others is *studying,* when, in reality, they are merely holding a book and allowing their eyes to occasionally skirt across the page. In most cases, this lie is not malicious; students believe that they are, indeed, studying. However, they have perfected hit-or-miss techniques that render inconsistent results. If you are one such student, what follows could very well change your approach to apprehending ideas from the printed page and improve your academic outcomes dramatically.

To seize knowledge while studying, you must assume an aggressive attitude and develop an effective study process comprised of many related activities. First, consciously commit to improving your attitude and study methods, recognizing that old habits will be difficult to break. Studying productively requires active involvement on your part. That is, you must become conversant with the author, questioning the value of material and deciding what is important to your learning task.

Second, assess the study task by "seeing the whole" and determining the most effective study methods to apply. For instance, if you were studying material for an oral presentation, you would probably select a topic, narrow the topic, do the necessary research, prewrite about the subject until a theme or thesis emerges, then spend days, even weeks, thinking about how to develop the thesis with proper support. In this example, you would not be able to study effectively (develop the assigned project) until you had conceived "the whole."

Third, once you understand the scope of the task, you should develop a study strategy that includes (1) blocks of study time; (2) apportioned study times that match the task's difficulty; and (3) a dedicated study place equipped with the tools necessary for college-level pursuits—that is, dictionary, thesaurus, pens, pencils, paper, texts, class notes, syllabi, course study guides, adequate lighting, a desk or table, a comfortable chair, and a typewriter or computer, if possible.

Fourth, understand that reading *does not* equal studying. Though reading is only one part of the study process, it is often the primary means by which you take in information to be learned. Studying requires that learners (1) develop a plan; (2) read; (3) write; (4) ponder/reflect while reading and writing; (5) recite; (6) review; (7) summarize; (8) translate text into familiar vocabulary; (9) record content, where possible, using charts, timelines, sketches, etc.; and (10) connect/integrate newly learned concepts with prior knowledge. Only when these activities happen as an *integrated* plan does effective learning occur.

Finally, when available and appropriate, you should avail yourself of learning resources in your college or community. Those resources may include professors, librarians, counselors, peer tutors, learning assistant center employees, and organized study groups. The time to take advantage of learning resources is early in the semester so you will not fall behind in difficult courses.

Follow this advice and you should see marked improvement in your academic performance. Moreover, you may also find that learning is more fun than ever before.

500 words

NAME ______________ CLASS ______________ DATE ______________

8 Developing a Study Plan

COMPREHENSION CHECK

GETTING THE FACTS

1. An effective study process is composed of (a) integrated activities. (b) independent activities. (c) unrelated activities. (d) unrestrained activities. 1. ____

2. The first step in an efficient study plan is to (a) make a commitment. (b) break old habits. (c) get help. (d) test yourself. 2. ____

3. The author contends that (a) reading takes longer than studying. (b) reading is not a part of studying. (c) studying does not equal reading. (d) reading does not equal studying. 3. ____

4. Students should take advantage of learning resources (a) just before a test. (b) just after a test. (c) at midterm. (d) just after the semester begins. 4. ____

5. Students often lie to themselves because they (a) want to fool themselves. (b) want to fool their teachers. (c) think they are studying. (d) don't think studying is important. 5. ____

GETTING THE MEANING

6. The main idea of this reading is that successful students (a) plan to be successful. (b) study endlessly. (c) avoid commitment. (d) encourage competition. 6. ____

7. A reliable study strategy is (a) attainable. (b) impossible. (c) short-lived. (d) open-ended. 7. ____

8. "Seeing the whole" allows the reader to (a) complete the task quickly. (b) seek help. (c) choose the most effective study method. (d) determine the value of the exercise. 8. ____

9. A good study plan (a) works for any subject. (b) is specific to the task. (c) takes little time or effort. (d) is very general. 9. ____

10. You could conclude that a specific study place is (a) unimportant. (b) optional. (c) desirable. (d) mandatory. 10. ____

WPM Rate for Reading Selection: ________
(See chart on p. 454)

Comprehension Score: ________
(to be filled in by instructor)

9

Learning to Remember

Take Susan and Mike. Both had equally good comprehension immediately after reading material assigned for the midquarter. Yet Mike got an *A* and Susan a *C*. How come? Susan forgot much of what she had covered. Mike didn't. He knew that immediate comprehension was not enough. He knew how to remember as well as how to read. That made the difference.

How can you improve your memory? Try these five essentials.

Desire it! Say to yourself before reading an assignment, "I want to remember what I'm reading. If I read with an active mind and earnest desire to remember, I will remember much longer and easier than if I read passively." To whet your desire, remember—this can change a *C* to an *A*.

Use it! A comedian walked across the stage several times during a show, carrying a heavy saddle. Finally someone asked him why. He replied, "Well, you can't ever tell when you might meet a horse." Most of us are more realistic. We carry an umbrella only when it's raining or looks like rain, not all the time. Remember this when you read. If you can think of a specific use for what you are reading, you have a real advantage. For example, before reading an interesting article, decide you're going to look for something to bring added interest to your coffee-break conversation. Or look for specific information to use in a speech, theme, classroom contribution, or out-of-class discussion. Always ask yourself, "Where and how can I use this material I am reading?" The more definite you can be, the better you will remember it. And the more immediate your use, the better. Using it in a speech later that day is better than using it next month.

Recite it! Often when you finish an assignment, you feel you know it well. Don't stop there, however. Close your book. Ask yourself some questions, such as, "What were the major causes of inflation discussed?" This reciting ensures a more active mental activity and gives you an immediate goal. This helps you remember more accurately and easily.

Review it! When you recite, you will discover main points and details that you have failed to learn. Open the book again and review those items so that you can fill in the gaps. For example, in studying linguistics, you remember *trachea, pharynx,* but not the technical term for that part of the throat containing the vocal cords. *Adam's apple* won't do. A review will fix the term *larynx* well in mind.

Associate it! Is it *attendance* or *attendence?* Try associating what you want to remember with what you already know. This link or association will often do your remembering for you. You know, for example, that you shouldn't get to a dance too early. The ideal advice? "At ten—dance." That's just the association you need to fix the correct spelling, *attendance,* in mind.

There they are. Use them conscientiously and intelligently. Let them help you transform those *C*s into *A*s, those *D*s into *B*s.

500 words

NAME ______________ CLASS ______________ DATE ______________

9 Learning to Remember

COMPREHENSION CHECK

GETTING THE FACTS

1. On the midquarter, both Susan and Mike (a) had equally good comprehension after reading the material. (b) got *A*s. (c) spent equal time in review. (d) got *C*s. 1. ____

2. *No* mention is made of (a) a comedian. (b) a cat. (c) an umbrella. (d) the desire to remember. 2. ____

3. You are advised to (a) use what you learn. (b) underline. (c) space your learning efforts. (d) take notes. 3. ____

4. Specific reference is made to (a) psychology. (b) linguistics. (c) philosophy. (d) sociology. 4. ____

5. This selection is chiefly focused on (a) the improvement of memory. (b) the beneficial results of remembering. (c) the difficulty of remembering. (d) the importance of memory. 5. ____

GETTING THE MEANING

6. The statement, "It's want-to, not IQ, that's important," could be used more appropriately to develop which point? (a) Use it. (b) Desire it. (c) Recite it. (d) Associate it. 6. ____

7. Spelling rules as aids in dealing with individual words could be discussed most appropriately under which point? (a) Desire it. (b) Recite it. (c) Associate it. (d) Review it. 7. ____

8. The story of the man carrying the saddle was used to illustrate the importance of (a) preparedness. (b) foresight. (c) a strong desire. (d) usefulness. 8. ____

9. The reference to Susan and Mike was to point up the importance of (a) reviewing. (b) remembering. (c) reading. (d) good comprehension. 9. ____

10. The student who used DURRA to help him remember the five steps is resorting to the advice (a) Associate it. (b) Desire it. (c) Recite it. (d) Use it. 10. ____

WPM Rate for Reading Selection: ________
(See chart on p. 454)

Comprehension Score: ________
(to be filled in by instructor)

10

The Goal—Adaptability

What's a good car? One that's speedy? Easy to handle? What about low initial cost, economy of operation, or riding ease? Perhaps no *one* factor provides a completely satisfying answer.

What's a good reader? Here, too, no one factor is enough. Speed isn't everything; neither is comprehension. More important than either one is the *ability* to *adapt*—to adapt rate to purpose and to a wide variety of reading materials. Adaptability, then, is the true mark of a good reader.

How do you measure adaptability? How better than by actually putting yourself into different reading situations to see how well you adapt? For example, using three articles of comparable difficulty, check your performance when reading normally, thoroughly, and rapidly.

To discover your normal leisure reading habits, read an article neither faster nor slower than you ordinarily do when you have some leisure and want to settle down comfortably with a magazine. Don't try to comprehend more or less than usual in that situation. When you have finished and taken the test, determine your reading rate and comprehension. Next, see how well you adapt yourself to the problem of getting meaning. In reading the next article, your purpose is to get as much comprehension as possible in a single reading. Keep track of reading time, but remember that it's comprehension you're after. With the last article, your purpose is to cover ground rapidly. Read it at your top rate. Although speed is your primary concern, check comprehension to see what price you ordinarily pay for haste.

These three sets of rate and comprehension scores provide a useful composite index of adaptability, a three-dimension picture of yourself as a reader. Careful analysis of these scores should reveal information of importance in directing future practice efforts and achieving maximum results. As Kettering once said: "A problem well-stated is a problem half-solved." In reading, that might well be paraphrased: "A problem *well-identified* is a problem half-solved."

For example, what about the range of reading rates at your command? Subtract your slowest rate from your top rate for that figure. Is it 200 wpm or more? If so, you're among the top 20 percent of adults *before* training in reading. If that figure is 50 wpm or less, you'll want to overcome your tendencies toward one-speed reading. And if your top rate is under 300 wpm, vocalizing and regressing are probably indicated.

Did you get comprehension when that was your purpose? And did you get details as well as main ideas and inferences? Was comprehension consistently good or did it vary considerably? Consistently good comprehension without considerable range in rate may indicate an unwillingness to recognize the importance of both depth and breadth as you read, an overlooking of Bacon's dictum: "Some books are to be tasted, others to be swallowed, and some few to be chewed and digested."

Such an analysis touches significant facets of this thing called *adaptability,* so important in defining a good reader.

500 words

NAME ______________ CLASS ______________ DATE ______________

10 The Goal—Adaptability

COMPREHENSION CHECK

GETTING THE FACTS

1. The good reader is likened to a good (a) car. (b) motor. (c) driver. (d) model. 1. ____

2. You are told to use articles of comparable (a) column width. (b) difficulty. (c) length. (d) subject matter. 2. ____

3. Mention is made of (a) Byron. (b) Ford. (c) Lamb. (d) Kettering. 3. ____

4. Reference is made to (a) stuttering. (b) word-for-word reading. (c) the tachistoscope. (d) one-speed reading. 4. ____

5. A speed range of 200 wpm or more was said to put you among the top (a) 60%. (b) 40%. (c) 20%. (d) 5%. 5. ____

GETTING THE MEANING

6. The primary purpose of this selection is to (a) define what is meant by a good reader. (b) define adapatability. (c) explain how to measure adaptability. (d) explain how to identify vocalizing difficulties. 6. ____

7. The emphasis in this selection is on (a) wisdom is power. (b) knowing thyself. (c) reading maketh a full man. (d) the reading man is the thinking man. 7. ____

8. The threefold check is intended to (a) eliminate reading difficulties. (b) identify reading difficulties. (c) test reading improvement. (d) determine reading potential. 8. ____

9. A vocabulary deficiency would be suggested by (a) consistently low comprehension. (b) consistently slow rate. (c) a drop in comprehension as rate is increased. (d) an increase in comprehension as rate is decreased. 9. ____

10. Difficulty with concentration would be suggested if 10. ____
(a) rapid reading brought better comprehension.
(b) rapid reading did not affect comprehension.
(c) normal rate brought better comprehension.
(d) comprehension remained fairly constant.

WPM Rate for Reading Selection: ________
(See chart on p. 454)

Comprehension Score: ________
(to be filled in by instructor)

11

Treat Causes, Not Symptoms

When you step into a doctor's office with a splitting headache, you expect more than an aspirin. That headache is usually a symptom of something that needs attention—something that is causing discomfort. A doctor, if he is to be genuinely helpful, must treat causes, not symptoms.

It helps to look at reading from this same vantage point. Suppose a student comprehends poorly and goes to a clinician for help. It will take more than the admonition, "Try to comprehend better," to bring results.

Poor comprehension is really a symptom—a symptom of what? That's the question which must be answered. Unfortunately the answer is likely to be complex, not simple. Many causes, not one, have to be examined.

For example, if a student reads that "Elizabeth is taciturn," he may not comprehend the statement because of a vocabulary deficiency. That's one important cause to check.

Sometimes a student may read a whole page or chapter and get very little? Why? Frankly because he was bored—had no real interest in it. Lack of interest, then, is another cause of poor comprehension.

Difficulty is still another factor accounting for low comprehension. The Flesch Reading Ease Score provides one method of determining difficulty, rating reading matter on a scale from 0 to 100 or from very easy to very difficult. Both word length and sentence length are used to determine difficulty.

A well-trained mechanic can often just listen to motor sounds and diagnose engine difficulties. He has had sufficient background and experience to do what one lacking that background would find impossible. In reading, also, low comprehension may be caused by inadequate background in a subject matter area.

And of course your reading rate affects comprehension. Reading either too rapidly or too slowly may affect comprehension adversely. For most students there is usually a "just-right" speed which provides maximum comprehension.

Lack of concentration is still another reason for low comprehension. Some readers have never developed proper techniques for dealing successfully with distractions, have never disciplined themselves to give concentrated attention to anything for any length of time. In this day of commercials, station breaks, and coffee breaks, we may be losing the ability to concentrate for extended periods of time.

This does not exhaust the list of causes, although those certainly deserve major attention. Other factors need to be kept in mind—temperature, noise, and movement, for example. Then there are the mechanics of reading—fixation patterns, regression patterns, vocalizings, word-for-word habits.

What does this add up to? Look closely and carefully at each of these possible causes. Try to decide which factor or combination of factors probably explains your low comprehension. Fortunately, without exception, you can do something about each of them. So set up a program for dealing with the causes underlying your symptoms. Then and only then can you begin to see good results.

500 words

NAME ______________ CLASS ______________ DATE ______________

11 Treat Causes, Not Symptoms

COMPREHENSION CHECK

GETTING THE FACTS

1. The article specifically mentions (a) a dentist. (b) a doctor. (c) an intern. (d) a receptionist. 1. ____

2. Poor comprehension is spoken of as (a) a symptom. (b) a disease. (c) a cause. (d) an accident. 2. ____

3. The Reading Ease Score mentioned was developed by (a) Flesch. (b) Fischer. (c) Flexner. (d) Garrison. 3. ____

4. The article mentions (a) a well-trained mechanic. (b) an experienced teacher. (c) a pilot. (d) a trouble-shooter. 4. ____

5. The article mentions (a) wage hikes. (b) coffee breaks. (c) bonus gifts. (d) hypos. 5. ____

GETTING THE MEANING

6. The central idea is to get you to (a) discover symptoms. (b) deal with causes. (c) improve comprehension. (d) check vocabulary deficiency. 6. ____

7. The allusion to station breaks was primarily to suggest (a) the importance of variety. (b) their effect on habits of concentration. (c) their encouragement of vocalization. (d) the importance of visual aids. 7. ____

8. A student who comprehends poorly (a) is reading too rapidly. (b) is not really interested. (c) is not concentrating. (d) may be doing none of these things. 8. ____

9. If your reading speed is not increasing, you should apparently try to (a) find out how to increase it. (b) try a new method. (c) discover why not. (d) work harder. 9. ____

10. Apparently, the most helpful move to ensure progress is (a) careful self-analysis. (b) extensive practice. (c) a higher goal. (d) more work on vocabulary. 10. ____

WPM Rate for Reading Selection: ________
(See chart on p. 454)

Comprehension Score: ________
(to be filled in by instructor)

12

"I Finally Got It!" or Capturing the Elusive Main Idea

Finding the main idea of a passage is a difficult task for some and nearly impossible for others. As a result, some dislike reading intensely and avoid it as much as possible.

The primary reason people miss the main idea is because many are passive readers who begin reading a passage at page one, paragraph one, and word one. These readers don't even read the title or subtitles that appear in the text and rarely are conscious of the words their eyes are seeing. Ultimately, they become frustrated, defeated, and say to themselves, "I don't get it!" and go on to the next reading task. But it need not be this way. Read on to learn a three-part approach that will make finding the main idea much easier.

First, be actively involved with the words on the page and the author of those words. You are probably wondering, "How can I be involved with words?" and "How can I be actively involved with someone who is not where I am or may, indeed, be dead?" The answers are simple: approach reading tasks with curiosity, searching for the stated as well as the suggested meaning of words. In addition, be committed to discovering the author's reason for writing and the impact those words and ideas will have on how you feel about the subject.

Unlike passive readers, active readers do the following things to ensure comprehension. They (1) mentally prepare themselves to receive information from print by clearing their minds of extraneous thoughts, (2) survey the passage, looking at the title and speculating about the content of the material, (3) develop questions and search for the answers as they read, (4) question the validity of the ideas presented and the credibility of the author, (5) stop periodically to review and ponder the relevance of the material, and (6) search for the links between ideas presented.

Second, ask *who* or *what* the paragraph is about to find the main idea. The *who* or *what*, the subject, is usually the most frequently mentioned or the most general noun in the passage. Then determine, What is the most general statement stated or implied about the subject? In other words, What happened to the subject? Then, using the subject, compose a statement, *in your own words,* that sums up the general idea.

Finally, pay attention to the function of sentences. Sentences in paragraphs fall into two categories: general and specific. A good paragraph has only one general sentence or, perhaps, one general sentence and a paraphrase of the same idea elsewhere in the paragraph. All other sentences support or provide proof for the general sentence. In other words, one sentence makes a claim and the other sentences back it up.

Continue this process for each segment of the reading assignment, adding up all of the individual main ideas when the process is complete to form the overall main idea of the passage. Use this process and the main idea will be easy to grasp.

500 words

NAME ______________ CLASS ______________ DATE ______________

12 "I Finally Got It!" or Capturing the Elusive Main Idea

COMPREHENSION CHECK

GETTING THE FACTS

1. Active readers (a) read aloud. (b) prepare themselves mentally. (c) read as rapidly as possible. (d) develop questions after they read. 1. ____

2. In a well-written paragraph, there are (a) more general than specific sentences. (b) more specific than general sentences. (c) an equal number of general and specific sentences. (d) no specific sentences. 2. ____

3. Those who say, "I don't get it!" usually (a) reread the selection. (b) ask for help. (c) move to the next task. (d) give up. 3. ____

4. When surveying, an efficient reader (a) reads thoroughly. (b) speculates. (c) does not guess. (d) rereads often. 4. ____

5. A main idea statement (a) must contain the subject. (b) is always stated. (c) restates the details. (d) provides support for the details. 5. ____

GETTING THE MEANING

6. The main focus is on (a) identifying supports. (b) getting the facts. (c) being a passive reader. (d) being an active reader. 6. ____

7. Efficient reading requires a partnership between the author and the (a) editor. (b) reader. (c) publisher. (d) teacher. 7. ____

8. Understanding the main idea is to comprehension as (a) water is to a river. (b) rap music is to youth. (c) skis are to snow. (d) the NBA is to basketball. 8. ____

9. Efficient readers are (a) born, not made. (b) made, not born. (c) especially gifted. (d) superachievers. 9. ____

10. Passive readers (a) question the author's credibility. (b) rely on effective reasoning. (c) expect a stated main idea. (d) confidently search for meaning. 10. ____

WPM Rate for Reading Selection: ________
(See chart on p. 454)

Comprehension Score: ________
(to be filled in by instructor)

13

Drawing Inferences or Fishing in the Author's Mind for What Is Not on the Page

Your plane has just arrived at the airport, and you notice that those greeting arriving passengers are wearing or carrying heavy coats. You also notice that the windows in the waiting area are covered with condensation. You think to yourself, "I am happy that I decided to bring my winter coat and gloves; I'll probably need them while I am here." Though no one has told you, you know that the temperature outside is probably lower than 40 degrees. But how do you know? What allows you to make those judgments? Prior knowledge! You were able to "read" the situation and make reasonable judgments based on previous experience. In other words, you were able to add up the clues and draw *inferences* about the situation. But being able to draw inferences is not a skill that everyone easily masters. Read on to learn how drawing inferences can improve your reading comprehension.

Making inferences about reading material as well as about experiences in your everyday life requires careful observation. Authors cannot possibly include all that they want the reader to consider about the subject. Not only would it make the passage too long to be easily digested, but also readers would become bored reading information that they already know. Therefore, authors include enough in a passage to trigger thoughts in the readers' minds, helping them understand and retain new concepts. Readers must be ever mindful that authors routinely do this and, more important, be prepared to search for the "triggers" or "links" imbedded in the text.

To detect inferences, you should employ the following strategies: search for and fully understand the main idea and details presented, examine the author's attitude toward the subject, and explore the logical, unstated judgments permitted by the facts and *suggested* by the information that is stated. For example, if you read the following account, what inferences could you draw?

> Around mid-day, Dr. Begay told the parents, cautiously, that their daughter would survive. She warned, however, that since it had been

less than ten hours since the surgery, the patient's condition could not be fully assessed. The doctor offered one comforting note: the patient could move her arms, fingers, legs, and toes.

Ask yourself a few questions. (1) About what time of day is considered "mid-day"? (2) Was the patient's condition ever life-threatening? (3) What are the chances that the patient is not paralyzed?

If you were able to answer *around noon* to 1, *Yes* to 2, and *Good* to 3, you have used inference. You answered the questions by applying prior knowledge to the situation described.

When studying unfamiliar material, read through it once focusing on finding the main idea and assessing the details. Then go through the material again to search for inferences that the author has imbedded. Remember, you have to be a detective of sorts to become a truly efficient reader.

500 words

NAME ______________ CLASS ______________ DATE ______________

13 Drawing Inferences or Fishing in the Author's Mind for What Is Not on the Page

COMPREHENSION CHECK

GETTING THE FACTS

1. Judgments based on clues are called (a) subtitles. (b) links. (c) theses. (d) inferences. 1. ____

2. Authors include enough information to (a) confound the thoughts. (b) suppress thoughts. (c) trigger thoughts. (d) obscure thoughts. 2. ____

3. To draw inferences, you must (a) skim. (b) read word-for-word. (c) examine the title. (d) understand the main idea. 3. ____

4. Inferences are (a) judgments stated by the author. (b) details that disprove the main idea. (c) questions in the reader's mind. (d) judgments permitted by the facts. 4. ____

5. When drawing inferences the reader should (a) ignore the facts. (b) rely only on the stated facts. (c) rely on prior knowledge. (d) disregard the author's biases. 5. ____

GETTING THE MEANING

6. This selection is essentially about (a) what was said. (b) what was suggested. (c) disregarding clues. (d) understanding details. 6. ____

7. To draw accurate inferences the reader must (a) fabricate information. (b) dismiss conjecture. (c) rely only on stated information. (d) "read between the lines." 7. ____

8. Good readers are (a) specialists. (b) risk takers. (c) not inquisitive. (d) not tenacious. 8. ____

9. "Imbedded" in the text means (a) stated. (b) implied. (c) contradicted. (d) disputed. 9. ____

10. Which is a reasonable inference about the sick-daughter scenario? (a) Surgery occurred after midnight. (b) Surgery was lengthy. (c) The victim is a child. (d) The doctor is inexperienced. 10. ____

WPM Rate for Reading Selection: ________
(See chart on p. 454)

Comprehension Score: ________
(to be filled in by instructor)

14

Summarizing

What is a summary? Is there a simple way to ensure that a summary contains all of the essential information presented in the original text? Is summarizing a valuable skill? These are legitimate questions that puzzle students everywhere. The answers are as follows: A summary is a brief report that covers the main points of a composition: Yes, there is a simple way to ensure that a summary contains the essential information presented in the original text; and, Yes, summarizing is a valuable skill because it forces you to identify, comprehend, and manipulate the primary information of a printed source. If your instructors require summaries or if you have volumes of texts to study and digest, you will find the following tips valuable.

Summarizing a text that you do not understand is impossible. Therefore, you must *study* the material to be summarized, making sure that you are able to identify the main ideas, supporting details, and essential vocabulary. When you are sure that you understand the material, employ the six-step process outlined below.

First, analyze the title and identify the subject of the material by asking, "Who or what is this material about?" and speculate about the essential point the author will likely make about the subject. If there are subtopics, read and analyze them, paying careful attention to the support the subtopics provide for the title. Next, study and analyze the illustrations. Then, read the first and last paragraphs of the material, including the author-supplied summary.

Second, while previewing try to anticipate the questions that will be answered in each subtopic and paragraph. One way is to convert the subtopics into questions, placing the traditional "question words," why, when, where, and how, in front of each subtopic. For example, if, in a selection entitled "Alaska's Vastness" one subtopic is Lakes of Alaska, you might ask *how, where, when,* and *why* about Alaskan lakes. Also, note the examples, descriptions, explanation, and definitions provided.

Third, identify the thesis or point of view, if given. If either is present, it is usually stated as a subtitle and/or at the end of the introductory paragraph.

Fourth, as you read, reduce each subtopic or section to its main ideas by identifying the most general statement in each paragraph and writing the idea on a piece of paper.

Fifth, rewrite the thesis and main ideas in your own words and arrange them in a paragraph. Avoid beginning the summary with *This article . . . (is about, talks about, is in reference to, deals with)* or *The author says. . . .* Simply begin by paraphrasing the thesis or point-of-view statement, then follow with paraphrased main ideas and essential details.

Sixth, often an instructor wants to ascertain your reaction to or interpretation of a text. When this is the case, decide how you feel about the subject, determine what, if any, impact the material has on your beliefs, and state that evaluation in a short paragraph, about 40 percent as long as the original text.

If you follow these directions, you should have no trouble composing an outstanding summary.

500 words

NAME ______________ CLASS ______________ DATE ______________

14 Summarizing

COMPREHENSION CHECK

GETTING THE FACTS

1. A summary is a (a) main idea. (b) technical report. (c) brief report. (d) thesis. 1. ____

2. A summary should contain (a) many details. (b) all supporting data. (c) essential information. (d) minor ideas and major support. 2. ____

3. How many steps are in the summarizing process described? (a) four (b) six (c) seven (d) eight 3. ____

4. Summarizing is beneficial because it (a) shortens study time. (b) helps you retain key information. (c) focuses on specifics. (d) focuses only on the subtopics. 4. ____

5. Which of the following reveals the subject of material? (a) who or why (b) what or when (c) why or when (d) who or what 5. ____

GETTING THE MEANING

6. The focus is on (a) examining details. (b) composing questions. (c) reviewing facts. (d) reporting key points. 6. ____

7. Summarizing forces the reader to concentrate on (a) specifics. (b) facts. (c) main ideas. (d) reasons. 7. ____

8. Summarizing (a) condenses information. (b) disburses information. (c) eliminates careful reading. (d) intensifies surveying. 8. ____

9. To paraphrase means to (a) restate. (b) copy. (c) delete. (d) defer. 9. ____

10. A summary should begin with (a) main ideas. (b) statistics. (c) general ideas. (d) the author's name. 10. ____

WPM Rate for Reading Selection: ________
(See chart on p. 454)

Comprehension Score: ________
(to be filled in by instructor)

15

Reading—On Screen

Reading is reading, is reading, is reading, right? WRONG!

Many factors influence how efficient readers read, some of which are purpose, difficulty level, the reader's experience with the subject, and the medium and format of the text. Efficient readers know they cannot read all material in the same way. They are aware that they must determine why they are reading and what they hope to glean from the experience. They also know they must assess the complexity and difficulty of the material, adjust their reading rate, and pay appropriate attention to *clues* in the margin and within the text. Also, efficient readers realize that what they know about the subject is a critical factor in how much they will understand and how hard they must work to make the reading experience useful. However, even the most proficient readers have found they need to hone their skills to match the medium and format of reading material, a task that often requires the most challenging adaptations.

For centuries, words appeared on a static surface: scratched in the earth; carved on rocks, leather, paper, or cloth; written on the sides of buildings; painted on billboards; etc. However, with the advent of technology, reading texts are appearing in places that require new and different reading skills and, often, manipulation of the environment. Today, students, business-people, and anyone who uses a computer must use a variety of strategies to ensure maximum comprehension and reduce the potential for fatigue and injury.

In traditional reading circumstances, readers adjust to the text as the publisher has presented it. If the font is difficult to read or the print too small, the reader uses a magnifying glass or puts on glasses to make the text more comfortable to read. If the material is too far away to read comfortably, readers either move the print source closer or move closer to the print source. If it is difficult for readers to see the print because of its color or the background on which it is written, the reader can do little to improve the situation.

Unlike reading from a static surface, reading from a computer screen allows readers to take more responsibility for the physical aspects of the reading process. If the font is difficult to read or the print too small, the reader can change the font size and style. If the material is too far away to read comfortably, the reader can manipulate the text size or move to a larger monitor. If it is difficult for readers to see the print because of its color or the background on which it is written, the reader can change the background and the color of the font.

On-screen reading allows readers to be active participants. So the next time you sit down to a computer, remember you are in control, to a large extent, of the way you will read what is before you. Take advantage of options that will make your reading experience more pleasant and rewarding.

500 words

NAME ______________ CLASS ______________ DATE ______________

15 Reading—On Screen

COMPREHENSION CHECK

GETTING THE FACTS

1. A factor specifically mentioned that influences reading efficiency is (a) font size. (b) readers's age. (c) reader's experience. (d) text length. 1. ____

2. Proficient readers hone their reading skills to (a) intimidate others. (b) challenge adaptations. (c) match the medium. (d) apply their experiences. 2. ____

3. For centuries, words appeared on (a) intangibles. (b) paper only. (c) cloth. (d) static surfaces. 3. ____

4. On-screen reading allows readers to be (a) bored. (b) monitored. (c) active listeners. (d) active participants. 4. ____

5. Reading from a computer screen allows readers to (a) take more breaks. (b) take more responsibility. (c) question the author. (d) multitask. 5. ____

GETTING THE MEANING

6. The main idea is that compared to reading from a static surface, reading on screen requires (a) better strategies. (b) different strategies. (c) more time. (d) a very fast computer. 6. ____

7. Efficient readers (a) adapt to the material. (b) have one proven approach to reading. (c) always read quickly. (d) always read slowly. 7. ____

8. One efficient way to customize text on the screen is to (a) e-mail the author. (b) print the text. (c) adjust the font color. (d) use an ergonomic keyboard. 8. ____

9. In traditional reading circumstances, who controls the presentation of text? (a) publishers (b) authors (c) readers (d) distributors 9. ____

10. When reading on-screen, a person who has difficulty seeing small text can make the task easier by being (a) passive. (b) understanding. (c) indifferent. (d) self-directed. 10. ____

WPM Rate for Reading Selection: ________
(See chart on p. 454)

Comprehension Score: ________
(to be filled in by instructor)

16

A Writing Center Approach to Composition

Her English professor outlined the second assignment of the semester—a descriptive paper. Karen's hands began to sweat, and her heart raced. Another essay less than a week since she struggled with the first. Karen had laboriously handwritten many drafts of her first paper. She did not have 32 hours to spend on the second one.

Karen met with her English professor, Dr. Hinz. He told her that repeated spelling and punctuation errors, syntax problems, and poor word choice cost her two grade levels. Defeated, Karen contemplated dropping the course. She said, "I don't think I am ready for this class. I don't have the time to write and rewrite the ten papers that are due this semester, so I am going to drop the course and take it another time." Dr. Hinz said, "Karen, you are a good writer. Go to the Writing Center and ask for assistance. You will learn to compose papers at the computer and use the tools that make composition faster and more efficient."

Karen went to the Writing Center, enrolled in a three-hour word processing immersion course, and settled in with Chris, who taught her the tricks of composing on screen. Writing has not been the same since. Karen learned to think of each writing assignment as a series of actions that lead to a completed project. Once she could see the assignment in manageable parts, Karen was able to think through the phases of the paper and work on each piece without feeling overwhelmed.

Before touching the computer, Karen learned to assess the writing task, think purposefully about the topic, and determine audience and point of view. Then, she sat down at the computer and let the ideas roll from her head onto the screen, not worrying about spelling, punctuation, grammar, syntax, or word choice. In fact, Karen soon resented the fact that she could not keyboard as fast as she could think. Once she completed the first draft, she spell-checked and printed it. She read the draft for a first impression, made revising notations, and set the draft aside to "rest." At the next session and for the first time, Karen revised a paper without rewriting the entire text. She added new ideas, deleted redundancy, used the thesaurus to find fresh vocabulary, edited for punctuation, eliminated passive voice, and checked the paper's word count, all on the computer.

Finally, Karen learned to use the human resources in the Writing Center to *test* her composition against the assignment. The staff asked Karen questions about the paper to help her see areas that needed strengthening and helped her detect subtle errors the word processing program could not identify.

This new approach to composition proved faster, more productive, and less frustrating. If you are using a computer only as a sophisticated typewriter or if you are not using a computer at all, visit the Writing Center on your campus for an introduction to writing the high-tech way.

500 words

NAME ______________ CLASS ______________ DATE ______________

16 A Writing Center Approach to Composition

COMPREHENSION CHECK

GETTING THE FACTS

1. Karen's second paper would be (a) argument. (b) descriptive. (c) biographical. (d) informative. 1. ____

2. With the first essay, Karen had (a) gone to the Writing Center. (b) completed it quickly. (c) struggled. (d) developed a good strategy. 2. ____

3. Dr. Hinz was (a) a Writing Center professor. (b) an advisor. (c) an English professor. (d) a computer professor. 3. ____

4. Karen's word processing immersion course was (a) a day long. (b) a semester long. (c) five days long. (d) three hours long. 4. ____

5. The staff in the Writing Center (a) edited Karen's paper. (b) revised Karen's paper. (c) asked Karen questions. (d) added redundancy. 5. ____

GETTING THE MEANING

6. The main idea is (a) Don't get in over your head. (b) English professors are considerate. (c) Writing Centers rely mostly on computers. (d) Writing Centers can help improve compositions. 6. ____

7. Seeing a writing assignment in manageable parts made the task (a) more frightening. (b) less frightening. (c) seem larger. (d) overwhelming. 7. ____

8. Word processing can help with (a) point of view. (b) audience. (c) subject. (d) spelling. 8. ____

9. Karen's professor said she was a "good writer" to (a) deceive. (b) persuade. (c) comfort. (d) clarify. 9. ____

10. Word processing programs (a) catch most errors. (b) catch select errors. (c) slow down the writing process. (d) are sophisticated typewriters. 10. ____

WPM Rate for Reading Selection: ________
(See chart on p. 454)

Comprehension Score: ________
(to be filled in by instructor)

17

Equity Under the Law

The 1990 Americans with Disabilities Act guarantees disabled people access to employment, public accommodations, transportation, public services, and telecommunications. Until that time, few standards existed to ensure that buildings, public transportation, streets and sidewalks, hotels, apartments, schools, parks, businesses, campgrounds, etc., were accessible to people who have a disability. As a result, a large segment of our citizenry could not participate fully and pursue many ideals of the American lifestyle.

However, over the past decade, our country has made progress in leveling the playing field for all Americans. Legislation, the first step, provided laws that protect our rights to equal access. Education and information, the second step, enlightened Americans about ways to remove barriers that exclude those with special needs. Finally, accepting others' differences and welcoming them into established circles demonstrated that all Americans, regardless of abilities, make a valuable contribution to our society.

At your college you may have noticed great diversity among student and employee populations. Such diversity enriches the college experience for all, but it may pose a challenge for people who have never interacted with those who are different from themselves. If you are one who feels awkward and uncomfortable when you meet people with a disability because you do not know how to interact with them, the following discussion will provide information you may find helpful.

Treat people with disabilities respectfully. Acknowledge their presence, as you would anyone's, by saying hello and engaging them in appropriate conversation. Make eye contact, if that is fitting, and allow the person to respond to you at her or his own pace. If you and the person with a disability share a common class, discuss how the course is going. However, do not touch or move assistive technology belonging to people with a disability without their permission. Moving or even touching a person's wheelchair, for some, is tantamount to touching the person.

If you suspect a person with a disability might need your assistance, always ask before providing help. For instance, if a person using a wheelchair approaches a closed door without an automatic opener, ask the person if he or she would like you to open the door. If a person using a wheelchair enters a room where chairs obstruct the aisle, offer to clear the pathway.

However, if a person with a disability is in imminent danger, alert the person immediately. For example, if a blind person is about to strike her head on a protruding shelf, say, "Stop! A shelf is protruding just above your head on the right." Or, in case of a fire, if a deaf person does not know why a warning light is flashing in the hallway, get the person's attention, write "fire" on a piece of paper, and gesture in the direction of safety.

Above all, do your part to create a receptive learning environment for your fellow students and yourself. Some of the most valuable lessons learned in college may not come from a textbook.

500 words

NAME ______________ CLASS ______________ DATE ______________

17 Equity Under the Law

COMPREHENSION CHECK

GETTING THE FACTS

1. The Americans with Disabilities Act was passed in (a) 1980. (b) 1989. (c) 1990. (d) 1999. — 1. ____

2. The first step in providing equal access for people with disabilities was (a) education. (b) enlistment. (c) legislation. (d) demonstrations. — 2. ____

3. According to this author, diversity (a) hinders. (b) accommodates. (c) impedes. (d) enriches. — 3. ____

4. You should treat people with disabilities (a) cautiously. (b) respectfully. (c) warily. (d) attentively. — 4. ____

5. If a person with a disability uses assistive technology, unless you have permission don't (a) move it. (b) walk past it. (c) refer to it. (d) look at it. — 5. ____

GETTING THE MEANING

6. This selection is primarily about (a) college diversity. (b) assistive technology users. (c) equal access. (d) equal pay. — 6. ____

7. Some people consider touching their wheelchair (a) stupid. (b) creative. (c) an invasion of their privacy. (d) an obstruction of their rights. — 7. ____

8. It is not appropriate to seek permission before intervening on behalf of a person with a disability when (a) in class. (b) you know the person. (c) danger is imminent. (d) the person is using public transportation. — 8. ____

9. This piece reveals that a flashing light is to (a) explain. (b) deter. (c) warn. (d) amuse. — 9. ____

10. The most essential ingredient in a receptive learning environment is (a) legislation. (b) acceptance. (c) comprehensive procedures. (d) new facilities. 10. _____

WPM Rate for Reading Selection: ________
(See chart on p. 454)

Comprehension Score: ________
(to be filled in by instructor)

18

Success on the Job

Graduating from college with honors and immediately lining up six interviews made Jennifer feel anything is possible. She bragged to friends and family that "work would definitely be much easier than college."

Jennifer was thrilled when she landed the job of her dreams, making a salary much higher than she expected, in a part of the country where she always wanted to live. However, the perfect life in paradise was short-lived. At first, her team was friendly and willing to help her learn the job, but by the second week, few people said more than "hello" to her. Since Jennifer was learning the layout of the city, she found it difficult getting to work on time and starting tasks early enough to get them finished by the deadline. The most troubling part of the "dream job" was Jennifer's trying to get her supervisor, Pam, to give her credit for having a brain. Pam wanted everything done the company way even though Jennifer had learned how to do things better and faster in college. However, having to work late three times in two months just because some big client needed a backorder was the last straw. When Pam fired Jennifer for lying and refusing to help her team complete the order, Jennifer stormed out and said, "You'll hear from my lawyer." How could the situation have gone from ideal to disastrous in less than sixty days?

Unfortunately, Jennifer's story isn't an isolated one. Getting a great job is not difficult for some people, but keeping that job and being a satisfied employee can be a real challenge. To avoid having an employment experience like Jennifer's, follow the advice below:

Develop the Right Attitude and Look the Part: Begin your job with a positive attitude and take pride in your work. Don't be afraid to tackle projects, exhibiting a "can do" attitude and avoiding those employees who might influence you in a negative way. Dress and conduct yourself in a manner commensurate with the company's image and standards.

Put the Business of the Business First: Organize your personal life so it does not interfere with your ability to do the job you were hired to do. Except in an emergency, do not conduct personal business while at work, and be willing to go beyond the minimum without complaint.

Be Ethical: Don't lie or help yourself to company resources, including long distance calls, supplies, and time for which the company is paying you to work.

Be Flexible: When you accept a position, you will likely become a member of an existing work team. Observe the way others work and strive to fit in. Learn as much as you can about the dynamics of the work environment before you challenge practices.

Be Ready for Work: Show commitment, enthusiasm, dependability, and leadership.

Successful employees contribute to the company, are cooperative, take pride in their work, and function well on a team. The kind of worker you become is up to you.

500 words

NAME ________________ CLASS ________________ DATE ____________

18 Success on the Job

COMPREHENSION CHECK

GETTING THE FACTS

1. Initially, Jennifer was (a) bored on the job. (b) challenged on the job. (c) happy on the job. (d) confused on the job. 1. ____

2. Jennifer was pleased with the job's (a) location and title. (b) title and salary. (c) salary and location. (d) title and benefits. 2. ____

3. At first, Jennifer's co-workers (a) shunned her. (b) excluded her. (c) bragged about her. (d) assisted her. 3. ____

4. Pam was Jennifer's (a) co-worker. (b) classmate. (c) boss. (d) client. 4. ____

5. Jennifer's first job ended up being (a) an ideal situation. (b) a "piece of cake." (c) a disaster. (d) a dream job. 5. ____

GETTING THE MEANING

6. This piece focuses on workplace (a) training. (b) politics. (c) leadership. (d) behavior. 6. ____

7. Jennifer implied she would (a) quit her job. (b) take legal action. (c) improve her attitude. (d) be more flexible. 7. ____

8. Jennifer had been (a) an average student. (b) a marginal student. (c) a mundane student. (d) an exceptional student. 8. ____

9. Conducting yourself commensurate with the company's image and standards demonstrates (a) apathy. (b) arrogance. (c) commitment. (d) coercion. 9. ____

10. Using company resources for personal purposes is (a) unethical. (b) expected. (c) a benefit. (d) advisable. 10. ____

WPM Rate for Reading Selection: ________
(See chart on p. 454)

Comprehension Score: ________
(to be filled in by instructor)

19

The Ethics of E-Mailing

At 4:30 P.M. on the Friday preceding a three-day weekend, all Paul wanted to do was put the finishing touches on a report that had taken him a week to prepare, clean off his desk, and review his schedule for next Tuesday's do-or-die budget briefing. The week had been grueling, and he was looking forward to a restful and fun weekend. One last sweep of his e-mail inbox revealed an urgent message from his supervisor telling him and the other three managers to reduce their travel requests for the coming year by an additional 10 percent and get the revised budgets to her by the end of the workday.

Paul was furious, and understandably so. He had followed company mandates to reduce his travel by 25 percent at the outset of the budget-building process. In addition, he and fellow managers had constructed an innovative strategy to maintain personal contact with clients via e-mail and phone to compensate for the reduced on-site visits. The request to cut an additional 10 percent from his travel budget seemed unreasonable.

Quickly, Paul fired off the following response:

KATHY, SARAH, AND TIM,

CAN YOU BELIEVE THIS X#*/@? OUR BOSS WANTS BLOOD! I HAVE CUT MY BUDGET TO THE BONE, AND THE WITCH STILL WANTS MORE. CALCO COULD SOLVE ITS TEMPORARY BUDGET PROBLEM BY FIRING *ELIZABETH THE GENERAL* AND REINSTATING OUR MEAGER TRAVEL BUDGET. WE ARE THE ONES MAKING SALES AROUND HERE; NOT HER.

LET'S JUST SHOW UP AT THE BUDGET MEETING ON TUESDAY AND TELL HER THAT WE NEVER GOT HER E-MAIL. MAYBE THE PREZ WILL STEP IN AND COME TO OUR RESCUE. HE KNOWS THAT THIS COMPANY WILL FOLD WITHOUT OUR ATTENTION TO THE CUSTOMERS.

WHAT DO YOU SAY?

PAUL

As soon as he hit the *send* key, Paul felt sick to his stomach. He knew that the reply would go to the sender rather than to Kathy, Sarah, and Tim. Paul's career with Calco was over!

Almost everyone has heard a horror story or two about an e-mailer sending a message to one or more people for whom it was not intended. The following might spare you a humiliating experience like the one described above.

First, never put anything in an e-mail message that you do not want the world to know. **E-mail systems are not secure.**

Second, be sure that you verify the intended recipient before executing the *send* command.

Third, don't use uppercase unless you want the message to "shout" to the recipient.

Fourth, when you receive an upsetting e-mail, take time out and count to ten before responding. Reread it and make sure that you understand the stated and implied content.

Fifth, if you think that you cannot respond professionally and appropriately by return e-mail, request time—several hours to several days, depending on the gravity of the situation—to consider a response.

Remember, a hasty reply in print is nearly impossible to recant. Carefully considering the impact of your intended message may prove to be the best investment you could make.

500 words

NAME ____________ CLASS ____________ DATE ____________

19 The Ethics of E-Mailing

COMPREHENSION CHECK

GETTING THE FACTS

1. Next week, Paul had to (a) prepare a report. (b) clean his desk. (c) review his schedule. (d) attend a budget meeting. 1. ____

2. Paul had had (a) a grueling week. (b) an urgent meeting. (c) a fun weekend. (d) a relaxed day. 2. ____

3. Paul's supervisor requested his (a) briefing. (b) budget. (c) report. (d) schedule. 3. ____

4. Paul accidentally sent the e-mail response to (a) managers. (b) customers. (c) his supervisor. (d) Calco's president. 4. ____

5. E-mail systems are typically (a) inaccessible. (b) painfully slow. (c) unsecured. (d) inconvenient. 5. ____

GETTING THE MEANING

6. The focus in this selection is on (a) taking responsibility. (b) establishing policies. (c) office politics. (d) dealing with a difficult boss. 6. ____

7. The upsetting e-mail caused Paul to respond (a) thoughtfully. (b) hastily. (c) proactively. (d) graciously. 7. ____

8. If Paul could have *recanted* his message, he would have (a) defended it. (b) renounced it. (c) verified it. (d) embellished it. 8. ____

9. Allowing time to pass before responding to an upsetting e-mail permits (a) intimidation. (b) immediacy. (c) defensiveness. (d) deliberation. 9. ____

10. The implication of Paul's misfortune is that e-mail is best reserved for (a) formal communications. (b) neutral content. (c) confidential messages. (d) medium security messages. 10. ____

WPM Rate for Reading Selection: ________
(See chart on p. 454)

Comprehension Score: ________
(to be filled in by instructor)

20

Evaluating Internet Information

Thanks to recent technology, researchers have options other than the books and journals available in academic libraries. The alternatives to traditional print resources—electronic research tools—are fast and easy to use, but some are also unreliable. Unlike the resources housed in libraries or indexed in databases where professionals have assessed their appropriateness, information available on the Internet is often unfiltered and meets no prescribed standards.

If you use the Internet, you must be prepared to assess the value of the infinite number of documents yourself. To be safe, Internet users should question the credibility of authors and the veracity of their compositions. Always seek answers to the following questions.

Who Wrote It? On some Internet sites, anyone can post an article on any subject. It is important for you to determine if the author is (1) well-known in the field, (2) one whom you recognize, and (3) held in high regard by authorities whom you trust. Also, determine if the Web site is linked to a reliable organization, if there is biographical information on the author, and whether the author provides an address, telephone number, e-mail address, and professional credentials.

Who Published It? Is the publisher reputable? On whose server does this document reside? Was the document prepared as part of a professional commitment to an institution or non-profit organization? Did the publisher pay the author for the publication?

Is It Current? When did the author write the document? If you are researching a new topic, considering information from a piece written five years ago would be a waste of time. However, if you are researching a topic where the date of authorship is irrelevant, e.g., a description of Michelangelo's painting of the Sistine Chapel, *when* the document was written is less important.

Is It Objective? Is the author's point of view neutral or biased? How the writer "sees" the subject determines how he or she will present the data. Is there a political, commercial, or personal benefit for the author that influences the point of view? Determine whether the publication is an advertisement or appears on an organization's site that would profit from disseminating the information. If the information is about a public figure, will the author benefit from readers adopting the document's point of view?

Are the Details Supported? Credible authors present backup research data to explain *how* they arrived at conclusions. A bibliography of related work also serves to verify findings and support the author's point of view.

Do Other Sources Validate the Content? You must also evaluate the depth of the author's knowledge on the subject. Does the author cite works of others to corroborate his or her point of view? Does the author discuss the pros and cons of the argument? If the author presents original ideas, does she or he discuss the limitations of the new orientation?

When doing research, remember that writers always have an opinion on their subject. Make sure the Internet information you select is credible and documented.

500 words

NAME ______________________ CLASS ______________________ DATE ______________

20 Evaluating Internet Information

COMPREHENSION CHECK

GETTING THE FACTS

1. Today, researchers, faculty, and students have options other than books and journals because of (a) large budgets. (b) endowments. (c) technology. (d) grants. 1. ____

2. Information available on the Internet is (a) often unfiltered. (b) excerpted from books. (c) always checked by a professional. (d) usually in the library. 2. ____

3. Researchers should question authors' (a) avocation. (b) intent. (c) profession. (d) credibility. 3. ____

4. It is important for you to determine if the author (a) is employed. (b) conducts research. (c) is known in the field. (d) maintains a Web site. 4. ____

5. Before using Internet information, determine if details are (a) documented. (b) original. (c) influential. (d) subdued. 5. ____

GETTING THE MEANING

6. The main purpose of this selection is to (a) teach. (b) warn. (c) illustrate. (d) enumerate. 6. ____

7. Before using unconfirmed Internet information, the researcher should (a) call the author. (b) call the publisher. (c) check with the Web master. (d) check other sources. 7. ____

8. A writer's opinion of a subject mainly influences the composition's (a) publisher. (b) currency. (c) content. (d) length. 8. ____

9. Using the Internet as a research resource (a) is cumbersome. (b) is time consuming. (c) places less responsibility on the researcher. (d) places more responsibility on the researcher. 9. ____

10. A bibliography attached to an Internet resource verifies (a) the site. (b) the publisher. (c) the content. (d) the author. 10. ____

WPM Rate for Reading Selection: ________
(See chart on p. 454)

Comprehension Score: ________
(to be filled in by instructor)

Navigating the Internet

GLOSSARY

Internet: a huge collection of computer and computer networks, worldwide

Search Engine: a tool for introducing terms you would like to search into databases

Database: an electronic holding tank of information

To complete the assignments that follow, you will need the help of search engines. These tools will allow you to type in the subject that you are interested in and identify "destinations" where you can find the information you seek.

Depending upon the browser you will be using (Netscape Navigator or Internet Explorer), you must double click the appropriate icon. When you double click, you will be launching your browser. In the window that appears, you will notice a white dialog box in which you will be able to point your mouse and click. You may now type in *Search Engines.* A series of different types of search engines will appear. You will see descriptions of each and it is up to you to choose the one you feel will work the best for you. Not all search engines work the same way. Therefore, when the list of search engines appears, choose the one that matches the kind of search you want to do. For instance, if you want to search for the name of a business in Hartford, Connecticut, Northern Light would be an appropriate choice. However, if you wanted to browse the Web by subject, you might choose Lycos, a site that also includes a section for newcomers.

Try a number of search engines when researching a topic. Through practice, you will refine your Internet searching skills.

Internet Assignments

Many Internet users select and use information without assessing it critically. The following exercises will help you become a savvy and judicious Internet user. Before beginning, read "Evaluating Internet Information," Ultimate Review selection 20, page 531. Then, complete the assignments, submit them to your instructor, and be prepared to defend the credibility and validity of your findings.

Easy

EXERCISE 1

Your instructor has asked students in your class to enhance their study skills. In addition to the helpful techniques presented in your texts, many sites on the Web contain useful information. Follow the directions below to become a more successful student.

1. Click on **Internet Start** or the Internet icon on your computer's tool bar.
2. Type in http://www.ucc.vt.edu/stdysk/stdyhlp.html.
3. Review the list of Study-skills Self Help Information.
4. Choose any three topics and study the concepts presented.

Based on your findings, write an e-mail that contains the following information to at least one of your classmates and copy it to your instructor.

A. The name of the study-skills topic you researched
B. A discussion of the most valuable information you learned
C. A discussion of how the information will contribute to your success as a student

EXERCISE 2

Your instructor has asked the class to research an invention that contributes to the safety of our everyday lives. You have chosen to report on the invention and evolution of the traffic light. Using appropriate search engines, answer the following questions.

1. When was the traffic light invented?
2. Who was its inventor?
3. What was this inventor's profession?
4. Where was the first traffic light installed?
5. What was people's reaction to the invention?
6. Why are the colors red, green, and yellow used in traffic lights?
7. How has the traffic light changed over time?
8. How do computers enhance the effectiveness of traffic lights?

Based on your findings, summarize answers to the questions above about the traffic light and discuss the impact this invention has had on modern-day lifestyles in a 300-word paragraph. Cite the sources of your search.

Moderately Challenging

EXERCISE 3

A friend has just been diagnosed with collagenous colitis. Neither you nor she has ever heard of the condition, and the doctor's packet of information has not arrived yet. You volunteer to research the condition on the Internet. Choose at least *three* sites and research the following questions:

1. What is the nature of the condition?
2. What are the symptoms?

3. What causes collagenous colitis?
4. Is it curable?
5. How long does the condition last?
6. What is the most effective treatment?
7. Is it contagious?
8. Are there long-term effects of the condition?
9. What restrictions, if any, must the patient observe?
10. What specialists are most effective in treating this condition?

Based on your findings and using the evaluative criteria in Ultimate Review selection 20, summarize the answers to the questions above in an e-mail to your friend. Ensure that the e-mail has an encouraging tone and that you present the findings in the most positive way. Cite the sources of your search.

EXERCISE 4

While watching television, you learned of two new allergy medications that pharmaceutical companies claim will bring your allergies under control. Your physician mentioned one of the drugs during your last visit, but you are skeptical. However, you are miserable, and, before discussing the possibility or using either drug, you decide to investigate.

Research *each* product on the Internet, making sure that you find the answers to the following questions:

1. What is the classification of the drug?
2. What are the side effects?
3. How long is the course of treatment?
4. How much does it cost per course of treatment?
5. What is its likely interaction with other drugs?
6. Are there restrictions while taking the drug?

Based on your findings and the information presented in selection 44, write a 200-word argument in favor of using one of the drugs and a 200-word argument against the drug your physician favors.

Challenging

EXERCISE 5

Several superstores in your community boast of their investment in civic projects and social initiatives. Choose at least four of these corporations and investigate their claims. Determine their level of *social responsibility* as discussed in selection 51.

1. How long has the corporation been in the community?
2. How does the corporation contribute to the quality of life in the city?
3. What percentage of its profits does the corporation return to your community?
4. Does the corporation promote equal job opportunities? How do you know?
5. Does it value diversity? How do you know?
6. What impact do the corporation's business practices have on the community?
7. To what extent, if any, does the corporation invest in the youth of the community?

Based on your findings and playing the role of a City Manager, write each of the corporations a letter extolling their contributions and thanking them on behalf of the community. Be sure to integrate answers to the questions above into your letter of compliment.

EXERCISE 6

Choose a corporation in a city at least 500 miles away that interests you. Assume that you have completed your course of study and are eminently qualified for a position that allows you to apply the knowledge you have gained to a very desirable job. Research the corporation on the Internet, using at least *three* sites to locate the following information.

1. What is the full name of the corporation and where is its homebase?
2. What is the name of its parent company?
3. Where are the corporation's location(s) in the city you are considering?
4. What is the mean income in the city?
5. How many employees does the corporation have at each site in the city of your choice? In the entire corporation?
6. What is the corporation's organizational structure?
7. What is the corporation's organizational culture?
8. What constitutes the employee benefit package? (For insights into this criterion, see selection 50, p. 395.)
9. How do salaries compare in the job category you are considering to similar jobs at *two* of this corporation's competitors? List the competitors and their locations.
10. What is the mean income in the city where the competitors are located?
11. Identify at least five non-work activities you enjoy and assess the availability of these activities in the city where you are considering the position.

Based on your findings, write a 500-word rationale for your decision to seek a job with this corporation or to seek a job with one of its competitors. Integrate the findings from all eleven criteria into the narrative of your rationale.

Vocabulary Post-Test A

Here's your chance to see how much you've improved in developing word mastery and building a bigger, more valuable vocabulary. As with Pre-Test A, this test contains one word drawn from each of the first 25 selections. Compare your score on the two tests—Pre-Test A and Post-Test A—to see what progress you've made.

1. cope	(a) capture (b) expect (c) deal with (d) state (e) push off	1. ____
2. solution	(a) solitude (b) outline (c) salve (d) explanation (e) separate	2. ____
3. terrain	(a) atmosphere (b) land (c) moisture (d) copy (e) trail	3. ____
4. expedite	(a) hasten (b) examine (c) spend (d) produce (e) fasten	4. ____
5. explanation	(a) examination (b) explaining (c) planning (d) pleasing (e) acting	5. ____
6. mere	(a) true (b) unusual (c) only (d) important (e) safe	6. ____
7. related	(a) discarded (b) began again (c) halted (d) restored (e) connected	7. ____
8. heed	(a) turn (b) down (c) notice (d) away (e) something	8. ____
9. brawls	(a) gashes (b) shouts (c) fights (d) bins (e) holders	9. ____
10. initial	(a) strange (b) desirable (c) beginning (d) intent (e) trial	10. ____
11. prefer	(a) foretell (b) comfort (c) do well (d) like better (e) keep	11. ____
12 endearment	(a) affection (b) expense (c) endorsement (d) energy (e) hope	12. ____
13. concise	(a) complex (b) brief (c) long (d) sturdy (e) exact	13. ____
		14. ____

14. respond	(a) retain (b) raise (c) spare (d) answer (e) pledge	
15. initiates	(a) investigates (b) helps (c) concludes (d) extends (e) begins	15. ____
16. superficial	(a) limited (b) extra special (c) trained (d) similar (e) perfect	16. ____
17. isolation	(a) likeness (b) range (c) solitude (d) softness (e) temptation	17. ____
18. miscalculations	(a) disappointments (b) changes (c) sums (d) wrong impressions (e) problems	18. ____
19. surpasses	(a) sells (b) surprises (c) enters (d) suggests (e) exceeds	19. ____
20. contortions	(a) contacts (b) conditions (c) trends (d) mistakes (e) twists	20. ____
21. hesitant	(a) hopeful (b) reluctant (c) weak (d) short (e) hearty	21. ____
22. insinuation	(a) intention (b) sly hint (c) suggestion (d) prediction (e) turn	22. ____
23. refuge	(a) shelter (b) trash (c) objection (d) failure (e) promise	23. ____
24. intruder	(a) enemy (b) friend (c) relative (d) trespasser (e) guest	24. ____
25. complicated	(a) loaded in (b) practiced (c) added (d) compared (e) involved	25. ____

Post-Test A Score: ________

Vocabulary Post-Test B

Here's a further chance to check your vocabulary development. This test contains one word drawn from each of the last 25 selections. Compare your Pre-Test B and Post-Test B scores to see exactly what progress you've made.

26. totally	(a) completely (b) helpfully (c) carefully (d) uncertainly (e) partially	26. ____
27. visualize	(a) picture (b) attempt (c) experiment (d) visit (e) try	27. ____
28. core	(a) discard (b) caretaker (c) most important part (d) beginning (e) neighbor	28. ____
29. flawless	(a) without fear (b) perfect (c) worn out (d) unbent (e) full	29. ____
30. disloyal	(a) unfriendly (b) disturbed (c) drunk (d) false (e) weak	30. ____
31. chief	(a) main (b) real (c) true (d) rare (e) strong	31. ____
32. capsized	(a) captured (b) killed (c) carried off (d) compared (e) upset	32. ____
33. devoted	(a) extended (b) judged (c) dedicated (d) decided (e) asked	33. ____
34. absolute	(a) solid (b) complete (c) strong (d) solemn (e) fair	34. ____
35. endeavored	(a) entered (b) tried (c) favored (d) aroused (e) ran	35. ____
36. stroll	(a) stand (b) push (c) come in (d) limp (e) saunter	36. ____
37. pose	(a) provide (b) put forth (c) cause (d) plead (e) send	37. ____
38. luxury	(a) splendor (b) fragility (c) limit (d) softness (e) warmth	38. ____

39. significantly (a) costly (b) fairly (c) surely (d) noticeably (e) frankly 39. ____

40. colleague (a) student (b) acquaintance (c) staff member (d) associate (e) graduate student 40. ____

41. portable (a) open-ended (b) waterproof (c) packaged (d) tied (e) easily carried 41. ____

42. fascinated (a) fastened (b) attracted (c) closed (d) prepared (e) pleased 42. ____

43. inexcusable (a) unearthly (b) rare (c) excellent (d) close (e) indefensible 43. ____

44. assertion (a) claim (b) falsehood (c) suggestion (d) belief (e) trial 44. ____

45. fierce (a) false (b) cruel (c) fancy (d) warm (e) fragmentary 45. ____

46. enormous (a) horrid (b) hopeless (c) twisted (d) complete (e) colossal 46. ____

47. convey (a) project (b) contrast (c) enter (d) expect (e) change 47. ____

48. collide (a) fight (b) combine (c) crash (d) unite (e) suffer 48. ____

49. attire (a) attempt (b) outfits (c) trial (d) tendency (e) field 49. ____

50. vicinity (a) signal (b) gesture (c) vacancy (d) vagueness (e) surroundings 50. ____

Post-Test B Score: ________

Acknowledgments

Mortimer J. Adler, "How to Read a Difficult Book" is reprinted with the permission of Simon & Schuster from *Great Ideas from the Great Books* by Mortimer J. Adler. Copyright © 1961, 1963 by Mortimer J. Adler.

Malcolm Boyd, "How to REALLY Talk to Another Person," from *Parade* Magazine, February 19, 1989. Reprinted with permission from *Parade,* copyright © 1989. Malcolm Boyd is the Poet/Writer-in-residence, Episcopal Cathedral Center of St. Paul, Los Angeles, CA.

Dr. Joyce Brothers, "How to Work for a Rotten Boss," *Parade* Magazine, April 4, 1993. Reprinted with permission from *Parade,* copyright © 1993.

Ann Carol, "The Gun," 1995, from *Bad Behavior* 1995 by Carol Ellis, edited by Mary Higgins Clark. Gulliver Books, Harcourt Brace, 1995. Reprinted by permission of Carol Ellis.

Cora Daniels & Carol Vinzant, "The Joy of Quitting," *Fortune,* February 7, 2000. Reprinted by permission of *Fortune* magazine.

Barbara Ehrenreich, "Good Health for Sale" from *Dollars & Sense,* 1996. Reprinted by permission of International Creative Management, Inc. Copyright © 1996 by Barbara Ehrenreich.

Robert Fulghum, "The Juggler," from *Uh-Oh* by Robert Fulghum, pp. 220–224. Copyright © 1991 by Robert Fulghum. Reprinted by permission of Villard Books, a division of Random House, Inc.

Natalie Goldberg, from *Writing Down the Bones* by Natalie Goldberg, © 1996 by Natalie Goldberg. Reprinted by arrangement with Shambhala Publications, Inc., Boston, www.shambhala.com.

Arthur Gordon, "Two Words to Avoid, Two to Remember," from *Reader's Digest,* February, 1974, pp. 69–72. Reprinted by permission of the author.

Ricky Griffin, "The Organization's Culture," from *Management,* Houghton Mifflin, 1999, pp. 170–173. Copyright © 1999 by Houghton Mifflin Company. Reprinted with permission.

James Herriot, "Watching a Veterinarian at Work." Copyright © 1972 by James Herriot. From *All Creatures Great and Small* by James Herriot. Reprinted by permission of St. Martin's Press, LLC.

Frank G. Jennings, "Words Can Be Slippery," from Frank G. Jennings, *This Is Reading,* Teachers College Press, 1965, republished by Plenum Publishing Corp., 1982, pp. 20–22. Reprinted by permission of the author.

Louise Andrews Kent, "Short Words Are Words of Might," copyright 1939, from *Weigh the Word* by Jennings, King and Stevenson, Harper, New York, 1957. Reprinted by permission.

Larry King, "The First Rule of Conversation," from *How to Talk to Anyone, Anytime, Anyplace* by Larry King. Copyright © 1994 by Larry King. Reprinted by permission of Crown Publishers, a division of Random House, Inc.

Malcolm X, "My Alma Mater," from *The Autobiography of Malcolm X* by Malcolm X with Alex Haley. Copyright © 1964 by Alex Haley and Malcolm X. Copyright © 1965 by Alex Haley and Betty Shabazz. Reprinted by permission of Random House, Inc.

Todd Mitchell, "The Road to Wellville," *USA Weekend,* March 17–19, 2000 is reprinted by permission of the author.

Robert L. Montgomery, "How to Remember: Some Basic Principles," from *Memory Made Easy,* Amacom, 1979. Reprinted by permission of the author.

William A. Nolen, "Watching a Surgeon at Work," from "The First Appendectomy" in *The Making of a Surgeon,* pp. 44–50, 1970, Random House. Reprinted by permission of Spectrum Literary Agency.

Mary Beth Norton, "Challenges to Racial and Sexual Discrimination," from *A People and a Nation,* Houghton Mifflin, 1999, pp. 401–404. Copyright © 1999 by Houghton Mifflin Company. Reprinted with permission.

Michael Osborn and Suzanne Osborn, "The Nature and Importance of Effective Listening," from *Public Speaking,* Houghton Mifflin, 2000, pp. 60–64. Copyright © 2000 by Houghton Mifflin Company. Reprinted with permission.

William Pride and O. C. Ferrell, "The Nature of Social Responsibility," from *Marketing: Concepts and Strategies,* Houghton Mifflin, 2000, pp. 81–85. Copyright © 2000 by Houghton Mifflin Company. Reprinted with permission.

Warren Robertson, "Ten Football Stars and Yours Truly," reprinted with permission from the October 1961 *Reader's Digest* and reprinted courtesy of *Sports Illustrated:* "The Reluctant All Star" by Warren Robertson, SI, 11/28/60. Copyright © 1960, Time Inc. All rights reserved.

Saki, "The Open Window," from *The Short Stories of Saki* by H. H. Munro, Viking Press, 1930.

John E. Schwiebert, "Short Stories," from *Reading and Writing from Literature,* Houghton Mifflin, 1997, pp. 133–38. Copyright © 1997 by Houghton Mifflin Company. Reprinted with permission.

Martin E. P. Seligman, "Two Ways of Looking at Life" from *Learned Optimism* by Martin E. P. Seligman. Copyright © 1991 by Martin E. P. Seligman. Reprinted by permission of Alfred A. Knopf, a Division of Random House, Inc.

Sharon J. Sherman & Alan Sherman, "Matter and Energy," from *Essential Concepts of Chemistry,* Houghton Mifflin, 1999, pp. 53–57. Copyright © 1999 by Houghton Mifflin Company. Reprinted with permission.

Stratford P. Sherman, "America Won't Win 'Till It Reads More," *Fortune,* November 18, 1991. © 1999 Time Inc. All rights reserved.

Brad Steiger and Sherry Hanson Steiger, "He Survived His Own Funeral" is reprinted with permission from *Animal Miracles* by Brad Steiger and Sherry Hanson Steiger. © 1999. Published by Adams Media Corporation.

Andrew Tobias, "The Dividends for Quitters," *Time,* October 12, 1992. © 1992 Time Inc. Reprinted by permission.

James Wilson and John J. Dilulio, Jr., "Bureaucratic Pathologies," from *American Government: The Essentials,* Houghton Mifflin, 1998, pp. 432–435. Copyright © 1998 by Houghton Mifflin Company. Reprinted with permission.

Ruth Woodman, "Father and the Tommyknockers," from *The Lion,* © 1961 Lions International. Reprinted with permission of *The Lion* magazine.